DATE DUE

~~MR 1 2 '93~~		
~~AP 19 93~~		
~~JE 18 93~~		
~~AP 18 94~~		
~~OC 13 '95~~		
~~NV 22 99~~		

DEMCO 38-296

Sail Like a Champion

Sail Like a Champion

Dennis Conner
and Michael Levitt

Illustrations by Tony Lush

St. Martin's Press
NEW YORK

DESIGN BY LAURA HOUGH

Library of Congress Cataloging-in-Publication Data

Conner, Dennis.
    Sail like a champion
  Dennis Conner and Michael Levitt.
        p.   cm.
      ISBN 0-312-07078-0
      1. Sailing. 2. Sailboat racing. I. Levitt, Michael. II. Title.
GV811.C568   1992
797.1'24—dc20   91-37988
                                                       CIP

First Edition: September 1992
10 9 8 7 6 5 4 3 2 1

Contents

Acknowledgments

The authors are indebted to Edward du Moulin and Jack Sutphen for their willingness to review these chapters. Also very much appreciated is the generous help of Tom Whidden, president of North Sails Group Inc., and David Dellenbaugh, marketing director, who made available the considerable educational resources of their company.

Yacht designer David Pedrick was an excellent source for the material that appears in Chapter 2, "Yacht Design," as was boatbuilder Eric Goetz, of Eric Goetz Custom Sailboats, in the preparation of Chapter 3, "Building and Equipping a Sailboat." Also appreciated was the help of Chris Bedford and Lee Davis, of Galson Technical Services, for sharing their knowledge of weather, the subject of Chapter 8, and Richard McCurdy, of Ockam Instruments, for making his company's resources available—specifically the writings of Jim Marshall and Steve Moore. Brian Doyle, of North Sails Cloth, applied both his engineering background and his impeccable sense of language in reviewing parts of the manuscript.

Others at North Sails who were generous with their thoughts and time include Bill Bergantz, of North Sails Cloth, Andreas Josenhans, Ched Proctor, and Tom McLaughlin, of North Sails East, Vince Brun, of North Sails One Design West, and David Curtis, Jud Smith, Steve Ulian, and Jim Brady, of North Sails Marblehead. The authors also thank David Perry for his critique of Chapter 9, "Rules," and, again, David Dellenbaugh for allowing us to use his video, "Learn the Racing Rules," made in conjunction with *Sailing World* magazine and Sea TV, as source material.

The authors acknowledge the unselfish help of Ben Hall, of Hall Spars, and Duncan MacLane, of MacLane Marine Design. Also, Alberto Calderon for his comments on Chapter 2, as well as Ed Baird, for kind permission to publish his chart found in Chapter 10. Thanks are due to Richard du Moulin, as well as Rick Viggiano, of Pro-Tech Marine, Scott Graham, of US SAILING, Larry Leistiko, of Computer Keels, and Arvel Gentry, of Boeing. It is also appropriate to mention Peter Smyth for his writing on the history of fiberglass boatbuilding and Accu-Weather for the use of its weather-forecasting software.

The authors also appreciate the guidance and vision of Michael Sagalyn, our editor at St. Martin's Press, David Sobel, and Ed Stackler. Also helpful at Dennis Conner Sports and Team Dennis Conner were Maria Flannigan, Jerry La Dow, Bill Trenkle, Chris Todter, Mick Harvey, and Cathy Harvey.

Last but first, Linda and Molly Levitt and Judy, Julie, and Shanna Conner.

1 | Beginnings

I was born in 1942 and lived at 2919 Talbot Street in San Diego's Point Loma section. The tiny house, where my sister still lives, is ordinary, to be kind, but it is a couple of blocks from the San Diego Yacht Club. This proximity set the stage for what followed in my life. My father was a commercial fisherman who fished for tuna, first for others and then in a boat of his own, the 45-foot *Victor I*. During World War II, he left the sea to build airplanes at the General Dynamics plant in San Diego, where he worked for more than thirty years until he died.

As a boy, I drifted down the hill to the San Diego Yacht Club. Despite its nearness, this place was far from my world. Nevertheless, it proved to be the magnet of my youth. Had I lived on another street or in another town, I could just as easily have hung out at a bowling alley, a pool hall, or worse. I often think how lucky I am that I lived near the yacht club and fell in love with sailing at an early age, because with my temperament, I would have been a very good bad guy.

The most obvious point of my personality—in sailing and out—is my tenacity. I called my first book *No Excuse to Lose,* written with John Rousmaniere in 1978. That title is a reflection of my tenacity. My friend Tom Whidden, now president of North Sails Group Inc., who has sailed with me in five America's Cup campaigns, characterizes my approach to sailing, as well as life, as "bludgeoning a problem to death."

In *No Excuse to Lose,* I claimed I wasn't a good sailor so I try harder. I made this claim because I wanted to appear modest. A better way to put this might have been, I am not a natural sailor. However, in the thirty-nine years that I have been sailing, I've won the Etchells 22 World Championship in 1991 and two Star World Championships. In 1977, I won all five races in the Star Worlds in Kiel, Germany, which I still consider my supreme accomplishment in the sport. I have sailed on four winning America's Cup boats and skippered three of them, and am, of course, best known as the only person to lose the Cup and then win it back. I have won an Olympic bronze medal in the Tempest Class, two Congressional Cups, and four Southern Ocean Racing Conferences (SORC). I got where I am by "bludgeoning problems to death."

This book, *Sail Like a Champion,* is a synthesis of what I've learned on the race course and in the course of life. The lessons that I've learned in sailing have stood me in good stead. These are hard-won lessons because sailing never came easily to me. I got where I am with sufficient talent and then simply by wanting it more and working harder to get it. And to keep it.

To the reader, there are advantages to this perspective, I think. Ted Williams, the baseball player who won six batting titles, was never a great hitting coach or more than an average manager. Perhaps Williams, who was born in San Diego and made his professional debut here, was too much of a natural athlete to be a good teacher. I am, however, a made sailor, not a born one. This book was written to help the average sailor become a much better one, and the good sailor, great. It ranges, literally, from the nuts and bolts of tuning and sheet leads, to go-fast tricks, steering, weather, tactics, sail trim, organization, leadership, crewing, yacht design, boatbuilding, and thinking like a winner.

This is primarily a how-to book: how any sailor, whether a cruiser or a racer, can improve his or her skills. Woven through it is my lifetime in sailing, anecdotal and candid information from some of the most exciting races in which I've participated.

The cruising or recreational sailor might ask at this point, What does Dennis Conner have to say to me? Plenty, I think. There isn't a "cruising" way to sail a boat and a "racing" way; there is only a right way and a wrong way. Both cruising and racing sailors have to trim sails properly, reef them, and sail in heavy and light winds. Both have to purchase the best and most appropriate boats and equipment, deal with designers and boatbuilders, and buy sails and deal with sailmakers. Both cruising and racing sailors have to know wind and weather, and how to steer a boat so they get to where they want to go, which can be Block Island, or the finish line first. Both types of sailors have to tune the mast so it remains standing and so the boat sails well. They must pack a seabag and be good shipmates.

Although *speed* is said to be a dirty word in some circles, I've yet to hear a cruising sailor brag, "This year it took me twenty-two hours to get to Catalina Island. Last year it took me a disappointing seventeen." Or, "I'm looking for a boat that's slower than my Puddlejumper 35." Indeed, many cruising sailors are making as much use of polar diagrams, developed with velocity-prediction programs (VPP), as are racers, and if they're not using such advanced go-fast techniques, their designer, boatbuilder, and sailmaker certainly are. A half-knot increase in boat speed—a realistic difference between good and bad sail trim—can save two hours during a twenty-four-hour passage. And if time isn't one of your major concerns, proper sail trim can make the boat heel less, adding to comfort afloat. It can also provide the proper amount of weather helm, making the boat easier to steer and your sailing more pleasurable.

A s noted, my good fortune in sailing and in life can be traced to the fact that my parents lived near the yacht club. Further, my father worked the sea and had an affinity for it, and he encouraged me to hang out around the water at an early age. I was your typical wharf rat. In those days, the San Diego Yacht Club was a more casual place. There wasn't a guard at the gate, protecting such treasures as the America's Cup, which I delivered to the club in 1987, after winning it back from the Australians.

There are those yacht club members who lament the changes that the America's Cup has brought. I understand those feelings and, in some ways, sympathize with them. The America's Cup has changed many lives it has touched. It has certainly changed mine.

Back in the early 1950s, I just walked into the San Diego Yacht Club without a proper invitation—indeed, without any invitation. Finally, when I was eleven, they made me a junior member. From their perspective, it probably seemed the easiest way to deal with a persistent problem. Compared with most of the other members, my folks were of far more modest means. My father became a member long after I did. He died in 1980, after I defended the America's Cup with *Freedom*—my debut as an America's Cup skipper.

Though I played Little League baseball, I wasn't Ted Williams. I loved to compete, and sailing was the arena in which I chose to express myself. When I first joined the yacht club, I desperately wanted a Starlet, a keelboat that was popular then. It was just a plywood box, with a fractional rig, and a piece of sheet iron for a keel, but somehow those pieces added up to $800. It might as well have been a million. Buying it was financially impossible for my folks or me. My father was not the type who went to the bank and borowed the money to give his kid a boat or tennis lessons. I sensed a difference between those kids with more affluent parents and me. Perhaps that distance from my playmates drove me harder in the sport.

I described that distance from my companions in *No Excuse to Lose*. Some people have read much into that remark—seeing it as the key to my character. Now that my wife, Judy, and I have raised our two wonderful daughters—Julie, a senior at Dartmouth College, and Shanna, a freshman at the University of California at Davis—and we have the resources to give them most anything, I know that what you don't give kids can be as important as what you give them. Earning it—wanting something like a Starlet so badly you'd do almost anything for it—drove me. Focused me. In my case, not being wealthy was a positive force.

Because owning a Starlet was beyond my means, I desperately wanted to crew on one. In time, I got my wish, and one of my fondest memories was running the hoist and putting the Starlet in the water for my skipper. Then I'd wipe it down with a wet towel and pretend it was mine. When I got older and bolder, I'd sneak off for a sail before the skipper's mother brought him to the club. Once a month, the yacht club would hold races where the crew was the skipper. What wonderful days those were.

These were my formative years, and from my perspective as a crew member, I watched and listened intently. I was putting myself together as a sailor and tried to do it with the best pieces. For example, the San Diego Yacht Club hosted the Star Worlds in 1958 when I was fifteen. The 22-foot, 8-inch Star, a William Gardner design that dates back to 1911, is one of the sport's oldest one-design classes. It is the oldest Olympic class, having been used since 1932. (In 1976, it was replaced by the Tempest, in which I won the bronze medal, but the Star returned in 1980.) Since its inception, the Star Class has tended to attract the sport's best sailors.

I can remember, as part of the welcoming ceremony for the Star Class, a clear-wood Star was placed in the swimming pool of the yacht club. It belonged to Leon L. Bothell, a member of the San Diego Yacht Club, and had the finish of a grand piano. After seeing such a boat displayed this way, it's little wonder that the Star has been a lasting fascination for me.

The club assigned a junior member to each boat to handle lines, wash the boats off, and be an errand boy. I was assigned to be the "boat boy" for Bill Buchan. For me, it was like winning the lottery. Buchan was the great Seattle sailor and boatbuilder who would go on to win the Star Worlds in 1961, 1970, and 1985. He also would win an Olympic gold medal in 1984. Buchan's father was crewing for him, but he was late arriving, so I got to sail with Buchan while he readied the boat.

Sailors were my heroes—people like Bill Buchan, Ash Bown, Malin Burnham, and Lowell North—and I took all they would give me and longed for more. I wanted to know everything. When I was twenty-one, I started crewing on *Carousel*, a 40-foot ocean racer owned by Ash Bown. Bown, who was brilliant on a boat, was like a second father to me, and I was always at his house asking him questions about ocean racing. His wife seemed less enthusiastic about my constant presence in their lives as she'd say things like, "Isn't it time to go home?"

Another great San Diego sailor to whom I paid attention was Malin Burnham. If Ash Bown was like a father to me, Malin Burnham was like an older brother. For Malin, things seem to come easily. From my perspective, he was to sailing what Ted Williams was to hitting a baseball. Malin, who had his own Star when he was fifteen, won the Star Worlds the next year, in 1945.

Malin would show up for a race and say, "What was it? Two weeks ago, I know we broke something...." Malin graduated from Stanford and was on the board of New York Life, and he had been flying around the country running his family's savings and loan. He had neither the time nor, likely, the temperament to "bludgeon a problem to death"—certainly not a sailing problem.

Then he'd hoist the main and notice the top batten was broken. He didn't have a spare, but he had an extra bottom batten, so somehow he found a hacksaw and cut the batten down to size. Maybe it was a little stiff for the top section of the sail, which needs the curve that a more flexible batten provides. And so the main had a hard spot, but wrong or right, the shape would have to do. Then he'd get a great start, go the right way, and win the race. Malin did it with tremendous talent, sufficient money, and very little apparent effort.

Then there was Lowell North, another San Diego sailing great. When Malin won his Star World Championship in 1945, his crew was the fifteen-year-old Lowell North. North was born in 1929. His father was a geophysicist, who worked in the oil business. The family settled in Newport Beach and then San Diego, where his father started working in electronics. The fifteen-year-old North was unenthusiastic about relocating, so to make the move more acceptable, his father gave him a Star. Burnham would receive an industrial-engineering degree from Stanford, while North received his degree in civil and structural engineering from the University of California at Berkeley.

On a sailboat, North had an unmistakable brilliance. He was, for example, the first person, as far as I know, to figure out how to use a compass on a Star for tactical sailing. The compass revealed to him how wind shifts influenced his heading. That is, the compass showed when he was being lifted, when he was being headed, and when it was advantageous to tack. To this day, the compass is still a sailor's best "crystal ball" for determining wind shifts.

North first used the compass in the Star Worlds in 1949 when he was nineteen. An example of his many talents is that he sailed the series in a Star he both designed and built. Being inexperienced in large fleets, he started poorly. Then as the forty-boat fleet went off to one side or the other, North sailed up the middle, tacking on headers as dictated by the compass (this is explained further in Chapter 8).

In this regatta in Chicago, he had four firsts and a second, and would have won the Worlds; however, in one race that he won, his boom touched the headstay of another competitor before the start, and he was disqualified.

Lowell won by being so much smarter than the rest. He won four Star World Championships and Olympic gold and bronze medals. This brilliance stood him well in the sailmaking business, too, when he founded North Sails in 1958.

When I was young, I was too small to crew on a Star, so I crewed in Lightnings—a 19-foot design by Sparkman & Stephens (S&S)—often for San Diego boatbuilder Carl Eichenlaub. I couldn't do enough for Eichenlaub. Whatever he said, I did, only more. That could be pumping up the tires in the trailer or sanding the mast. I had a great attitude.

In my formative years, San Diego seemed rich in sailing and sailing talent. I didn't know this was unique; I thought people everywhere were consumed by sailing. Part of the reason for San Diego's focus on sailing is the climate. In San Diego, life is an endless summer, and people can and do sail all year. One season of San Diego sailing is the equivalent of at least two seasons in many other places.

Then, too, there is the consistency of the conditions. San Diego is not Long Island Sound, Newport, Rhode Island, or Lake Geneva, Wisconsin. While it is not a windy place, the wind is relatively consistent. San Diego sailing requires less anticipation of wind shifts and more of an emphasis on boat speed. Sailing fast—drag racing—is what people from San Diego do best, and since major regattas tend to be held in places with consistent winds, I think San Diego sailors do inordinately well.

Also, the day-in, day-out consistency of the wind means equipment and techniques can be tested thoroughly. Compare that with Long Island Sound, where weather that is here today may be gone tomorrow and not be back for two weeks or until next season.

Many exciting and important developments in sails and sailing techniques happened when I was growing up in San Diego, and it was exciting to be a witness—often a participant—in some of them. For example, Carl Eichenlaub and I were in one Lightning and brothers Manning and Merritt Barber were in another when Elton Ballas, of Ballas Sails, developed and tested the decksweeper jib. The decksweeper jib, which puts the foot of the headsail on the deck, helps to prevent the air from leaking under the sail, from the high-pressure windward side to the low-pressure leeward side. It creates what is termed an end-plate effect (see the induced-drag discussion in Chapter 2). Ballas lopped 7 inches off the luff, while leaving the leech and foot alone. This allowed the foot to drape on the deck, effectively sealing off the space where air can leak. Eichenlaub and I appropriated the decksweeper jib for our own use and won a number of races before people caught on to what we were doing.

Similarly, Eichenlaub and I were there when the Barber brothers figured out what's become known as the Barberhauler. A Barberhauler is a short line, a small block and tackle, or the tail of a sheet that moves the headsail's lead outboard. In light winds and lumpy seas—a common San Diego condition—a Barberhauler can make as much as a 1-knot difference. The brothers, who are identical twins, still live in San Diego and share a dental practice that I use.

Eichenlaub, Malin Burnham, and Lowell North were gifted sailors who would become known worldwide. Then there was Alan Raffee, a man who substituted tenacity for ability and got almost as far as these three. Raffee was the proverbial bull in a china shop or, in this case, a Lightning. I got to know Raffee, who owned a carpet business, through Lightning sailing with Eichenlaub on Mission Bay in north San Diego. I was nineteen then and attending San Diego State College. Raffee would get into trouble, with a rule violation or other matter, and I'd go over and try to help. He didn't even know how to look things up in the rule book. In the realm of sailing, he was so needy but, all the same, very, very likable—a thoroughly generous man.

During one such conversation, he asked me what I was doing for work during my summer off from college. I told him I didn't have the slightest idea, and he said come and see me. I went, and he said, "What can you do?" I told him I didn't know. Then he asked me how much money I thought I was worth. I told him at least $300 a month. He said, "Here's the first lesson I'm going to teach you about business. I'll give you $275, because I have to keep something for myself."

So there I was in the carpet business, and soon enough, I was in management. In truth, Raffee hired me to sail on his Lightning. I was put in charge of his boat, and my meteoric rise in his company was amazing. I got my own office. It sure beat working for a living.

That's not to say there wasn't an inordinate amount of work involved. Raffee was the one who taught me to bludgeon a problem to death. His unexpressed philosophy of life was: If a little is good, a lot is a lot better. He would have me sand every blemish, every pinprick, every bit of subatomic dust from the bottom of his boat. He'd be out there helping me, too. I can remember one New Year's Day, lying upside down in his carport, sanding the bottom of his boat to glossy perfection. His car, a new Pontiac convertible, was out in the rain. I even used a magnifying glass to help search for imperfections. Then we'd go out on the race course and compete on about the same level as Malin Burnham and Lowell North.

In 1968, for example, Raffee and I needed only to beat Lowell North in the final race of the Olympic trials in San Diego to make the Olympic team. We were ahead of North, too, when we hit a mark. In those days if you hit a mark, you were out of the race. North went on to the Olympics in Acapulco that year and won the gold medal.

Raffee taught me so much about sailing, business, and life. He taught me to fly high—figuratively and literally. Raffee had his own plane, and often we'd fly to regattas. He taught me to fly the plane, too, and eventually I got a pilot's license. Raffee was killed when his plane crashed on the way to a ski vacation. I never piloted an airplane again.

Marty Gleich was made of similar stuff. I first met Gleich sailing Lightnings and later sailed with him on his Redline 41, *Hallelujah*. He was from the East Coast originally. He made his money in real-estate development and later mortgage banking. He was always well dressed in suits or a tweed sports jacket with leather patches on the sleeves. To me he looked professorial. He had thick glasses—even with them, he could barely see. Gleich was one of the most organized men I've ever met. He always had with him a little black book that had every hour of every day marked off for meetings, things to do, and notes. Now such things are common, of course, but this was the first one I'd ever seen. That impressed me. Through Gleich and Raffee, I learned how attention to detail can pay off on the race course.

Gleich wasn't simply interested in sailboat racing; he was fascinated by it. When he wanted to learn how to race better, he left his business in San Diego and went to New York to work as an intern at the yacht-design firm of Sparkman & Stephens. And Gleich was no kid. He lived in New York for six months and worked on Madison Avenue, basically sharpening Olin Stephens's pencils.

If Raffee and I got to the boat at 8:30 A.M. for an 11 A.M. start, Gleich had already been there for an hour. He had two copies of the race-committee circular—in case one got wet—and had read it.

The moral of this story is that there are many ways to succeed. Guys like Raffee and Gleich were trying so much harder than Malin. They didn't have any of Malin's skill, but they were down at the boat early; their boats were in perfect shape; and they had the race circular—two copies of it—and had read it.

I'm not Malin and I'm certainly not Lowell. I'm most like Raffee and Gleich. But I've taken pieces from all of them to make myself a sailor. When I finally owned a boat—I purchased a Star when I was twenty-eight years old—my boat was perfect. It was four years old, the oldest boat in the fleet. I didn't have any money, so I'd use toothpaste to polish the bottom. I got there early—I was the first one down there in the morning at 7 A.M. I had the race circular—two copies of it—and I had read it. The next year, I won the Star World Championship, beating Lowell North in the process.

Twenty-two years later, my approach to the details of sailing has not changed.

One of my strengths in sailing is that I've worked my way from the bottom of the ladder—or the bottom of Raffee's boat—to the top. Doing every job on a sailboat—from wet-sanding, to working the foredeck, to wiggling the tiller—has helped me immeasurably with how I treat my crew and skipper a boat. I understand the crew's jobs; I know what's easy and what's hard, and I know when a job has been well done and when it hasn't. This perspective has also helped me in writing this book.

Once I had the tiller or wheel, however, I never let go. My last significant experience as crew, rather than as helmsman, was back with Ted Turner on *Mariner*. This was in 1974, when I was thirty-one. Later that summer, I crewed for Ted Hood on *Courageous*. That was a season of contrasts, for while Ted Turner could hardly keep quiet long enough to take a breath, Ted Hood hardly uttered a word. As I began to take on a leadership role on the water, though, I realized that neither style was right for me. Thus, I have had to develop other techniques. Leadership is one of the subjects explored in this book.

As Tom Whidden noted, I'm persistent. Others have been less kind in describing my tenacity. Ted Turner, owner of the Turner Broadcasting Company, including Cable

News Network (CNN), disparaged my America's Cup effort in 1980 with *Freedom* as "professional" and accused me of ruining the sport. To set the stage for that remark, Turner was sailing *Courageous* that year in an encore performance, after defending the Cup in 1977 with the same boat.

Turner and I started in the America's Cup wars together back in 1974 on *Mariner*. I was thirty-two, from Southern California, and Turner was thirty-four, from Atlanta. Turner, who was named skipper of *Mariner,* invited me to be his number-two man. Later, I learned he made the same offer to Robbie Doyle, who at the time worked for Ted Hood, then the dean of sailmakers. Both of us accepted.

Turner's invitation to this prestigious competition was, primarily, the two SORCs he won; the first in a Cal 40, *Vamp,* in 1964 and the second in 1970 in *American Eagle,* a converted 12-Meter. Perhaps more important, Turner had logged thousands of miles in that America's Cup 12-Meter, which he used to win the World Ocean Racing Championship in 1970. It is likely that at the time, he had more miles in 12-Meter racing than anyone in sailing.

My invitation to the America's Cup stemmed primarily from my winning the Star Worlds and the Congressional Cup, America 's premier match-racing series, held in Long Beach, California. Turner and I were, unquestionably, the Young Turks of the America's Cup, a new generation that was both geographically and socially thousands of miles away from the New York Yacht Club and the East Coast establishment, which championed, orchestrated, and, in those days, almost totally funded the America's Cup.

Listening to Turner on *Mariner* was an education in itself. Turner, who has been called the "Mouth of the South," had most of an Ivy League education, as he was asked to leave Brown University before completing his senior year for some infraction of the rules. A complete southerner—despite being born in Cincinnati (his family moved to Savannah, Georgia, when he was nine)—he would describe complex Civil War campaigns, quote Shakespeare, speak Greek or Latin, or spout dirty limericks in his high-pitched, rapid-fire southern accent while steering the boat. There was a darker side to him, however. Should the crew miss a tack, or wrap a spinnaker around the forestay, everyone on Narragansett Bay would know about the error as well as about the bungling crew member's flawed character. He'd bellow things like, "You simple son of a bitch, you piece of dogmeat!" That's how he described his best friend, Marty O'Meara, who was sailing on the boat. Nevertheless, the crew would walk on water for him. I would have, too, and I can't even swim.

Turner is the most charismatic person I've ever known. If he had been a

Civil War general, we'd probably all be speaking in that high-pitched southern way of his.

Mariner was awful, a failure of the test tank. With a slow boat, Turner had to resort to trickery—surprise—to win races in 1974. There was, for example, the time Gerry Driscoll, skipper of the 12-Meter *Intrepid*, tried to pass us to windward.

We were sailing our stablemate *Valiant*, as *Mariner* was in the shop in search of a new personality. Driscoll was then fifty years old and a boatbuilder. Like me, he was from San Diego and a member of the San Diego Yacht Club, and like me, he had won a Star World Championship. (As a point of interest, when Driscoll won his Star Worlds in 1944, his crew was the fifteen-year-old Malin Burnham.) As *Intrepid*, a two-time winner of the America's Cup, started to pass us in 20 knots of wind, Turner indicated I should take hold of the wheel with him. We had luffing rights, and we exercised them—without mercy. Both Turner and I spun the wheel, and *Intrepid* was unable to respond in time to the luff. The collision resulted in a substantial hole in *Intrepid*'s side. The wound in *Intrepid* was repaired, but not so in Driscoll. From then on, he gave us a very wide berth. He probably thought we were crazy. Turner thought it was the greatest thing he'd ever seen.

Turner would eventually be removed from the helm of *Mariner*, and I was handed command. My relationship with Turner was never the same after that. No one likes to be "fired," and an America's Cup firing is a particularly public event. He was angry, and not surprisingly, a large measure of that anger focused on me. His summer was ending; mine, as it turned out, was just beginning.

To Turner's great credit, when he told his crew he was no longer skippering *Mariner* and would be sailing the second boat, *Valiant*, he urged them to stand behind the effort and to sail with me. Most of them were his great friends who had sailed with him for years. They were a loyal band. Turner said anyone who quit out of sympathy for him would never again sail with him.

When I assumed command of *Mariner*, I cobbled together a winning record. I won three races and was ahead in two others. Nevertheless, we were "excused" from the competition, as the New York Yacht Club called it, leaving the competition to *Courageous* and *Intrepid*. *Courageous* was being co-skippered at the time by Bob Bavier, the New York publisher of *Yachting* magazine, who defended the Cup with *Constellation* in 1964, and Ted Hood, the famous sailmaker from Marblehead, Massachusetts, whose sails had powered every America's Cup defender since 1958.

While my wife, Judy, and I were packing to return home to San Diego,

I received a telephone call from Bob McCullough, head of the *Courageous* syndicate. He was also the New York Yacht Club's vice-commodore. *Courageous,* like *Mariner,* was the first generation of 12-Meters built in aluminum. Common wisdom had it that building a 12-Meter in aluminum rather than wood was, as Turner might have put it, as great an advantage in the America's Cup wars as the ironclad *Merrimac* and then the *Monitor* enjoyed over the wooden warships in the Civil War. Nevertheless, *Courageous* was then involved in a monstrous struggle with the wooden *Intrepid.*

When I met with McCullough, he invited me into the cockpit of *Courageous* to be starting helmsman. McCullough is a large man with a commanding presence. He said, "Young man, I don't want you to feel as though we're putting any undue pressure on you. I don't want you to feel as though you have to dominate [*Intrepid*] at the start. Just as long as you're comfortably ahead...." For a thirty-two-year-old, that was an amazing call to arms. Nevertheless, I thought I could do it. After all, I was up against Driscoll, and after the collision, he seemed scared of me.

When I joined *Courageous,* the chain of command was somewhat confused. I was to start the boat, Ted Hood was to sail it upwind, and Bavier to sail it downwind. Eventually, Bavier would leave the boat, and Hood would be named skipper. *Courageous* defeated *Intrepid* by one thin race in the trials and then went on to defend the America's Cup that year against *Southern Cross,* the first of the Alan Bond–led Australian challengers. Ten years later, of course, Bond would "own" the America's Cup, when his *Australia II* beat *Liberty,* which I skippered, thus ending the longest winning streak in sports.

In 1977, Turner purchased the same *Courageous.* I desperately wanted to skipper a 12-Meter that year in the Cup competition, but the helm of *Enterprise,* the only boat I had a chance to sail, was offered to sailmaker Lowell North, one of my boyhood heroes from San Diego. Frankly, it hurt being left out. I would have killed for the helm of that boat, but how could you not pick Lowell? He had just won the 1976 SORC on *Williwaw,* had Olympic gold and bronze medals, and had won four Star World Championships. He was great. Lowell sailed *Enterprise* with Malin Burnham.

With no invitation to the 1977 America's Cup, I returned to the Star Class for the Worlds in 1977 and the Tempest Class for the Olympics in Kingston, Ontario, in 1976. From Eichenlaub I had learned a little about building boats, and for the Star Worlds, in particular, I decided to push the construction of the boat as much as I could. I went to Leonhard Mader, then the hot builder in the Star Class. His shop is about 60 miles east of Munich, Germany, in, essentially, a cow pasture. I spent a month there—primarily with a scale—supervising the building of my Star. I made sure his building crew squeegeed out every drop of resin. As we will see in Chapter 3, the fiber-to-resin ratio is a very important indicator of strength. I also insisted that they put the boat in the mold on Friday and wouldn't allow them to remove it until Tuesday. I wanted to be sure the boat had adequately hardened. Removing a boat prematurely from a mold can cause it to sag or twist out of shape.

I didn't speak any German. The boatbuilders thought I was nuts. But then, too, the great Soviet sailor Valentin Mankin was there, doing the same thing. So in this cow pasture 60 miles east of Munich were two of us: one communist, one capitalist, both nuts. I won the Star Worlds that year, with five firsts, giving me my second championship in that class.

Just before the 1977 Star Worlds, I received a call from Ed du Moulin, head of the *Enterprise* syndicate. He asked if I would be interested in skippering *Enterprise* in the 1977 America's Cup, replacing Lowell North. I have great respect for Lowell and for his second-in-command, Malin Burnham. If they couldn't beat Turner, I figured, how could I make a difference? Plus, I remembered how furious Turner was when I replaced him on *Mariner*. I didn't want Lowell and Malin mad at me, too. They're my friends; we live in the same town and sail at the same club. As it turned out, Lowell would be off the boat before the summer was over, replaced by Malin.

A sad thing, I think, for the sport of sailing and the America's Cup is that after being relieved of command, Lowell North never returned to sailing with the same fire, enthusiasm, and brilliance he had shown before. His fire was at least partially extinguished. As I said, the America's Cup has changed many lives it has touched.

Turner sailed brilliantly that 1977 summer against *Enterprise* and *Independence,* skippered and designed by Hood. Turner seemed determined to erase the *Mariner* blot on his record. He then successfully defended the Cup against *Australia*, the second Alan Bond–led challenger.

For the 1980 Cup, Turner again sailed *Courageous;* I sailed *Freedom.* Turner's thoughts seemed elsewhere. By then he owned the Braves and Hawks, Atlanta's professional baseball and basketball teams, respectively. Also, he was very involved in starting his television network, which is so successful today. He didn't have the time and, seemingly, the energy, enthusiasm, and money to spend on the Cup.

Beginning with *American Eagle,* then *Mariner, Valiant,* and *Courageous,* Turner had logged tens of thousands of miles in 12-Meters. If I had steered a 12-Meter in a dozen real races, I would have been surprised. So while preparing *Freedom* for 1980, I logged 180 days at sea. I needed at least to close the experience gap with Turner. More important, I believe that in sailing, as in life, practice makes perfect. A key to my success, which will be explored in this book, is that I steer boats: from the moment we leave the dock, through the hours and hours of testing, through the practice races and the actual races, and then while racing to the dock at the end of the day's races. I am practically affixed to the wheel. People who sail regularly with me rarely hear the words: "Here, you take it." To me, that is a waste of time—time that one should spend on honing his or her skills for competition.

It is understandable why Turner would criticize me for racing it my way. When he accused me of ruining the sport with my tenacity, I think he was really saying, "Well, look, if I spent the same amount of time as Dennis does, I could beat him." Or, "Make Dennis spend the same time that I do, and then I'll beat him." Turner wanted this to be a contest of skill and sailing ability: a "one-design" contest for sailors. I said, "Come on now. I don't see that in the rules anywhere. I thought this was a race where the fastest boat and the best skipper, sails, crew, and organization win."

Since I lost the America's Cup in 1983 and won it back four years later, the sport of sailing has changed significantly, some might say unrecognizably. One enduring America's Cup story describes a visitor's question to a member of the New York Yacht Club, after being shown the America's Cup, the 8-pound silver trophy that anchored the club on New York's West Forty-fourth Street until the autumn of 1983. The visitor asks, "What will the club replace the trophy with when it is finally lost?" The response was, "The head of the man who lost it."

I faced the press alone on September 26, 1983, after losing the America's Cup 4–3. Nowhere to be seen were any members of the New York Yacht Club for whom I had tried so hard. I was devastated; I fought to keep the tears from running down my face. I tried to represent my yacht club, my country, and myself the best I could, but it was not to be.

When I looked in the mirror the day after losing the America's Cup, my eyes were a little bloodshot from shedding a tear or two. My head may have hurt, but it was still firmly attached to the rest of me. In time, I could get on with my life. I was able to say to myself, I did my best. I tried my guts out every day. I did nothing but work on this program. I had the best crew, built three boats, and had the best sails. I had no excuse to lose. I just got beat.

I have since come to realize that losing the Cup was the best thing that happened to the America's Cup and inarguably to the sport of sailing. As a result, sailing is front-page news in much of the world. Certainly not all of it is pretty or kind, but the sport of sailing is better understood, appreciated, and is of interest to far more people than it ever was before.

2 | Yacht Design

No one would ever confuse me with a yacht designer. I have been sometimes a witness, sometimes a patron, sometimes the beneficiary, and sometimes the victim of yacht-design technology. I have gained a knowledge of yacht design through firsthand experience with a number of boats. The live-and-learn philosophy characterizes my approach to understanding yacht design.

Also, my lifeblood is fast design, and this is coupled with a consuming curiosity about why some boats are fast and others are slow. When something works, I want to know why. When it doesn't, I want to know why not.[1]

Besides that, what I bring to yacht design is a direct association with some of the best and worst boats of our time. That includes *Mariner, Courageous, Freedom, Australia II, Stars & Stripes '87,* and *Stars & Stripes '88,* the catamaran. They were racing boats all—and hybrid America's Cup yachts at that—but the principles of yacht design are universal (if not universally understood).

The differences between a racing boat and a cruising boat are in emphasis—the choices—not in principles. A cruising designer makes different choices than a racing designer, but the playing field, the sea, is the same. The difference between a 12-Meter and a boat shaped to the International

---

[1]The authors appreciate the kind help of yacht designer David Pedrick in the preparation of this chapter. Pedrick was part of my design team, along with Britton Chance and Bruce Nelson, when we regained the America's Cup in 1987. He was also a member of my 1992 America's Cup design team, along with Nelson and Alberto Calderon. Calderon also contributed to this chapter.

Measurement System (IMS) Rule have to do with how committees of rule-makers see boats, not how the sea does.

Is a knowledge of yacht design important to sailors? It is fundamental—whether you sail a Sunfish, an Etchells 22, or a 35-foot cruising boat. The boat you have or the one you think you want represents hundreds or even thousands of hard choices that began with yacht design. For example: How tall is the rig? How deep is the keel and what is its shape? How long is the waterline? How much ballast is there, where is it concentrated, and what is the displacement? Where is the mast positioned? How much sail area does it carry, and how is the sail area distributed? Where is the engine placed? I could list a thousand more examples. You can buy a boat without understanding yacht design or knowing someone who does, but I doubt you'd buy the best boat for you.

You can sail a boat without understanding yacht design, but you absolutely can't sail one well. You want more weather helm to get more feel in light air, move the mast back or rake it aft. That's yacht design. You want to get your dinghy planing, move the crew back, bring the centerboard up, and pump the sails once. That's yacht design. You want the crew on the high side in heavy air to flatten the boat or on the low side in light air to reduce wetted surface and to give the sails some shape. That, too, is yacht design. You want to go fast or ease motion in a seaway, get the weight out of the ends. You think that Etchells 22, fresh out of the box, is ready to win the worlds? Not likely without you or someone you hire properly sanding and painting the bottom and shaping the keel and rudder. Again, that is yacht design.

I've never met a racing champion or an accomplished cruising sailor who wasn't knowledgeable about yacht design, boatbuilding, maintenance, sails, equipment, technique, weather, strategy, and (if a racer) tactics.

I took an interest in yacht design beginning in 1974. In early June of that year, boatbuilder Bob Derecktor, at the controls of his hulking crane, which dominates the Mamaroneck, New York, waterfront, hoisted a new, bright red 12-Meter out of the blocks. The boat, called *Mariner*, was now on its way to the America's Cup wars. As tactician, I was there at the launching, along with several others, including skipper Ted Turner and designer Britton Chance. *Mariner* would, in time, change the face of the America's Cup, but not in ways we could have imagined when seeing her take wing for the first time.

We were so young back then. I was thirty-two, and Turner and Chance,

Sail Like a Champion

16

thirty-four. Also, as time would tell, we weren't very good in this facet of the sport. When we started sailing the boat, we couldn't even tack the headsail without someone getting injured.

With this design, Britton Chance was challenging Olin Stephens, the dean of yacht design. Stephens, then age sixty-six, had dominated America's Cup yacht design since before the war. He collaborated on the design of *Ranger,* the last of the J-Class boats, which defended the Cup in 1937. He designed such winning America's Cup 12-Meters as *Columbia* in 1958, *Constellation* in 1964, and the brilliant *Intrepid* in 1967. In 1970, he stumbled with the oversized, overweight *Valiant.* Fortunately for the longest winning streak in sports, the then thirty-year-old Britton Chance was there with a redesign of Stephens's *Intrepid,* which successfully defended the Cup. *Intrepid* was Britton Chance's variation on Olin Stephens's brilliant design; *Mariner,* on the other hand, began with a blank sheet of paper.

As *Mariner* rose 15 feet into the air, we peered up at her, first in awe—looking up at a boat of that size from that perspective is always astonishing—and then with considerable surprise. Although I was inexpert in such matters, the back of the boat was unlike anything I'd ever seen. It was blunt rather than pointed.

The day was blustery, as I recall it, not the best time to be launching a package of this size and presumed worth. Despite the wind, Derecktor, who can make the launching of a boat a performance, easily settled the 60,000-pound, 66-foot aluminum boat into the murky water that surrounds his boatyard.

DISPLACEMENT

As one can imagine, a boat of that size makes a considerable hole in the water. According to Archimedes, an object will sink until it displaces an amount of water equal to its weight, about 60,000 pounds of water in the case of *Mariner* and other 12-Meters of the era. Yacht designers refer to the amount of water a boat displaces as displacement and use the terms *weight* and *displacement* interchangeably, which we will do in this book.

There is a dynamic (moving) quality to displacement as well as a static (stationary) one. When a boat moves through the water, the hull moves a corresponding amount of water out of its way, like a seagoing bulldozer. To put this another way, for every boat length *Mariner* travels, it must push 60,000 pounds of water out of its way.

When the water first encounters the hull of a boat moving at maximum

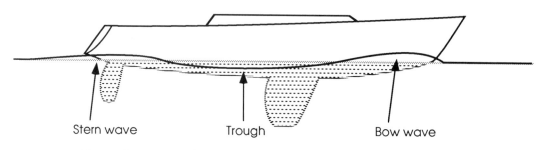

Stern wave   Trough   Bow wave

FIGURE 2.1. *Bow- and stern-wave pattern when moving at or near hull speed.*

speed (known as the boat's hull speed), the water is pushed up into a bow wave (see FIGURE 2.1), like snow before a snowplow.

Like a knife, a hull gets wider, and as it does, the water speeds up to get around it. To understand this increased speed of the water, imagine a boat anchored in a drainage ditch. The water moves past the anchored boat, rather than the boat moving past the water. As the water moving past the anchored boat encounters the widest area of the hull, it has less space on either side to move through the ditch. Will the water speed up—keeping the water flow continuous—or slow down—backing up the flow? The water speeds up, since all the water is pushing from behind in order to get past the boat. With this increase in the speed of the fluid comes a decrease in pressure, according to a principle of physics known as Bernoulli's law.

This speeding up of the fluid to get around the widest part of the hull and the resulting decrease in pressure create suction—such as on the top of an airplane wing or on the lee side of sail. When this suction is at its maximum amidships, where the hull is widest, it pulls the water and the boat down into a trough, or hole, in the water (see FIGURE 2.1).

Although the water speeds up to get past the widest part of the hull, once it has passed that part, it cannot be going faster than its initial speed. Thus, the water slows to its original speed. Also, the water that was sucked downward amidships now rises up with the increase in pressure to form a stern wave that closes back around the boat. The stern wave is slightly smaller than the bow wave. There are also a few trailing waves astern of the yacht that grow smaller until they disappear after a few more oscillations.

WAVE-MAKING RESISTANCE

As energy from the wind is required to make wind-driven waves, energy from the boat is required to make boat-driven waves. (A sailboat's energy comes from the deflection of wind by the sailplan and the deflection of water by the underwater foils.) The energy used in wave-making acts as a limit to boat speed and is felt by the boat as a resistance—an impediment to motion. Suppose you have a car with a 100-horsepower engine, and its top speed is 80 miles per hour. When you turn on the air conditioner, the top speed may drop to 77 miles per hour. It takes energy to make the waves that form around a hull—and the bigger the waves, the more energy it takes—which reduces the energy that can drive the boat. This diminishes a boat's top-end speed.

When it is windy and the boat is moving fast, the wave-making resistance, as this is called, can account for about 60 percent of the total resistance; the rest comes from frictional drag, form drag, induced drag, etc. (to be discussed later). Obviously, a theme of yacht design is to reduce drag, or resistance, and to increase the driving forces.

The horizontal distance between wave crests is called the wavelength. With wind-driven waves, the greater the wavelength—or greater the horizontal distance—the faster the wave form moves through the water. This relationship between wavelength (distance apart) and speed is expressed in a formula: wave speed = 1.34 x square root of wavelength. Little waves—that is, those with a small horizontal distance between crests—move slowly; big waves move quickly.

It is the same with boat-driven waves: the farther the bow and stern waves can be pushed apart by the hull, the faster the resulting wave form moves through the water, and the faster the boat. A boat that cannot plane—a displacement boat—is trapped in its wave train; thus, the faster the wave train moves, the faster the boat moves. This is expressed in the formula for hull speed: hull speed = 1.34 x square root of waterline (LWL). (Note that the two formulas are identical.) Thus, for displacement boats, the (horizontal) distance between bow and stern waves is a very real limit to boat speed.

Think of the wave train around a boat as a conveyor belt carrying the boat. The faster the conveyor belt moves, the faster the boat moves. To put this another way, the farther apart you can push the bow and stern waves, the faster the conveyor belt moves, and the potentially faster the boat. Obviously, the longer the waterline, the farther apart are the waves. This is a main reason why a boat that is longer on the water is faster than one that is shorter on the water.

When a boat is moving at hull speed, there is a bow and stern wave on either side of a trough (see FIGURE 2.1). When a boat is moving slower than hull speed, however, there are more waves overlapping the hull. At half speed, for example, there will be two troughs, or four waves. The increase in the number of waves when sailing at reduced speed is because of the relationship between the horizontal distance between waves and their speed. As the boat is moving slower, the horizontal distance between waves decreases and, thus, more of them overlap the waterline.

In addition to waterline length, the displacement of a boat is critical to wave-making resistance, or drag. A heavy boat sits deeper in the water. This increases the size of the waves. It is similar to a snowplow: a snowplow with its blade on the ground moves more snow out of the way and makes a bigger "wave" than one with its blade 8 inches above the ground. A heavy boat that sits deeper in the water moves more water out of the way than a light boat that doesn't sit as deep. Thus, with a heavy boat, the waves are bigger. More energy is required to make bigger waves, making for more resistance.

A useful measure of both displacement and sailing length is the displacement-length ratio. The formula is:

$$D/L = \frac{\text{displacement (in long tons)}}{(.01 \times LWL)^3}$$

A long ton is 2,240 pounds. To convert 10,000 pounds to long tons divide 10,000 by 2,240, which equals 4.46 long tons. LWL is waterline length.

A cruising boat might have a displacement-length ratio of 300; a 12-Meter, 260; a light boat, like an IOR 50-footer, in the 200 range. The new International America's Cup Class (IACC) is less than 100, and an ultralight displacement boat (ULDB) is 60 to 90. (These displacement boats are still limited by hull speed; however, a ULDB needs less wind and/or less sail area to get to hull speed.) Other factors that influence wave-making resistance are the beam of the boat, the fineness of the entry (how pointed or blunt the bow), the distribution of the underwater volume, the depth of the hull, and so on.

By way of contrast, a planing boat, like a Laser, is light enough for its length (D/L is 69 with crew), moves fast enough, and develops sufficient lift from its hull form to leave its stern wave behind and climb nearly over its bow wave. As a result, it encounters less wave-making resistance and less frictional resistance (discussed below). Due to the lift, the boat skims or planes above the surface—hence the designation planing hull.

If you look behind a Laser when it is planing, you can often see a small wave or lump in the water. This is the stern wave, which the Laser has outrun. A stern wave is most apparent in waterskiing. With a planing powerboat, there is a lump in the water, well behind the boat, where the stern wave is. The length of a waterskier's rope is made longer to avoid this stern wave, which can easily trip the skier.

Returning to *Mariner*, the focus of this boat was on wave-making and sailing length. Britton Chance's radical 12-Meter was an attempt to fool the ocean into thinking the waterline was longer than it actually was—to push the bow and stern waves farther apart, to make the "conveyor belt" carrying the boat move faster. To trick the water, the designer kept the back of the boat artificially full and then chopped it off abruptly where required by the 12-Meter rule.

If Chance was enthusiastic about this concept, the ocean was vastly less impressed. There were early indications that this might be so. When we first left Derecktor's yard to go to the commissioning, *Mariner* was dragging an inordinate amount of trash. Rather than the hull smoothly releasing such flotsam, it seemed to be hauling it along in its wake. The crew took to describing this phenomenon as a "bone in her tail"—a variation on the more familiar expression "a bone in her teeth."

Thus, though *Mariner* was a bold experiment, she turned out to be slow, and the summer of 1974—Turner's and my debut in the America's Cup—started badly and got worse, at least until I was invited to join *Courageous*. As a result, considerable acrimony developed between the yacht designer and the skipper. Then when I replaced Turner as skipper of *Mariner*, there was tension between Turner and me. Chance was pointing his finger at Turner and the crew for the failure of the boat. He'd come to the dinner table with a three-page list of things to do to make the boat faster. He was right about most of these ideas, but despite his and everyone's best efforts, our basic lack of boat speed was an insurmountable handicap.

Mariner sailed in the June trials without much success. Then the boat was shipped back to Derecktor's yard, where the back end was to be rebuilt. Bob Derecktor, who built the boat originally, is a rough-and-ready man who, in addition to being a very talented boatbuilder, is a very talented sailor. Derecktor, in fact, was sailing on *Mariner*. When *Mariner* returned to the shed, he took out a felt-tip pen and just roughly sketched out this huge expanse—the area Chance worked so hard on—that was to be cut away. Then his work force took out their power saws and attacked the aluminum hull. It was shocking to see an America's Cup boat, even a very slow one, treated this way.

Mariner missed the July trials while the back end was being reshaped into a more normal configuration. The *Mariner* crew pitched in with Derecktor's work force to help prepare the boat for the August trials. In those days; America's Cup crews weren't paid, but we put in seventeen- and eighteen-hour days sanding the bottom and doing other tasks. Compared with Derecktor's work force, we were rank amateurs. Late one evening, Derecktor came in and saw one of his workers sanding across the boat instead of fore and aft. He shouted, "Gabriel! How many times do I have to tell you, sand fore and aft, not up and down." Well, this guy had had enough. He threw down his sanding block and shouted, "F— Derecktor! F— America! F— the America's Cup!" and stormed out.

FRICTIONAL RESISTANCE

This is a good place to talk about the importance of a smooth hull. I have sanded my fair share of hulls in my time, and I know that kind of frustration. On more than a few occasions, I've wondered, Is a perfectly smooth bottom really worth it?

Earlier we commented that as a displacement yacht nears hull speed, wave-making resistance accounts for as much as 60 percent of the total resistance. At lower speeds, frictional resistance is the major cause of resistance. There is friction where the water touches the hull. (In Chapter 4, we will see there is also friction where the air touches the sail.) Both water and air have a certain amount of viscosity, or stickiness. The viscosity of water is why glasses come out of the dishwasher with water spots.

Because of this viscosity, or stickiness, the water that touches a moving hull stops and is, in essence, carried along by the hull. The next layer of water flowing past the moving hull is slowed by the braking action of the first, but is not slowed as much as the first layer. The next layer of water is slowed by the braking action of the second, but is not slowed as much. And so on. This area where water is stopped and gradually increases speed is termed a boundary layer. Outside the boundary layer, the water is unaffected by the passing of the hull. The drag due to the viscosity is called frictional resistance, or viscous drag.

The boundary layer around a hull gradually thickens toward the stern of a boat to about 1 to 2 percent of the waterline (LWL). Thus if the waterline is 44 feet—about the length of a 12-Meter waterline—the boundary layer, an area of turbulent water, can be as much as 5 to 11 inches thick at the back. With all that turbulent water, how much of a difference can a perfectly smooth bottom make?

From time to time, coatings have come along supposedly to reduce the drag due to the viscosity of water, or viscous drag. I can, for example, remember Lowell North in the late 1960s, dispensing a soaplike product from the bow of his 5.5. Using the soap, which is slippery, was an attempt to reduce frictional resistance. While this method of dispersal was declared illegal by the International Yacht Racing Union (IYRU) Rule 63(a), racers have been known to apply soap to a boat's bottom just before a race. There was, for example, a team that went over *Courageous* every morning with rollers, applying a soapy product. The soap would dry, and the hope was that it would decrease skin friction before it would completely wash off the hull.

Then in 1986–87, along came Rivlets, from the 3M company. Rivlets is a plastic-film coating with microscopic parallel grooves, designed to decrease the viscous drag of air on aircraft. We used this experimental film on *Stars & Stripes '87*. It wasn't easy to use. The grooves had to match the flow of water around the boat, which varies. Also, cracks appeared between the adjacent sheets. Nevertheless, the designers felt there was a decrease in viscous drag of 2 to 4 percent. I wasn't convinced, but I recognize the crew believed in it. Their belief, I felt, could be a psychological edge for us. Whether truth or fancy, Rivlets and similar coatings have since been outlawed under Rule 63(b) of the IYRU Rules.

Because of the undesirability of skin friction, many racers won't paint a boat's bottom before a big race. They'll paint it at least three weeks before and then wet-sand it. I don't believe in that; I think you want to wait for the paint to harden, for a week at the most, before sanding it. New paint, however, is no slower, I believe, than old paint, provided it is hard and smooth.

The honest answer is, I don't know if a perfectly smooth bottom makes any difference or not—just as I couldn't tell if Rivlets made any difference. However, my philosophy of life is, When in doubt, do it! If you don't sand with 600-grit or even 1000-grit paper (see Chapter 3), you can bet the next guy has—and so have I.

If I didn't have time to sand the entire boat, I'd concentrate on the front quarter, where the boundary layer hasn't had time to form or isn't very thick. Here, the flow along the hull is relatively smooth, what a yacht designer describes as laminar flow. In a small boat, like a dinghy, laminar flow and the slightly more agitated transitional flow can extend along a fair portion of the hull. So a larger percentage of a dinghy should be sanded.

WETTED SURFACE AND
FRICTIONAL RESISTANCE

The smoothness or lack of smoothness of the skin, or hull, is not all that accounts for viscous drag. The greater the wetted surface—the more boat in contact with the water—the greater the frictional resistance. Reducing wetted surface during the yacht-design process is especially important for sailing in light winds. Since the mid-1960s reducing wetted surface has been a trend in yacht design, for racing boats as well as cruising boats. One sign of this is the predominance of fin keels, as opposed to full-length keels. A long traditional keel, however, does give a yacht a kinder motion, but it is slow, particularly in light winds.

The Cal 40, a racer/cruiser designed by Bill Lapworth in 1964, is considered the pivotal boat in the trend to the fin keel as well as the separate spade rudder (see FIGURE 2.2), both of which reduce wetted surface. Before this, sailboats had contiguous keel/rudders. Asking one lifting surface to steer, create lift, and carry ballast meant the foil was much larger than it had to be. As such, it showed much greater wetted surface.

Another advantage of a separate fin keel and spade rudder is that the keel could be optimized as a lifting surface, as could the rudder. Also, moving the rudder back gave it more leverage, making it more effective in steering the boat. Thus, both lifting appendages, the rudder and the keel, could be smaller—front to back—decreasing wetted surface, viscous drag, and induced drag (discussed later in this chapter).

FORM DRAG

Similar to viscous drag, form drag is associated with the bluntness of a boat's form. For example, a 66-foot, 60,000-pound 12-Meter has more form drag than an eight-person rowing shell, which is similar in length.

A blunt shape has to push more water aside than a more streamlined shape. It takes extra energy to force the water to go around a blunt shape, when compared with a pointed shape.

Form drag is also influenced by how rapidly the boat curves as it broadens to the widest part of the hull and how quickly it narrows again toward the back. Too steep a curve and the water can't easily negotiate it. When the water is unable to follow the curve, the flow can separate—break away from the contours of the hull. Then there is a further increase in drag, or resistance, due to energy expended creating vortices in the separated flow.

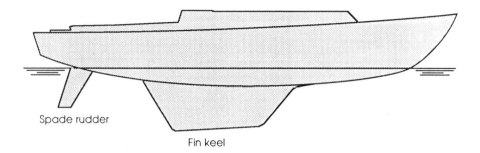

Spade rudder

Fin keel

FIGURE 2.2. *The Cal 40 was the forerunner in the trend to a separate fin keel and spade rudder.*

Decreasing form drag is the reason yacht designers work very hard to design a boat with a fair hull, that is, one without sharp or abrupt curves, or bumps. It is also why boatbuilders work so hard to build a fair boat and then to enhance its fairness with microballoons (discussed in the next chapter). Bumps, or areas of unfairness, cause the water to turn additional curves, creating turbulence, or form drag, which, like viscous drag, slows a boat.

ADDED RESISTANCE IN WAVES

Waves also cause resistance, at least when sailing upwind. When a boat is sailed upwind in a seaway, each wave slaps the hull, that is, exerts a force on the boat. (When you are sailing downwind, following seas give the boat a shove from behind.) The shape of the boat—its displacement, beam, and susceptibility to pitching (the alternate rising and falling of the bow)—determines how much the vessel's progress will be affected by wave action. A boat with excess weight in the ends is more likely to pitch excessively in waves; one with weight concentrated in the center pitches less.

INDUCED DRAG

A sail turns the wind. This turning results in high-speed flow and low pressure on the leeward side of the sail and low-speed flow and high pressure on the windward side. A keel turns the water, too, and the result is the same: a high-speed and low-pressure side and a low-speed and high-pressure side. In

Chapter 8, we will see how the wind blows from a high-pressure system to a low-pressure system (see FIGURE 8.2). Like water running downhill, this is a natural tendency. Putting high pressure on one side of a sail or keel and low pressure on the other side creates instability. The fluid—be it air or water—wants to leak from the high-pressure side to the low-pressure side to equalize the pressure, and it looks for ways to do this. The easiest path is to go over the top or under the bottom of the sail, or under a keel. This leakage is termed induced drag. (Recall from Chapter 1 that the decksweeper jib, with its foot touching the deck, helps prevent the air from leaking.)

Whether applied to sails, a keel, or an airplane wing, this leakage manifests itself as a vortex—a spinning, or circulation, of considerable strength. It takes significant energy to cause this tornadolike spinning. The energy is lost or wasted; it cannot be used to create forward motion. As such, induced drag is slow, and yacht designers work hard to minimize it.

The profile, or aspect ratio, of the foils (in a sailboat, the foils include the sailplan, keel or centerboard, and rudder) has an impact on induced drag. The higher the aspect ratio of the foils, the less the induced drag; see the top boat with the high-aspect (deep and thin) keel in FIGURE 2.3. The low-aspect-ratio (or shallow and long) keel beneath it has a much longer tip and thus shows more induced drag. This is why practically all foils on

FIGURE 2.3. *Keel aspect ratio and induced drag.*

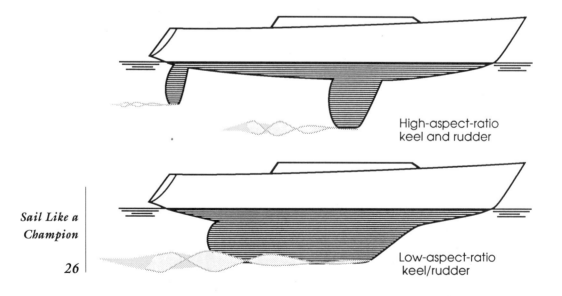

High-aspect-ratio keel and rudder

Low-aspect-ratio keel/rudder

yachts, be they racing or cruising boats, have grown taller and thinner, or show a high aspect ratio. (As mentioned, one still sees an occasional cruising boat with a contiguous keel/rudder. Such a keel offers greater strength in the event of a grounding—since its attachment to the hull is much longer and therefore stronger than that of a fin keel—and the motion it provides is more seakindly. However, this configuration is becoming rarer.)

Aspect Ratios and Sailing Angles

As a rule, the higher the aspect ratio, the faster a boat is to windward. Of course, if a keel is too deep, it is more likely to bump against the bottom. Also, at a certain point, racing rules—the International Offshore Rule (IOR), for example—punish extreme draft. This is presumably because the rule-makers don't want boats running aground and wish to avoid the structural hazards inherent in extreme appendages on a boat. Similarly, a rig reaches a point of diminishing returns. A rig that is too tall is difficult to support and probably doesn't allow you to go much faster to weather.[2] Also, at some point, racing rules penalize exaggerated rig height.

Off the wind, however, foils with high aspect ratios are a disadvantage. This is why, for example, the centerboard on a dinghy is raised. Turning to sails: When sailing downwind, there is little or no lift from the sails. At this orientation, there isn't low speed and high pressure on the weather side and high speed and low pressure on the lee side. Downwind, sails are wind-blocking devices, like a kite, and their drag is what moves sailboats. A low-aspect-ratio sailplan (short mast and long boom) is the best shape to block the wind or maximize drag.

When reaching, both lift and drag contribute to speed, and this is one reason a reach is the fastest point of sail. The optimum sailplan for a reach is somewhere between that of a high-aspect-ratio (beating) shape and a low-aspect-ratio (running) shape. The keel should be deep when reaching, as well as when beating, but for a different reason. A keel, in addition to providing lift, carries ballast (discussed below). The more ballast and the lower it is carried, the straighter the boat stands. Because heeling is a limit to how much sail a boat can carry, a boat that heels less can carry more sail.

---

[2]If the rig is 100 feet tall with a boom that is 20 feet wide, by the time you get to the top of the triangle, or rig, there isn't much sail area. Also, what little sail area there is at the top of the triangle is fairly ineffective behind the disturbed flow around the mast.

These very different rigs and keels for the three wind orientations are some of the reasons why yacht design is such a challenge, whether a designer is creating a racing boat or a cruiser. Usually, racing boats focus on windward sailing, as beating is emphasized in competition. (The popular Olympic course, for example, has three weather legs, two reaching legs, and one running leg.) The result of this upwind emphasis in competition is a high-aspect-ratio sailplan and lifting surfaces (keel and rudder). Alternatively, designers may draw what is termed "horses for courses": the ultralight displacement boat (ULDB) for the downwind Transpac is an obvious example. Cruising boats focus on reaching, which requires a less high-aspect-ratio shape in the underwater foils and the rigs. However, all boats need some windward ability for safety; at some time, a boat might have to beat off a lee shore in a big breeze.

LIFT FROM A KEEL

Put a sail at an angle to the wind—what is known as an angle of attack—and the sail turns the wind. The result of turning the wind is the now familiar pressure differential: high-speed flow and low pressure on the leeward side of the sail and low-speed flow and high pressure on the windward side. This causes strong pulls, or suction, on the leeward side and smaller pushes on the windward side. It is possible to represent these pulls and pushes by a single vector (a line showing magnitude by its length and direction by its compass orientation) that acts through the center of effort in the sail(s). In FIGURE 2.4, that vector is S_{Total}, which stands for total-sail force. If there were no drag from the sails and the rig, S_{Total} would be perpendicular to the apparent wind.[3] Because of this drag, it is slightly aft of perpendicular.

Without a keel, or centerboard, a boat would not be able to sail closer to the wind than a broad reach, that is, approximately the angle between the apparent wind and the S_{Total}. These underwater appendages work in a way that is similar to a sail. The angle of attack of the keel, or centerboard, stems from leeway, the difference between the boat's centerline and the course made good (see FIGURE 2.4). Like a sail, a keel has a high-pressure side

[3]The wind you feel when the boat is moving is the apparent wind. The wind you feel when the boat is stationary is the true wind. Both the direction and the speed of the apparent wind differ from the true wind. This is because the apparent wind is the vector sum of the true wind as well as the boat speed and heading (see FIGURE 4.9).

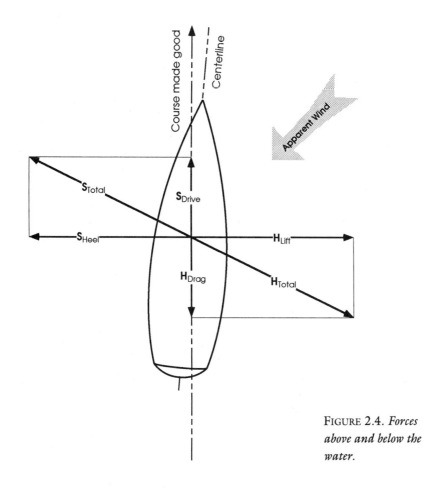

FIGURE 2.4. *Forces above and below the water.*

where the fluid (water) moves past it relatively slowly. The keel also has a low-pressure side along which the fluid moves by at a greater speed. (The boat in FIGURE 2.4 is on starboard tack. The high-speed, low-pressure side of the sails is on the lee, or left, side. However, the high-speed, low-pressure side of the keel is on the right side.) Again, the results are pulls and pushes on the keel, although in the opposite direction to the sails. The pushes and pulls in the athwartships direction can be reduced to one vector—see H_{Lift}, which stands for hydrodynamic lift. The vector acts at the keel's center of lateral resistance.

Lift isn't free, however. As noted above, the generation of lift induces a corresponding force, often termed drag or resistance. This hydrodynamic drag (H_{Drag} in the figure) comes from the hull primarily but also from the keel (centerboard) and the rudder. The result of this hydrodynamically induced drag is to rotate H_{Lift} back to H_{Total}. The ability to create a significant hydrodynamic side force (H_{Lift}) at a small leeway angle with a modest drag penalty (H_{Drag}) allows a yacht to make headway to windward.

RIGHTING MOMENT FROM A KEEL

A keel, in addition to providing lift, also carries ballast. The ballast helps balance the heeling force of the sailplan. In FIGURE 2.4, we reduced the forces in the sailplan to one force, S_{Total}. It is also possible to break that force into two equivalent forces: S_{Drive} and S_{Heel}. S_{Drive} is the part of the sail force that drives the boat forward. Opposing it is the sum of all the drags: wave-making, frictional, form, and induced. The less drag, the longer the S_{Drive} vector; this shows graphically why yacht designers work so hard at reducing drag, or resistance. Also note that when S_{Drive} exceeds H_{Drag}, such as in a puff, the boat accelerates, until drag builds a corresponding amount. When H_{Drag} exceeds S_{Drive}, such as in a lull, the boat slows, until lift from the sailplan and keel build.

S_{Heel} is perpendicular to the boat's direction of travel. It is this force that causes the boat to heel. Upwind, the heeling force (S_{Heel}) is roughly four times greater than the forward force (S_{Drive}). That fact alone explains the importance of hiking on a weather leg on a centerboard boat, or putting crew on the rail in a keelboat. The more you can flatten the boat to make the keel (centerboard) more vertical, the longer the S_{Drive} vector, and the faster the boat. Also, the fact that only a small component of the total force generated by the sails when sailing upwind is in the drive direction explains why upwind sailing is slow.

The ballast in the keel exerts a righting moment that helps balance heel (S_{Heel}). In fact, without this ballast—or in a dinghy without weight on the rail or, better yet, a hiking crew—the boat can tip over.

The keel lowers the vertical center of gravity (VCG) of the overall yacht; the lower the VCG, the more stable the boat. This is clearly seen in the scientific concept of moments, or weight times distance. To illustrate this: There are seesaws that have movable balance points (see FIGURE 2.5, top). A 60-pound child 6 feet from a balance point can balance a 180-pound adult 2 feet from the balance point (60 x 6 = 360, 180 x 2 = 360). Applying this principle to keels, the more weight you can pack low in the keel, the greater the righting arm (see FIGURE 2.5, bottom). The result is the boat can carry more sail and is more powerful.

In effect, weight aloft is bad; weight low is good—at least in a displacement boat. Lessening weight aloft is why rigs and sails have grown much lighter, in both racing and cruising boats, and more expensive. The obvious example is the carbon-fiber masts and booms in the new International America's Cup Class. While I applaud the achievements in physics and engineering, I don't salute the $500,000 price tag of such rigs. Since failures occurred—at least six masts failed from 1991–1992, including one of ours—the leading edge is now accompanied by a painful learning curve. Furthermore, the America's Cup is a match race, and all the top boats had similar rigs. So the new material does nothing for the speed of one boat relative to another and leads to excessive costs as well.

FIGURE 2.5. *The principle of "moments" or weight times distance.*

A 60–pound child 6 feet from the fulcrum balances a 180–pound adult 2 feet away.

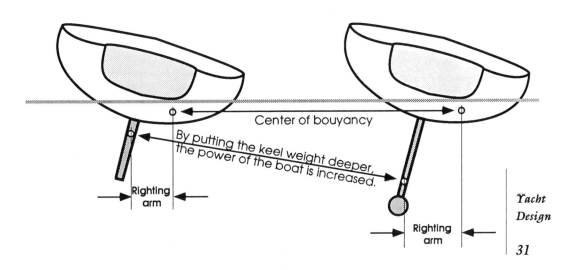
Center of bouyancy
By putting the keel weight deeper, the power of the boat is increased.
Righting arm
Righting arm

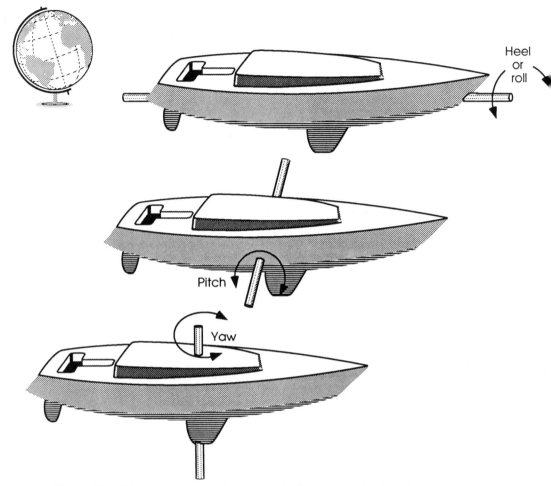

FIGURE 2.6. *A boat can move on three axes or in six directions in three-dimensional space.*

MOTIONS OF A SAILBOAT

As should be apparent from the above, a heavy mast causes a boat to heel more. A heavy keel—better yet, one with the weight low—causes a sailboat to heel less. Heeling is one of three motions a sailboat makes.

Imagine a sailboat supported as a globe is. One imaginary line, or axis, can run from the bow to the stern (see FIGURE 2.6, top). Supported this way, the boat can heel, or roll. It is the keel's job and/or the crew on the weather rail to minimize this movement.

An axis can also run athwartships (see FIGURE 2.6, center). Supported this way, the boat can pitch. Moving the crew forward and back affects the boat's pitching, as does keeping weight out of the ends of the boat. In Chapter 5, we will see that crew weight should be concentrated at this axis, or center of pitching, to minimize pitching.

Finally, an axis can pass vertically through the boat, causing it to yaw (see FIGURE 2.6, bottom). Yaw is linked to helm balance. A rudder has two jobs: to steer the boat, obviously, but also to complement the lift of the keel. This is why a sailboat is rigged to have 3 to 5 degrees of weather helm. When you must move the tiller or wheel 3 to 5 degrees just to make the boat track straight, the rudder has an angle of attack, too, and is able to create lift, like a keel. (This will be discussed further in Chapters 5 and 7.) A sailboat's attitude is an ever-changing combination of motions around these three axes. All of these motions affect boat speed.

AUSTRALIA II

Australia II, which beat *Liberty,* the boat I skippered in the 1983 America's Cup, is an interesting example of increasing the righting moment and reducing induced drag. Normally, the fat part of the keel is against the hull, and the keel narrows at the bottom (see the Cal 40 in FIGURE 2.2). This tapering—with the longer chords at the top—is reminiscent of how a wing leaves the fuselage of an airplane and obviously is the easiest attachment to engineer.[4] (Buildings, for example, don't have narrow bottoms and wide tops.)

Australia II, however, had an upside-down keel (see FIGURE 2.7). The fat part—the longest chords—is at the bottom rather than the top. This reverse taper allowed more lead to be packed at the bottom of the keel, increasing the righting arm (see FIGURE 2.5). This lowered the vertical center of gravity, making the boat stiffer and a better sail-carrying platform. Also, where the keel joins the hull, called the fillet, is a high-drag area, and making this attachment smaller (that is, cleaner) decreased drag there.

A problem, however, was that this huge tip down low showed an increase in induced drag. A high-aspect-ratio shape, such as a keel with short chords and a deep draft, can lessen induced drag. This shape wasn't possible because the International Rule, used to rate a 12-Meter, has a draft limit of 9 feet, 2.5 inches for these boats, which is not generous. Also, with

---

[4]Chord is the measurement of the keel front to back; height is its measurement top to bottom, also called depth.

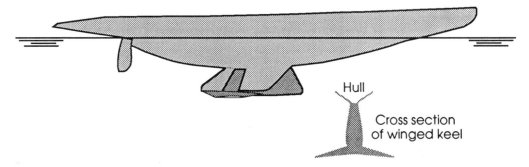

FIGURE 2.7 *The upside-down winged keel of* Australia II.

the fat part of the keel carried low, a high-aspect shape wasn't possible: a keel can't be fat down low to carry more lead and thin to have a high-aspect shape.

To decrease induced drag—the flow escaping from the high-pressure side of the foil to the low-pressure side—airplanes sometimes have "fences," or more sophisticated "winglets," on their wing tips. Wings, or fences, are described by aerodynamicists as multiple-lifting surfaces. Multiple-lifting surfaces can produce lift with less induced drag. Ben Lexcen, in essence, used this technology on *Australia II*; he affixed winglets on the keel to help prevent induced drag. Like a decksweeper jib, the wings cut off the area where the flow can leak from the high-pressure side to the low-pressure side. Also, winglets can produce lift in their own right, making the foil—the keel—even more efficient.

Just as significant, Lexcen made these winglets out of lead, which allowed him to pack even more weight at the very bottom of the keel, further increasing the righting arm. Then, he angled the wings down. This increased draft when the boat heeled, improving speed to weather. This was a way to get around the limitations of increased draft, under the rule. When the boat was measured upright, the wings didn't extend beyond the draft limit of 9 feet, 2.5 inches. When the boat heeled under sail, it had a deeper keel, further reducing induced drag and increasing the righting moment.

Most observers would say the intent of the rule was for the boat to sail in 9 feet, 2.5 inches of water. *Australia II* could not, but the Australians, led by Alan Bond and Warren Jones, were better able to make their case for the new keel shape than the New York Yacht Club could make its case against it.

The 12-Meter rule, like most rating rules, allows a designer to make

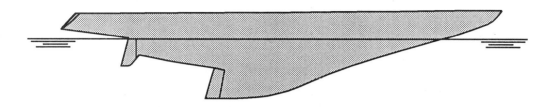

FIGURE 2.8 Courageous, *designed in 1974, had a profound influence on America's Cup yacht design until* Australia II, *designed in 1983.*

various trade-offs in hull dimensions and sail area. The formula[5] is:

$$\frac{L + 2D + \sqrt{SA} - F}{2.37} = 12$$

From the formula and the relationships or penalty section of the rule, a boat can be long on the water and show increased ballast but less sail area if the designer wishes to emphasize heavy-weather performance. Alternatively, it can be short on the water and show less ballast but more sail area if the designer wishes to emphasize light-air performance. With *Australia II* showing increased stability over the traditional 12-Meter, Lexcen traded waterline length and displacement for more sail area. With a stiff boat, he could well afford to do that. Being shorter on the water, the boat had some wave-making limits, but this was easily overcome by her increased stability and her ability to carry more sail area. These trades were as brilliant as the winged keel, if more subtle, and all of them made for a breakthrough boat.

Australia II, a product of computer modeling, was a giant step taken in a time when American yacht designers were taking baby steps with what the press referred to as "*Courageous* clones." *Courageous* (see FIGURE 2.8) was designed by Sparkman & Stephens, for the 1974 America's Cup. She suc-

---

[5]L is similar to sailing length, or waterline, but it is measured 7 inches above the load waterline, to get an idea of the shape of the overhangs, fore and aft. Overhangs can translate to sailing length when the boat heels. D is the difference between the skin girth and the chain girth. The skin girth follows the lines of the hull. The chain girth bridges the hollows. This measurement penalizes the removal of displacement from the center of the boat. It accounts for the wineglass-sectional shape of 12-Meters. SA is mainsail area and 85 percent of the headsail. F is the average of three freeboard stations—freeboard corresponds to the height of the deck. Additionally, the rule defines various relationships; for example, for a given waterline length, you must have a certain amount of displacement; otherwise there is a penalty.

cessfully defended that year and defended again in 1977, when redesigned by Ted Hood. *Courageous* is one of only three boats that have defended the America's Cup twice: the others are *Colombia* in 1899 and 1901, as designed by Nathanael Herreshoff, and *Intrepid* in 1967, as designed by Sparkman & Stephens, and in 1970, as redesigned by Britton Chance. *Courageous* was so successful that all defense candidates, as well as most challengers, came out looking like her. That continued into 1983. *Courageous,* in fact, was very competitive in 1983, as sailed by John Kolius. What we Americans were doing for design for the 1983 Cup pales by comparison to *Australia II.*

To set the stage for the loss of the Cup in 1983, I was in awe of Olin Stephens back in 1980, when he designed *Freedom* for me. Olin Stephens was, in my mind, the most talented designer. He knew the most about yacht design, had the most experience, and had created the most winning boats. He was also the most acceptable from the fund-raising perspective. All the deep-pocket guys from the Northeast thought he was the master. I never really got to know him well, but he was like a god to me, too; it was thrilling just to be in his company. It wasn't Olin and Dennis. He was "Mr. Stephens" to me. Despite that distance, I liked him.

In the 1980 America's Cup, my first as skipper, we could do no wrong. We had a good boat in *Freedom*—a *Courageous* clone—and even better sails. We easily beat *Courageous* and *Clipper* and sailed the America's Cup against *Australia I,* a boat similar to *Courageous,* which had, however, an inventive bendy mast. The bendy mast was a clever way to get extra and unrated sail area (discussed in Chapter 5). *Australia I* won one race in the America's Cup match—something that hadn't been done by a challenger in ten years. I was, I have to admit, surprised when immediately after the series, the Australians sold the boat.

While the significance escaped me then, I understand it clearly now. The Australians decided they couldn't beat us by copying us. They would start the design process fresh. That led them to computer modeling, where the computer was used to test shapes. A computer can test shapes much faster than a towing tank or obviously by building a full-size boat, and at a much lower cost. It was the speed and low cost of computer testing that allowed Lexcen to develop the radical winged keel.

For 1983, Olin Stephens was semi-retired, but his firm, Sparkman & Stephens (S&S), penned *Spirit* for our syndicate. Also for 1983, Johan Valentijn, who worked for S&S before establishing his own design office in Newport, drew *Magic* for us. I wanted two designers in the program. So we got *Spirit* and *Magic,* which never measured up.

Magic, in fact, never measured in. Johan Valentijn, her designer, was creative but disorganized, and not particularly good with details. Even if his *Magic* had been a competitive 12-Meter, I still couldn't have raced her in the America's Cup. Johan had read the 12-Meter Rule, but he'd never read the America's Cup Deed of Gift. According to the Deed of Gift (but not the Rule), "The competing yacht or vessel, if of one mast, shall be not less than forty-four feet nor more than ninety feet on the load waterline."[6] *Magic* was 2.9 inches too short. I was glad no one ever found out about that because we would have looked incredibly stupid. I didn't learn about it until much later. In those days, designers kept their rating certificates secret, even from the skipper and crew. If I wanted to know what we had to do to add 3 inches of sail area, they could tell me to remove 200 pounds of ballast, or whatever. That was about it.

When these two boats proved to be slow, we tried to get S&S and Johan Valentijn to work together in 1983 on a third boat, but the collaboration proved impossible. That was discouraging. So Johan designed *Liberty*.

After *Australia II* was measured at Cove Haven, we had sketches of the radical boat with the trick keel, yet our technical people were unable to figure out exactly what the winged keel did. That was discouraging, too. They may have been threatened by it, but they didn't understand it enough to copy it. As should be apparent, the winged keel did plenty. It gave the America's Cup a new home and caused the Australian boat and yacht design to fly.

An interesting question is, Would I have built a yacht with a winged keel if the idea had been presented to me? I think not—particularly as the defender of the longest winning streak in sports. I've never been interested in being the first, the pioneer. Give me a competitive design, and I think I can do all right with it. My experience is that people on the leading edge pay the price more often than they reap the rewards.

I've been very wrong about this approach, too. For example, I chose not to build *Ganbare,* one of the most famous One Tonners of my generation. In 1973, Doug Peterson, a schoolmate of my wife, Judy, showed me drawings of a yacht he designed. He hoped I would be interested in building and campaigning the boat in the One Ton North Americans, which were to be held in May of that year at the San Diego Yacht Club. Peterson spread the drawings out on the hood of my car at the San Diego Yacht Club. It was hard not to laugh. "Oh, Doug," I said, "I can't build this."

---

[6]The "ninety feet" was the waterline length of Michael Fay's *New Zealand*, which challenged for 1988, discussed at the end of this chapter.

The drawings were ridiculously crude; the boat itself was also small. One Tonners of that day were long; the Ranger 37, *Munequita,* for example, which won the 1973 SORC, was 37 feet overall. Peterson's boat, which he called *Ganbare*, was 34 feet overall. Peterson, also, was virtually unknown as a yacht designer.

I said no, but Carl Eichenlaub obviously saw more there than met my eye because he agreed to build the boat. Peterson had to scrounge for paint and could only afford one cockpit winch. Then the boat didn't measure in, so Carl taped lead on the deck forward of the mast to bring its rating down. (This brought the bow down, which under the International Offshore Rule decreases rating.) I didn't sail this series, but after a couple of races, I phoned the yacht club to see who was leading. *Ganbare* was. I thought it had to be a fluke. The boat won the North Americans. After the win, Peterson again offered me the boat for the ridiculously low price of $20,000. Again, I turned him down. Later that year, Peterson and Lowell North sailed *Ganbare* in the One Ton Cup, the world championship, held that year in Sardinia. They would have won the series, except for missing a mark. Peterson went on to have a significant career in yacht design. I eventually built two of his boats, *Stinger* and *High Roler*, and sailed on several others. Peterson was one of Bill Koch's designers in the 1992 America's Cup.

RATING RULES

Rating rules are mathematical attempts to allow boats of different sizes and types to race together on a level playing field. Rules also generally try to reward "wholesome" and "desirable" qualities, while penalizing "unwholesome" and "undesirable" qualities. Obviously, not everyone agrees on the definitions of those attributes, and that is one of the major problems with rating rules. Various racing rules include the International Offshore Rule (IOR), International Measurement System (IMS) Rule, Performance Handicap Racing Fleet (PHRF) Rule, Midget Ocean Racing Club (MORC) Rule, the International Rule used for 12-Meters, 6-Meters, etc., and the new International America's Cup Class (IACC) Rule. Time-allowance systems are often adjuncts to rating rules; for example, one boat gives another so many seconds per mile in Time on Distance, used in IOR racing in the United States, or so many seconds per the time spent on the race course in Time-on-Time, used elsewhere.

Level racing, such as the America's Cup, Maxis, Ton Cups, or the IOR

50 Class, usually dispenses with time systems.[7] All competing boats have been built to a maximum rating number, and so they race on equal footing. One-design boats, of course, typically race without a handicap. When various One Designs compete together, as they often do in club racing, Portsmouth Numbers, a fairly primitive rating system for one-design boats, are sometimes used.

IMS, quite popular in the U.S. and becoming more popular internationally, uses a single general-purpose handicap or, more commonly, permits organizers to match the handicap to local conditions and time spent on various points of sail. This handicap can be determined by average conditions or by selecting a handicap before or immediately after a race.

All rules consider such measurements as waterline length, sail area, beam, draft, displacement, shape of the ends, stability, etc. Often there are corrections for freeboard, type of propeller, the distance of the engine from the center of the boat, centerboard, movable appendages, and so on.

To explain a few of these common measurements briefly, sailing length—the effective waterline at speed—is usually the most important factor in a rating rule. As mentioned, waterline length establishes the distance between bow and stern waves. A problem for rule-makers, however, is determining the effective sailing length of a vessel. With substantial overhangs and fine ends, length varies with speed and heel. Therefore yacht designers have long focused on trying to fool the water and the rule-makers in this area.

Wave-making, as indicated, is a major consideration at moderate and high speeds. Yachts, however, spend much of their time at lesser speeds. At low speeds, increased sail area becomes a more important speed-producing factor. Thus, the rating of a yacht is typically increased when sail area is exaggerated. There are, however, many ways to distribute sail area: masthead rig, fractional rig, sloop, split rigs, etc. Thus, to be sure that sail area is rating fairly, the International Offshore Rule, for example, devotes sixteen pages to this subject.

Beam also figures in most rating rules. Obviously, increased beam increases resistance—the amount of boat touching the water. This wetted-surface drag makes a boat slower, particularly in light air. Beaminess also

---

[7]America's Cup yachts used to rate 12-Meters; now they rate 42-Meters under the new International America's Cup Class (IACC) Rule. A Maxi rates 70 under the IOR. Also under the IOR, a One Tonner rates 30.55, a Two Tonner rates 35.05, and an IOR 50 rates 40.05. (The 50 designation of the latter class has to do with its length overall.)

increases form drag. This increase in wetted-surface and form drag speaks for a credit in rating. On the other hand, exaggerated beam can improve stability. A beamy boat shows good initial resistance to heeling. (Once a beamy boat starts heeling, however, it tends to heel excessively.) As stability—or sail-carrying ability—is addressed in other ways, excessive beam is given a credit, at least under the IOR. The IOR uses the inclining of the boat to determine stability, or its sail-carrying ability.

Draft contributes to speed in two ways: The greater the span of the keel (depth), the more lift and less drag, which is important when sailing upwind. Also, the lower the ballast, the greater stability, which is significant when beating and reaching.

International Measurement System Rule

The International Offshore Rule (IOR), which began in 1969, has its roots in the former Royal Ocean Racing Club (RORC) Rule used in England, and the Cruising Club of America's (CCA) Rule, used in this country. The impetus for the change to a worldwide rule was the popularity of such international competitions as the Admiral's Cup, a team race in England, and the various international level-racing competitions, such as the One Ton Cup. The IOR incorporated many of the RORC hull measurements and many of the CCA rig measurements.

The switch from the CCA to the IOR had a greater impact, I think, on a generation of American yachts than on British yachts, as it is far more difficult (and expensive) to modify a hull than a rig. Also, from the clear perspective of hindsight, the majority of sailors did not have plans to race internationally. Yet they saw their local game changed radically due to decisions made far away. This topic has fueled conversations at yacht clubs for more than twenty years, and of late there has been a significant decline in IOR racing.

That said, I enjoy IOR racing and the international competition it fostered. I also enjoy the thoroughbred yachts it produced. My affection for IOR competition, often described as Grand Prix, and IOR boats is not a universally held view, however. Many sailors prefer a dual-purpose boat: a cruiser/racer. The cruiser/racer has become something of a rallying cry. Behind that is a corresponding desire for less rigorous competition.

For these and other reasons, American yachtsmen began turning away from the IOR and started looking for a new way to rate yachts. The IOR depends on measurements, taken at certain points on the hull, which causes designers to make considerable tucking and bumping, or distortions, to satisfy the rule. Over time, designers learned to alter the hull at the measurement points, and elsewhere, to achieve an advantageous rating while preserving boat speed. As such, there are those who disparage the IOR as a "connect-the-dots" rule. Many designers have learned to "connect the dots" in a similar, if not identical, fashion, and for this reason the IOR is considered "type-forming"—a rule that spawns similar boats.

A disaffection with the rule and with the boats that it seemed to encourage were among the reasons for a scientific look at yacht racing and yacht design. From 1975 to 1977, a $400,000 grant, called the Pratt Ocean Race Handicapping Project, funded a research project at Massachusetts Institute of Technology. It was a three-pronged approach: It studied the time-allowance systems (discussed above). Further, it developed a hull-measuring device—a so-called black box—for describing more accurately the physical characteristics of a yacht. It developed a velocity-prediction program (VPP) to equate better the physical characteristics of a yacht, such as sailing length, beam, and displacement, to its speed. A Dutch aerospace VPP was very helpful, incidentally, in the design of *Australia II*.

The result was the Measurement Handicapping System (MHS), implemented in the United States in 1978, which has since become the International Measurement System (IMS). In November 1985, the International Offshore Racing Council, the governing body of the IOR, adopted the IMS as an alternative rule to the IOR. The idea was that Grand Prix boats (Admiral's Cuppers, Maxis, and IOR 50-footers) will use the IOR. True dual-purpose boats (racer/cruisers) will use the IMS. This has been implemented, particularly in the United States.

A great strength of IMS is the black-box measuring device that very accurately takes the lines of a hull. An electronic wand touches a boat at defined points, and the measurement relationships are stored in the computer. The black box "knows" where it is and "knows" where the wand is. Obtaining full lines, as the IMS hull-measuring device can do, makes it possible to determine very accurate numbers for sailing length, displacement, wetted surface, vertical centers of gravity, and buoyancy. Also, the great accuracy of the IMS measuring device discourages the bumping or other distortions common to IOR boats. A bumpy boat is like a bumpy road; it doesn't lend itself to driving fast. Without bumps and tucks, IMS boats are often faster than their IOR brethren.

After the hull lines are determined by the IMS black box, then the IMS VPP uses aerodynamic and hydrodynamic principles to equate shape with speed for various wind angles and wind velocities. One very important measurement from the VPP is the velocity made good (VMG). VMG is the component of boat speed directly toward the wind (upwind) or directly away from the wind (downwind). The rule-makers use the information to determine a series of handicaps in seven wind velocities, 6, 8, 10, 12, 14, 16, and 20 knots, and standard combinations of these for statistical averaging. (Similar handicaps are provided for boats that don't use spinnakers.)

Sailors can also use this information to develop "target boat speeds," which tell you how fast a boat of your type should be going in different wind speeds and at different wind angles. As such, target boat speeds are like a report card.

Simply considered, if the VPP says you should be doing 6.25 knots when beating in 20 knots, and you are only sailing 6 knots, perhaps something should be done differently. Maybe the sails are trimmed wrong or are too small for the conditions. Or perhaps the steerer is pinching the boat. If slow of target, as in the example, the steerer might try falling off the wind a bit. Then when the speed increases to the target, come up again. This will be discussed more fully in Chapter 7.

A complement to IMS are the IMS regulations. These regulations govern accommodations, permitted building materials, crew weights, and sail limitations. They address the racer/cruiser philosophy of the rule and are more controversial. They don't countenance such allegedly high-tech materials as carbon fiber and titanium. There are those who object to such bans, because some boatbuilders can fabricate rudder shafts better and cheaper in carbon fiber than in lower-tech materials. Also, titanium blocks are much lighter and stronger, if slightly more expensive, and are a staple of many hardware manufacturers.

The IMS isn't a perfect racing rule. It is type-forming—it encourages a certain shape of boat—but it is probably less type-forming than the IOR. Also, the VPP is fairly primitive. Since *Australia II* in the America's Cup of 1983, the VPP has become a key part of designing any America's Cup yacht, indeed most yachts. There are, I can tell you, differences in VPPs as there are differences in computer programs. A VPP uses mathematical equations, and although I am not a mathematician, I know some equations are better than others.

Also, the more motions a VPP can solve for, the more accurate it is. Earlier (in FIGURE 2.6), we described three axes a boat can move around. Supported in three ways, a boat can move in six directions in three-dimensional space: the bow can go up and down, called pitching; it can heel or roll to leeward or to windward; or it can yaw, steer up into the wind or down. Some VPPs used in the 1992 America's Cup can solve all six equations, as well as include a measure of rough-water effects, which obviously gives more accurate numbers.

A strength of IMS racing, however, is its greater openness to change, a more ad hoc philosophy. If some element of yacht design seems to be undervalued or overvalued, it is studied and changed if appropriate.

AMERICA'S CUP OF 1988

The 1988 America's Cup was a political challenge. It was also a design challenge; however, few remember that. The politics first.

Newport, Rhode Island, never appreciated the America's Cup until it lost it. Until recently, one could say San Diego didn't appreciate the Cup until it almost lost it. When I challenged for the America's Cup through the auspices of the San Diego Yacht Club (SDYC) in 1986–87, less than $300,000 came from the SDYC membership.

To the victor, of course, go the spoils. America's Cup spoils can be considerable. Western Australia reportedly grossed $700 million from the 1986–87 event. Recognizing the economic and public relations windfall of an America's Cup, the Western Australia government spent over $50 million on improvements to the waterfront and to the towns of Fremantle and Perth. According to a study conducted by CIC Research Inc. for the America's Cup Task Force, a group of community leaders from San Diego, the America's Cup would add $1.2 billion to the local economy and create 9,126 extra jobs in San Diego County. While recent numbers cut that figure in half, due to the recession of the early 1990s, the 1991 war in the Persian Gulf, and the decrease in challenging syndicates, the America's Cup represents a sizable boost to a local economy.

If the spoils go to the victor, what about selecting the venue? When our syndicate won the Cup in 1987, Malin Burnham and I didn't immediately name the site of the next races. Our syndicate had signed a management agreement back in September 1985 with SDYC. A year before the competition started, SDYC was worried about the costs of keeping the America's Cup should our group win it and the costs of staging the next event. The agreement protected the yacht club from financial liabilities of being the trustee of the Cup. In turn, our syndicate got marketing rights in order to pay the bills. An America's Cup Committee would be named to decide, among other things, the venue and dates of the next competition. Under the management agreement, our syndicate nominated the committee members, and SDYC could accept or reject them but could not name its own committee.

Malin and I hoped that the San Diego Yacht Club, where both of us have sailed all our lives and both of us had served as commodore, and the city of San Diego would make an emotional and financial commitment to help keep the trophy. While we were raising money in other parts of the country for 1986–87, we were often asked if we would consider holding the event elsewhere. We said we'd consider it but made no promises. Hawaii, where we trained in preparation for the Cup, had been very good to us. Hawaii was also very eager to stage the event, and the lobbying was intense. Also, it is a wonderful place to sail, like Western Australia, only better. In Western Australia, you only get the big winds in late summer; in Hawaii you get them year-round.

We entertained bids from Hawaii and other places. In truth, it was never our intention to take the America's Cup out of San Diego. We feared, however, that if we gave the Cup to the San Diego Yacht Club and to the community, we'd never get their support. Why pay for something you've already been given? It's similar to what I said in Chapter 1: there is a difference, I believe, between being given a boat when you're a kid as opposed to wanting one so badly you would do almost anything for it.

Admittedly, the venue question wasn't handled well; the yacht club was mad at me because they thought I was conspiring to take the Cup out of San Diego. I was mad at the yacht club and the city for what I saw as a lack of support.

Malin and I named an America's Cup Committee, made up of local sailors and others from around the country. We hoped the committee would make the best decision for the event. SDYC rejected this committee and tried to name one of its own. The question of committee membership was ultimately decided by binding arbitration on July 19, 1987. A new committee, which we submitted and SDYC accepted, was chaired by Gerry Driscoll, a member of SDYC, manager of the 1986–87 Newport Harbor Yacht Club America's Cup challenge, and skipper of *Intrepid* in 1974. (Driscoll's *Intrepid* was the boat that Turner and I rammed with *Valiant* in the 1974 America's Cup.) Also on the committee were Gene Trepte and Charles D. Hope, both former commodores of the San Diego Yacht Club, and Kim Fletcher, a member of the San Diego Yacht Club and president of Home Federal Savings & Loan in San Diego. From outside of San Diego came John Marshall, my design director in 1986–87; Harry Usher, the former executive vice-president of the Los Angeles Olympic Organizing Committee; and Gary Jobson, a winning America's Cup tactician and TV commentator.

Meanwhile, as we struggled internally—it could best be characterized as a lover's quarrel—Michael Fay, head of the impressive New Zealand syndicate in the 1986–87 America's Cup, had his lawyer Andrew Johns take a long look at the America's Cup Deed of Gift, the document governing the contest, under the jurisdiction of the New York State court system. Eventually, Fay found a loophole.

There was a 12-Meter Worlds in Sardinia in June 1987, less than five months after the Cup competition. During the event, a meeting of the 12-Meter Owners' Association was held. Fay, whose team would win the regatta, was an extremely active participant at the meeting. He had numerous ideas about how to develop 12-Meter racing and how to market the next America's Cup. He was also planning his end run on the America's Cup. Fay is so clever; he kept everyone off guard.

After Sardinia, Fay and his attorney Andrew Johns flew to San Diego. He called Dr. Frederick A. Frye, commodore of the San Diego Yacht Club, who invited Fay and Johns to lunch at the San Diego Yacht Club on July 17. Frye, a busy pediatrician, was late for lunch. While waiting for Frye, Fay and Johns were entertained by Doug Alford, vice-commodore of the San Diego Yacht Club. Fay told Alford that Mercury Bay Boating Club, his yacht club, was going to challenge San Diego one-on-one for the America's Cup in a boat that was 90 feet on the water. Alford was shocked and blurted out, "I guess we can respond with a 90-foot catamaran." Interesting words, those.

Once Frye joined them, they had a pleasant lunch, by all accounts. After coffee, Fay and Johns expanded on their challenge to Frye and Alford. The boat would have a 90-foot load waterline (the maximum under the Deed of Gift), a draft of 21 feet, a beam waterline of 14 feet, and a maximum beam of 26 feet. The competition, Fay said, would start in ten months, according to the timing specified in the Deed of Gift. Frye, too, was shocked. He responded, "We'll be in touch."

Fay didn't wait for an answer. By August, if not well before, he commenced building his boat.

When Fay first made this challenge, no one really appreciated that he was right. The yacht club, Malin Burnham in particular, just wanted him to go away. They concluded this was a bad joke and tried to shrug it off. It became readily apparent that Fay's challenge was legal. Then everyone got concerned, but they didn't have a plan.

The San Diego Yacht Club didn't formally respond to Fay until August 8. On this day, SDYC and the new America's Cup Committee rejected the terms of the New Zealand challenge. On August 31, 1987, Fay filed a brief with the New York State courts. For the first time in the then 136-year history of the oldest trophy in sports, the America's Cup entered the legal system, where it would remain for an unhappy and prolonged period. The next day, September 1, the court issued a restraining order, preventing the America's Cup Committee from naming the venue and dates of the next defense.

This restraining order was lifted on September 9. On September 11, the committee selected San Diego as the sight for a "normal," multichallenger America's Cup regatta in 12-Meter yachts in May 1991. San Diego Mayor Maureen O'Connor said the city pledged its full support for the event.

Fay's right to mount his challenge was argued before Justice Carmen Beauchamp Ciparick of the New York Supreme Court. Eleven weeks later, on the day before Thanksgiving, Judge Ciparick announced her decision: "...Mercury Bay Boating Club has tendered a valid challenge and that San Diego Yacht Club must treat it as such in accordance with the terms of the Deed."

I was in Australia on business at the time of the decision. While I wasn't happy about it, I accepted the decision of the umpire. I decided to fly to Auckland, where Fay, a merchant-banker, runs Fay, Richwhite & Company, to congratulate him. Fay is like the Donald Trump of New Zealand. He seized the moment and called a press conference where I could properly humble myself. That's what I did. I thought it was the right thing to do, to offer my congratulations. Fay was, in truth, very gracious.

I might not have liked what Michael Fay did, but I have much respect for him. From my perspective, he was ruining what I had worked so hard to help bring to fruition—a great sailing event, which the 1987 America's Cup in Perth, Western Australia, certainly was. I also hoped that the next America's Cup regatta would be a "normal" event (with multiple challengers using 12-Meters) held in San Diego, where my friends, family, and fellow members of the San Diego Yacht Club and the community could enjoy it.

So Fay upset my plans. What he did wasn't in my best interests. Nevertheless, I understood exactly what he was trying to do; he was trying to win the America's Cup by any legal means. We did the same thing in trying to defend the Cup by any legal means. Fay found a loophole in the rules large enough to drive a monohull 90 feet on the water (130 feet overall) through. His mistake was in thinking that this was the only loophole. We found another large enough to drive a 60-foot catamaran through. I don't think it was any more complicated than that.

That brings us to the catamaran. The decision to build the catamaran was expedient. We had no money and little desire to mount another campaign so soon after the previous one. My guess is that Fay counted on our lack of money and enthusiasm. I'd been chasing the America's Cup since I lost it in 1983; that was almost four years. Also, before that, I had put in the better part of six years preparing for a successful defense in 1980 and then trying to defend it in 1983. I'd neglected my family, friends, and business.

Despite what Fay would later say, we didn't know what type of boat he was building. The dimensions he supplied could also describe a multihull. We thought the catamaran was fast enough to beat whatever he was building. Also, we felt we could build it in the limited time remaining. Most important, we thought it was legal under the Deed of Gift. Eventually the courts agreed with us.

Expedient or not, I wasn't an eager participant. The 1988 America's Cup was a lose-lose situation for me. If I won in the catamaran, everyone would say, "Ho-hum, Dennis won in a cheater boat." If I lost, they'd say, "There's goes Dennis losing the America's Cup again." Several of my friends advised me not to get involved and to let someone else organize the defense and drive the boat.

For example, Randy Smythe, a leading multihull sailor, was on the team. He'd won an Olympic silver medal in the Tempest Class and was a Formula 40 champion—both boats are multihulls. Smythe could just as easily have steered the boat.

Also, I wasn't enthusiastic about sailing this type of boat. Like many monohull sailors, I thought that multihull sailors were speed freaks, in their Hobie 18s. Initially, I was as guilty of this prejudice against multihull sailors as anyone. That prejudice was, I think, one of the reasons why our response to Fay's challenge was unpopular.

Finally, Malin Burnham and other members of the yacht club came to me and asked me to participate in the defense. After everything the yacht club had done for me throughout my life, it didn't seem like an appropriate time to quit just because I found the prospects distasteful.

After I got the opportunity to sail the boats, I developed a newfound respect for catamarans and catamaran sailors. Catamaran sailors are very good in their own way. It's true they don't have to know the tactics of sailing a dinghy, but in many ways, they have their own tactics that are just different, not inferior.

Unfortunately, the catamaran we designed and built never received the attention that I think it deserved from the technical standpoint. The cat featured a solid wing rather than a soft sail. The wing was 107 feet tall, showed 1,860 square feet of "sail" area, and weighed 2,000 pounds. Nothing like it had ever been built before or has been built since.

Both the wing and the hulls were based on the *Patient Lady* series of C-Class catamarans—specifically *Patient Lady V*, a two-time winner of the International Catamaran Challenge Trophy, better known as the Little

America's Cup. The *Patient Lady* series of six catamarans was designed primarily by Dave Hubbard and Duncan MacLane. Joining these two in the design effort for the 1988 America's Cup were Gino Morelli, Bruce Nelson, Britton Chance, and Bernard Nivelt. John Marshall was the design director, as he was in 1986–87.

A C-Class cat is 25 feet overall and about the same length on the water, has a 14-foot beam, and shows a 300-square-foot wing, which is about 40 feet tall. *Stars & Stripes '88* was 60 feet overall and 55 feet on the water, had a 30-foot beam, and showed, as mentioned, a mast 107 feet tall with 1,860 square feet of sail area. Downwind sail area with a reacher totaled 4,100 square feet. The displacement of *Stars & Stripes '88* was 7,000 pounds, making for a displacement-length ratio of 19. You can't get much lower than that! To put that into perspective, a Laser has a ratio of 69, and a C-Class catamaran, a ratio of 24. *New Zealand*, the boat we sailed against, also had a remarkably low displacement-length ratio of about 51.

A catamaran is a displacement boat in that the hull doesn't develop sufficient lift to plane. (The windward hull may lift out of the water—what is called flying a hull—but the loaded hull does not plane.) That said, a very light boat like this, or like *New Zealand*, has less trouble with wave-making resistance than does a heavier boat. (You will remember that at speed, wave-making resistance accounts for 60 percent of the total resistance in a displacement monohull.)

Also, the catamaran was designed to fly a hull in about six knots of wind. When a catamaran like *Stars & Stripes* is floating on both hulls, both of them sink about 13 inches. When flying a hull, however, the displacement from the windward hull is transferred to the leeward hull. The cat picks up the displacement of water it needs to float—recall Archimedes—and at the same time has less of a penalty in terms of wetted surface. With the windward hull flying, maybe the leeward hull sinks an additional 7 inches. This puts 20 inches of one hull in the water versus 26 inches for two hulls. As a result, the boat gets the volume of displacement needed to float but with a 20 or 25 percent reduction in wetted surface. The boat goes faster. Also, with the waves normally hitting one hull rather than two, pitching is reduced when flying a hull.

If a normal displacement boat can go 1.34 times the square root of the waterline, due to wave-making resistance, a catamaran like *Stars & Stripes '88*, which is much less troubled by wave-making resistance, can move at a speed equal to four times the square root of the waterline. The wind speed necessary to reach top, or hull, speed was remarkably low. For example, *Stars & Stripes* could go 21 or 22 knots in 10 knots of wind. That is two times wind speed.

Also, the wide beam of the boat, 30 feet, makes for a stable sail-carrying platform. Heeling a 30-feet-wide, 60-feet-long catamaran like *Stars & Stripes '88* is like trying to heel a tennis court.

The wing sail was exciting. It was built by Scaled Composites, Inc., out of carbon fiber (discussed in Chapter 3), which was layered over foam. Scaled Composites, in Mojave, California, previously built *Voyager*, the airplane that flew nonstop around the world.

The wing had three elements (see FIGURE 2.9). The main wing was element 1, and behind it was a 20 percent flap. It is helpful to think of element 1 as the front and middle of a headsail, and element 2 as the leech or back of the headsail. There were eight separate flaps comprising element 2, each of which was independently adjustable. Then came a vertical slot, like the slot between a main and a jib, and a second flap, which was element 3. Element 3 is the equivalent of a mainsail.

FIGURE 2.9 *The solid-wing sail on the catamaran* Stars & Stripes '88.

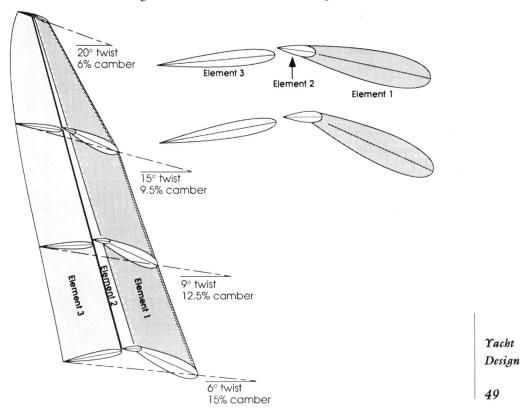

A soft sail stretches; obviously a solid wing doesn't. Stretching, as will be discussed in Chapter 4, is slow since it dissipates energy, rather than transforming it into forward motion. Also, a soft sail represents a huge compromise in shape. The shape of the back, or leech, is influenced by the shape of the front, or luff, and vice versa, and both are influenced by the shape of the middle. A wing broken up so many ways allows very precise shaping of the foil. Such aspects as camber, or depth; angle of attack, or how hard the sheet(s) is trimmed; and twist, or angle of the back of the sail, are precisely adjustable. (Camber, depth, and twist will be described more fully in Chapter 4.) Because of better shape, the winged sail worked harder than a soft sail.

Also, the nicely rounded leading edge is a much more forgiving shape for the introduction of the foil to the wind. Watch the telltales on the leading edge of a normal (soft) headsail. Whenever the weather and leeward telltales aren't flying straight back, the wind isn't hitting the sail precisely at the leading edge. When this happens, you get a small bubble of separated air, which is slow, like eddies around a hull. If the bubble grows too large, it can burst, and the entire airfoil can stall—that is, cease to produce lift. Aiming a thin sail directly into the wind is as difficult a task as trying to aim a piece of paper into the wind. If you don't aim it precisely, the wind blows on one side or the other, causing the paper, or sail, to flag. A rounder leading edge, like that on an airplane, or that on this cat, is a much more forgiving shape.

The result is that the wing showed more lift and/or less drag and higher maximum power per square foot of sail area.

Those are just numbers, however. The catamaran was a joy to sail, as fast and as much fun as any sailing experience I've ever had. We built two catamarans for 1988, one with a solid wing and one with a soft sail. I enjoyed sailing them so much that I kept the one with a soft sail and sail it often around the country.

3 | Building and Equipping a Sailboat

From the new International America's Cup Class (IACC) yachts to maxis, to cruising boats, to dinghies, fiberglass dominates boatbuilding. This was not always so, however. Once upon a time, boats—or at least the material to make them—grew on trees. Sailors showed little enthusiasm in making the switch from wood, which had nearly a six-thousand-year history in boatbuilding.

If sailors were unenthusiastic about fiberglass, the boatbuilding establishment was even less keen on the material. It never took much capital to get into fiberglass boatbuilding. All that was required was a mold, a bucket of resin, some inexpensive fiber, and a few tools one can purchase at the corner hardware store. The result, when the ingredients were mixed, was a chemical reaction that produced a plastic boat. In fact, the proper term for fiberglass is fiber-reinforced plastic (FRP), a good descriptive name.

Compare that with the huge investment in craftspeople and woodworking machinery required of traditional boatbuilders. To protect its "turf," the National Association of Engine and Boat Manufacturers (NAEBM) considered banning the use of fiberglass in the 1950s.

Though once slow to warm to the "new" material, boatbuilders and their customers now wholeheartedly embrace the philosophy of "Better living through chemistry." Today, most boats are built with fiberglass. Some of them, like the Bounty and Triton, are more than thirty years old and still going strong.

Not all fiberglass boats are built the same. There are over-built Bounties and Tritons that will probably outlive us all, but there are also fiberglass boats that don't survive a season. An IOR 50-footer I heard about recently didn't survive its maiden voyage. Others fail less spectacularly. They are heavy in the ends so they pitch excessively, making them uncomfortable and slow, or are heavier than they need to be and, likewise, are slow. Alternatively, boats are built too light, and they flex. With each flex of the hull, the forestay slackens, and the draft of the headsail becomes deeper. This is the equivalent of easing the sheet on each puff. As a result, energy that could produce forward motion is wasted. Also, such flexing of the hull can eventually cause the fiberglass laminate to fail.

A racer absolutely has to understand boatbuilding. This is because no two fiberglass boats, even one-design boats, are exactly alike, and those differences can make one boat fast and another seemingly identical boat slow. A cruising sailor who is looking for value should understand boatbuilding, too. This is because one boat might be a great value and provide years of trouble-free use, while another may be more trouble than it's worth.

The reasons for the predominance of fiberglass are familiar. Fiberglass requires less maintenance than other boatbuilding materials. Also, fiberglass, the raw material, is inexpensive to buy and easy to work with, making the boats cheaper to build and own. The material has a good strength-to-weight ratio. Fiberglass doesn't rot and is unaffected by parasites like marine borers. Fiberglass is not completely waterproof—witness the problem of blistering due to osmosis (more on this later)—but is still comparatively impervious to water.

Other boatbuilding choices exist. There is still the occasional cold-molded wood boat, whose epoxy resin glue makes it fiberglass masquerading as wood. Rarer still is the plank-on-frame wooden boat, valued by traditionalists. The only other popular choice is aluminum, still used in one-off construction of larger cruising sailboats.

The first fiberglass boat I can recall seeing was the Cal 40 (a Bill Lapworth design, discussed in Chapter 2). I saw the Cal 40 in the mid-1960s in San Diego. I wasn't impressed. I can recall saying, "What a dog!" There was something shocking to the eye about those early fiberglass boats. They had all the warmth of a Clorox bottle, to which they were often compared. You felt you needed to wear sunglasses just to be around one of these hulls.

My opinion of fiberglass began to change when I saw how fast the Cal 40 was. This 40-footer was as fast upwind as the wooden 46-footers of the day, and it could fly downwind, even surf down waves easily, something I don't remember seeing very often before this kind of boat came along (see FIGURE 2.2).

The Cal 40 made a believer out of me and, in time, a believer out of the sailing world. It was my "weapon of choice" for a number of years.

Since the Cal 40 was a wholly new design, I don't know if it was fast because of its fiberglass construction or because of its design (see the previous chapter). My guess is both. However, the fiberglass Star Alan Raffee had built for us in New Jersey for the 1968 Olympic Trials was a triumph of material. It was one of the first—if not the first—fiberglass boats in the Star Class. As you may recall, I worked for Raffee, in his carpet business, beginning in college. We were Lightning sailors who eventually decided to compete with the "big boys" in their Stars. We took delivery of the boat in April 1968 and didn't even know how to put it on the trailer. The first time we tried, we placed it on the trailer backwards.

Despite being complete novices in the class, Raffee and I enjoyed such speed that we only needed to beat Lowell North in the final race of the Olympic trials in San Diego to make the Olympic team. While ahead of North in that race, we hit a mark, however, and were disqualified. I don't think we just ran into the mark. I have some vague recollection of match-racing with North in the final race and finding ourselves in a maneuver where hitting the mark became unavoidable. Raffee and I were way out of our league; all we had going for us was a very fast fiberglass boat. North took our Star to Acapulco for the Olympics to help him tune up. The synthetic hull was, by all accounts, faster than *North Star*, Lowell's wooden Star, but North used his boat in the Olympics because he had such affection for it. North won the gold medal that year.

A couple of footnotes to the above story are interesting, I think. The alternate on the 1968 U.S. Olympic team was John Marshall. Marshall, a young graduate of Harvard University, sailed our Star to help North get ready for the competition. North was impressed by Marshall and offered him a job in his sailmaking organization. Marshall would go on to be a president of North Sails and sail with me in the 1980 and 1983 America's Cups. He was my design director in the America's Cups of 1986–87 and 1988.

One other thing I remember about the 1968 Olympic trials that is neither a boatbuilding nor design story but says something about what would become the design of my life. I postponed my wedding—for the second time, at that—when the dates for the Olympic trials were changed.

FIBERGLASS BOATBUILDING HISTORY

Fiberglass dates back to 1836 in France. A patents application was filed for a glasslike substance softened by steam, which was to be used for weaving. Then, early in the 1900s, a fiberglass insert was used to stiffen shirt collars. Thirty-five years later, there was modern fiberglass, made from molten glass, thus the name. It was called A-glass.

The first fiberglass boat was probably a Snipe, produced by Ray Greene, of Toledo, Ohio, in the 1930s. Greene built Snipes to put himself through Ohio State University. He used urea and melamine resins and ordinary cloth for strength. To cure or harden the resin and cloth, he employed a small autoclave, a device that supplies heat and pressure. In time, resins could be made to set at room temperature without pressure.

Jumping ahead more than fifty years, boatbuilders are again using heat and pressure to cure boats, in particular those made of materials like carbon fiber. For example, the new IACC yachts employ heat and pressure.[1]

By 1942, Greene was building polyester resin fiberglass-reinforced boats. Polyester resin is still in use today; it is the most commonly used type of resin.

After World War II, common building materials like wood, aluminum, and steel weren't readily available, so fiberglass found an expanding place in manufacturing, including boatbuilding. The first production fiberglass powerboat was probably the Gar Form runabout, built by Gar Wood, Jr., beginning in the spring of 1946. Some two thousand copies were eventually sold. The first production fiberglass sail boat was likely the Bounty, a 40-footer, built in 1959 by Fred Coleman, in Sausalito, California. The Bounty was made, at least at first, with preimpregnated fabrics, known as "pre-pregs," to be discussed later.

Another significant early fiberglass sailboat was the Triton, a Carl Alberg–designed 28-footer, built in Bristol, Rhode Island, by cousins Clinton and Everett Pearson. More than a thousand were built. Also important was the Columbia 29, a Sparkman & Stephens (S&S) design, built in the

[1]My IACC yacht was built by Eric Goetz Custom Sailboats in Bristol, Rhode Island. The authors kindly acknowledge the help of Eric Goetz in the preparation of this chapter.

early 1960s in Costa Mesa, California, first by Glass Marine and then by Columbia, as the company was later called. Costa Mesa, in Southern California, would become a mecca for building fiberglass boats.

As noted, the boating public was very skeptical of these early fiberglass boats; consumers doubted the durability of the material. In the face of the skepticism, many of the first boats were overbuilt by a significant margin, which largely accounts for the three-decade-long life of some of these vessels.

The September 1962 issue of *Yachting* magazine contained an article titled "A Report on Long Term Durability of Fiberglass Boats." It described tests conducted by the U.S. Coast Guard on three experimental fiberglass 40-foot patrol boats, built ten years earlier. These fiberglass boats were compared with steel vessels of the same size, age, and type. The boats saw similar service. The fiberglass boats required one-fifth the maintenance costs of the steel boats. The conclusion was that fiberglass is superior to other boatbuilding materials. This article represented the end of the wooden-boat era.

CHEMICAL PROCESS

The chemical reaction that makes fiberglass boats possible is called polymerization. Polymerization works this way: something soft (fiberglass cloth) is made hard by the addition of a liquid (a resin) and a catalyst to kick off, or start, the chemical reaction. Often an accelerator is added to hurry the process along. The resins then form a matrix around the cloth.

Resins

The resins commonly used in boatbuilding—polyester, vinylester, and epoxy—are made of long molecules. The molecules are, in turn, made of atoms, which, while chemically linked fore and aft, aren't cross-linked. The catalyst, most often methyl ethyl ketone (MEK) peroxide, starts a chemical reaction where the long, skinny atoms cross-link. This cross-linking begins to turn the liquid resin into a solid. Since the resins are brittle, they are reinforced with fabric, typically fiberglass or some modern variation.

The resin forms a matrix around the fabric. This is the laminate—thin layers of material bonded together. Ideally, both elements work together when the structure is stressed. For example, when you run your shiny new fiberglass boat into a dock, the resin matrix limits surface damage. As such, it is a first line of defense. The resin matrix must also stretch enough to transmit the load to the stronger fibers. Some resins, like polyester, stretch very little (1 percent) before breaking. Other resins, like epoxy, can stretch 4 to 7 percent before breaking. With a greater range between the yield strength and breaking strength, boats made with epoxy resins tend to be longer-lived than those made of polyester resins. This is one reason why better boats use epoxy resins.

Other duties of the resin are to prevent water from penetrating the laminate and to act as a glue to hold the laminate together. Also, the resin provides a chemical resistance to things like oil in the water. Lastly, the resin also makes for the glossy finish prized in fiberglass boats. For the resin to fulfill these important functions, the laminate should have a high resin content, particularly in the outer layer. On the other hand, as we will see, for the molding, or laminate, to be strong, the fiber-to-resin ratio must be high. Boatbuilders can reconcile these contradictory requirements by choosing high-quality resins.

Fiberglass

A-glass (melted window glass) is no longer used in boatbuilding. E glass was the next fiberglass choice. Developed as an electrical insulating material, E glass was and is inexpensive and, thus, the vast majority of boats are made of E glass. Next came S glass and R glass, produced in the United States and Europe, respectively. Among other qualities, S glass and R glass are lighter, stronger, and stiffer than E glass. Lighter, stronger, and stiffer are key attributes in boatbuilding materials. Usually, these qualities are accompanied by a fourth property, more expensive. For example, S glass and R glass are at least five times more expensive than E glass.

Kevlar

Other fibers, in addition to fiberglass, are used as a reinforcement cloth in boatbuilding and, of course, in other manufacturing. Among them is Kevlar, familiar for its use in high-tech racing sails. Kevlar, Du Pont's name for aramid fiber, comes in two forms: Kevlar 29 and 49. While sailmakers most often use the lighter Kevlar 29, boatbuilders most often use 49.

Kevlar, developed by Du Pont as Fiber B (which made an unsuccessful appearance under that name in sails in the early 1970s), is used in tire cord, as well as in bulletproof vests. As with R and S glass, the aerospace application of Kevlar preceded its marine utilization. Kevlar has twice the strength of E glass but is at least ten times more expensive.

Carbon Fiber

Carbon fiber, the stiffest material used in boatbuilding, shows good resistance to stretching (that is, tensile strength). The fiber also shows good resistance to vibration and fatigue. Carbon, however, doesn't have good impact resistance.[2] Thus, it is often paired with another cloth featuring good impact resistance, for example, Kevlar or S or R glass.

The International America's Cup Class yachts are made of carbon fiber and feature carbon-fiber rigs, as mentioned in the previous chapter. Many cruising sailboats use carbon-fiber rigs, too. One of the first was the Freedom line of cruising sailboats, designed by Garry Hoyt, and dating back to the 1970s. The boats feature unstayed carbon-fiber masts, typically in the cat-ketch configuration. More recently, Ted Hood, through his Little Harbor Marine, is beginning to make his popular Stoway mast for cruisers out of carbon fiber. The reason for the shift from aluminum to carbon in both cruising and racing boat masts is to limit weight aloft. Recall that the more weight aloft, the more the boat heels, which is slow as well as uncomfortable (see FIGURE 2.5, top). Carbon fiber is also used in boatbuilding for steering wheels, rudders, and rudder shafts. Making such parts from lightweight carbon fiber helps to get weight out of the back end of the boat, which decreases pitching (see FIGURE 2.6, center).

Although carbon fiber is more common today, it was nearly banished from the scene, as was fiberglass. In the 1979 Fastnet Race, five carbon-fiber rudder posts failed in the most deadly race in ocean-racing history. (This race will be discussed later.) Also, a sixth carbon rudder, belonging to Sir Edward Heath, the former prime minister of Great Britain, failed earlier in moderate winds in the 287-mile Channel Race.

The failed rudder posts, however, were made of carbon fiber over an aluminum mandrel, or core. In 1979, designers and boatbuilders were

---

[2]Engineers typically measure impact resistance as the energy required to break a material. Impact resistance is determined using a notch-impact test, where a hammer swinging as a pendulum is allowed to smash into the sample, breaking it. The height to which the hammer continues swinging (the energy left over after breaking the sample) is measured. For materials like Kevlar with high-impact strength, the hammer doesn't go very far after breaking the sample. Thus, boats made of such materials are stronger.

unsure of the new carbon-fiber material and assumed that one plus one is two. They took the strength of carbon and the strength of aluminum and added them together. Carbon fiber is very stiff, and aluminum bends easily. When the rudder posts were stressed, the carbon fiber alone took the load. There was no synergy between the two materials.

Since then, carbon fiber, either used alone or with a complementary material like Kevlar, has had a growing impact in boatbuilding. Its lack of general acceptance stems from the fact that the material is more difficult to work with than other fibers. Most important, however, is its cost: carbon is from twenty-five to one hundred times more expensive than E glass, depending on the type of carbon fiber. What distinguishes one carbon fiber from another is the carbon content, which can vary from 91 to 95 percent, along with the price.

STYLES OF REINFORCEMENT

Materials such as E glass, R glass, S glass, Kevlar, and carbon fiber come to the boatbuilder in several forms. Among them are a chopped-strand mat (CSM), rovings, fabrics, and pre-pregs. The form of the material provided to the builder has a direct impact on how the boat is built and, in some cases, how well it is built.

Chopped Strand Mat

To make chopped-strand mat (CSM), strands of fiberglass are chopped into small pieces. The pieces, about an inch in length, fall randomly on a mat on a moving belt. A binder sticks the fiberglass to the mat. In Chapter 4, we will discuss the importance of matching cloth strength to sail load, to prevent distortion, or stretch. This is a theme of modern boatbuilding, too. Due to the random nature of the fibers in the CSM, however, the mat's strength cannot be tailored very accurately to the load.

One way boatbuilders address the random orientation of the chopped-strand mat is to lay one mat one way and rotate the next 90 degrees, to make what is called a cross-ply laminate. This improves the strength of a laminate built with CSMs, but when compared with other styles of reinforcement, a CSM laminate still isn't strong.

Since CSMs are easy to work with (for example, the mats are easily saturated with resin) and are relatively inexpensive to manufacture, they are popular. Although this ease of use makes life better for the boatbuilder, it can compromise overall laminate strength. As noted, one measure of strength is the fiber-to-resin ratio. A typical CSM laminate might show 30 percent fiber and 70 percent resin—a low ratio.

E glass, the least expensive fiberglass reinforcing, commonly comes to the boatbuilder in the form of a CSM. The boatbuilder must then cut the mats to size and lay them up by hand. This building technique, called contact molding, is discussed later in this chapter.

Rovings

The glass can be gathered into strands, and the strands gathered around a spool. This is similar to the spinning of wool. The resulting fiberglass material is known as a roving of glass. The rovings can be used in a chopper gun, a manufacturing tool that chops the fiberglass and then sprays it onto a mold with resin and hardener. Combining all the processes in one manufacturing tool eliminates the need for the cutting and fitting of a mat or for the mixing and applying of a resin and catalyst. A chopper gun is the easiest way to lay fiberglass, which makes the resulting boat comparatively inexpensive. This lay-up technique is commonly paired with inexpensive rovings of E glass.

Boats built with chopped-strand mats or rovings and a chopper gun can be perfectly acceptable, particularly if the fiberglass-to-resin ratio is high or if the boats are built thick enough. However, while thickness can translate to strength and, perhaps, longevity, it also means excess weight. That may not be an acceptable trade if you value speed. The quality of the boats built of these materials also depends on the skill of the person doing the work. Generally, the materials aren't used generously or well.

Fabrics

Rovings can also be woven into fabrics, sometimes called woven rovings. The weaving produces a fabric that is lighter and stronger than a CSM. All materials, however, lose strength when woven, as the handling involved in the weaving process places stress on the individual strands, weakening or even breaking them. Taking more care in the weaving process can minimize this. Since the emphasis of E glass is low cost, the material doesn't usually lend itself to more costly but less damaging weaving techniques. Careful weaving is reserved for costly materials.

Careful weaving and more expensive materials allow a higher fabric-to-resin ratio. This is because the resulting woven fabric is thinner and easily accepts resin; thus, resin doesn't have to be liberally brushed on to "wet out" the fiber. Being thinner, it is also easier to work with, thereby requiring less resin. Woven rovings give a bidirectional or unidirectional strength orientation, allowing the designer or builder to match more accurately the strong fibers to the load. Again, in better boatbuilding, as in better sailmaking, the strongest fibers are matched to the load.

As mentioned, E glass comes in this woven roving form, as does better R and S glass. Fabrics can also be combinations of materials, such as Kevlar and carbon fiber. This Kevlar-carbon weave, for example, offers the stiffness of carbon fiber with the good impact resistance of Kevlar at a considerable savings of weight.

Pre-Pregs

If the resin and catalyst are preimpregnated at the factory rather than at the boatbuilding site, the material is called a pre-preg. The resin is usually epoxy, and the pre-preg comes to the boatbuilder in rolls in catalyzed form, meaning that the catalyst is added and the chemical reaction (polymerization) is already occurring, although slowly. Pre-pregs are refrigerated to slow the chemical reaction until building begins. With proper refrigeration, pre-pregs have a shelf life of about six months. Pre-pregs can be woven or nonwoven fiber.

Pre-pregs are particularly appropriate for use with a core material, such as a honeycomb. Since the chemical reaction is occurring, the pre-preg is tacky. Due to the stickiness, a honeycomb or some other core material easily sticks to it. The bond becomes permanent through the application of high heat and high pressure. Heat causes the material to kick off—the chemical reaction to accelerate—and the pressure holds the laminate, or layers, together as if in a huge clamp. The high pressure prevents the formation of voids, actually microscopic holes, that can weaken the strength of the laminate.

A stock fiberglass boat built with E glass in the chopped-strand mat (CSM) form might have a fiber-to-resin ratio of 30 to 70. Resin is easy to apply; it nicely fills microscopic holes and voids in a laminate, but it adds little strength. On our pre-preg America's Cup boat, our boatbuilder, Eric Goetz Custom Sailboats, in Bristol, Rhode Island, achieved a 60 to 40 ratio. Again, the higher the ratio, the stronger the boat.

CORE MATERIALS

Stiffness is critical in boatbuilding. A boat that flexes causes the headstay to loosen, which makes the headsail deeper. This is the equivalent of easing the sheet in a puff. Also, flexing can wear out the laminate; it's like bending a wire back and forth until it breaks easily. Further, as discussed in Chapter 2, the keel imposes a righting moment, which creates a torque at the joint where the keel and hull meet. In addition, the boat flexes when it falls off waves, stressing the hull. The best antidote to all of these forces is stiffness—a resistance to bending.

Stiffness is easy to achieve in manufacturing. All that must be done is to make the laminate thicker. However, thicker usually means heavier, which isn't acceptable from the perspective of speed under sail and, to a lesser degree, manufacturing costs. To save weight—particularly weight in the ends to decrease pitching (see FIGURE 2.6, center)—fiberglass boatbuilders, starting in the late 1970s, began replacing some of the relatively heavy fiberglass with a much lighter core material. This could be a balsa core (the popular J-Boats, for example, have balsa wood cores), and foam cores, such as polyvinyl chloride (PVC). More recently, a popular choice is honeycomb, made of such materials as aramid (Kevlar) paper, carbon, cardboard, etc. (see PHOTO 3.1). The result is a sandwich: two pieces of fiberglass, Kevlar, or carbon-fiber "bread" surrounding a core, which can be considered the "meat."

Sandwich construction in boatbuilding is like the I beam used in building and bridge construction. Shaped like a capital I, the I beam has two parallel steel skins and a steel flange that keeps the skins apart and parallel. An I beam is stiffer and lighter than a solid steel beam. In molding a boat, the core is the flange. It holds the skins apart and parallel. Then the inner and outer skins and the core work together. Like an I beam, the resulting structure is stronger, stiffer, and lighter than a solid material.

Increased speed wasn't the only factor that led to the shift from heavy to lighter boats and to an increased use of sandwich construction. With the oil embargo in the early 1970s, the costs of petroleum-based resin and fiber went up dramatically. The price of resin, for example, tripled. Even at that price, it wasn't readily available. Using core materials, which replaced some of the fiberglass, was one answer to the shortage.

In Chapter 2, I commented on how uncomfortable it is to be on the leading edge. Nevertheless, I find myself there from time to time, usually on other people's boats. One night I was uncomfortably on the leading edge of boatbuilding on arguably the worst night in ocean-racing history—certainly the worst night in my ocean-racing history. I skippered *Williwaw* on the

Building and Equipping a Sailboat

61

PHOTO 3.1 *Core materials are being affixed to* Insatiable*'s deck. The dark core material is Nomex honeycomb; the white material is high-density foam, which is where the hardware will be positioned; the gray material on the cabin top is lower-density foam.* (Courtesy of Eric Goetz Custom Sailboats, Inc.)

U.S. team in the 1979 Admiral's Cup. The last race of the Admiral's Cup and of its companion regatta, Cowes Week, is the Fastnet Race. During this race, an awful storm savaged the fleet. Sadly, fifteen sailors lost their lives, and twenty-three boats were abandoned.

The weather disturbance that caused this tragedy first spawned tornadoes in the Ohio valley, capsized ten racing boats in Newport with 35-knot winds, and killed two people in Massachusetts. The low-pressure system, which would, in time, measure a dramatic 27.93 inches on the barometer (see Chapter 8), then raced across the Atlantic toward Ireland for its rendezvous with the Fastnet fleet. Here 302 boats, ranging in size from about 30 to 82 feet, were racing from Cowes, England, to Fastnet Rock, 10 miles south of Ireland, and then to Plymouth, England—some 605 sea miles.

I was scared that night of August 13th–14th, during the height of the storm. We had to take our main down because it was too windy. We had only a storm jib up. As a headsail alone stresses a mast while a mainsail or storm trysail helps to support it, that was hard on the rig. However, we were just trying to survive. Certainly, a storm trysail would have been the best sail for such extreme conditions, but unbelievably, we had left it in the van by mistake.

Twelve or thirteen people were on *Williwaw,* and half of them were unable to function because it was so rough. I remember crew member Greg Gillette being particularly strong. He lives in Hawaii and is used to those conditions. Also Jim Pugh, the yacht designer, was very strong. He grew up in Lymington, on the south coast of England, not far from where we were that awful night, and is no stranger to heavy weather. I wasn't feeling that well, although I tried to keep it to myself. It is not, I believe, a great idea for a skipper to appear weak, particularly on a night such as this. I get seasick, though only at night. I am, however, less troubled by it these days.

We had our spreaders in the water from time to time—well beyond that at least once. A canvas bag of winch handles and spare blocks was below decks on the cabin sole. In one knockdown, the bag was lost out of the companionway. That bag didn't roll uphill. The keel would have to be up in the air for the bag to fall out of the companionway.

I never told anyone about it, but I was unable to sleep. I feared the boat was going to break up. To keep weight out of the ends—to minimize pitching—the cockpit sole was built with a sandwich construction: fiberglass surrounding a Nomex core. When you walked on it, the floor would give way a little; when you jumped on it, it would vibrate. I had visions of a huge wave crashing into the cockpit and blowing out the floor. If that had happened, we would have sunk. Nevertheless, the sandwich construction proved adequate. My worries were for naught.

One important lesson of that race bears mentioning. A rule of the sea is to stay with the boat. Of the twenty-three boats that were abandoned, eighteen of them were still floating after the storm ended. Their construction was adequate. Sadly, in many instances, the crews broke before the boats, by taking to life rafts prematurely. The only conclusion that should be drawn from this is that remaining with the boat is a good, if not perfect, rule.

PRODUCTION BOATBUILDING WITH A FEMALE MOLD

Production boats are typically molded *inside* a female mold. In contrast, one-offs—which include high-tech maxis as well as boats built by amateurs—are typically molded *over* a male mold.

Female molds—in essence a slightly enlarged boat—are reusable, and therefore lend themselves to production boatbuilding. Female molds also allow the introduction of a gelcoat, the protective, shiny, and sometimes colorful outer layer. A gelcoat is usually made of polyester resin. The gelcoat should be smooth and hard when the boat comes out of the mold, which means, among other things, that the outer skin doesn't require extensive finishing. Less labor at the end is a boon to cost-conscious production boatbuilders.

However, the gelcoat picks up any flaws in the surface of the female mold in which the hull sits, so the finish of the mold is critical. It must be impeccable. Boatbuilders usually make female molds out of fiberglass and spend much time and effort making them perfectly smooth. The cost, it is hoped, is amortized over a long production run.

Contact molding is the most commonly used technique in production boatbuilding. Since production boats are created inside a female mold, the boats are built from the outside layer (the gelcoat) to the inside. First, the gelcoat is sprayed on a waxed mold or, alternatively, is brushed on. (The wax helps to separate the boat from the mold.)[3] The gelcoat resin has to be sticky—show a fairly high viscosity—so as not to flow into the bottom of the mold. The gelcoat cures, or hardens, and then is typically covered with a surface tissue—a light fabric, usually made of the same fiberglass as the rest of the boat. The tissue helps to protect the gelcoat from the heavier fiberglass layers.

Then laminating begins. Most commonly, E glass, in either chopped-strand mat (CSM) or woven roving form, is cut to size and then placed in the mold by hand. It's like hanging wallpaper. The boatbuilder wets the mold or previous layer with the sticky resin, and attaches the new layer to it. Next, an ordinary paintbrush is used to draw the resin up through the new cloth, thereby saturating it. Usually several layers of fiber are applied. Each layer is then rolled to consolidate it with the earlier layers.

If the boat designer calls for core material, the boatbuilder molds the outer skin, as described, and then attaches the core, which, again, can be balsa wood, foam, or a honeycomb made of aramid (Kevlar), carbon, card-

---

[3]A practical note: If you purchase a new production boat, it is important that the waxy outer layer is rubbed off. The boatbuilder should attend to this but doesn't always do it or do it well. Also, although shiny gelcoat finish looks wonderful, its relative degree of porousness makes the water bead, which increases the size of the boundary layer (see Chapter 2). If the boat is dry-sailed (not stored in the water), I advise wet-sanding shiny surfaces—at least those that touch the water—with 1,000-grit paper until they are dull. If the boat is kept in the water, I'd seal the gelcoat—again, at least the part that touches the water—with at least one coat of an epoxy-based primer and an antifouling paint. For specifics, talk to your paint dealer.

board, etc. This makes the laminate thick, and thickness translates to stiffness. (As mentioned, using a core also offers considerable savings in weight when compared with building with solid fiberglass.) This joint—where the fiberglass skin joins the core—is carefully checked for voids, and then the innermost fiberglass skin is fabricated. This joint, too, is checked for voids.

With CSMs, the designer typically specifies only the thickness of the laminate. With more sophisticated woven fabrics, the designer might specify cloth weight, fiber orientation, number of layers, and even the desired fiber-to-resin ratio. Also specified are the locations of turning blocks or winches that might require extra reinforcing (for instance, wood blocks or high-density foam used as a backing).

In addition to increasing the stiffness of the construction by way of extra thickness or a core material, stringers and ribs can be used (see PHOTO 3.2). They are typically laminated in during the lay-up process. (Bulkheads, too, can strengthen fiberglass hulls. They are, however, glassed into place after the hull is finished.) Once proper laminate thickness is achieved, a top coat and sometimes another surface tissue finish the hull.

PHOTO 3.2 *Ribs, stringers, and bulkheads help to increase stiffness.* (Courtesy of Eric Goetz Custom Sailboats, Inc.)

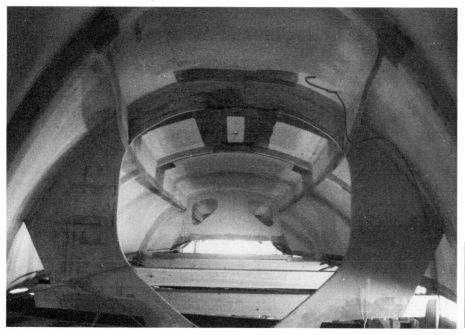

The curing process has three stages: 1) The gel stage is when the material is no longer liquid and cloth but is not yet a solid. 2) The hardening stage can take several hours, before the boat can be safely removed from the mold. Even then, careful support is necessary; otherwise the boat can twist or sag out of shape. (In Chapter 1, I described my trip to Germany in 1976 to oversee the construction of my Star. I insisted that Leonhard Mader mold the boat on a Friday and wouldn't allow him to remove it from the mold until Tuesday. I wanted to give it as much time as possible to harden, to hold its shape.) 3) Finally, there is the maturing stage, which can take anywhere from several days to weeks. Heat can hurry any of these stages along; this is particularly true of the lengthy maturing interval.

An alternative manufacturing method with a female mold is the use of a chopper gun, discussed earlier. This is particularly appropriate when molding large, simple shapes.

ONE-OFFS WITH A MALE MOLD

A male mold is usually used in the molding of one-off custom yachts, like America's Cuppers, as well as in boats constructed by amateur builders. The process starts with frames, spaced 2 or 3 feet apart (see PHOTO 3.3). A 75-foot America's Cup boat has about twenty-five carefully shaped frames. The precise shape of the frames comes from the designer's lines. Our Cup designers, for example, gave our builder, Eric Goetz, full-size computer-drawn patterns on Mylar plastic, to shape the boat precisely. One set corresponds to the inside dimensions of the hull and is used to build the twenty-five wood frames. The second set corresponds to the outside dimensions and is used to check that there is a proper buildup of material, that is, the proper hull thickness.

These frames are set up on a support structure, made of heavy wood. Before building begins, the frames are carefully checked for accuracy, to ensure that they correspond to the yacht-designer's lines. Then the stem and stern pieces and backbone are fitted to the frame. The boatbuilder covers the frames with battens. Finally, there is what amounts to an upside-down wood boat, although spaces are left between the battens. Prior to fiberglassing, the boatbuilder checks the mold for fairness. High spots are sanded or planed; low spots are built up.

The male mold must be strong and fair but need not show a perfect finish (as must the female mold). This is because the molding technique doesn't lend itself to a gelcoat, and the male mold isn't normally used again.

PHOTO 3.3 *In a male mold, the frames are spaced two or three feet apart—their shape comes from the designer. The frames sit on a support structure, or "stong back." Here the frames are being covered with battens, and next the inner skin, core material, and outer skin will be draped over the mold.* (Courtesy of Eric Goetz Custom Sailboats, Inc.)

In the absence of a gelcoat, the boatbuilder must sand the hull and carefully finish and paint it after removing it from the mold.

As mentioned earlier, the designer's job includes specifying the laminate thickness and, in some cases, the orientation of the fibers, the amount of resin, etc. In a project as complex as an America's Cup boat, this is done through finite-element analysis, a sophisticated computer engineering model of the stresses and strains of a boat. In addition, the finite-element analysis also isolates spots where extra reinforcing is necessary, for example, under a winch or turning block or where the bilges turn. Such areas require a buildup of material. This buildup is the boatbuilding equivalent of a clew patch in a sail. In either case, extra material disperses the load.

In the bygone days, boatbuilders laminated the core and outer skin first. After this hardened, they removed the boat from the mold, and molded the inner skin. These days, boatbuilding with a male mold starts at the inner skin and progresses to the outer skin.

For stiffness, custom boats, like production boats, use additional mater-

Building and Equipping a Sailboat

ial: cores, stringers, and ribs. Some custom racing boats also feature a space-frame, made of aluminum or carbon, to isolate the forces of the keel, rig, etc., from the rest of the boat. As far as I know, designer Ron Holland and his then brother-in-law, Gary Carlin, the boatbuilder, were the first to use this technique.

PRE-WET AND PRE-PREG BOATBUILDING

Carbon fiber is presently the ultimate material in boatbuilding. It is used, for example, in hulls of America's Cup boats; maxis; IOR 50s; rudder shafts and rudders in some racing and cruising boats; chain plates; and rigs for cruising and racing boats. There are two ways to work with carbon fiber: pre-wet and pre-preg.

In pre-wet manufacturing, the carbon fiber is passed through a resin-impregnation machine just before the carbon fiber is to be used. This wets the fiber with resin. Then a roller squeegees the excess epoxy resin—carbon is invariably paired with epoxy resin—in a process reminiscent of a wringer on an old-fashioned washing machine. Then the boatbuilder lays the pre-wet fiber, which is gathered in tufts, over the mold (see PHOTO 3.4).

In pre-preg manufacturing, the epoxy is preimpregnated into the fiber at the factory by an expert, and the material is refrigerated until used.

The pre-wet or pre-preg pieces can be as long as the entire boat. These full-length pieces are called zeros, since they are parallel to the centerline of the boat, that is, oriented at zero degrees (athwartships would be 90 degrees). In the America's Cup boats, some of the zeros are 75 feet long and 39 inches wide. Not all the pieces are this long, of course. (Also, the more inexperienced the builder, the shorter the pieces used.)

First, boatbuilders put the inside carbon-fiber skin over the mold. Next typically comes the Nomex honeycomb, made of Kevlar, varying from 30 to 50 millimeters, that is, 1-3/8 to 2 inches thick in the case of the new America's Cup yacht. With these boats, the lay-up of the hull—the inner skin, core, and outer skin—required about four to five weeks.

At each stage, the boatbuilder puts down a peel ply over the laminate, a breather cloth, and then a vacuum bag loosely covers the hull. Then air between the bag and the hull is pumped out with a vacuum pump. As the air is removed, the vacuum bag squeezes the laminate harder and harder, like an enormous clamp. This consolidates the laminate, eliminates microscopic voids, and squeezes out the excess resin, which drains into the felt-like breather cloth. This pressure makes the laminate stronger. (The peel

PHOTO 3.4 *The bow of* Capricorno *is laminated with carbon fiber in the pre-wet form.* (Courtesy of Eric Goetz Custom Sailboats, Inc.)

ply helps prevent the laminate from sticking to the vacuum bag.)

In these America's Cup hulls, the vacuum can be drawn to the pressure of 1 atmosphere—about 14.7 pounds per square inch. To put this another way, 1 atmosphere of pressure is the equivalent of 3 feet of lead over every square inch of the boat. In addition to being pressurized, the laminate is cooked to more than 200°F to hurry along the chemical reaction.

The rules limit the amount of heat and pressure in these America's Cup hulls. For example, the maximum cooking temperature is 203°F (95°C), and maximum pressure is 1 atmosphere. The reason for the limitations is to contain costs. With pressures higher than 1 atmosphere, a vacuum bag isn't sufficient. A more costly autoclave is necessary. Very few autoclaves can accommodate something 75 feet long and 18 feet wide—the size of an America's Cup yacht. Also, above 203°F or so, normal tooling, as in a wooden mold, can't be used, or more fire-resistant materials are required.

Small parts for these America's Cup boats, like rudder posts, spinnaker poles, chain plates, and rigs, can be heated at higher temperatures (288°F) and higher pressures (up to 5 atmospheres).

Building and Equipping a Sailboat

Important to the quality of the finished product is how the fiberglass or carbon layers overlap. The pieces must overlap, not abut one another, for strength. If too many overlaps occur in the same place, the result is a bump on the inner skin. Then after the core is affixed, the bump increases in size. Next, after the outer skin is attached, the bump increases again. This is the boatbuilding equivalent of turning a molehill into a mountain. A bumpy boat is like a bumpy road; you can't go fast. This is why it's important that a boatbuilder avoid, whenever possible, a concentration of overlapped materials. Also, this is another distinguishing feature between a well-made boat and a poorly built one.

Once the hull is out of the mold, boatbuilders smooth areas of unfairness with microballoons, a type of nautical putty. Microballoons are an epoxy mixture, used on fiberglass and aluminum boats alike. Aluminum, which distorts when welded, requires a thicker coating of microballoons than fiberglass.

Stinger was a Doug Peterson–designed boat built for me in aluminum by Carl Eichenlaub. This was Eichenlaub's first aluminum offshore boat, and he learned how to do it by doing it. He bent the aluminum plates that cover the hull with a machine he built. Essentially, he had his workers running over the plates with a forklift. Eichenlaub is clever; he figured this all out and did it so well, too. *Stinger* was built upside down. Then Eichenlaub welded a pipe on the front and on the back. The boat looked like a turkey on a barbecue spit. Then with forklifts, he rolled the boat over. Next, to make the hull fair, his workers attacked the boat with microballoons and putty. Eichenlaub built this boat in twenty-two days and built *Inflation,* an identical boat, for Greg Gillette—the same Greg Gillette who was so strong in the 1979 Fastnet Race—in the same amount of time.

Stinger probably had 6 to 7 millimeters of microballoons over the entire hull, which is about average for an aluminum boat. By way of comparison, the carbon-fiber America's Cup boats built by Goetz carry about 1 millimeter. The former is obviously six or seven times the weight of the latter. Also, the America's Cup boat used a special material, Microlite, rather than microballoons, for fairing. This material is harder and weighs half as much as microballoons. This means the coating is twelve to fourteen times lighter on the America's Cup boat than on an aluminum boat. The point of this story is: the lighter the "blanket" around a boat, the faster it is.

Incidentally, we won the 1975 SORC with *Stinger.* When I finished the Nassau Cup Race, the last race of the series, Ted Turner was on the dock to take our dock lines, along with another man. Turner and I hadn't talked much since I replaced him on *Mariner* in the America's Cup the previous summer. After taking *Stinger*'s lines, Turner told me he was going to buy my boat. I told him I wanted $60,000 for her. He agreed to my price; the deal was penned on a cocktail napkin.

Then Turner said, "Since you don't have a boat to sail, I've got a new one for you." He introduced me to Jesse Philips, a Dayton, Ohio, industrialist, who would be taking his *Charisma,* an S&S-designed 54-footer, to England for the Admiral's Cup, in the summer. I removed my personal gear off *Stinger,* gave Turner the keys, and went to take a look at *Charisma.* I sailed aboard her in the 1975 Admiral's Cup, my first.

ALL FIBERGLASS BOATS AREN'T CREATED EQUAL

As should be clear, fiberglass boatbuilding is not an exact science. It is a labor-intensive activity, and like snowflakes and people, no two fiberglass boats, be they cruisers, racers, or production boats, are exactly alike.

For example, mast steps may be in different places, which can make a significant difference in weather helm and how the boat sails (see Chapter 5). Some boats are lighter, some heavier. That can depend, for example, on the amount of materials used in the boat. Also, some are fairer than others. That can be influenced by how long the boat remains in the mold when curing. Some boats are stronger; others are weaker. That can be due to the fiber-to-resin ratio.

Most of these things, however, are invisible to the naked or uneducated eye. What you can do is ask the builder about the fiber-to-resin ratio, about the curing time, about the thickness of microballoons, about the construction method and materials. While this doesn't guarantee you a better boat, at least the builder or salesperson will know that you are knowledgeable about boat construction. It might help.

Better yet, before buying a production boat, weigh it if possible. The variations will surprise you. If speed is what you want, buy the lightest boat you can find. That said, a light boat may not prove as durable.

I often raced with Eichenlaub in Lightnings when I was growing up. Eichenlaub built the boats we raced, and one lesson he taught me was the importance of racing a minimum-weight boat. If the boat is too light for class rules, use lead or whatever to get it up to minimum weight. The problem is that all boats, even fiberglass boats, absorb water and gain weight. Also, boats are like magnets. After a while you don't even notice the 10 pounds of tools or 6 pounds of foul-weather gear, or three-year-old sodas

Building and Equipping a Sailboat

you're carting around. You need to start light to stay light. You wouldn't, for example, run a foot race with a six-pack of soda under your arms. Similarly, don't race a boat with unnecessary gear.

Also inspect a boat you are interested in buying for fairness. A long batten bent around a hull can show areas of unfairness. A boat with bumps is likely to be slow. Further, unfair curves can be a sign of shoddy workmanship. Also look at the seams. Are they straight, which can be a sign of good workmanship, or crooked? If, for example, I was buying a J/24 or an Etchells 22, I'd drive the dealer nuts comparing boats. I'd select a dealer or even go to the manufacturer—if I could get in the door—to see the largest selection of boats. I'd weigh them, if possible. Also, I'd carefully inspect every inch of the hull. Certainly, not every dealer is going to welcome such scrutiny and be so accommodating, but I'd try to find one who wouldn't mind.

Obviously, buying a custom boat gives you greater license to monitor the building process. In building my recent America's Cup boat, for example, I visited the boatbuilder as often as I could, though Eric Goetz Custom Sailboats in Bristol, Rhode Island, is a continent away from where I live in San Diego. I enjoyed meeting the people doing the work. Building a fiberglass boat is tough, dirty work, and doing it well is an art form. Also, what the boatbuilders do affects me directly, and I want them to know I appreciate the job they do. Even my daughter Julie came down from her junior year at Dartmouth to join me at Goetz's Christmas party.

Of course, I hoped to get something out of the experience, too. I hoped the builders would make me a better boat. Believe me, I was well aware that just down the street, Goetz's work force was building a mold for a boat for my America's Cup defense rival, Bill Koch.

BLISTERING

Even fiberglass boats absorb water. In addition to increased weight, the result is often a blister, sometimes called boat pox. This was recognized as a serious threat to fiberglass boats in the mid-1980s. The blisters, seen in the gelcoat, can vary from the size of a quarter to the size of a pinhead. The cause is osmosis, where fluid moves through a porous structure (the fiberglass) to another fluid (for example, moisture in the bilge). (The process is similar to skin wrinkling in the bathtub.) This allows water to permeate the hull and saturate the fiberglass laminate. Pressure builds up, which can result in a blister. The blister can rupture and in extreme cases can threaten the integrity of the hull.

A study conducted at the University of Rhode Island identified several water-soluble materials that can be present in the fiberglass boatbuilding process and can allow water to saturate the laminate. The study, titled "The Prevention and Repair of Gel Coat Blisters," was funded by the U.S. Coast Guard through the auspices of the American Boat Builders and Repairers Association (ABBRA).[4] ABBRA is working to improve the quality of the laminate and to remove the identified impurities.

Before the release of the study, multiple layers of epoxy, at least 15 millimeters thick, were found to be an effective treatment for blisters. The epoxy presents a barrier to water penetration. This treatment, first used in 1984, remains one of the most successful.

The study identified three stages of the problem: Type I is superficial, that is, pinheads; Type II is more significant damage, with cracking up to halfway through the laminate; and Type III shows cracking and delamination. With Type III damage, the boat may be unseaworthy, though it is repairable, if at no small cost. To determine severity, a core sample may be necessary.

For treating Type I blisters, the blister is penetrated, and is ground away along with some of the surrounding gelcoat. The surface is cleaned up, rinsed off, and then allowed to dry. The report emphasizes that for the treatment to be most effective, the drying time of the saturated laminate is critical, from 30 to 128 days. That can end the sailing season, in some cases; so if possible, it is a repair better left for the end of the season.

In place of treating the blister with epoxy, alternative methods include coating the affected area with topside alkyd or polyurethane paint. Although the repair won't last as long as epoxy, subsequent blistering is reported to be less severe. Alternatively, the area can be repaired with an air-curing gelcoat. The latter is a job best left to a professional, as is probably the repair of the more severe Type II and certainly Type III problems.[5]

The study described preventive measures, as well. Among them are sanding areas that are normally underwater and applying two coats of alkyd or polyurethane marine-topside paint. This paint does not provide a barrier, as does the epoxy treatment discussed above; rather, a component of the

---

[4]The report is available from ABBRA. Contact them at 1(203)967-4745.

[5]With Type II blisters, the area is ground down, as with Type I blisters, although more of it is removed. Next, noncorrosive E or S glass is used to replace the fiberglass. It is important that the fiberglass not have soluble binders. These binders are on the list of impurities identified in the ABBRA report. Type III problems may require rebuilding the hull.

paint reacts chemically with the polyester in the gelcoat, inhibiting water migration. The paint should be applied every one to three years. The heavier the use of the boat and/or the warmer the water in which you sail, the more frequent the application. Also important as a preventive measure is keeping the bilges dry and humidity out of the boat. This represents a second source of fluid—the requirement for osmosis.

CARPENTRY AND FIBERGLASS BOATBUILDING

There is more to a boat than just the fiberglass hull. I doubt anyone bought a fiberglass boat because they liked the look, feel, or aroma of fiberglass. Fiberglass has to be one of the world's most synthetic—most processed— materials. People buy fiberglass boats for any number of practical reasons, but not because they love the material. I think it was L. Francis Herreshoff, the famous yacht designer, who described the inside of a bare fiberglass hull as "frozen snot."

Thus boat carpentry lives on, particularly in high-end yachts. When you're talking about a fine fiberglass yacht, much time, effort, and money are spent camouflaging the fiberglass with wood. That ranges from the interior furnishings to the teak decks.

Consider the interior furniture, which can vary from a production to a custom boat, and from a racing boat to a cruiser. International Offshore Rule (IOR) boats tend to be like seagoing college dormitories, which perhaps accounts for their limited popularity of late. International Measurement System (IMS) boats show nicer accommodations, as the rule tries to weigh the accommodations in view of performance. Some fine cruising yachts can show furniture and fit and finish as elegant as a drawing room in a mansion.

One obvious measure of the quality of a yacht is the wood used in the interior. This includes hardwoods, for corner posts, locker frames, and drawer faces. Some favorite hardwoods used in fine boatbuilding are cherry, butternut, teak, and mahogany. Bulkheads, on the other hand, are stronger and lighter when made in plywood.

There are differences in plywood. When looks count, such as with below-deck furniture and teak decks, the thicker the plywood, the better. Thicker plywood—1 millimeter, close to 1/16 of an inch—allows proper sanding and finishing and permits the builder to fair the plywood sheets nicely into the solid corner posts.

In some racer/cruisers, there are fool-the-eye tricks with plywood veneers over foam cores. These items look and feel like solid tables, for example, and have the stiffness of a solid table, but at a fraction of the weight. (This is the I beam principle again.) Therefore, they compromise sailing performance less.

For those who favor teak decks, thickness counts there, too. Teak veneer can vary from 1/4 to 5/8 of an inch. That 1/4-inch teak might not last as long, and wood that thin doesn't allow proper bungs, the wood plugs that cover countersunk screws.

Thickness isn't the sole measure of veneer quality, however. Grain and color are important, too. The grain can be startling or subdued; it can match other panels in color or can contrast with them. It can have an abundance of mineral—the black lines in wood—and knots, or be free of them.

Another measure of furniture, be it in the drawing room or in the main saloon, is joinery: how cleanly two pieces of wood are cut and fitted together. Is the joint clean? Is it strong? Do the two pieces of wood show the same grain and color? The best joints maximize the gluing surface, use the strength and geometry of the wood to resist further movement, and appeal to the eye. The joints can be showy, like a dovetail, or subtle, like a tongue and groove.

One of the beauties of wood is that it was living when harvested and retains many of those characteristics. The challenge of working with wood is also that it retains many of those characteristics, particularly in the marine environment. Wood swells when it is moist, contracts when it is dry, and warps—all according to the type of wood, the direction of the grain, and the strength of the joint. The boatbuilder must engineer this growth and contraction into each piece. Boatbuilders have to allow for expansion around drawers, for example. It is even important in such areas to allow for the thickness of the varnish.

Whether the location is on deck or below, there are those who think screw heads shouldn't be obvious, except where access is necessary. Also, structural members, like chain plates or knees, shouldn't be apparent. There are, of course, tremendous differences between yachts and yachtsmen, and not everyone cares about visible screw heads or obvious engineering details. A boat can vary from a piece of sports equipment (that's probably closest to my bias), to an extension of the home, to one's home itself.

EQUIPPING A BOAT

After you have the boat, then comes the equipment. You have to equip the boat, as well as yourself. The bits and pieces, from a compass to a boat-speed indicator to a kelp stick to radar, can be expensive. These high- and low-tech items can make your sailing more interesting and more comfortable, or can burden you with responsibility and easily empty a bank account.

It's beyond the scope of this book to rate the wide variety of products available. Also, features change frequently, so what's considered the best today may not be next season. To help in equipping your boat, however, we provide these general equipment lists, some of which were taken from the 1986–87 *Stars & Stripes* America's Cup campaign. It includes items from both the racing boat and the tenders. The list doesn't pretend to be exhaustive; nor is all of it necessary. Use it solely as a guide.

Racing Boat

Item	Quantity	Remarks
Magnetic compasses	2	
Electronic compass	1	Accurate; helpful in determining lifts and headers
Complete instrumentation		
Boat-speed indicator		
VMG indicator		
Heading indicator		
Mark-heading indicator		
True-wind-speed indicator		
True-wind direction		
Apparent-wind speed		
Apparent-wind angle		
Heel angle		Placed athwartships and fore and aft
Timer		
Electronic range finder	1	For determining aheads and behinds
GPS	1	For position locating
VHF radio	1	
Local harbor and ocean charts	1 set	

Item	Quantity	Remarks
Binoculars with hand-bearing compass	2	
Hand-bearing compass	2	
Stopwatch	1	
First-aid kit	1	
Flashlights	6	
Searchlight	1	
Life jackets		One per person
Required safety equipment		Per racing category, contact national sailing authority for ORC lists, also local authorities for PHRF lists, etc.
Felt-tip pens and markers; black and in colors, waterproof and water-soluble	Several	For marking courses on bulkheads, etc. (see Chapter 8)
Diving masks, goggles, and fins	1 set	
Running lights	1 set	
IYRU Rule book and protest flag	1 each	
Dock lines	4	
Towing line	1	
Fenders	4	
Anchor	1	
Anchor rode	1	
Reels of various lines		
Fire extinguishers	1	
Yacht ensign	1	
Harness for bowman	1	
Kelp Stick		For removing weeds, etc., from keel and rudder
Light list	1	
Tide and current table	1 set	
Weather fax	1	
Dividers, parallel rules, etc.		
Code flags and alphabet charts	2 sets	

Item	Quantity	Remarks
List of race committee signals	1	Cones, signal-code flags, boat numbers for start recalls
Current stick		(See Chapter 10)

Coast Guard–required equipment

Item	Quantity	Remarks
Life jackets		Based on boat's capacity
Fire extinguishers	as required	
Horn and whistle	1	
Bell	1	
Distress signals and flare gun	as required	
Heaving-life ring	1	
Towing lights and day signal	1 set	
Anchors	3	
Anchor rodes	2	
Chain	30 feet	
Searchlight	1	
First-aid kit	1	
Stretcher or hoisting litter	1	
Man-overboard light	2	
Fixed and portable pumps	1 each	
Flashlights and batteries	numerous	
Oil-discharge placard		A sign prohibiting the dumping of oil must be mounted near engine compartment
Waste-discharge placard		
Numbers		Registration numbers required by Coast Guard and/or state
Complete tool kit		

Sailmaking kit

Tools	Hardware	Materials
Scissors	S.S. O-rings	Sq. yd. of each cloth
Needles	Duct tape	2" Dacron tape (3 oz.)
Palm	Seizing wire	Nylon webbing
Awl, pic, or spike	Pins (tacks)	2 Yds. Dacron insig. cloth
Hot knife	Spare slides	Light thread
Pliers	Spare hanks	1/4" or 1/2" double-sided seam tape

OPTIONAL

Seam ripper	Waxed twine	Heavy thread
Razor knife	Bee's wax	
Hammer	Grommets	
Grommet set		
Punch		

Clothing

Foul-weather gear (two-piece for ventilation)
Boots
Boat shoes (two pairs)
Short pants (a number appropriate to length of voyage)
Long pants
Heavy jacket or float coat
Heavy sweater
Shirts (long sleeve)
T-shirts
Cap or hat (2)
Woolen or polypropylene hat for cold weather
Sailing gloves
Flannel shirt

Personal items

Sunglasses (2)
Sunscreen
Personal overboard light and whistle

Toothbrush and paste

Comb, brush, other necessary toiletry items

Thermal polypropylene underwear (for cold locations)

Wristwatch, preferably with a countdown timer

Seasickness medication that you have tried and found effective:

a) Transderm Scop (available by prescription only)

b) Dramamine or Marezine (both available over the counter) or Meclizine (by prescription only)

c) Phenergan (available by prescription only)

4 | Sails

My first boat was a derelict, a 9-foot dinghy of no apparent type. My father must have found it floating in San Diego Bay. He gave it to me when I was four. It had a 15-foot mast, which separated into two parts, probably for easy storage in a small garage. It leaked terribly. The boat also had a round bottom, which, combined with the leaks, made it essentially unstable. I had no money to fix the leaks or the boat.

Whoever designed this boat must have known how to swim. I couldn't swim then and can't now. My father allowed me to use it, provided that I wore an oversized life jacket that dwarfed me. My mother has photos of me barely visible in this overstuffed flotation aid. When the boat tipped over, which it did regularly, I was unable to right it. I would just have to hang onto the boat the best I could and wait until someone came along to tow me in. To this day, my inability to swim can probably be linked somehow to the helplessness I felt while waiting for a tow in a life preserver that made movement impossible.

Practically every time the tiny boat tipped over, the mast would separate into two pieces. The sail would usually rip, which would prevent me from going sailing. That was the worst thing that could happen to me.

Herb Sinnhoffer ran Sinnhoffer Sails within the boundaries of the San Diego Yacht Club. At the time I'm speaking of, Sinnhoffer was selling his business to Elton Ballas. Both Sinnhoffer and Ballas were Penguin sailors; the 12-foot Penguin, like the Star and Lightning, was a popular class in San Diego at the time. Ballas was an innovative sailmaker. He was the first one, as far as I know, to figure out the advantages of the deck-sweeper jib, which limits induced drag.

To get my ripped sail fixed, I used to go bother Sinnhoffer and then Ballas. I was a pest, and the worst kind at that, because there was no way they could get me to go away except by helping me. While hanging around, I tried to make myself useful. I swept floors, washed cars. I'd do anything.

I loved sailing, and so I loved my sail. So great was my affection for this tired, patched, and threadbare sail, I used to sleep with it. Similarly, I would study pictures of sails in magazines for hours, trying to figure out what made them work. That love of sails has stood me well. To this day, my expertise in the sport is primarily sails.

In 1956, when I was 14, Ballas took me as his crew to the Penguin Nationals in New Orleans. This was my first trip to the "big time," and it left an impression on me. I still cherish those memories.

SAILCLOTH

My dinghy sail was cotton, the material used in sailmaking for more than a century. It is significant that the yacht *America,* which won a noted race around England's Isle of Wight in 1851, used cotton sails—one of the first yachts to do so. The English schooners and cutters used flax sails, cotton's predecessor.

Both cotton and flax are plant fibers. Flax comes from the plant stems, while cotton comes from the seed case. What made cotton more desirable than flax was that it stretches less. Sailing to windward requires flat sails. The fact that cotton stretches less than flax helped *America* to win this race. The Hundred Guinea Cup, as the trophy *America* won was then called, became the America's Cup.

After World War II, synthetic fibers, developed for the war effort, found an application in sailmaking. The first was nylon, still used in spinnakers, and next Orlon. I remember that during the trip to New Orleans, Ballas told me about Skip Boston, a sailmaker in Detroit, who made the fastest Penguin sails out of Orlon.

In 1957, when I was fifteen, I borrowed a Penguin from a friend, Bob Andre, and borrowed my grandmother's car. I wasn't old enough to have a driver's license, but with my crew, Dave Reed, we drove across the country to Lake St. Clair near Detroit. The Penguin was number 5440, and I remember calling it "Or Fight," after the famous territorial slogan, "Fifty-four–Forty or Fight. "

We won the Penguin Junior Nationals for sailors under eighteen years old. Before driving home, I stopped at the Boston sail loft, in Mt. Clemens, near Detroit. I can remember being shown the Orlon sailcloth, racks and racks of the stuff. It was yellow, as Kevlar is today. As an impressionable fifteen-year-old, I thought, There's gold in them-thar hills. Somehow I purchased enough Orlon cloth to make two Penguin sails. I don't remember how I paid for it as I had no money. Not only had I borrowed my grandmother's car to make the trip, but I had to borrow gas money from her.

I took the Orlon sailcloth back to San Diego. With the help of a Portuguese seamstress who worked for Ballas, I made my first sail. I can't remember the seamstress's name, but I do remember what she looked like: she was heavyset and very formidable. I talked her into sewing the sail by promising I'd wash her car for the rest of the summer or the rest of my life. The sail was a disappointment, as I remember it. It certainly wasn't as good as Ballas could have made. Nevertheless, I was immensely proud of this sail. It was mine.

Dacron

Orlon proved to be but a passing fancy in sailmaking. Dacron came next. Its use in sails was spearheaded by Ted Hood, a young sailmaker from Marblehead, Massachusetts, whom I would sail for in the 1974 America's Cup. Hood began using Dacron in 1953. The material, a by-product of oil refining, was invented in England in 1941 and called Terylene. Du Pont purchased the rights and called it Dacron; polyester is the generic name.

In San Diego, Lowell North, who started in sailmaking in 1958, championed the use of Dacron. North built Dacron sails that were blue in color for Star boats and for a smaller version, the Starlet. This was, no doubt, a marketing idea as blue sails eventually sailed off into the sunset. They were distinctive, however. North would eventually build a loft next to Ballas and next to the San Diego Yacht Club on Anchorage Lane. That loft, his first of what would be more than fifty worldwide, is still there.

I saw North put a mast on top of the building and work on sail shape. Lowell was always on the forefront. To be close to Sinnhoffer, then Ballas, and then to watch North offered me extraordinary exposure to some of the best thinking in sailmaking.

Dacron would have a long reign in sailmaking. Indeed, it is still used in triangular cruising sails (main and jibs), in one-design applications, and, most recently, in spinnakers. The switch to Dacron in the 1950s and early 1960s was occasioned by the fact that the material would not mildew like cotton. That said, the primary reason for Dacron's long life was that it stretched less than the cotton sailcloth it replaced.

Low stretch is the most desirable feature in a triangular sail. In increased winds, a sail stretches and gets deeper, and the draft moves aft. This shape creates more power, which causes a boat to heel more, which reduces the forward force, or drive. A sail with low stretch will hold its designed shape longer than a sail that stretches more.

Mylar

In 1975, laminated sails appeared. Lowell North used them on *Pendragon*, an IOR ocean racer. A more significant appearance was in 1977, when North used Mylar genoas on *Enterprise,* the 12-Meter he sailed for a time in the America's Cup trials. North laminated (glued) a Mylar film to woven polyester. In time, there would prove to be a synergy in this recipe, as a Mylar sail stretches less than a Dacron sail. Also, it weighs significantly less. If low stretch is the first principle of triangular sails, light weight is the second. A Mylar sail could weigh half as much as a Dacron (polyester) sail and show the same low stretch.

Sailcloth weight is measured in ounces per sailmaker's yard (SMY). This is the weight of cloth of a section 28.5 inches wide by 36 inches long.

Weight aloft affects a boat's degree of heel and how well it sails. This principle is most clearly expressed in an object's moment, an engineering term defined as weight times distance (see FIGURE 2.5). The practical importance of the moment of a boat's rig is that the vessel heels and pitches more when called upon to balance sails that weigh 76 pounds than sails that weigh 38 pounds (see FIGURE 2.6). This is the primary reason why sailmakers have worked so hard in the last decade to make sails lighter.

Recently, cruising sailors, like racers, are turning to Mylar sails, too—in particular Mylar headsails. With small crews, it is much more desirable to handle a lighter sail than a heavier one. Reducing weight aloft is important to cruisers, too, as their boats typically trade stability for increased accommodations.

Furthermore, sailmakers have worked hard to make Mylar cruising sails feel softer to the touch, and though delamination was sometimes a problem in bygone days, such failures are rare today. Sailmakers consider Mylar every bit as durable as polyester. Finally, the difference in cost is no longer dramatic: a Mylar sail is only about 10 percent more expensive than a polyester one.

Although Mylar eventually became a significant improvement in sailmaking, it wasn't when Lowell North first used it in the 1977 Cup. Ted Turner, sailing *Courageous,* won the June trials. North won the July trials, and it was during this round that North unveiled his new Mylar genoa. Ed du Moulin, who ran the *Enterprise* syndicate and later ran my syndicates in 1980 and 1983, thinks something significant happened at the end of the July trials that unfortunately went unnoticed at the time. Turner won the last race of the series with a brand-new Hood Dacron headsail. Du Moulin says that the Hood polyester sail was faster than the North Mylar sail, "but we were dazzled by our technology." With this sail and others like it, Turner won the August trials and defended the America's Cup.

The lesson of this story is that while saving weight is significant in sails, it should never be done at the expense of shape.

Kevlar

Kevlar is the miracle material used to stop bullets in bulletproof vests. We used some Kevlar sails in the 1980 America's Cup on *Freedom*. In a Mylar sail, a Mylar film is laminated to a layer of woven polyester. In a Kevlar sail, the Mylar film is laminated to a woven fabric that has Kevlar fiber in one direction and polyester in the other. If a Mylar sail could be half the weight of a polyester sail—with the same degree of low stretch—a Kevlar sail could be one-fourth the weight.

Kevlar sails first appeared in the early 1970s, under the name Fiber B. In this manifestation, the Kevlar yarns were in both directions: the warp and fill. Directions like warp and the fill are textile terms related to the weaving or manufacturing process.

In FIGURE 4.1, note that the warp direction is the longest direction in a roll of fabric. The warp yarns are the long yarns, which unroll from a spool and pass through the loom during the weaving process. They can be 100 yards long or longer. The fill yarns pass back and forth through the warp yards and are perpendicular to them. They are typically 28.5 inches long (a sailmaker's yard), or even less. The bias direction is 45 degrees to the fill and warp. Normally, there are no threads running in the bias direction; thus sailcloth is most likely to stretch when pulled in this direction. To avoid bias stretch, sailmakers try to aim the strong warp or fill threads to the loads that are applied to the sail. (This principle of matching material strength to load was also discussed in Chapter 3 in the context of boatbuilding.)

In the Fiber B days, running Kevlar in both the warp and the fill caused the Kevlar yarns to abrade each other. Thus, such sails often failed. In the second coming of Kevlar, as signaled by *Freedom* in the 1980 America's Cup, the Kevlar threads ran in the fill direction only. The warp was

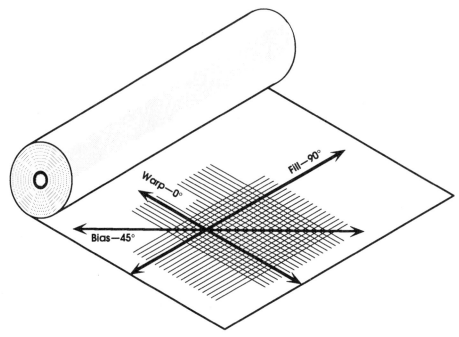

FIGURE 4.1 *Cloth directions.*

polyester. Then the Kevlar threads were oriented to the load.

Similar to Mylar, when Kevlar first appeared, there were problems gluing the Mylar film to the woven (Kevlar and polyester) substrate. The material would delaminate. For example, the early Kevlar sails on *Freedom* did have some problems. Our famous Number 10 mainsail, made by North, was fast but falling apart. I only used that sail when I really needed some extra speed. It had patches all over it to try to hold it together. Nevertheless, we continued to use it whenever we had to win a race.

In the weaving of sailcloth, it is possible to make one of the threads, either the short fill yarns or long warp yarns, particularly strong. This is done primarily by limiting crimp. Crimp refers to the serpentine path that yarns take when they cross other yarns. The problem with crimp can be seen with a crimped telephone cord. When you pull on the telephone cord, it gets longer. If the wind and sail-control devices pull on the crimped threads in a sail, the sail stretches out of shape.

Sailmakers and cloth manufacturers have discovered that crimp can be limited to one direction rather than two. Thus, the uncrimped direction is low stretch while the crimped direction is higher in stretch. Then, if the low-stretch side, either the warp or fill, is oriented in the same direction as the load, the sail will stretch less. FIGURE 4.2 shows warp-oriented cloth. In this application, the warp threads could be low-stretch Kevlar, for example, and woven to minimize crimp. (One way to minimize crimp is by using thick yarns in the uncrimped direction and very thin yarns in the crimped direction.) These strong and relatively uncrimped Kevlar threads would be oriented to the load (see the arrows in FIGURE 4.2).

The loads in sails mainly radiate from the attachment points. In triangular sails, these are primarily the head and clew, with lower loads encountered at the tack. The most common response of sailmakers to such radiat-

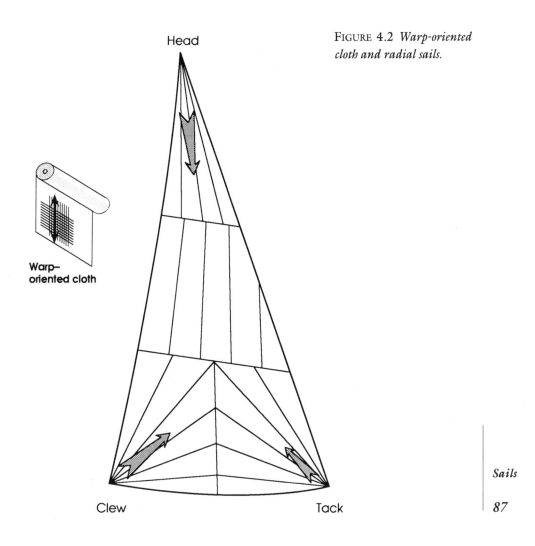

FIGURE 4.2 *Warp-oriented cloth and radial sails.*

ing loads is to create a radial sail (see FIGURE 4.2), that is, a sail in which many overlapping wedge-shaped pieces of cloth radiate out from the attachment points.

FIGURE 4.3 *How luff and foot curve shape sails.*

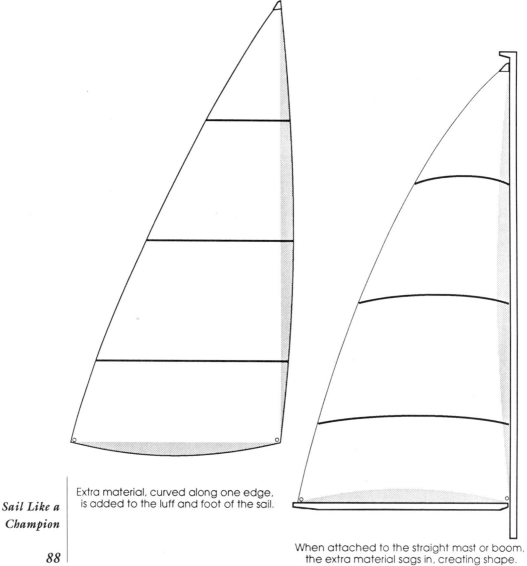

Extra material, curved along one edge, is added to the luff and foot of the sail.

When attached to the straight mast or boom, the extra material sags in, creating shape.

HOW SAILS ARE SHAPED

Turning a two-dimensional piece of cloth into a three-dimension airfoil shape requires some technique. Sailmakers shape headsails with luff curve; mainsails with luff and foot curve; and triangular sails, as well as spinnakers, with what is called broadseaming. With luff curve, extra material is added to the luff. When attached to a straight mast, the extra material sags into the sail, creating shape (see FIGURE 4.3). Similarly, foot curve is extra material at the foot. When attached to a boom, the extra material pushes shape into the sail. The above two methods are rather primitive ways to shape sails.

With broadseaming, sailmakers cut a curve on one panel of cloth (the broadseam). The adjacent panel is straight. (See FIGURE 4.4 for broad-seaming on cross-cut, or horizontal, sails.) In vertical sails, such as those in FIGURE 4.2, the broadseams run vertically. When the curved panel is sewn to a straight one, shape is forced into the sail. In a deeply curved spinnaker, both panels may have broadseams. Due to the shape, a broadseamed sail will not lie perfectly flat on the floor.

FIGURE 4.4 *How broadseaming shapes sails.*

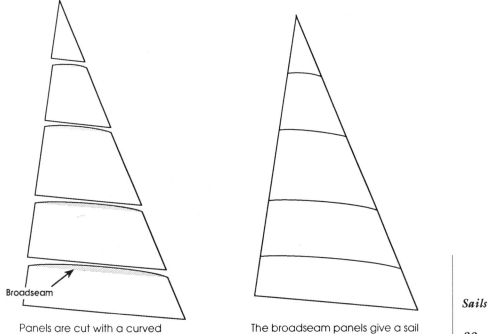

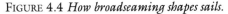

Broadseam

Panels are cut with a curved
edge known as a broadseam.

The broadseam panels give a sail
shape in three dimensions.

Ballas taught me about broadseaming. When I bought the yellow Orlon cloth from Skip Boston, one quality I found exciting was that the cloth came in 18-inch panels rather than in the traditional sailmaker's yard (SMY) of 28.5 inches. I recognized that this sail would have more seams and, thus, more opportunities for broadseaming. I'm not taking credit for this idea—Ted Hood had been doing it for years—but realizing this as a boy was exciting.

LIFT-DRAG RATIO

In Chapter 2, we saw that sails and a keel (or centerboard) turn the flow. The result of this turning is high speed and low pressure on one side of the foil and low speed and high pressure on the other. This creates pushes and pulls in a sail, which can be reduced to one vector (see, for example, S_{Total} in FIGURE 2.4). If there was no drag from the sails, rig, etc., this lift vector would be *perpendicular* to the apparent wind. Because of drag, a force *parallel* to the apparent wind, lift is slightly aft of perpendicular.

FIGURE 4.5 shows these vectors on a mainsail. It is worth noting again how lift is perpendicular to the apparent wind, whereas drag is parallel to it. The sum of these two vectors is the total force on a sail, which is slightly greater than perpendicular to the apparent wind.

FIGURE 4.5 *The sum of the lift and drag vectors is the total sail force, or S_{Total}, as seen in* FIGURE 4.5.

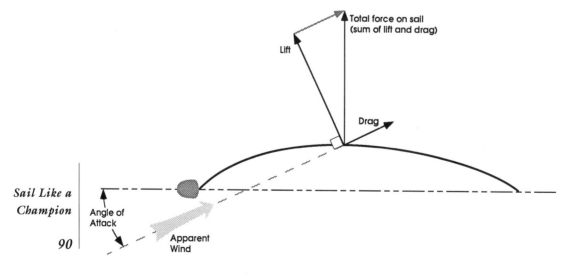

To generate lift, the wind must be turned. To turn the wind easily, trim a sail. When you first trim a sail, lift goes up much more quickly than drag. If you continue trimming a sail, however, at some point the turn becomes too sharp. Rather than the wind following the sharp curve of the sail, the wind spins off, like a driver who tries to negotiate a hairpin curve with too much speed. When the curve starts to get too sharp, drag increases much more rapidly. (To a sailor, drag is felt as increased heel.)

So upwind sail trim and steering are a balancing act between maximizing lift and minimizing drag. This can be accomplished through more or less sail trim or through steering lower or higher. Or, most often, both. (It is difficult to separate sail trim from steering; thus both subjects are discussed in this chapter as well as in Chapter 7, "Steering.")

Lift versus drag is measured in the lift-to-drag ratio, discussed in Chapter 2. When sailing upwind, usually the higher the ratio, the better you are, at least until the boat is overpowered.[1]

TELLTALES

While it is good for sailors to be aware of the lift-to-drag ratio, there isn't an instrument that reads it as such. Telltales—small tufts of yarn placed on the headsail near the luff—are an adequate substitute.

First a word on telltales: If the leading edge, or luff, of the headsail is aimed perfectly into the wind, both windward and leeward telltales stream aft. If, however, the headsail's sheet is eased too much or the course steered is too close to the wind, the leading edge of the headsail is no longer aimed perfectly into the wind. Rather, the wind—what aerodynamicists term the stagnation streamline—is striking the windward side of the sail. This results in separated, or unattached, flow on the windward side. The windward telltales react to this bubble of separated flow by flipping up or down. In due time, the sail will luff. If, on the other hand, the sail is trimmed too tight or the course steered is too low, the luff of the sail is aimed so the wind—or stagnation streamline—strikes the leeward side. Now the bubble of separated flow is on the leeward side, and the telltales on that side no longer stream aft.

In summary, telltales show attached flow. When the flow is attached on both sides of the sail, the wind is hitting the leading edge of the sail. At such

---

[1]Downwind, sailors want to maximize drag. When reaching, both lift and drag create movement in the desired direction. This is one reason why a reach is the fastest point of sail.

times, both windward and leeward telltales stream aft. When the flow isn't attached, the telltales on one or the other side of the sail flip up. (Later we will see that without attached flow, such as when running, telltales won't work.)

When the windward telltale is just flicking (the leeward telltale would be streaming aft), that signals the highest lift-drag ratio. When both windward and leeward telltales stream aft, however, lift is at its highest but at the expense of increased drag.

One could conclude that steering with the windward telltale just flicking is optimum. There are times, however, when more lift is needed, even at the expense of more drag, for example, when you want to accelerate to hull speed or when the boat is slowed by waves. At such times, you might sail with both telltales streaming.

Most sailmakers know where to place telltales. If not, you should probably find another sailmaker. Locate the telltales on a headsail 12 to 24 inches back from luff; the bigger the boat, the farther back. While I prefer to see three pairs (a pair one-quarter down from the top, one-quarter up from the bottom, and in the middle), the middle telltales are the most important. Sometimes the sail has a very fine entry at the bottom, and it stalls there (the bottom lee telltale flags). Usually, the top telltale isn't visible to the helmsman steering from the high side (the proper side on which to steer; see Chapter 7).

It is helpful if clear plastic windows frame these telltales, making it easy to discern the weather telltale from the leeward one. By convention, the telltales on the starboard side are slightly higher than those on the port side, and the yarns are colored green and red, respectively. More important is that the steerer and sail trimmer know which telltale is which without having to think about it. Yarn makes the best telltales, and these yarn telltales should be affixed to the sail with sticky-backed material. I've tried using other materials for telltales, audiocassette tape, for example. That worked well until it got wet.

Whether made of wool or another material, wet telltales sticking to the sail are very frustrating. The only remedy for that is to have a crew member free it with a shake or two of the sail, or to use a halyard or a boat hook to scrape it off. Telltales shouldn't be so long that they foul on the luff.

Telltales should be on every sailboat, small and large, racer and cruiser. More sophisticated and more expensive—and only appropriate to larger boats—is electronic instrumentation. Wind and boat-speed indicators allow you to sail by target boat speeds (discussed later in this chapter and in Chapter 7), which are a great aid to proper steering.

AN OVERVIEW OF SAIL SHAPE

Sails have three- and two-dimensional qualities. The three-dimensional measurements are draft, draft location, twist, and angle of attack. The two-dimensional measurements are sail area and aspect ratio. Proper sail trim requires an understanding of all of these measurements. First, these terms will be defined generally; then we'll get specific when discussing headsails, mainsails, racing and cruising spinnakers, and spinnaker specialty sails.

Draft

When an airplane needs power, while landing, for instance, the curvature, that is, the depth of the wings, is made deeper through the extension of flaps. Similarly, when added power is needed in sailing, such as when you are heading upwind in light air and sloppy seas or when reaching or running in all but the heaviest winds, the curvature of the sails is made deeper. Power increases as sail depth, or draft, increases.

The amount of depth, or draft, is described as a percentage of the sail's width at a given point. (A sail's width, or luff-to-leech measurement, is called its chord.) Thus, a 1-foot depth in a sail with a 10-foot chord is a 10 percent depth (see FIGURE 4.6). Fuller sails, with a 17 percent depth, for example, generate more power, that is, more lift and more drag. This shape is appropriate to light air since fuller sails help the boat to accelerate.

As the wind increases, the desired headsail shape is flatter, for example, 10 percent. A flatter sail generates low lift and low drag. Flatter is faster in drifting conditions because light winds lack the energy to round a deeply curved sail.

In a headsail, the sail designer has the major effect on sail depth. Using

FIGURE 4.6 *How depth is determined.*

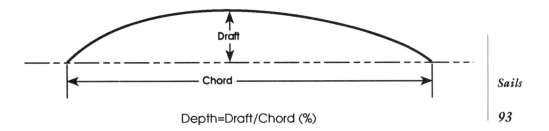

Depth=Draft/Chord (%)

luff curve and broadseaming, the designer makes, for example, a Number 1 headsail fuller than a Number 2. The Number 1 is therefore a better sail for lighter winds since it has more shape and more power, and is, of course, larger. Similarly, a Number 2 is fuller than a Number 3. The sailor initially controls depth in a headsail by changing to the appropriate sail for the wind and sea conditions. Then, within the range of a given sail, shape is primarily governed by mast bend, sheet and halyard tensions, and lead angle (athwartships, in and out, as well as forward and back). A main, which isn't normally changed as the wind increases, has numerous controls (mast bend, outhaul, flattening reef, reefing, etc.) that affect sail depth.

Draft has a vertical component, too; a mainsail, for example, has more draft at the top than at the bottom. Obviously, since little sail area is at the top of a triangle, more power is needed there. Increased power at the top is accomplished through increased depth.

Draft Location

After the amount of draft (depth), the next most important factor in sail design and sail trim is where the point of maximum draft falls along the chord of a sail. Determine draft position this way: Locate the point of maximum draft (see FIGURE 4.7). Then compare the location or distance of the draft (from the leading edge) to the overall chord of the sail. Draft position is thus location divided by chord, expressed as a percentage. If the draft is 4-1/2 feet back and the chord is 10 feet, draft is 45 percent. For a headsail, the 45 percent depth position is about average.

A sail with the draft aft (48 percent, for example) has a flatter leading edge. This can make the sail closer winded—particularly if the wind is moderate and the water relatively smooth. As such, a draft-aft sail can show a higher lift-drag ratio. The draft-aft shape can, however, round the back of

FIGURE 4.7 *How draft position is figured.*

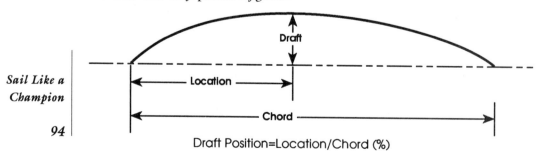

the sail. While this is not a problem in moderate air, in heavier air the wind can separate at the point of maximum draft. When this happens, the lift-drag ratio decreases.

When sailing upwind, steering takes precedent over sail trim. A draft-aft headsail, for example, while more efficient, is more sensitive to imprecise steering. This is why this shape is only appropriate when steering is easy, in moderate winds and smooth seas, or when the steerer is particularly gifted. A draft-forward sail is slower upwind but more forgiving of less skilled steering. This is discussed further in Chapter 7.

As the amount of draft varies in the vertical direction, so, too, does the draft position. The draft should be farther forward in lower sections—where due to friction on the water (addressed next), wind velocity tends to be less,

FIGURE 4.8 *Wind velocity increases with height.*

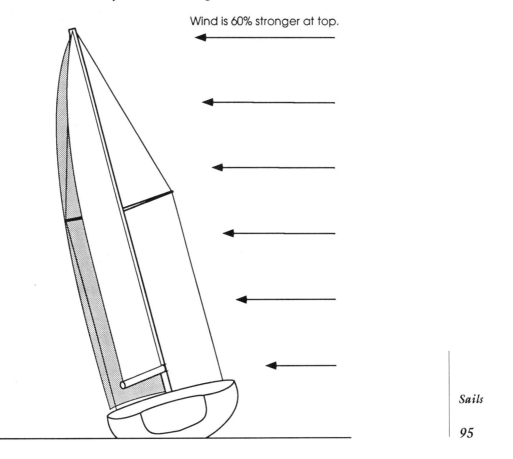

Wind is 60% stronger at top.

and the angle of the apparent wind farther forward. Conversely, the draft should be farther aft in upper sections—where the wind is stronger and thus its angle farther aft.

Twist

Friction occurs when wind passes over water. This friction slows the wind, particularly at the surface. There is, thus, more wind at the top of the mast than at the bottom. (In FIGURE 4.8, note how the arrows are shorter at the bottom than at the top.) Studies, in fact, show the wind blows 60 percent greater at the top of a 40-foot mast than at deck level.

FIGURE 4.9 *Apparent-wind triangle.*

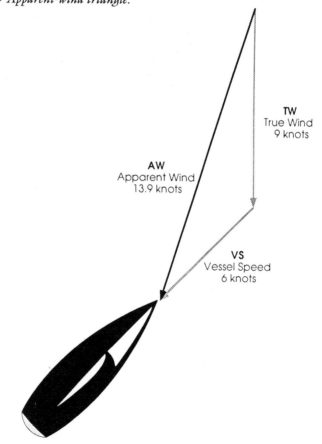

TW
True Wind
9 knots

AW
Apparent Wind
13.9 knots

VS
Vessel Speed
6 knots

FIGURE 4.9 shows the apparent-wind triangle, which is familiar to many sailors. The true-wind vector, side TW, represents the angle (and speed) of the wind that one experiences when the boat is stationary. Then the boat begins to move. Vessel speed and direction are represented by vector VS. Once the boat begins moving, the wind that the boat senses is different from the true wind. This is the apparent wind, or AW. If the wind speed and/or boat speed change, the apparent wind changes, too, in both direction and speed.

Returning to the sail with more wind at the top than the bottom: As the velocity increases with height, there is a corresponding change, or twist, in the apparent-wind angle. (In FIGURE 4.10, note the difference in the apparent-wind angle, top to bottom.) That twist in the apparent wind can be as much as 3 to 5 degrees in a 40-footer. This means the top of the sail is in a 3-to-5-degree lift. In essence, the top is close-reaching and the bottom beating. Thus, the top of the sail needs to be eased, as on a close-reach; the bottom needs to be trimmed hard, as on a beat.

To account for this vertical shift in the apparent wind, sails are designed and trimmed to twist off toward the top. It is important that the twist in the

FIGURE 4.10 *As the wind increases with height, the apparent wind changes direction.*

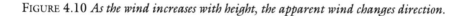

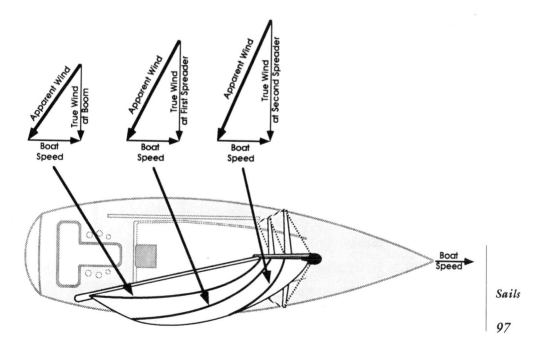

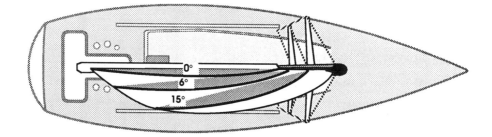

FIGURE 4.11 *Twist as measured in a mainsail.*

sail match the vertical twist in the wind. This is accomplished in a headsail, for example, by moving the lead forward and back and watching the telltales. The goal is for the telltales up and down the luff of the headsail to luff at the same time (more on this later). Also, how hard the jib sheet is trimmed affects twist.

In a mainsail, twist is controlled by mainsheet tension and by the vang. Twist is easiest to see in a mainsail. Measure twist by comparing the angles of the chord lines of a sail to the centerline of the boat at various heights (see FIGURE 4.11). Simply put, twist is the leeward sag of the back or leech. Note that near the boom, the sail isn't twisted, while at the top it shows, in this example, 15 degrees of twist.

Why isn't, you might ask, that twist 3 to 5 degrees? This would match the vertical variation in the true-wind direction between the deck and the masthead of our typical 40-footer. The answer is that twist also affects power in a sail, and this function takes precedence over the vertical twist in the wind. In this context, it is simplest to think of twist as a power-off (brake) and power-on (accelerator) device. More twist, or more leeward sag, and the sail has less power—the "brake" is on. Less twist or less leeward sag, and the sail has more power—the "accelerator" is pushed.

Due to the words *more* and *less,* twist is confusing to many sailors. So this principle bears repeating: The *less* a sail twists—the straighter its back— the more power. The *more* the sail twists—the *more* the back sags off to leeward—the less power it shows. If I wanted more power in the main in FIGURE 4.11, I could trim the vang. Then the top might only fall off (twist) 10 degrees rather than degrees 15, making the sail more powerful.

Why the lack of twist corresponds to an increase in power has to do with what was touched upon earlier. A sail that doesn't twist as much asks the wind to turn more, which up to a point, can increase the lift-drag ratio.

This is why in light to moderate winds, sails show less twist, or the accelerator is pushed down. On the other hand, a sail that twists more asks the wind to turn less. This decreases lift—as does stepping on the brake—which is appropriate when the boat is overpowered in heavier winds.

Angle of Attack

The angle of attack is the angle between the apparent-wind direction and the sail's chord line. For a given heading, wind speed, and boat speed, the angle of attack increases as the sail is trimmed or the lead is brought inboard (see FIGURE 4.12). Sail-control devices that can bring headsails inboard and outboard include the jib lead, crosshauls, and Barberhaulers, or in a main the traveler and, to a lesser degree, the mainsheet.

The import of angle of attack is that the more a sail is trimmed, the more power, or lift, it develops. This is because the more the sail turns the wind, the greater the potential force. Sir Isaac Newton said that for every action there is an equal and opposite reaction. The action of trimming the sail or steering farther off the wind without easing the sails causes a reaction: lift and drag. You trim the sail a little more or fall off more without easing the sails, and you get more of a reaction: more lift and maybe more drag but, it is hoped, a higher lift-drag ratio. Then you trim the sails a little more, and the wind reaches a point where it can't negotiate the curve of the sail. At that point, drag goes up much faster than lift, and the lift-drag ratio falls precipitously.

Sail Size

An important two-dimensional measure is the size of the sail. There is a direct relationship between sail size and power—at least until such times as the boat can't carry the extra sail and heels too much, or steers poorly, or both. Of course, in an offshore racing boat, the rating rule that governs the hull design and sailplan comes into play: excess sail area usually results in a penalty. In one-design boats, sail area is usually controlled in some way.

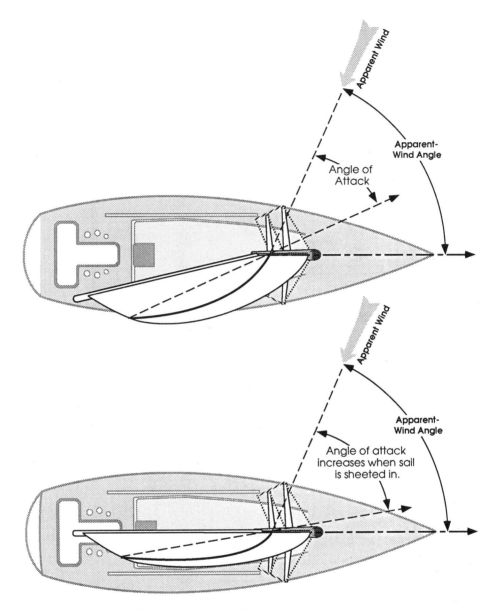

FIGURE 4.12 *Angle of attack increases as the sail is trimmed or the lead brought inboard.*

Aspect Ratio

Aspect ratio is another important two-dimensional measure in a sail. In a modern boat, whether for racing or cruising, the aspect ratio of sails has climbed steadily along with the aspect ratio of the rigs; that is, the vertical dimension of the sailplan has grown. This is because high-aspect-ratio sails make a boat faster upwind, as we saw in Chapter 2. Off-the-wind, low-aspect-ratio sails are faster. This accounts for the slightly lower aspect ratio of the sails and rigs on cruising boats, where upwind performance is less important.

Now that we are familiar with the three- and two-dimensional characteristics of sails, let's turn to the individual sails.

HEADSAIL SIZES AND SHAPES

There are many ways to describe a headsail. To determine headsail size, imagine a line perpendicular to the luff through the clew (see FIGURE 4.13). This is LP, or the luff-perpendicular dimension. Then, compare this distance with the J measurement, the distance between the mast and the forestay, measured at the deck. The amount by which the headsail overlaps the mainsail is expressed as a percentage, derived from the ratio LP/J. If LP is 15 feet and J is 10 feet, for instance, the overlap is 150 percent.

The amount of overlap in a headsail roughly determines the sail's number. For example, under the International Offshore Rule (IOR), a Number 1 genoa is usually 150 percent. (In Performance Handicap Racing Fleet it can be 155 percent.) A Number 2 is anywhere from 130 to 140 percent. A Number 3 has an overlap of 95 to 100 percent. As one can guess, a 95 percent headsail does not overlap the main. Until heeling or steering, etc., becomes a problem, a big sail (one with more sail area) is faster. Such a sail offers more lift and probably more drag, but likely a higher lift-drag ratio.

Aspect ratio is another term used to describe a headsail. A useful way to figure aspect ratio is to divide the headsail's luff length by its overlap (see FIGURE 4.13). As described in Chapter 2, a high-aspect shape minimizes induced drag.

The aspect ratio of a Number 1 genoa is 2.3–1. That is a low-aspect-ratio sail; however, in light winds, maximum sail area and a high lift-drag ratio is more important than a low-drag high-aspect-ratio shape. A Number 2 has an aspect ratio of 2.5–1. Modern offshore racers carry Number 3 jibs with an aspect ratio up to 3.75–1. Since drag translates to heeling, as mentioned, this is important in the heavy winds where the Number 3 works.

Since a Number 3 is flown in the heaviest winds, it is the most highly loaded headsail. This is compounded by its sheet lead, which pulls more directly down on the leech, or back, than does the lead for a Number 2 or 1. In summary, the Number 3 is often the most highly loaded sail on a boat, including the main, which has a lower aspect ratio (about 3.5–1). Not sur-

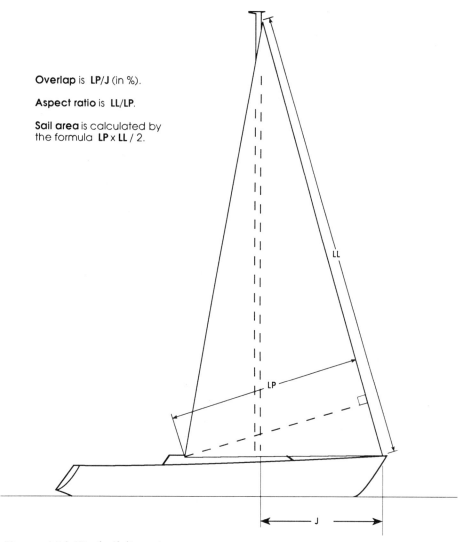

Overlap is **LP/J** (in %).

Aspect ratio is **LL/LP**.

Sail area is calculated by the formula **LP x LL / 2**.

FIGURE 4.13 *Headsail dimensions.*

prisingly, the Number 3 was the first sail to benefit from low-stretch Kevlar construction.

Lastly, sail area is measured by the formula LP x LL/2. This is also shown in FIGURE 4.13.

HEADSAIL CONTROLS

The sail designer has the first—as well as most important—word about sail shape in a headsail, primarily through broadseaming (see FIGURE 4.4). As mentioned, a Number 1 is cut fuller than a Number 2, and so on. A fundamental decision a sailor has to make is the choice of headsails.

Sail selection controls power—depth and draft location—as well as steering. A sail used beyond its range causes the boat to heel too much. This typically generates too much weather helm. As will be discussed in the next chapter, weather helm should be somewhere between 3 to 5 degrees. Also, a sail used beyond its wind range stretches. If it stretches too much, even once, or is too often stretched, the stretch can become permanent. This ruins a sail.

To determine which sail to use when, start with your sailmaker. Based on the weight of the cloth, its construction, the weight of your boat, etc., the sailmaker should provide customers with a safe working load number and an effective working range. For example, the range of the light Number 1 is from 5–10 true, and its safe working load is up to 12 knots true. That is the starting point only. You should then test the sails against other boats, either in a regatta or a dedicated testing session (see Chapter 5).

From such testing, write down which sail you used when and whether it was fast. Also note the cross-over points; when to change from the Number 1 to the 2, for instance, can be a critical decision. Eventually, you will develop a chart that might look like the one below. (We include jib leads and halyard position, which will be discussed later. Because jib-lead location and halyard position depend on arbitrary numbers, they are left blank. Within the range of a sail, halyard tension increases with the wind.)

Sail	Wind Range	Jib Leads	Jib Lead	Halyard Position
Light Number 1	2–13	8–10 degrees		
Medium Number 1	6–20	7.5–9.5 degrees		
Heavy Number 1	14–24	7.5–9.5 degrees		
Number 2	21–27	9–11 degrees		
Number 3	24–35	9–11 degrees		
Number 4	31–45	11–12 degrees		

The choice of headsails is straightforward in a small one-design boat as there are usually but one or two choices.

Once the decision is made about the correct sail size, then four devices control headsail shape: sheet tension, jib leads (adjusted forward and back and in and out), halyard tension, and headstay tension.

Sheet Tension

Tensioning the sheet removes twist, making the sail more powerful, and increases the sail's angle of attack, which also makes the sail more powerful. A deep, powerful sail is good in moderate winds, but normally not so good in heavy winds or drifting conditions.

If I want to point, such as when the water is flat, or when trying to cross another boat, or when sailing too fast for my targets (see Chapter 7), I would overtrim the headsail a bit and steer a little higher so the windward telltale is flicking or jumping every other second or every two seconds. (This, you will recall, signals the optimum point on the lift-drag curve.)

If I wanted to foot, to head off the wind so I could power through choppy seas, or if I was sailing too slowly for my targets, I'd ease the jib sheet a bit. Then, I might sail with both telltales streaming aft. (This is when lift is maximized, though at the expense of increased drag.) The proper amount of sheet tension varies from boat to boat and according to wind speed.

Also, when the boat becomes overpowered, you can ease the jib sheet a little, creating more twist. This, as described, depowers the sail. By this point, you should be considering changing headsails. If you are close to a turning mark, however, this technique might eliminate the need for a sail change, since it depowers the sail. You should also twist the headsail by putting the lead out and moving it aft if the mainsail shows too much backwind.

Jib Leads: Fore and Aft

Moving the headsail's lead forward and back is one way to control twist (see FIGURE 4.14). Moving the lead forward decreases twist, which powers up the sail. Moving it back increases twist, which depowers the sail. Again, sails are twisted for two reasons: to match the vertical twist in the wind and to control power in the sail.

Addressing the vertical twist in the wind, first: choose a starting point for the genoa car that looks correct in view of the foot length of the sail. Don't worry too much about this position, as it is only a rough approximation. After the lead is established, observe the telltales as the boat slowly turns into the wind. The goal is to have the genoa's telltales, from the top to the bottom, break simultaneously.

If the top telltales break first, the sail is twisted too much. Move the

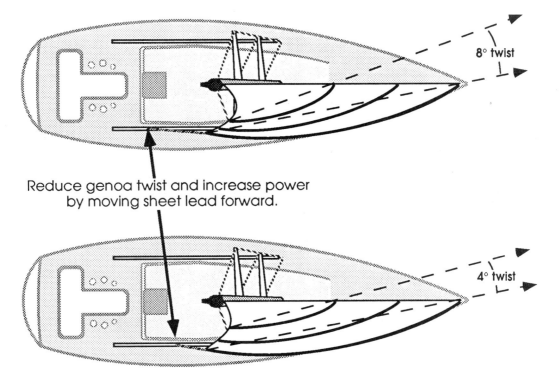

Reduce genoa twist and increase power
by moving sheet lead forward.

8° twist

4° twist

FIGURE 4.14 *Headsail lead location and twist, that is, power.*

lead forward. Conversely, if the bottom ones break first, the sail needs more twist. Move the lead aft. FIGURE 4.14 shows how twist increases and decreases by moving the headsail lead back and forward, respectively.

It is a good idea to mark lead positions (both beating and close-reaching) on a chart, like the previous one, as well as on the sail's clew (see the next chapter), so the correct setting is obvious every time the sail goes up. In an America's Cup program, determining genoa-lead location never ends. Also, sails age and stretch, and Mylar and Kevlar sails, in particular, wrinkle and shrink; with such size changes, lead position changes over time, too.

When it comes to power, more twist means more leeward sag of the leech, and this, like stepping on the brake, decreases power in sails. Thus, moving the lead slightly aft from the optimum position can decrease power. This can be appropriate in heavy winds. Less twist means more power in a sail. Thus, moving the lead slightly forward from the optimum position above increases power. In moderate winds this helps the boat to accelerate to hull speed.

Sails

Jib Leads: In and Out

Inboard and outboard lead adjustments determine power, that is, angle of attack, and twist. In an IOR boat, the light Number-1 genoa (150 percent overlap) will typically sheet at 8 to 10 degrees off the centerline when beat-

FIGURE 4.15 *Lead locations and spreader angle for a typical IOR boat.*

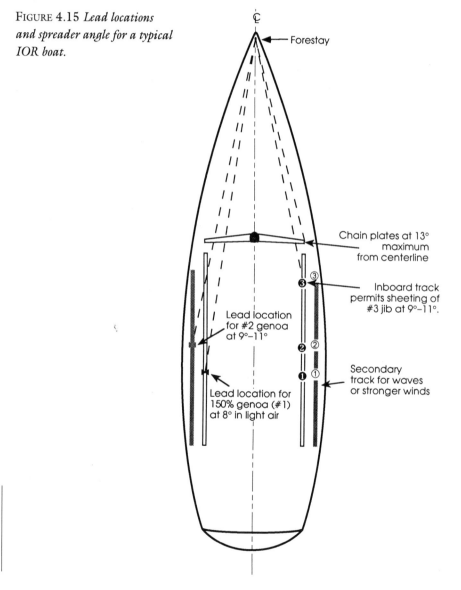

Forestay

Chain plates at 13°
maximum
from centerline

Inboard track
permits sheeting of
#3 jib at 9°–11°.

Lead location
for #2 genoa
at 9°–11°

Secondary
track for waves
or stronger winds

Lead location for
150% genoa (#1)
at 8° in light air

ing (see FIGURE 4.15). The smaller number (8 degrees) is appropriate when seas are smooth; the larger (10 degrees), when there are waves. A medium and heavy Number 1 will sheet from about 7.5 to 9.5 degrees when beating, again depending on seas. A Number 2 genoa (130–145 percent) will sheet at 9 to 11 degrees. The Number 3 jib (nonoverlapping) will also sheet at 9 to 11 degrees. (Use these degree numbers as a guide only, as designs vary. Also, some boats won't lend themselves to some angles, due to the placement of shrouds, deck hardware, etc.) As a rule, as the wind comes up, move the lead farther outboard, thus decreasing angle of attack and power. In very light winds, the lead goes out also.

This is why most racing boats will have an inboard and outboard track. Cross-hauls and Barberhaulers can adjust the lead angle of the genoa sheet, in addition to the track location. Cross-hauls and Barberhaulers pull the lead inboard or outboard, respectively. By moving the lead a half to a full degree toward the centerline, there will often be a small improvement in pointing in very flat water. This gives the headsail a narrower angle of attack.

In big seas when pointing is secondary to keeping the boat moving, an outboard lead in combination with slightly eased sheet will be better than just easing the sheet. When bearing away to a reach, move the lead outboard and forward. At such times, an outboard lead can, in fact, make as much as a 1-knot difference in speed.

The technique of moving the leads in and out is used when tacking too, particularly if the boat has leads that are readily adjustable in and out. The leads are kept out on a tack, and then as speed increases, they are moved inboard.

When the headsail overlaps the main, as it does in a masthead boat until you use the Number 3 jib, the headsail has a considerable effect on the main. This is seen, for example, in backwind. A fractionally rigged boat has such a small foretriangle that the sails overlap almost all the time. Thus, due to this overlap, a fractionally rigged boat requires more playing of the jib leads than does a masthead boat—this is particularly so when it is windy. By playing the leads, I mean both in and out and forward and back. Also, when the wind is heavy, it is more important on a fractionally rigged boat that main and jib twist match, that is, the sails show the same degree of twist top to bottom.

In my San Diego office, there is a picture of *Stars & Stripes '87*, sailing in Perth. The picture is taken from directly above. We must be going upwind in 35 knots true, 44 apparent. I can tell wind speed by the jib. It's our Number 7. It's hard to believe we're going upwind because the sails are twisting off at 45-degree angles—a reaching angle. That's an example of over-twisting sails in very heavy winds. Also, both main and jib have about the same degree of twist.

With a fractionally rigged boat, like a 12-Meter, the new International America's Cup Class, or an Etchells, jib trim is important due to its affect on the main. Compared with mains, however, the headsails on these boats are relatively small. Is jib trim so important in its own right? To put this another way, how effective is a jib on a fractionally rigged boat?

The relative lack of importance of jib trim in a fractionally rigged boat occurred to me in the fifth race against *Kiwi Magic* in the America's Cup Challengers finals in January 1987. We were ahead 3–1 in the series. On the second windward leg of this race, our Number 6 headsail disintegrated, when we had a forty-five-second lead. I knew exactly what to do: I dropped the traveler and footed off. This allowed me to sail at 8 knots, close to the target boat speed for this amount of wind. The trim was reminiscent of sailing a single-sail Finn or a Laser upwind in heavy air. The main just sat over the stern quarter while the crew worked frantically to change the headsail. To compound our problems, we were within two minutes of the layline when this occurred, so I had to tack while the crew changed the headsail. This put us on port tack with no rights, no headsail, a low course, and slightly diminished speed.

Kiwi Magic approached us on starboard. The questions were: Could we cross them on port with only a mainsail? And do we dare? The answer was simple: If we don't try it, the race would likely be lost.

Our jib went up just when the two boats came together. We pointed higher, and they had to tack underneath. This cut our lead from forty-eight seconds to fourteen seconds, but we were still ahead. If this had happened in a race involving a masthead-rigged boat, the other boat would have passed us in thirty seconds.

The moral of this story is that while jib trim in a fractionally rigged boat is important; it's not as important as mainsail trim. In my America's Cup career, I've spent an inordinate amount of time testing jibs. If I had to do it again, I'd spend more time testing mains.

Whether fractional or masthead rig, the jib leads affect mainsail trim, too. Thus, check main trim after setting up the jib. View the headsail's effect on the main by the degree of backwind. A little backwind is often unavoidable, but if the main starts flogging as if it's luffing, move the jib leads outboard or trim the main harder. Move the traveler up. Usually, the best response is to move the jib's lead out or not trim the jib sheet quite so hard. This is because moving the traveler up can create too much weather helm, which, in turn, can cause the boat to heel too much and unnecessarily increase leeway.

Halyard Tension

Comparatively stretchy Dacron (polyester) sails are still very popular with cruisers, and with polyester sails, halyard tension is the primary tool for draft location. More halyard tension moves the draft forward; less moves it aft. Because the wind pressure on genoas pushes the draft aft, more halyard tension is necessary as the sail reaches its upper wind range. For Number 2 and 3 genoas, the maximum draft should be about 35 to 40 percent back from the luff.

In choppy seas, move the draft forward with more halyard tension. If draft is forward, the lift-drag ratio is likely lower, but the boat will likely show a wider steering groove—a 10-degree margin of error as opposed to 5 degrees or less. A draft-forward sail will make fewer demands on the steerer's skill and concentration. Draft-forward is an excellent setting for cruisers, as this shape places fewer demands on steerers, be they people or self-steering devices. For cruisers or racers, this is also a good shape at night when steering is less precise.

Determine the width of your steering groove by slowly turning into the wind. Note the compass heading when the windward telltales luff. Then turn off the wind. Note the compass heading when the leeward telltales sky. If the range is 5 degrees or less, that is a very narrow groove; 10 degrees is a wide groove. (This is discussed further in Chapter 7.)

Draft-aft, which allows a higher lift-drag ratio, is a good shape for maximum pointing in flat water. To get this shape, apply little halyard tension to allow the draft to move aft. At such times, the boat will likely show greater top-end speed and point higher, but will be less tolerant of steering error.

A sail has to be stretchy on the luff for halyard tension to have much effect on draft location. Thus, low-stretch Mylar and Kevlar sails rely more on headstay tension for draft location (see below). With these sails, tighten the halyard just enough to remove horizontal wrinkles.

Headstay Tension

Headstay tension affects the draft position, too. In a boat with a masthead rig, the permanent backstay controls headstay tension. With a fractional rig, the running backstays do. More mast bend, like more halyard tension, moves the draft forward. Less mast bend, like less halyard tension, moves the draft aft.

Headstay tension also affects overall depth, particularly in the upper

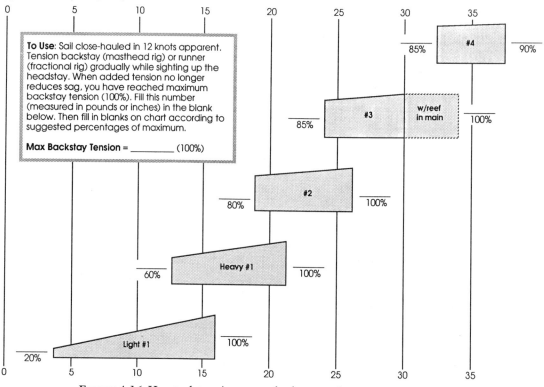

Apparent Wind Speed (knots)

To Use: Sail close-hauled in 12 knots apparent. Tension backstay (masthead rig) or runner (fractional rig) gradually while sighting up the headstay. When added tension no longer reduces sag, you have reached maximum backstay tension (100%). Fill this number (measured in pounds or inches) in the blank below. Then fill in blanks on chart according to suggested percentages of maximum.

Max Backstay Tension = _____ (100%)

FIGURE 4.16 *How to determine proper backstay tension.*

and middle parts of a sail. Less headstay tension means a fuller headsail, good in light winds and a chop. More backstay or runner tension means a flatter headsail; good in a breeze. (Obviously, at some point, the physical integrity of the mast takes priority over sail shape!)

Headstay tension also has some effect on twist. When the headstay sags, the leech rotates to windward somewhat. This reduces twist. Reducing twist makes a sail more powerful. Reducing twist can be good in medium winds, but more twist is better in heavy winds.

The light Number 1 requires the least tension on the backstay (if a masthead rig) or on the runner (if a fractional rig). The Number 4 requires the most. See FIGURE 4.16 to determine the proper amount of backstay tension.

Even with the most powerful hydraulic backstay adjuster, it isn't possible to get a headstay perfectly straight. With more wind, the headstay sags more, and the direct effect of this is to make the headsail fuller. That isn't desirable in heavy conditions. The greater the sag, the narrower any sail's performance band. This is true for all headsails on all types of boats. Incidentally, in special circumstances, increased sag is helpful. This includes those times where there are leftover seas (more sea than wind), or when trying to make a flat sail work in winds *below* its range.

In 1977, Lowell North reasoned that a straight headstay was important to upwind performance. With *Enterprise,* his America's Cup boat, he worked hard to get the headstay perfectly straight. One way he did this was by decreasing the J-measurement, the distance from the forestay to the mast, from 24.3 feet—which is practically the standard on a 12-Meter—to 22.5 feet. Straight or not, the result was a slow-tacking boat. The overlap of a 12-Meter genoa is fixed at 16 feet. So North's crew had to move an equal-sized sail through a smaller foretriangle. The boat also had a main with an oversized roach—extra sail area at the back—something else with which North experimented. It would load up, even before the mainsail was fully sheeted in. I used *Enterprise* as a trial horse in 1980. Even in a straight line, the boat was slow. In this case, North's innovation wasn't successful. The brilliance of North has always been his faculty for improvement. His lack of success in that America's Cup was due, in my opinion, to a relative lack of restraint. North perhaps tried to accomplish too much, from a straight headstay, to Mylar sails, to mainsails with huge roaches.

HEADSAIL TRIM WHEN REACHING

Jib reaching at 35 to 65 degrees to the wind requires unfortunate compromises. When reaching under headsail, move the jib's lead as far outboard as possible. In fact, a lead 2 feet beyond the rail would be about right. That, obviously, isn't possible. Another problem is that the genoa, when called upon to reach, tends to twist too much and loses power. Thus, the lead has to go forward as well (see FIGURE 4.14), to reduce twist. This causes the sail to be too deep, particularly at the foot. Nevertheless, that's about as good as you can get it.

When overpowered on a reach, move the lead back as well as out. This increases twist. When the wind comes up, you can also make the headstay tighter, as long as it doesn't ruin main trim or threaten the mast.

When reaching, the sheet is the primary sail-trim tool. You sail on the telltales. Both windward and leeward telltales should be flowing aft most of the time. If your boat is particularly weight-sensitive, a trick when reaching is to run the sheet across the cockpit. Then, the crew can trim the headsail from the high side.

Because of the above compromises, some offshore boats use a special high-clewed reacher, sometimes called a jib-top. A high clew means a shorter leech. This allows the reacher sheet better control of twist than is possible with a genoa and its longer leech. On close reaches, lead the reacher sheet to the stern. On broader reaches, the lead should go forward, thereby reducing twist and increasing power. To fine-tune the lead location, get the telltales on the luff to break evenly. Finally, a reacher typically requires more back stay tension than would a genoa used at the same wind orientation.

This chart of headsail controls can make headsail trim more comprehensible.

Control	Primary Effect(s)	Action
Sheet tension	Twist and angle of attack	Twist: for more twist (less power and less weather helm), ease sheet; for less twist (more power), trim it. Angle of attack: more sheet tension increases the angle of attack, increasing power; less sheet tension decreases angle of attack and power.
Jib leads, fore and aft	Twist	To determine proper twist, slowly turn the boat into wind. If bottom telltales on headsail break first, lead goes back. If top telltales break first, lead goes forward. Also use twist to control power. Move lead slightly forward for more power, aft for less.
Jib leads, inboard and outboard (athwartships)	Depth, angle of attack, twist	Moving lead inboard can improve pointing in flat water and smooth seas; moving lead outboard can improve speed in rough water and light winds. Also moving lead outboard and aft can make headsail work better when used at the top of its effective wind range.
Halyard tension	Draft location	More halyard tension, particularly in polyester sails, moves draft forward, allowing a more forgiving shape for the helmsman. Less halyard tension, draft moves aft. This can improve pointing and top-end speed but proper steering becomes critical.

Control	Primary Effect(s)	Action
Headstay tension	Draft location	More mast bend (by tensioning back stay, etc.), draft goes forward. This provides a more forgiving sail shape. Less mast bend, draft goes aft, which is less forgiving but improves pointing ability and top-end speed.

OPTIMIZING SAIL TRIM

With the number of variables involved in sail trim, it is important to record fast settings for various wind speeds, angles, and conditions. Then, of course, fast settings can be repeated on subsequent days. This is discussed in the next chapter.

A good memory helps, too. Good sailors have a good memory for sail shape. I'm not good with people's names, but I can recall the shapes of the forty jibs we used on *Freedom* in 1980. To me, sails are the engines of my race boats, and I remember them. To develop a good eye for three-dimensional shape, measure sails. I've used a Sailscope, an inexpensive plastic device sold by North Sails, to measure draft and draft location. Then I try to record which depth and draft location are fast and which are slow, and under what conditions. For example, is this headsail, with a depth of 18 percent and a draft location of 43 percent at the center draft stripe, faster in 9 knots of wind than one with a draft of 13 percent and a draft location of 50 percent?

The America's Cup competition of 1980 was a relatively easy time for me, at least in the trials, and I spent much of my time studying and working on sails. This practice developed my eye for fast shape. Studying sails is an ongoing process, however. Ideas change. Sails are flatter now than they used to be, particularly at the bottom, and my eye has had to adapt to that.

Already, however, there are intimations that the future will be different. Michael Fay's *New Zealand*, the 133-footer that raced our catamaran in the 1988 America's Cup, had a sophisticated computer system that monitored sail shape. This was first tried on *Kookaburra*, the boat we beat in the 1987 America's Cup.

As I understand it, aboard *New Zealand* were three lightweight video cameras mounted at or near the top of the mast, which would record the sail geometry every three-tenths of a second. The boat had oversized draft stripes on the sails to facilitate the camera's viewing of certain three-dimensional measurements, such as depth, draft location, angle of attack, and twist. The actual sail geometry then went into a computer for comparison with shapes that had proven to be fast before in similar wind and sea conditions. Thus, if the boat wasn't reaching its optimum speeds, target-sail shapes could be called up on the computer screen for comparison. Then depth, draft location, angle of attack, and twist would be modified until they matched the standard shape on the computer screen.

MAINSAIL SIZE AND SHAPE

Size is fundamental to sails. The more sail area, the faster the boat is until it is overpowered or steering becomes difficult. Usually the size of the mainsail is decided by the yacht designer, although booms can be made longer and masts replaced. In a mainsail, sail area is determined by the formula:

$$\frac{\text{Luff Length x Foot Length}}{2}$$

Aspect ratio also makes a difference. The aspect ratio of a mainsail is calculated as luff length divided by the length of the foot. Mains have followed the trend toward high aspect ratios for better upwind speed. The result is that most modern-racing mains have evolved to an aspect ratio of 2.9 to 3.5. Cruising boats show similar numbers; typical ratios are 2.7 to 3.4. Note that if racing rules did not penalize high aspect ratios, sails and the spars they sit on would likely be taller.

MAINSAIL CONTROL

Sailors have much more control over a mainsail than a headsail. A jib has five controls, while a main has almost twice that number. Also, two of a mainsail's sides, the luff and the foot, are completely held by the mast and boom, respectively. Compare that with a headsail that has only one side completely fixed or a spinnaker that has none. Then, battens provide good control of the mainsail's leech, the free side. Further, full battens are now becoming more popular on racing boats, and are very popular on cruising boats.[2] Full battens give even better control of the leech.

[2]At this writing, full battens are permitted by the International Measurement System (IMS), Performance Handicap Racing Fleet (PHRF), and Midget Ocean Racing Club (MORC); only the IOR doesn't permit them.

Because of all this control, a mainsail typically spans a range of conditions from no wind to a near gale. A racing boat might have seven or more headsails to cover that range.

TWO JOBS OF A MAINSAIL

A mainsail, like a headsail, must drive the boat. In recent years, as mains in fractionally rigged boats have grown much larger, and headsails, smaller, the mainsail's role in driving the boat—creating more lift and less drag when sailing upwind, both lift and drag when reaching, and drag when running— is more important.

The main must also help to steer the boat. While the main doesn't steer as well or as quickly as the rudder, it does steer with less negative impact on speed. A main with a tight leech (no twist) turns the wind more. This increased turning of the wind is similar to turning the rudder more. The result is that the boat turns into the wind more; this, of course, is weather helm. While weather helm can be desirable in light winds, it isn't when the wind blows. In heavy winds, the main's leech is loosened by easing the sheet, allowing the sail to twist or sag off, minimizing weather helm.

On small one-design boats, the driver usually plays the main. This allows the rudder and the main to complement one another when steering. In larger boats, steering and playing the main are separate jobs. With less skilled crews, the skipper is always saying things such as, "Ease the main!" or "Trim it!" A better mainsail trimmer watches for too much weather helm, that is, beyond the 3 to 5 degrees, discussed in the next chapter. Then the main is eased before the driver has to ask for it. Similarly, if there is too little weather helm, the mainsheet trimmer trims the main to increase helm.

MAINSAIL DRAFT

Draft in mains is measured in the same fashion as it is in headsails (see FIGURE 4.6). The rules are the same, too: A full main (depth equal to 15 or 16 percent of chord at the center draft stripe) gives more power for acceleration, like a fuller jib. A full main is the proper shape for light winds. A flatter main (10 to 11 percent) allows better top-end speed, like a flatter jib. This is the most desirable shape in heavy winds, or when opting to point rather than foot, or in very light winds.

Mains are fuller in the head than in the foot, as described. The shape adds power where the sail chords are so short. The top of a main ought to be about 5 percent deeper than the middle in quite light air and 10 to 15 percent deeper for winds from roughly 6 to 18 knots. The middle and top are about the same depth in stronger winds. The bottom quarter should be approximately 20 percent flatter than the middle in medium winds and perhaps 10 percent flatter in both light and strong winds.

MAINSAIL DRAFT POSITION

The maximum draft of a mainsail should be in the middle of the sail, or at 48 to 50 percent aft. Draft position, however, is dependent on other aspects of sail shape. For example, when increasing twist for heavy-air sailing, the draft should be moved forward as much as 5 percent. When decreasing twist to increase lift in lighter air, the draft will move aft—as far as 55 percent in some cases. The front of the main has draft requirements of its own. There is disturbed flow around a mast, so the front of the main must be full enough to get out into the clean air flow to leeward of the mast. At the same time, the front of the main must be flat enough to work at a very large angle of attack.

MAINSAIL TRIM

Fine-tuning of the main has to wait for headsail trim. One of the reasons is that headsail shape depends so much on mast bend for draft position, particularly with Mylar and Kevlar sails that aren't affected that much by halyard tension. While mast bend is important to mainsail shape too, other devices on the main (the Cunningham, for example) can positively control draft location. In many ways, mast bend for genoa shape sets the parameters for trimming the main.

A racing main typically has nine controls that influence three-dimensional sail shape, including, draft, draft position, twist, and angle of attack. Further, two-dimensional shape is controlled by sail size, as specified by the yacht designer. Sailors control size with the flattening reef and then reefing. The controls work as follows.

Battens

An important part of mainsail trim occurs before the sail is even raised. That is the selection of battens. With short so-called IOR-style battens, I firmly believe in carrying battens of varying stiffnesses and flexibilities. Then, if I think the mainsail should have more curve in light air for more power, I might put a more flexible batten in the top one or two pockets. For less curve in heavy air, I'd put in less flexible battens. No top racer would go to the race course with just the battens supplied by the sailmaker. A batten can break; anything can happen. Conditions change, and a batten that looks good in light winds may look terrible in heavy. Incidentally, many sailmakers now include an extra top batten or two of a different stiffness when you purchase a sail.

There are two families of battens: IOR-style and full. While my exposure to full battens is limited to the soft-sailed catamaran, used as a trial horse for the 1988 America's Cup, and my International America's Cup Class (IACC) yacht, I'm impressed with them. They are quieter, improve sail durability, make a main easier to flake on a boom, permit a smooth shape, allow more roach, and hold shape well in light air.

On the negative side, full-batten sails weigh more than sails with IOR-style battens. Full-batten sails also require special engineering, or they can jam at the luff. Further, they can cause the sail to chafe against the shrouds when running or broad-reaching, and they require more hand-detailing by the sailmaker. This makes sails with full battens more expensive. However, their long life can offset the increase in cost.

Mast Bend

Luff curve is important to the shape of a main, as it is with a jib. When a main with a curved luff is affixed to a straight mast, the extra sail area pushes shape into the sail. However, if you bend the mast so that its curve matches that of the main's luff, shape is removed (see FIGURE 4.17).

Mains are very sensitive to mast bend. Less than half an inch of bend on a main with a 40-foot luff can change the shape of the sail. This is why practically all racing boats and most cruising boats will have adjustable backstays to bend masts. An extreme example of mast bend was seen on the Maxi boats in the most recent Whitbread Round the World Race. They would bend their masts up to 4 feet to flatten the main. Obviously, that puts enormous loads on the mast; the hull, which supports the mast; and the sails. In less extreme examples, mast bend would typically range from .25

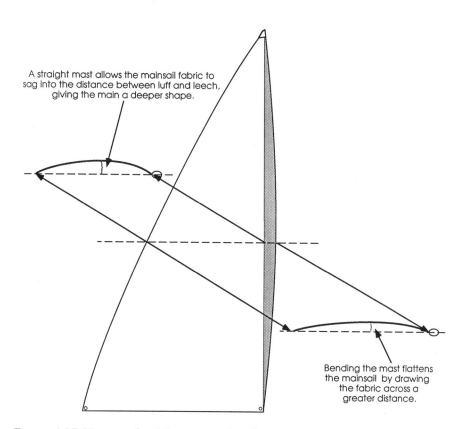

A straight mast allows the mainsail fabric to sag into the distance between luff and leech, giving the main a deeper shape.

Bending the mast flattens the mainsail by drawing the fabric across a greater distance.

FIGURE 4.17 *How mast bend flattens a mainsail.*

percent of mast height or less (equal to 1.5 inches in 40 feet of luff length) to 2 percent (approximately 10 inches).

No matter how a mast is bent, it should bend the proper amount and in the right place. This requires consultation with your sailmaker. The luff curve should match mast bend. If the sailmaker locates luff curve in the middle of the sail, and the mast bends near the top, this compromises sail shape. Similarly, if the sailmaker figures on 9 inches of mast bend and you only bend the mast 3 inches, shape suffers. Such considerations explain why a good sailmaker asks customers about mast bend before building a sail.

A main, particularly one made of low-stretch materials, such as Mylar, Kevlar, or yarn-tempered Dacron, can be overbent.[3] A wrinkle extending

[3]Yarn-tempered Dacron—Duroperm is another trade name—is a heavily finished polyester used in some one-design classes that don't allow Mylar or Kevlar sails.

from the clew to the middle of a mast is a sign of overbend; indeed, it is called an overbend wrinkle. That said, mains are now flatter in the lower sections. It is not uncommon or wrong to see overbend wrinkles near the boom.

Mainsheet

As indicated, the mainsheet primarily controls twist and then when sailing off the wind, angle of attack. More mainsheet tension removes twist, less increases it.

The test for the proper degree of twist for a main is similar to that for a jib. First, ease the traveler. If the top of the main backwinds first (due to air-flow off the jib), the sail has too much twist. The main needs mainsheet trim to remove twist. If the bottom backwinds first, the sail needs more twist, so ease the mainsheet.

An easier (if less exact) way to determine proper mainsheet tension, and thus twist, is to trim the mainsheet so that the top batten is parallel to the boom. (Note that this is the proper orientation when sailing off the wind as well.)

In maximum pointing conditions—smooth water and a medium breeze—you can sometimes trim the main so the top batten pokes to weather somewhat. This, however, is only appropriate with a masthead rig. The full-hoist genoa on a masthead rig steers the wind flow onto the lee side of the upper leech, thereby reducing the danger of stall. With a fractional rig, there is no headsail in front of the upper batten to steer the wind.

Another trick to determine twist is to put a telltale on the top batten—better sailmakers will do this as a matter of course. This telltale should flow aft at least half the time. If, however, the telltale curls off to leeward more than half the time, the sail needs more twist, so ease the sheet.

A hint about twist helped me to win my first Star Worlds. In 1971, I bought Alan Raffee's Star for $3,000. I sailed that boat in the Worlds, in Seattle. There was a practice race before the regatta, and I did terribly. So, too, did Bill Buchan, another of my boyhood heroes, who had won the Star Worlds the year before as well as in 1961.

After our dismal showing in the tune-up race in 1971, Buchan and I got to talking. He asked if I always sailed with so little tension on my main-sheet. I paid attention to that. In the first race, I trimmed my main a little harder, which reduced twist as well as increased the main's angle of attack. Both of these actions can make a sail more powerful. I had a second and fifth to show for it and the series lead. I had another fifth in the third race.

From then on, I just covered Lowell North and stayed out of trouble to win my first Star Worlds.

Traveler

The traveler controls angle of attack, which affects the power in the sail, heel, and steering. Ideally, you want 3 to 5 degrees of weather helm. If you have more than that—if you're overpowered—drop the traveler. This increases forward force and drive. If you need more helm and power, in light winds, for example, raise the traveler to windward. Never raise it so much that it moves the boom above the centerline, however. Note that I said the boom and not the traveler. Often to get the boom on the centerline, the traveler must be well to weather.

In my Star boat, I found that I never used the traveler, so I eventually removed it. Stars have such a low boom that I just trimmed the mainsheet to a pad eye in the center of the boat, which put the boom on the centerline.

When reaching in heavy winds, judicious use of the traveler—easing it in puffs and trimming it in lulls—can spell the difference between the helmsman maintaining control or losing it. Broaching can be the result of losing control (see Chapter 7). Sometimes the mainsheet is eased at the same time. Easing the main increases twist, and easing the traveler decreases angle of attack—all of which decrease power in the sail.

Outhaul

Tensioning the outhaul flattens the sail, particularly in the bottom half. Luff curve, mast bend, and broadseaming nullify the effects of the outhaul in the top half.

Proper sail trim calls for the foot of the mainsail to be very flat when you are sailing upwind—even if this leads to overbend wrinkles. A main should be flat near the boom to minimize induced drag. Obviously, there is a big hole under the boom where the flow can easily escape from the high-pressure windward side to the low-pressure leeward side. As stated often, this leaking equalizes the pressure differential. To minimize leaking, a sail is not powered up near the hole, or boom, with increased shape, or draft. Rather, it is kept flat. To put this another way, if the difference between the high-pressure side and the low-pressure side is not that great—the result of a lack of shape—there is less induced drag.

In the J-Class era of the America's Cup (1930–37), boats had very wide booms, called Park Avenue booms, to stop the flow from leaking. In many ways, such booms were like the winged keel, or fence, on *Australia II* (see Chapter 2).

Shelf Foot and Flattening Reef

Downwind, of course, depth at the foot is important; recall that drag moves boats downwind. Off the wind, you want 20 to 25 percent foot depth. A shelf foot, an extra panel of cloth sewn to the foot, is a good way to add area at the foot. The extra panel of cloth folds up when tensioning the outhaul and opens when the outhaul is eased. Without a shelf foot, you can ease the halyard and the outhaul to add some depth.

Another way to get some shape at the foot is to put in some extra broadseaming at the bottom seam or two (see FIGURE 4.4). This extra shaping does not disappear with outhaul tension. The flattening reef, a small reef line 1 or 2 feet up the leech of the mainsail, removes this extra area when sailing upwind.

Vang

The vang is much like a mainsheet, in that it pulls down on the boom and controls twist. As a twist-control device, the mainsheet is only effective, however, when sailing upwind, whereas the vang affects the leech of the mainsail throughout the boom's arc. That means when reaching and running, too.

We put a semicircular vang on *Freedom* in the 1980 America's Cup. This is an idea I first saw on Starboats, probably done by Lowell North or Bill Buchan. You typically want no vang when sailing upwind—the mainsheet governs twist then—and maximum vang at 100 degrees apparent where you want to eliminate twist to expose the most sail to the wind. By raising the vang car track aft near the centerline—where you want no vang—and lowering it where the boom is when the boat is sailing at 100 degree apparent—when you want the most vang—it is possible to create an "automatic" vang.

On an overpowered reach, leave the outhaul tight to flatten the sail and to lessen weather helm. Make sure someone plays the vang to keep the end of the boom out of the water. When the boat begins to heel too much,

Sails

121

dump the mainsheet. Be careful not to overvang in light and medium air. In these conditions, the weight of the boom usually provides enough leech tension.

On heavy-air runs, however, be sure to have a good bit of vang. As noted in Chapter 2, a sail is a wind-blocking device when sailing downwind, and drag, not lift, is what's important. Without sufficient vang on a heavy-air run, however, the twisted upper leech can stop merely blocking the wind and develop sufficient lift. This, however, is lift in a direction you don't want to go. The lift at the top of the mast can steer the boat to weather and over-whelm the helm. The result is often a broach (see Chapter 7). So if the top batten twists off beyond 90 degrees with respect to the centerline of the boat, trim the vang. Do this if you think your equipment can handle it, and the boom doesn't go in the water. Another solution is to trim the mainsheet.

Cunningham

The Cunningham, named for Briggs Cunningham, who skippered *Columbia*, an America's Cup defender in 1958, works the same as halyard tension in a jib. Either control moves the draft forward and back. More Cunningham tension moves the draft forward; less moves it aft. Of course, the main has a halyard, as does the jib, so the obvious question is, Why not use the halyard to accomplish the same thing? The reason is that mains on racing boats are full on the hoist, and the black band on the masthead defines the top limit. An upward pull on the halyard would likely bring the main above the black band. This is a violation of the racing rules. A downward pull on the Cunningham accomplishes the same thing. A cruising boat might not have a black band painted at the top of the mast, but an upward tug on the halyard can bring the halyard shackle into the sheave, fouling the halyard and/or damaging the sheave (see Chapter 5).

The Cunningham works with mast bend. For example, when bending the mast, the draft often moves aft. More Cunningham tension moves the draft forward again.

Leech Cord

Upwind, the leech cord isn't exactly a sail-trim device. It is there to keep the leech from fluttering—called motorboating for the sound it makes. Flutter-ing decreases a sail's useful life. Trim the cord just enough to still the motion. Off-the-wind, however, this control has some sail-trim advantages, which will be discussed next.

REACHING AND RUNNING WITH THE MAIN

Save for the vang and maybe the leech cord, nearly all the controls tightened on the mainsail when sailing upwind are loosened when reaching or running. Ease the outhaul, Cunningham, and backstay (be sure, however, that the headstay doesn't get too loose). Also ease the mainsheet and drop the traveler. If the sail has a leech cord, you might want to pull on it to increase the pressure on the leech of the sail. This bends the battens and gives the sail a bit more camber, that is, shape, or depth, which is good when reaching or running.

In 12-Meters, we developed a leech cord that, rather than traveling down the leech from the top, started about halfway up the leech. It then went over the top of the headboard and down the luff. It was adjusted at the mast. The top of the sail could then be closed without closing the bottom. This helps to prevent the top batten from twisting off, decreasing the tendency to roll on a windy reach (discussed above). The advantage is that you don't have to vang as hard to close the top of the sail. Also, it is easy to overvang a mainsail. As mentioned, use maximum vang when the boat is sailing at 100 degrees to the apparent wind. Beyond 100 degrees apparent, there is little pressure on the sail, since at this point, the sail ceases to produce lift and is only a wind-blocking device. With so little pressure, it is easy to overvang. As a guide, keep the top batten in line with the boom. This, you will recall, is the same rule as when sailing upwind.

When reaching, ease the main until it luffs and then trim it until the luffing stops. Downwind, however, a main is primarily a kite and as such, it doesn't luff. This complicates sail trim. So you have to use the apparent-wind angle. In general, the boom should be no more than 90 degrees to the apparent wind and usually a bit in from that. This keeps the sail from chafing against the spreaders and shrouds, which is very hard on the sail.

This chart will help to summarize the above points.

Control	Primary Effect(s)	Operation
Battens	Sail depth	Use more flexible top battens in light air to obtain more depth or shape, less flexible battens in heavy air.

Control	Primary Effect(s)	Operation
Mast bend	Sail depth	More bend flattens main. Less makes it deeper.
Mainsheet	Twist; angle of attack when sailing off the wind	Ease main sheet for more twist and smaller angle of attack. Trim for less twist and increased angle of attack.
Traveler	Angle of attack (power)	Traveler to weather increases angle of attack, or power. Traveler dropped to leeward decreases angle of attack.
Outhaul	Sail depth at the bottom of the sail	With increased outhaul tension, bottom of sail flattens. With decreased outhaul tension, bottom gets fuller.
Shelf foot	Depth or shape	Opens when outhaul is eased—adds shape or depth when sailing off the wind. Ensures that downwind sail shape is continuous from head to foot.
Flattening reef	Depth or shape	Easing flattening reef adds depth or shape. When tensioned, shape is removed.
Vang	Twist	Tension for less twist (more power); ease for more twist (less power).
Cunningham	Draft position and depth	More Cunningham, draft moves forward, which flattens sail. Less Cunningham, draft moves aft and deepens the sail.

SPINNAKER MATERIALS

Advances in spinnaker design are less dramatic than in triangular sails. Much of this has to do with materials. For example, most spinnakers are nylon, as they have been for nearly forty years. Nylon, developed by Du Pont in 1938, shows significant stretch but as a result is very strong. In the case of a spinnaker, this means the sail doesn't break (rip) very easily. This is important in downwind sails, like spinnakers, as the stretch of nylon acts as a natural shock absorber when the sail fills suddenly. Also, sailmakers have long used the stretch of nylon to help shape sails. Until the appearance in sailmaking of computer-aided design (CAD) and computer-aided manufacturing (CAM), most of the seams in a spinnaker had little or no shape, or broadseaming. The stretch of the material provided most of the shape, which is an inexact science. Today, spinnakers built by better sailmakers are shaped by broadseaming (see FIGURE 4.4).

There have been some recent attempts to use Mylar, Kevlar, and, most recently, polyester in spinnakers. These materials show promise, particularly in reaching sails where lack of stretch is important.

SPINNAKER WEIGHT

In light winds, a spinnaker can sag under its own weight, so the weight of spinnakers is obviously important. Spinnaker cloth is typically available in weights of .5, .75, 1.5, and 2.2 ounces per SMY. The lightest weight, .5 ounce, is sometimes the only sail on smaller boats and is the only light-air sail on most boats. The heaviest weight is the storm chute on the largest boat. The standard spinnaker is usually .75 ounce. The actual cloth weighs about .25 ounce more than these designations due to the finishing process where Melamine, urethane, and/or silicone are impregnated after the weave is heat-set.

All spinnakers on America's Cup boats are typically the same color combinations. This makes it hard for a competitor to recognize a sail. On the other hand, if a competitor knows your green and white spinnaker is .5 ounce and your blue-and-white is .75, he or she can easily match your sail choice when you start to gain. Thus, it is a good idea to have all your spinnakers look the same.

Nonetheless, good sailors can often tell the difference between spinnakers by the color saturation of the fabric: the .5 ounce is slightly lighter in color than the .75. Also helpful is the attitude of a sail—that is, how high it flies. A lightweight sail tends to fly higher than a sail made from heavier cloth.

I can remember racing against *Intrepid* with *Courageous* in the 1974 America's Cup trials. We had a comfortable lead at the weather mark and set the .75-ounce spinnaker. Halsey Herreshoff, our navigator, noticed that *Intrepid* had up a .5 ounce—he could tell because the sail was floating higher than ours. They were gaining on us. As a result, we kept trying to encourage Bob Bavier, the skipper of *Courageous,* to change to the .5-ounce chute to match them, but he wouldn't. I think that may have been the proverbial straw that broke Bavier's back. He was off the boat the next day, and Ted Hood was given command.

SPINNAKER DESIGN

The loads in a spinnaker radiate from the corners, as in triangular sails, and spinnakers were the first sails to show radial construction. In offshore boats, the tri-radial spinnaker is a standard. Tri-radial spinnakers, which feature three radials in the three corners, joined by one or more horizontal center seams, date back to the mid-1970s. We used a tri-radial spinnaker on *Courageous* in the 1974 America's Cup. In some one-design classes, like the Soling, an Olympic dinghy, cross-cut spinnakers (with all horizontal panels and seams) still predominate.

More recently, America's Cup yachts, as well as cruising boats, have begun to use asymmetrical spinnakers. With asymmetrical sails, the luff (front), or leading edge, is longer than that on a symmetrical spinnaker. The foot and leech are shorter. This configuration moves the spinnaker's clew away from the mainsail, reducing interference between the two sails. Actually, a normal spinnaker doesn't want to fly symmetrically when reaching. It is only the racing rules (IOR, IMS, etc.) that insist it be symmetrical. Such asymmetrical reaching sails are legal in America's Cup racing.

In the 1992 America's Cup, boats used asymmetrical spinnakers primarily on the reaching legs four, five, and six. The true-wind direction on legs four and six was about 135 degrees; on leg five, it was 100 degrees. Legs two and eight (to the finish) were downwind. The familiar symmetrical spinnakers were often used then. While asymmetrical spinnakers are faster when reaching, jibing them (the technique is discussed later in the chapter as well as in Chapter 6) is difficult and seems awkward. I, for one, missed the dip-pole jibe that was used much less often in this America's Cup.

SPINNAKER SIZES AND SHAPES

The size of the boat's foretriangle determines spinnaker size. Offshore boats, be they racers or cruisers, usually follow the International Offshore Rule (IOR) limits for spinnaker luff length (SL) and spinnaker maximum width (SMW). The maximum size of spinnakers is computed using the formulas below.

$$(SL) = .95 \, (\sqrt{I^2 + J^2})$$

$$(SMW) = 1.8 \times J$$

(Note the I dimension runs from the deck to the top of the mast. J, as noted, is the distance from the genoa-tack fitting to the mast.)

These are maximum-size spinnakers. Racing rules as well as design considerations allow a spinnaker to be smaller than the maximum. Also, if a boat is not a racer—or if the yacht designer or sailor thinks the speed increase is worth the penalty allocated by the rule—spinnakers can be larger. As the rig's aspect ratio has climbed on racing and cruising boats, so has the spinnaker's aspect ratio. Cruising boats in the late 1970s had spinnaker-aspect ratios—SL/SMW—of about 1.75, while racing boats were about 1.8. Today cruising boats have aspect ratios of about 1.83, and racing boats about 1.9. The high-aspect sail is better for reaching but is an inferior runner. As a result, extra long so-called penalty poles—the rule controls spinnaker width by the length of the pole—are more common.

Under the International Rule, used to rate a 12-Meter, you can get a longer J—which allows a longer spinnaker pole—by decreasing the length of the mainsail's boom. In some America's Cup campaigns, we've spent considerable time testing a longer pole versus a shorter boom. In light air, the longer spinnaker pole tested faster. It seems to increase the separation between the spinnaker and the main. In heavy air, however, the shorter pole and longer boom tested faster. We ended up going with the standard J of 24.3 feet and a standard-length pole.

The most popular type of symmetrical spinnaker is the all-purpose spinnaker. The all-purpose spinnaker is a good compromise between reaching and running. The design is most effective for a wind direction of 90 to 150 degrees off the bow. Since these angles are most common, this accounts for its popularity. Many cruisers own an all-purpose spinnaker—rather than a specialized cruising chute (discussed shortly)—as it is a better compromise between reaching and running.

What enables the all-purpose spinnaker to span this range is its balanced profile from head to foot. The head is not excessively full as in the runner (as we will see) or excessively flat as in a reacher. No matter what the wind speed, the all-purpose design usually shows a maximum-size luff (SL) and maximum width (SMW).

Reaching spinnakers are appropriate when the wind direction is between 65 to 120 degrees apparent. There are full-size (maximum SMW), a recent development, and reduced-girth (less than maximum SMW) reaching spinnakers. Which size is right depends on the aspect ratio of your rig, the boat's stiffness/stability, the wind speed in which you intend to use the sail, and, finally, the wind angle(s) for which you want the sail optimized. If only one reacher is aboard, it will usually be between 90 and 95 percent SMW.

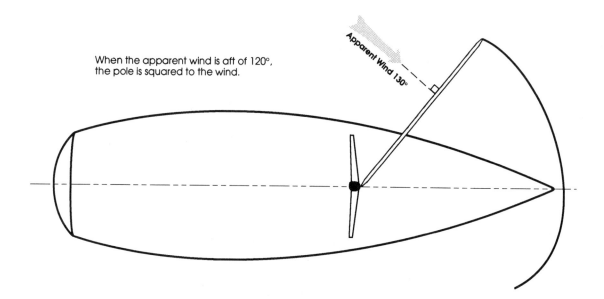

When the apparent wind is aft of 120°, the pole is squared to the wind.

Apparent Wind 130°

FIGURE 4.18 *Spinnaker-pole angle when the apparent wind is aft of 120 degrees.*

Running spinnakers are appropriate for wind angles ranging from 130 to 180 degrees. When running, projected area is the key quality for speed. A sail with the greatest width and least depth has the greatest projected area. However, the sail with the most projected area is very difficult to fly. Fullness, or good depth, means easy flying. This requires a compromise between projected area, or flatness, for speed and fullness for stability.

SPINNAKER TRIM

With symmetrical racing spinnakers, there are five major controls: guy, sheet tension, tweaker (lead location), topping lift (outboard-end pole height), and the device that controls the height of the inboard end of the pole. The guy controls the spinnaker's angle of attack. When broad-reaching or running (when the apparent wind is 120 degrees or farther aft), the pole should be 90 degrees to the apparent wind (see FIGURE 4.18). When reaching (when the wind is forward of 120 degrees), the spinnaker pole should be 75 degrees to the apparent wind (see FIGURE 4.19). The latter

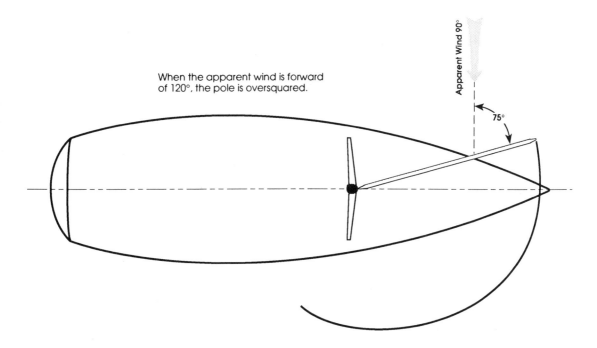

When the apparent wind is forward
of 120°, the pole is oversquared.

Apparent Wind 90°

75°

FIGURE 4.19 *Spinnaker-pole angle when the apparent wind is forward of 120 degrees.*

angle keeps the spinnaker flatter, a better shape for reaching.

The spinnaker sheet's primary job is to control the curl of the spinnaker's luff. Once the guy angle is properly set, sheet tension keeps the spinnaker filled. The sheet should be eased until the sail nearly luffs, that is, until the leading edge breaks. Telltales should be mounted on the two luffs of a spinnaker as they are an early warning of luffing. They are a better warning, too, since easing the sail to a curl diminishes spinnaker area. Because telltales need attached flow to work (discussed earlier in this chapter), they only work on a reach, however. On a run, the sail must be eased to the curl from time to time.

A secondary job of the spinnaker sheet is to control power, or the twist of the leech. When reaching, you want to ease the sheet enough to get the spinnaker out toward the front of the boat, rather than off to the side. A spinnaker in front of the boat decreases heeling and maximizes the forward force of the sail. In a puff, ease the sheet farther. A puff causes the apparent wind to move aft (see velocity-lift discussion in Chapter 7), so the sheet is eased with the apparent shift. When running in heavy air, the spinnaker can be overtrimmed to help choke it down.

Another way to control power with the spinnaker sheet is by adjusting its lead location. Move the lead forward and back to adjust power. For example, when reaching in light winds, the sheet lead should be forward. This adds foot depth and decreases leech twist, thus adding power. (Recall that moving the lead forward in a genoa also increases foot depth, decreases twist, and increases power, as shown in FIGURE 4.14.) In moderate-air reaching conditions, move the sheet aft to open the leech and limit foot depth. In heavy-air reaching, move it farther aft, to increase twist and to keep the bottom of the sail quite flat.

If you don't have a track that allows you to reposition the spinnaker sheet block, use a tweaker line—a line with a block on the end of it that is led to a convenient and suitably strong spot on the boat. The block holds the spinnaker sheet, and the tweaker line is tensioned. This pulls the spinnaker sheet down to where the tweaker line is located.

When running in light and moderate air, the sheet lead should be led to the rail under the boom. In windy conditions, the lead should be even farther forward. This position depowers the spinnaker by presenting less area to the wind.

Pole height at the outboard end ensures that the luff shows the proper orientation to the wind. As with a genoa, you want the spinnaker luff to break along its entire length at the same time. Watch the telltales, and if the top telltales break first, raise the pole. If the bottom telltales break first, lower the pole. To put this simply, move the pole up or down toward the telltale that breaks first.

The amount of draft is important, too. For example, as stated, a runner is a compromise between being flat for speed and being full for easy flying. If more speed is needed and the sail is flying well, you might try flattening the sail somewhat. To flatten the sail, particularly at the top, raise the clews, that is, the spinnaker pole. Alternatively, if easier flying is needed, you might want to make it fuller. To deepen the sail, lower the spinnaker pole. The rule is: Pole down, the spinnaker gets fuller; pole up, the spinnaker gets flatter. Such fine-tuning of depth is likewise important to an all-purpose sail, which is called on both to reach and to run.

Finally, the inboard end of the pole should be even with the outboard end. The pole should be horizontal. This chart can help to summarize the above points.

Control	Primary Effect(s)	Operation
Guy	Angle of attack	When running, pole should be 90 degrees to apparent wind. When reaching, pole should be at 75 degrees.
Sheet Tension	Controls luff	Works in conjunction with guy. Ease until telltales break or until luff curls. When reaching, ease sheet to get spinnaker in front of boat; ease it farther in puffs. When running in heavy air, use more sheet tension to choke spinnaker. (See tweaker, below.)
Pole (outboard end)	Twist, draft, and position	If top breaks first, raise pole, draft moves aft, and sail gets more powerful. If bottom breaks first, lower it; draft moves forward and sail gets less powerful.
Tweaker	Power (twist)	When reaching in light wind, move lead forward; in moderate air, move lead aft; in heavy-air, move lead farther aft. When running in light and moderate air, move lead under boom; in heavy air, move lead farther forward.
Pole (inboard end)	Draft position	Inboard and outboard ends of pole kept at same height.

SPINNAKER SPECIALTY SAILS

When reaching, a staysail is often flown on an offshore boat. Two types are commonly used: a Dazy for masthead boats and a special little staysail (SLS) for fractional boats. The Dazy is full on the hoist and has a length perpendicular (LP) of about 80 percent (see FIGURE 4.13). (A 100 percent LP, you will recall, would fill the foretriangle.) The SLS is the same shape as the Dazy, except its overlap is 70 percent. A staysail can be effective when the wind varies from 90 to 120 degrees.

These specialty sails are best used when the wind is moderate and the seas are smooth. A staysail can be made to work in heavy air by luffing or reefing the main. Also, the staysail itself should be luffed in puffs. Its trim should never compromise spinnaker trim or steering, however. The staysail should be excessively twisted at the top (lead farther aft than optimum, as shown in FIGURE 4.14). Its tack moves from the centerline of the boat to the weather side as the apparent-wind angle broadens to 120 degrees. (Racing rules, however, often address tack positions, so consult them first.) If the spinnaker collapses, the staysail often has to be luffed. If it continues to compromise spinnaker trim, drop the staysail. A small boat doesn't typically use a staysail (or blooper). Often, the jib is left up when reaching if it doesn't compromise the trim of the spinnaker.

Bloopers are used on masthead boats to balance a spinnaker when running in moderate to fresh breezes. Trim the blooper's sheet through a block at the end of the boom, rather than to the back of the boat. In heavy winds more than in moderate conditions, the halyard has to be raised to keep the foot out of the waves. A blooper adds significant sail area, so it isn't appropriate in heavy winds. (When to use or strike a blooper depends on how well your boat steers and how good the crew is.) A blooper isn't normally used on a fractionally rigged boat. The working jib (Number 3) strapped on the centerline with both sheets can also stop rolling.

CRUISING SPINNAKER

The cruising spinnaker is a design of the last twelve years. This designation has come to describe a variety of downwind sails built out of .75-ounce cloth. These cruising spinnakers are asymmetrical, as are the specialized reaching sails on America's Cup yachts. They show a defined luff, leech, and foot. They are, in fact, somewhere between a spinnaker and a genoa. As these sails have a high clew, the helmsman can clearly see under the sail, allowing good visibility forward. Cruising spinnakers don't use a spinnaker pole, which makes handling easier. A sail-sock device facilitates setting and stowing the sail; such a device is particularly desirable in boats over 25 feet. The overlap of a cruising spinnaker is typically 170 percent (see FIGURE 4.13).

TRIMMING THE CRUISING SPINNAKER

Cruising spinnakers can be adjusted at the tack to help change the draft location as a function of the wind angle. When close-reaching, the tack of the sail should be level with the pulpit. When beam-reaching, the tack should be level with the gooseneck of the boom. When broad-reaching, the tack should be between the gooseneck and the first reef point. As the tack goes up, the draft goes aft.

Cruising chutes don't do well when overtrimmed. For that reason, they aren't particularly effective at close-reaching angles. The less wind there is, however, the closer one can sail to the wind with a cruising spinnaker. One or two sheets attached at the clew are the only extra equipment these sails need, although a whisker pole on the clew can help stabilize the sail in light winds.

The cruising spinnaker is asymmetrical, like a genoa, and as such has an unvarying luff and leech. Thus, such sails are often taken down before jibing, then are raised again on the opposite tack. If you have a sail-sock device and are comfortable using it, this is often the conservative approach to jibing. It is, however, possible to lead the sheet around the headstay as the helmsman slowly jibes the boat. (This is discussed more fully in Chapter 6.)

5 | Boat Speed

I began skippering ocean racers when I was sixteen, a tender age. The first boat I ran was an Owens cutter, a 40-foot Cruising Club of America (CCA) design called *Dolphin*. The boat belonged to Gerry Bill, of San Diego. Looking back at it, I realize I was one of the early so-called hired guns that populate the upper echelon of sailboat racing these days. This group includes Paul Cayard, John Kolius, and Chris Dickson—my America's Cup rivals. In my day, however, people weren't paid for such things, at least as far as I knew.

Gerry Bill liked to race. However, he didn't have the time or energy to do it as well as he'd like, so I got to fill that role. Ash Bown, the noted San Diego sailor, had an Owens cutter, too. Bown, an early hero of mine, was one of those rare sailors who knew where to go on the race course. I don't know how he knew; he just seemed to know everything. I could never beat him by trying to go the right way. The only chance I had to beat him was through boat speed. This has become a theme of mine.

One example of this was faster sails or, to be more precise, bigger sails. I'd study what Ash Bown did with sails aboard his *Carousel*, then go to Elton Ballas, the local sailmaker, and have him make me the same sail, only bigger. Ballas, as mentioned, figured out the decksweeper jib. The decksweeper jib, with its low clew that puts the foot of the sail on the deck, prevents high-pressure air from the windward side from leaking under the headsail to the low-pressure leeward side. As such, the decksweeper jib limits induced drag, discussed in Chapter 2. I can't say I completely understood the principle of the decksweeper jib or induced drag when I was a teenager, but since Bown had a decksweeper jib, I went to Ballas and said, "I want the same thing, only bigger!"

Before an Acapulco race on *Dolphin*, I brought an old genoa to Ballas. I had him cut it off horizontally and sew a huge foot onto it to add sail area at the bottom. The foot was so big that it couldn't really be controlled. It used to go flop, flop, flop on the deck. I spent hours putting in vertical take-up seams in an attempt to control this oversized foot roach.

I mention this for two reasons: I'm still a firm believer in boat speed, and in the interest of boat speed, I'm a firm believer in copying others to get it. Improving rather than inventing has been a secret of my success. I don't know as much about sails as Ballas did or Lowell North does. I'm not as smart as Ash Bown was on the race course. I don't know as much about yacht design as David Pedrick, Bruce Nelson, and Alberto Calderon, or the late Ben Lexcen. I take what they invent, try to find out all I can about how it works, and just try to make it better. I don't mean me, alone; I mean the team: the yacht designers, sailmakers, consultants, and sailors. My management style is to give people the opportunity to do creative work and then push them to do their best. As the world well knows, I didn't invent the winged keel; Ben Lexcen did. I just tried to make it better with *Stars & Stripes '87*, through the efforts of David Pedrick, Bruce Nelson, Britton Chance, John Marshall (my design director), and numerous consultants.

In a perfect world, I'd be fast and smart, and I've spent my life working on both. If I had to make a choice, however, I'd be fast. Smart in sailing means anticipating the wind, its direction and strength, and placing your boat accordingly. There are gifted guessers, as Ash Bown was, and less-gifted guessers, like most of the rest of us. However, no one is going to guess right all, or even most, of the time. If you doubt this, ask yourself why the currently recognized experts in smart sailing don't win all or even most of the time. Or why meteorologists, with all their sophisticated computer codes and freon-cooled super computers, aren't more accurate in predicting the weather. Fast, on the other hand, is pure boat speed, and speed can make up for a multitude of sins.

Note that one of the reasons that fast is better than smart in sailing is because major sailboat regattas often take place in areas characterized by steady winds. That can be San Diego, Newport, Perth, or San Francisco. Sailing in places where the wind is predictable removes much of the mystery from the sport, allowing for a more level playing field.

Figuring out the winds and other subtle wind indicators on Long Island Sound can take a lifetime. For example, Long Island Sound locals like my friend Ed du Moulin say dew on the deck in the morning means a southwest sea breeze in the afternoon, as do cobwebs in the rigging. Or birds walking the beach or flying low means foul weather. You can't figure that out by Saturday morning's race if you arrive in Oyster Bay on Friday evening. A home-court advantage in a place like this is often difficult to beat. On the other hand in steady winds, boat speed often triumphs.

Fast sailing includes tuning, mast bend, proper amount of weather helm, boat trim, boat preparation, and practice. These subjects are the focus of this chapter. (Other elements of boat speed include sails, discussed in Chapter 4; crewing and practice, in Chapter 6; and steering, in Chapter 7. Smart sailing is the focus of Chapters 8, 9, and 10.)

Boat speed is not just a concern for the racer. As noted, an increase in speed of a half knot over a twenty-four-hour period—an easily attainable difference between good mast tune and bad, good helm or bad—can save you two hours or more of sailing in a day. "What's the hurry?" you say. "I'm a cruiser." Few of us have unlimited free time. A faster boat allows you to wander farther in a weekend, or to stay longer at your destination before pushing off for home. It also is, as I see it, much more fun to sail fast than slow. It just feels better. Also, a slow boat is like a marginal, unwashed, or smoky car; to my mind, it looks incongruous. Finally, speed under sail is a measure of ability, the equivalent of a low handicap in golf or an A ranking in tennis. I don't see how one can sail well without sailing fast. It's part of good seamanship.

MAST TUNING

Boat speed begins with mast tuning. The themes of tuning are straightforward or, more accurately, straight athwartships. The mast should be vertical in the boat, that is, without sideways bend or lean. Also, you want to control the degree of weather helm, by adjusting the entire mast forward or back and/or the degree of rake or lean. Furthermore, unless you are a very conservative cruising sailor—a belt-and-suspenders type—you want to be able to shape the mainsail using mast bend. Finally, you want the mast to stay upright.

These rules of mast tuning are easier said than done because many of them have exceptions, and some that address tuning the rig are contradictory. For example, good mainsail shape depends on bending the mast, but if you bend the mast improperly or too much, it can break. Then there are the many types of rigs, such as masthead or fractionally rigged boats, and they are held aloft in any number of ways. Also, there are many ways to bend or to straighten a mast, some of them simple, some of them extremely complex.

Because of these differences, I'll start by offering general tips on mast tuning, and I'll also address the big picture. A valuable source for tuning a specific sail to a specific boat is your sailmaker. If your sailmaker doesn't have published tuning guides for the boat you sail or can't or won't help you, you should probably find another sailmaker. This is because sail design, mast tune, and sail trim go hand in hand. A sailmaker who doesn't recognize this can't be much of a sailmaker.

Position the Mast in the Center of the Boat

Start by determining if the mast partners—the hole in the deck that the mast penetrates (assuming this is a keel-stepped mast)—is in the precise center of the boat. In Chapter 3, we learned that boats vary, even production boats that come from the same mold. Very often, the hole for the mast isn't centered, which makes it difficult to get the masthead vertical, that is, with-

FIGURE 5.1 *Determining if the mast is centered in the boat.*

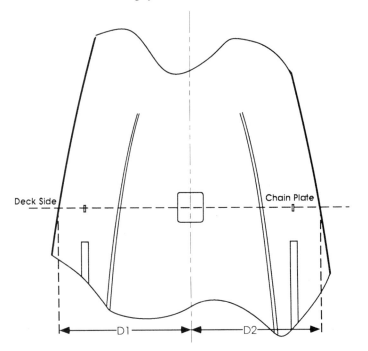

out athwartships bend or lean. An off-center hole isn't typically a big problem, because the mast can usually be centered in the boat without too much trouble. If you aren't aware of it, however, an off-center hole can be a big problem because the mast will resist all efforts to tune it properly. With improper tune, you'll never be fast. Also, the rig can bend in ways it wasn't designed to bend, perhaps causing it to fail.

There are two ways to determine the location of the mast partners. First, with the mast out of the boat, take a string or a chalk line from the forestay to the measured midpoint of the transom. Then it is easy to tell if the mast partner is off by a quarter of an inch or so. The second technique is to measure from the center of the partners to either side of the boat (see FIGURE 5.1). This can be done with the mast stepped. If the measurements (D1 and D2) are the same, the hole is in the center.

If the center of the partners is off to one side, steps must be taken to ensure that the mast is placed evenly along the centerline—not necessarily in the center of the hole. If the hole is larger than the mast, this is usually not a problem. Use wedges, either wood or hard rubber, strategically placed on the port or starboard sides of the mast, to center it. If the hole is the same size as the mast, the hole must be enlarged. If you are not handy, this job is better left to a professional. When you are done, use wedges, on either side of the mast to center it and to lock it in place. The mast need not touch the partners or the wedges, but there shouldn't be more than 1/16-inch gap. If it is more than that, add or increase the size of the wedges.

Most masts on offshore boats are keel-stepped, as are the masts on such popular one-designs as the Etchells 22, Lightning, and Sonar. With a keel-stepped mast, it is also important to determine if the mast step, like the partners, is in the center of the boat. This, too, should be measured. You want the butt (bottom) of the mast, the mast at the partners, and the top of the mast to be on the same plane running fore and aft. (Later, we will see that the butt, the mast at the partners, and the top will vary when the plane runs athwartships.) Some masts are stepped on deck—Thistles and Solings are two popular one-design examples—and for deck-stepped masts, you must determine if the deck step is in the center of the deck.

Shrouds of the Same Length

With the mast on sawhorses, check the lengths of the shrouds. They should be the same length. Tie a line to both of the shrouds and tension the line, which will tension the shrouds evenly. Measure them under tension. If one shroud is a quarter of an inch longer than the other, take up one turn on the turnbuckle of the longer shroud. You want to begin tuning with the shrouds the same length. They probably won't stay that way because masts are rarely straight (discussed later), but you do want to start with all things equal.

Fore-and-Aft Location of the Mast

The fore-and-aft location of the mast is important, too. In an offshore-racing boat, the J measurement—the distance from the forestay to the mast—is defined in your rating certificate. Or the J measurement may be listed in the sailplan for your boat provided by the builder or designer. Be certain that the mast location fore and aft corresponds to the J measurement. If not, move the mast step forward or back. The fore-and-aft location of the mast is fixed in many, but not all, one-design classes as well.

Some one-design classes allow you to vary the fore-and-aft location of the mast. Also, this can be done in offshore-racing boats, provided the boat is remeasured. It can usually be done with impunity in a cruising boat. Moving the entire mast back increases weather helm—the tendency of the boat to steer into the wind—by moving the boat's center of effort aft (shown later in FIGURE 7.1). Moving the mast forward decreases weather helm. Ideally, you want the boat to sail with 3 to 5 degrees of weather helm when heading upwind. This means to counteract weather helm and to sail straight, the wheel or tiller will be angled 3 to 5 degrees off center in the direction that drives the boat down or away from the wind.

Three degrees of weather helm corresponds to light air, five degrees to moderate-to-heavy air. The proper amount of weather helm gives the rudder lift, and this lift complements the keel's lift. Lift from the rudder and lift from the keel make the boat work itself to weather. (With lee helm, the rudder and keel are fighting each other.) Seven degrees of weather helm can be acceptable, but once you approach ten degrees, that is a sign that something is wrong because the rudder is creating too much drag, along with the lift. When reaching, more weather helm is acceptable. When running, little or no weather helm is best.

Mast location and the proper amount of weather helm are controlled by tuning and are best checked when sailing. This will be addressed later in the chapter. When locating the mast fore and aft, you have to start somewhere, however, and a good place to start is by copying others. For example, in a one-design class, like a Star, you can tell where the mast is fore and aft by watching a competitor drop the mainsail. You want to copy someone who is fast and who has an aggregate on-board weight—skipper and crew—that approximates the weight of you and your crew. In the Star class, the rules fix boom length. Thus, where the boom falls on the deck when the sail is dropped gives a good indication of fore-and-aft location.

When I was starting in the Star class, I'd watch, for example, if the boom stuck out 2 inches or was even with the transom. Then I'd position my mast accordingly. Bill Buchan, the great Seattle Star sailor and boat-builder, was someone I particularly liked to copy. Buchan is such a good guy that he never seemed to mind.

Similarly, you should pay attention to the equipment your competitors use. When I was more inconspicuous and when sailing was a less serious pastime, I enjoyed walking the parking lot or the staging area, chatting with competitors, comparing equipment, and seeing how boats were set up.

Items I would pay attention to could be obvious or subtle. If a competitor has new sails from a different sailmaker or new sails from the same sailmaker—newness can usually be determined by the color—and suddenly he or she is fast, the new sails could be an obvious reason why. Or if this person has a new mast or certainly a new boat, this could be why, too.

In sailboat racing, know thy competitor—not just their names but their brand names. Also, try to get an idea of the positions of important elements like the mast and leads (the latter was discussed in the previous chapter). It is very important to learn from others. I learned to be a good sailor by studying people such as Bill Buchan, Ash Bown, Malin Burnham, Carl Eichenlaub, and Pete Bennett. If I had had to reinvent all the wheels, I'd be an inferior sailor.

Attaching the Standing Rigging

After properly locating the mast in the partners and on the step, attach the headstay and backstay. Keep them loose in the beginning, although tight enough to hold the mast up. Attach the upper shrouds next; keep them loose as well. The rig may have lower shrouds. There can be one set of lowers or two. If two sets of lowers are used, the forward lower shrouds should be a little tighter than the back lowers.

Next check to see if the mast is vertical, not leaning to one side or the other. If it isn't vertical, the entire mast may lean like the Tower of Pisa or it may bend, even into an S. Remember that we want the masthead, the mast at the partners, and the butt end of the mast on the same plane—through the center of the boat.

To determine if the masthead is vertical, take the main halyard and run it to the gunwale on one side. Apply a little tension and then mark the halyard. Be certain, however, that the main halyard's sheave—the grooved wheel where the halyard exits the mast—is in the center of the mast; sometimes it isn't. Then move the halyard to the same place on the other side and apply the same tension. I've used a fish scale to be certain I'm applying equal tension on both sides. This measurement can also be done with a tape measure hoisted on the main halyard. Verify that the measurement is the same side to side; if the measurement is the same, the masthead is vertical. Usually, the measurement isn't the same. If it is unequal, take up on the appropriate upper shroud until it is. Once the mast is in the center of the boat and vertical, wedge it in place at the partners so that it can't bend sideways.

When Athwartships Bend Is Fast—The Exception to the Rule

Athwartships lean is generally slow. If the mast leans to one side or the other, the effect is the same as heeling the boat. Exaggerated heeling caused by excessive sideways lean of the rig requires the crew to depower the sailplan prematurely. That is the equivalent of taking your foot off the accelerator.

On the other hand, bend at the top of the mast can be fast on some boats in some conditions. With a fractionally rigged small boat, like the popular J/24, a little bit of sideways bend can be fast when windy. In a breeze, the unsupported tip falls off (see FIGURE 5.2, where the dotted line is straight). With the top of the mast sagging to leeward, the middle of the mast pokes to windward. This pokes the main's middle to weather, which opens the slot (the area between the main and the jib). At the same time, the back, or leech, of the main is twisted off, depowering it. Also, the sideways bend helps to flatten the main—which is good in breezy conditions. If a small fractionally rigged boat is tuned so the top of the rig falls off the proper amount, this automatic correction is faster than sail trim that relies on the reaction of a crew member. If the boat is tuned so the rig falls off too much, you can lose the rig and, of course, the race.

With a masthead rig or a larger fractional rig, avoid lateral tip bend since the mast can easily fail. In 1974, I campaigned a 32-footer, called *Carpetbagger,* in the Southern Ocean Racing Conference (SORC) in Florida and the Bahamas. The previous year, a bigger sister of this boat had dominated the SORC, so I was optimistic about my chances. As I had little money, the company gave me a very favorable deal to buy and

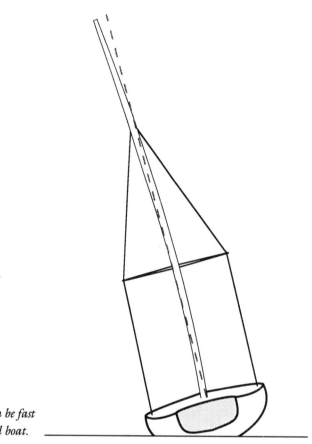

FIGURE 5.2 *Lateral bend can be fast on a small fractionally rigged boat.*

campaign the boat. Nevertheless, I did it with mirrors, not money.

The 32-footer had a masthead rig, and I was no expert on tuning it. In a tune-up race before the SORC, the top of the mast was bending off to leeward due to pressure from the jib. Also, with each flex of the mast, the headsail would get fuller. We tried to tune it—to keep the mast in column—but couldn't stop the tip from bending off. I decided not to worry about it. It didn't look right to me, but I concluded that the designer and builder knew more about it than I did.

Then the mast broke 4 feet from the top. With no money and a broken mast, I had to beg for help. There was a little factory near the St. Petersburg Airport, and I persuaded this guy to help me reconstruct the mast. He found some tubing and somehow spliced the mast together. It turns out the attachment point for the shrouds was in the wrong place.

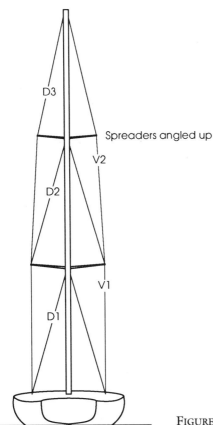

D3

Spreaders angled up

V2

D2

V1

D1

FIGURE 5.3 *Vertical and diagonal shrouds.*

This series did not prove to be a good one for me. I think I finished eleventh in my class, out of fifteen.

Another point to draw from this story is that side bend causes the headstay to sag, which increases headsail depth. This is undesirable when sailing upwind in a strong breeze (as mentioned in Chapter 4).

Multiple Spreaders

Some boats have multiple sets of spreaders (see FIGURE 5.3). The rigging used in multiple spreaders is usually labeled V for vertical shrouds and D for diagonal shrouds. These wires are respectively termed V1 and D1, V2 and D2, etc., as you go up the mast.

Tensioning the Shrouds Before Sailing

Before the rig is tensioned, make sure the spreaders are angled up or horizontal, never angled down as they can fail. Note that the spreaders in FIGURE 5.3 show the proper orientation. Determine their angle from a position off the boat and behind.

Set the upper shrouds first, so the masthead is vertical. Use the halyard or a measuring tape to determine this; if the distance is the same side to side, the mast head is vertical.

If you have a rig with multiple spreaders, work on the diagonals next, starting at the bottom. The D1s should hold the bottom of the mast straight under load—more than 25 degrees of heel. The D2s should pull the mast back to vertical (see FIGURE 5.4). Be careful not to overtighten the

FIGURE 5.4 *Over-tightening the D2s.*

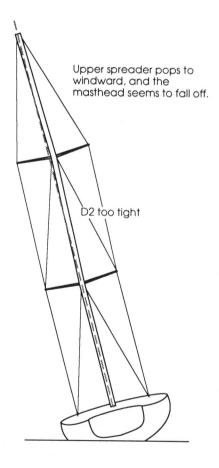

Upper spreader pops to windward, and the masthead seems to fall off.

D2 too tight

D2s, however. If you do, it can appear that the D3s are too loose when in actuality the D2s are too tight. Again, use the halyard or a measuring tape to check that the mast is vertical. Also, sight up the mast from the gooseneck, to see if the top or middle is out of column.

The leeward shrouds should have no slack when the boat heels 20 degrees. Some books say you can check this at the dock by heeling the boat 20 degrees with a halyard led through a block on the dock, but this can be hard on the halyard, the masthead, and, even, the dock. It is better to tune the rig when sailing, and the best time to do this is with the wind in the 12- to 15-knot range—that is, the top end of the Number 1 headsail. This puts maximum pressure on the rig. Don't, however, start with the heavy Number 1 in this amount of wind; as will be discussed later in this chapter, work up to this size sail.

If you have one set of lower shrouds, remove all slack and then apply a bit more tension. The lowers should not be as tight as the uppers. With two sets of lowers, the front lowers, as indicated, should be tighter than the back lowers. The back lowers can be fairly loose.

Mast Rake

A mast can be raked, that is, the entire mast leaned aft. In effect, this is similar to moving the mast back. Raking the mast moves the center of effort (CE) of the sails aft. Increasing rake increases weather helm; decreasing rake decreases weather helm. This principle is clearly seen in the rig of a windsurfer, a rudderless sailboard. Rake the windsurfer's rig back, and the board turns into the wind. Lean the rig forward, and the board turns away from the wind.

Use the amount of weather helm to determine rake. Recall that you want 3 to 5 degrees of weather helm when sailing upwind so that the rudder's lift complements the keel's lift. The length of the headstay determines rake.

Sail shape also influences the amount of rake. In a Star, Flying Dutchman, Soling, or Etchells, the length of the mainsail's leech, or trailing edge, determines rake. These boats sail best with as much rake as possible. You've reached the limit of rake when the main can't be properly trimmed.

The weight of the crew affects the amount of mast rake, too. The heavier the crew, the more rake you can carry, since the heavy crew is better able to flatten the boat when necessary, decreasing weather helm. For example, in the 1990 Etchells 22 Worlds, held in Perth, Western Australia, I sailed with the sizable duo of Bill Munster, my longtime Star crew, and Andreas Josenhans, the gentle giant of North Sails East. From my America's Cup experience in Western Australia where I sailed two hundred days, I expected it to be windy. That proved accurate as five of the six races saw winds averaging 18 knots; the sixth saw much heavier winds.

The Etchells 22 is a three-person keelboat. It is 22 feet on the water, 30 feet, 6 inches overall, and weighs about 3,300 pounds. Our combined crew weight was 800 pounds, or 266 pounds per man. I opted for bulk—weight on the rail—because I reasoned that in heavy winds, I could keep maximum rake. Also, I wouldn't have to depower the sails as early or as much as would a lighter crew. We were the heaviest crew in Perth by 75 pounds; next came John Bertrand and crew. It was Bertrand, you may recall, who beat me in the 1983 America's Cup. The regatta marked Bertrand's return to competitive sailing. With 800 pounds on the rail, my guess is that we carried more mast rake than any boat in the fleet. I ended up second to Chris Law, who sailed on *White Crusader* in the 1986–87 America's Cup. Peter Gilmour, starting helmsman on *Kookaburra* and skipper of *Spirit of Australia* in 1992, finished behind me in third. Then came Bertrand.

In the 1991 Etchells Worlds, sailed six months later in San Francisco Bay, I once more had a sizable crew in Bill Munster, again, and Norm Reynolds. We would win the worlds this time.[1]

Might, as you've doubtless heard, makes right. Whether you subscribe to that or not, in a sailboat, might also makes rake.

Mast Bend

A mainsail is called a triangular sail. In truth, the sail shows an exaggerated leech (roach), and a curved luff (luff curve). The amount of luff curve can vary considerably. Masts are bent because of luff curve. For example, when the crew bends the mast so it matches luff curve, the mainsail grows flat (see FIGURE 4.17), particularly at the leading edge. This is typically done when sailing upwind. Off-the-wind, the crew straightens the mast or even allows it to lean forward. Then mast curve no longer matches luff curve, which makes the sail fuller.

As mentioned in Chapter 4, a full sail has high lift and high drag, which

[1]The Etchells class has since passed a weight limit of 628 pounds (285 kilos) for skipper and crew.

is a good reaching shape. (When reaching, both lift and drag contribute to boat speed.) The high-drag (full) shape is also appropriate when running. When beating, however, you want to maximize the lift-drag ratio. A flatter sail can show more lift and less drag.

Certainly the most extreme and famous example of mast bend was *Australia I*, the boat I raced against with *Freedom* in the 1980 America's Cup. I first learned something was going on with the Australians while having breakfast at Handy Lunch on lower Thames Street in Newport, across from Williams & Manchester Shipyard. I was enough of a regular at Handy Lunch that they had a "Freedom Burger" on the menu. Gary Hooks, who owns Handy Lunch, told me the Australians were doing secret work across the street. I started snooping around and learned it had something to do with the mast, but I couldn't find out exactly what.

Then I saw it. *Australia I* had a mast with greatly exaggerated bend. The bendy mast, which actually was seen earlier in the summer on the British challenger, *Lionheart*, allowed *Australia I* to carry extra—and unrated—sail area at the top of the mast and to control it through exaggerated mast bend. Upwind, the mast was bent well aft, flattening the main. Downwind, it was straightened, allowing for an extra-large and extra-deep sail.

Also, a bendy mast decreases induced drag, discussed in Chapter 2. There is, you will recall from Chapters 2 and 4, leakage from the high-pressure windward side of a sail to the low-pressure leeward side. Similarly, there is leakage from the high-pressure side of the keel to the low-pressure side (see FIGURE 2.3). This is induced drag. In Chapter 2, I commented on how this leakage, whether above or below the waterline, manifests itself as a spinning. In aviation, this spinning is called a tip tornado. The energy required to cause this spinning is considerable and can't be used by the sail or keel in creating motion.

The tip of a triangular sail isn't very effective. C. A. Marchaj, the aerodynamicist and well-respected author who developed the bendy mast for the *Lionheart*, determined in a wind-tunnel test that the luff of a mainsail on a 12-Meter can be reduced at the top by 15 percent without any noticeable effect on performance. In similar tests, Marchaj determined that if you bend the top of the mast, induced drag is decreased, with a 4 percent increase in performance.

This means a mainsail that is shaped more like a U than a V, or triangle, is superior. The U, or elliptical shape, is common to an airplane wing, and since *Lionheart* and then *Australia I*, even the contours of triangular sails have become rounded. So, too, have the profiles of keels.

Sailmakers make a mainsail more elliptical by emphasizing roach—the extra sail area along the leech that extends beyond the straight line from head to clew—and by adding extra area at the top of the sail. They then support the extra roach area with battens—the best support comes from full-length battens. Of course, full-length battens aren't always allowed. They're prohibited in 12-Meters or in boats that race under the International Offshore Rule (IOR). Full-length battens are allowed, however, in other racing rules, such as the International Measurement System and in the International America's Cup Class (IACC). Of course, they are permitted and popular with cruising boats.

Before we raced *Australia I* in the 1980 America's Cup, we had an executive meeting to discuss the bendy mast. The question was, Do we try to copy it or ignore it? It was decided there was neither the time nor the money to copy it. We just hoped we were good enough in other areas to offset the advantages of a bendy rig. *Australia I* with her bendy mast won one race that year—a challenger hadn't won a race in ten years. We won the next four races and the Cup competition, 4-1.

From the perspective of sail shape and reducing induced drag, all boats, be they cruisers or racers, should have some way to bend a mast. This is because mains are hypersensitive to mast bend, as discussed in the previous chapter.

Of course, how much you bend your mast depends on the type of mast, its construction, and its support, as well as the integrity and age of the hull. For example, a mast with a small section and thick walls can be bent more and more safely than a large-sectioned thin-walled mast. Also, the former shape presents less windage, that is, less disturbed flow around the mast. Some big boats will use small-sectioned masts for these reasons and will support them with three sets of spreaders, even more. The added support allows the small-sectioned thick-walled mast to be lighter than a large-sectioned thin-walled mast with single spreaders.

When I won the SORC in 1975 with *Stinger*, I had a one-spreader rig, about as big as a telephone pole. It probably would have stood up in a hurricane without rigging. Lowell North, who sailed with me on *Stinger*, was, I believe, embarrassed by the size of the rig.

Around this time, Lowell North and Tim Stearns were making advances in rig design. North, the great sailmaker, Star-boat sailor, and innovator that he is, took a small rig and glued carbon-fiber strips to the sides to give the mast some strength athwartships. I saw this being done at North's San Diego loft. Stearns is an engineer, who wanted to make advances in the sport. The two of them got together and modernized sailboat rigs. They produced rigs that are fundamentally what we see today: small sections, thick walls, and well-supported by multiple spreaders and jumpers. Lowell understood that a lighter mast, supported by more and longer "branches" (spreaders and rigging), means less windage and less pitching (see FIGURE 2.6, center).

A disadvantage, however, is that the long branches don't allow the headsail to be trimmed in as much as it should be. This is true with modern IOR boats and the IACC boats. As a result, the headsail is "light"—the windward telltale flicks—much of the time. (This will be discussed further in Chapter 7, "Steering.") Nevertheless, less windage and less pitching seem to outweigh a light headsail.

Although I think the sport has benefited immeasurably from Lowell North, I never wanted to be Lowell North. By nature, I've always been more conservative; I've never been the one to embrace new things. I saw so many people at the leading edge have problems. Lowell had problems with some of those early masts. As I've said before, my experience is that people on the leading edge pay the price more than they reap the rewards.

Ways to Bend a Mast

My roots are in a 22-foot Star boat, as are Lowell North's. I believe that one of the big edges we enjoyed in ocean racing back in the late 1960s and early 1970s was an understanding of mast bend and other aspects of sail trim. This is how we were able to win so many races. We sailed against big-boat sailors who, while having much better equipment than we could afford, lacked the critical small-boat experience. In a small boat, things like mast bend, sheet angles, etc., can make such a difference.

There are dozens of ways to bend a mast. Deckblocking is most common. Here the mast at the partners is shoved forward with a wedge behind the mast. Alternatively, with a deck-stepped mast, the butt can sit on a shim placed at the back, or the front of the mast can be shaved off at an angle. Under compression, the high back or lowered front throws the front of the mast forward, causing the mast to bend. Other design elements that control mast bend include degree of taper at the top, local reinforcing, and angle of the spreaders. Spreaders angled aft allow the mast to bend, while those angled forward limit it. See FIGURE 5.5 for the various ways to bend rigs.

The typical main for a typical offshore boat is designed for 1 to 2 percent mast bend, with 1.5 percent being about average. Thus, if the mast is 50 feet high, 1 percent bend is 6 inches. That is a typical amount of bend for a main cut for a conservative masthead rig. A whippy fractional rig might have a sail designed for 9 inches of bend, which is 1.5 percent. Of course,

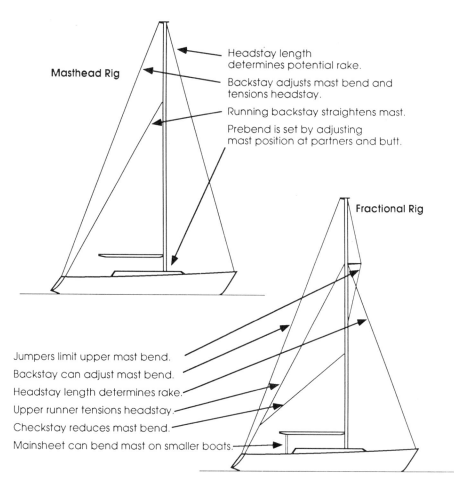

Masthead Rig

Headstay length
determines potential rake.

Backstay adjusts mast bend and
tensions headstay.

Running backstay straightens mast.

Prebend is set by adjusting
mast position at partners and butt.

Fractional Rig

Jumpers limit upper mast bend.
Backstay can adjust mast bend.
Headstay length determines rake.
Upper runner tensions headstay.
Checkstay reduces mast bend.
Mainsheet can bend mast on smaller boats.

FIGURE 5.5 *How masthead and fractional rigs are bent.*

before you bend your mast at all, be certain your boat, mast, and sails are up
to it.

If you don't know how much bend your mainsail was cut for, bend the
mast without Cunningham tension until you see a hint of overbend wrinkles. These are wrinkles that radiate from the luff to the clew. If the overbend wrinkles are even, from the top to the bottom of the sail, then mast
bend and luff curve match. If all the wrinkles are coming from the lower
section, the mast is being bent too much. If they are in the top section, the
likelihood is you will have to increase prebend, discussed below. (Another
way to determine the degree of bend is to use the chart in FIGURE 4.16.)

Prebend

Normally, bend depends on the relative positions of the butt of the mast, the location of the mast partners, and the tip. If the mast is aligned in the fore-and-aft direction, it is straight. Move any of these elements, and the mast bends more or less.

Prebend is mast bend applied through the rigging. It is different from mast bend caused by pressure in the sails. Prebend involves alteration of the shrouds, forestay, jumpers, etc. (see FIGURE 5.5).

Offshore boats use prebend to lock the mast rigidly. Start bending a mast, and it usually bends easily. At some point, however, it develops a resistance to bending. It locks up and becomes quite stable. That point is the rig's "sweet spot." Of course, bend it just a little more, and it can break. Prebend, if done correctly, also starts the mast bending high or low, which is helpful in matching sail shape to mast bend.

Prebend is important in one-design classes, too, where boats don't normally have different suits of sails for light, medium, and heavy winds. Asking one set of sails to span such a range requires prebend, particularly in light air.

As described in the last chapter, two rules characterize mainsail trim upwind: the draft (deepest part) of the mainsail should be at 50 percent—or halfway between luff and leech—and the top batten should be parallel to the boom.

A mainsail has roach, that is, extra material beyond a straight line from head to clew. It also has luff curve, that is, extra material beyond the straight line from head to tack. When the wind is moderate, the leech, or back, of the sail is pressed to leeward by wind pressure. This, in turn, bends the top of the mast. The bending through wind pressure pulls the extra material—the luff curve—at the front of the mast, placing the draft at 50 percent. In the absence of sufficient leech pressure in light winds, the extra material remains bunched at the luff. Thus, the draft of the main is farther forward than 50 percent (see FIGURE 5.6, top). In one-design boats, which are usually fractionally rigged, the mainsheet alone is usually enough to bend the mast. However, if we use the mainsheet to do this, the top batten will poke too far to windward, which is undesirable. If we prebend the mast, however, by pushing the mast forward at the partners and/or tightening the backstay, the mainsail grows flat, particularly at the leading edge (see FIGURE 5.6, bottom). Also, the draft goes to 50 percent, which is optimum, and the top batten maintains the proper orientation.

How a rig is prebent varies by class rules and whether the mast is deck- or keel-stepped. For example, unless prohibited by class rules, keel-stepped

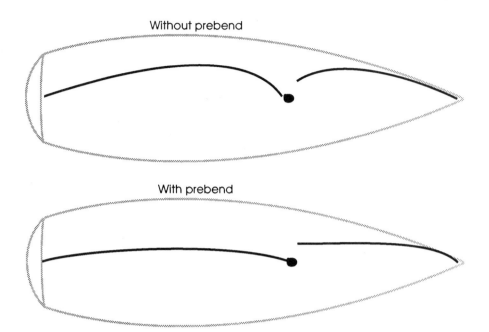

Without prebend

With prebend

FIGURE 5.6 *How prebend influences sail shape.*

masts allow deck blocking at the partners. Most commonly, a hard rubber or wood wedge is placed behind the mast through the deck partners. This arcs the mast forward at the deck, causing it to bend low (see FIGURE 5.7).

Prebend also affects the headsail. In anything but the lightest winds, the headstay sags back and to leeward. This headstay sag is addressed in the design of a jib, which has a hollow cut in luff. Obviously, it is difficult to get the headstay to sag in light air, particularly in a small fractionally rigged boat. Prebend, however, induces headstay sag (see FIGURE 5.7), letting the jib assume a fast shape. The result of prebend in both sails is apparent in FIGURE 5.6, bottom.

Boats with deck-stepped masts often have two headsails, a light-air sail designed for a straighter headstay and a heavy-air sail designed to fit a headstay that sags under load from heavy winds. Alternatively, in light air, some crews run the spinnaker halyard, to the stem head at the bow and tighten the halyard, allowing the headstay to sag. Suffice it to say, there are many other stratagems to prebend masts in classes that don't encourage prebend or outlaw it.

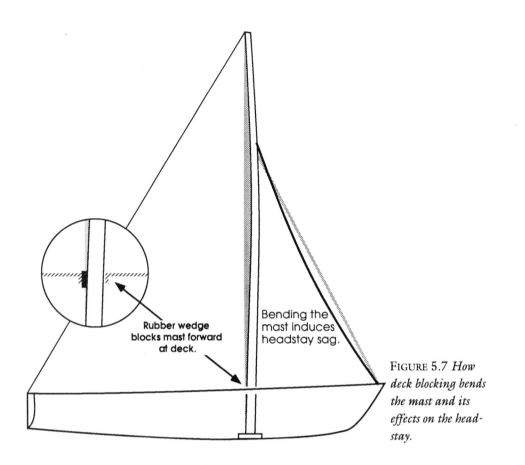

Rubber wedge blocks mast forward at deck.

Bending the mast induces headstay sag.

Figure 5.7 *How deck blocking bends the mast and its effects on the headstay.*

Marking the Degree of Weather Helm

Weather helm can be an important reference in mast tuning: 3 to 5 degrees is best. How do you know, however, how much helm you have? With the boat out of the water, measure the distance from the trailing edge of the rudder to the center of the rudder post. This is W (see Figure 5.8). Then use the trigonometric sine values in the figure to determine R.[2] Finally, move the rudder off centerline the required distance from 0 degrees to 5 or 6 degrees. Then mark the corresponding distances.

Use tape pieces on the wheel to correspond to the various rudder angles. With a tiller, use lines scribed in the cockpit. Play in the wheel or tiller will compromise the measurement. It will also compromise steering, so if possible remove the play.

[2]This is a good approximation for the small angles we're concerned with here.

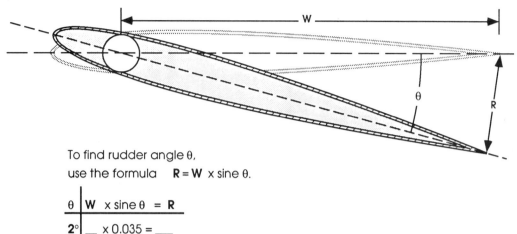

To find rudder angle θ,
use the formula   **R** = **W** x sine θ.

θ	**W** x sine θ = **R**
2°	__ x 0.035 = __
4°	__ x 0.070 = __
6°	__ x 0.105 = __

FIGURE 5.8 *Measuring rudder angle.*

TESTING RIG TUNE UNDER SAIL

Now we are ready to go sailing and test the tune of the rig. Before leaving, however, put the cotter pins back in the turnbuckles, so you don't lose the mast.

Speaking of cotter pins, never bend them completely back to lock them in. Those neat little circles make cotter pins too difficult to remove in an emergency, such as a dismasting, where the fallen rig can severely damage a hull. Cotter pins should only be split to about a 45-degree angle. Then the ends should be clipped off a little bit with a wire cutter and filed until smooth. This helps to keep sails, sheets, etc., from catching on them. Lastly, cotter pins should be taped.

The optimum condition to check tuning is in 12 to 15 knots of wind, which is typically the top limit of the heavy Number 1 genoa. This amount of wind and size of sail put maximum load on the rig. If the wind is less, you can try powering—assuming you have an engine—to increase the apparent wind. If the wind is too light, you're probably wasting your time. If you don't have an engine, do the best you can or wait for a better day.

Don't start with a heavy Number 1 in 12 to 15 knots of wind, however, but start with the mainsail alone. Go through the exercise described below and then add the Number 3 genoa. Again go through the exercise, then change to the Number 2, and finally test tuning with the heavy Number 1. This can help to prevent a rig failure.

The goal when checking tune under sail is to get the mast in column, that is, without sideways bend or lean. To address tuning a one-spreader rig, start sailing upwind on starboard tack, for example. Then sight up the mast from behind to see if it's falling off at the top. Tack onto port and sight up the mast again. If nothing seems amiss, tighten the starboard upper shroud, which is unloaded on port tack. Do it a few turns and carefully count the turns. Then put the pins back in and tack onto starboard. If the mast is now straight, the adjustment was correct. If, however, it is still leaning to leeward or is hooked to windward, adjust the unloaded (leeward) shroud accordingly. Tack back and forth—putting back the cotter pins each time—until the mast is straight.

Finally, the shrouds should be taken up quite tight—do it the same amount on each side. Some people think the unloaded leeward shrouds should be floppy since this doesn't put extra strain on the mast, but this isn't true. As discussed in prebend, you need considerable tension from both windward and leeward shrouds to lock the mast in place.

With a multispreader rig, you have to adjust the diagonal shrouds—the Ds—as well. Some crews do this when sailing, by hoisting an agile crew member in a bosun's chair, but this can be dangerous. It is safer but less accurately done at the dock. Remember that the forward lower shrouds should be tighter than the aft lowers.

MAST TUNE AND WEATHER HELM

Getting the mast straight isn't the whole story. Helm is an important variable, too. You should start to feel weather helm when there is about 5 knots of apparent wind. If you take your hand off the tiller or wheel, the boat should head into the wind. At 10 or 12 knots, the boat should require 3 or 4 degrees of helm to steer straight, and at 14 or 15 knots, 5 degrees. Use the tapes on the wheel or the marks in the cockpit (see FIGURE 5.8), to determine the degree of weather helm. When sailing in winds at the top end of the Number 1, typically 12 to 15 knots, you have to start thinking about decreasing helm. This can be accomplished by increasing twist—allowing the back of the sail(s) to sag to leeward. Increasing twist can be accomplished by moving the genoa leads aft (see FIGURE 4.14), and/or easing the genoa sheet, and/or easing the mainsheet.

What happens, however, if there is no helm at 5 knots, or—less desirable still—lee helm (that is, the tendency of the boat to turn away from the wind)? You can move the mast back or more likely rake it aft, as the latter doesn't normally the affect rating of the boat under the rating rules. To rake the mast aft, you'll probably have to drop sails first. (If the wind and sea conditions are too rough, return to the dock before raking the mast.) Also ease the shrouds, because you probably can't move the mast at the step with so much load on the rig. Alternatively, you can move the mast aft at the partners. Then ease the headstay and take up the backstay. From there, tuning starts afresh. (Remember, if you've changed the fore-and-aft location of the mast, the boat may have to be remeasured.)

In light-air places like San Diego, you can set your boat up differently. For my Etchells 22 in San Diego, I have more rake—which moves the center of effort of the sails farther behind the center of lateral resistance of the keel, giving me more weather helm in light winds. If, however, I lived or raced my Etchells in Newport, Rhode Island, I'd have less rake. In Newport, the wind averages 12.7 knots (see Wind Rose, FIGURE 8.1), while in San Diego, it is 6.9 knots. Also, in Newport, a 22-knot day can occur nine times in May, five times in June, three times in July, etc. That's one-third of the time in May. In San Diego, you have one heavy-air day a month. The odds are you aren't going to be out sailing that day. If you are, everyone else is going to be in the same boat—so to speak—as you.

CODING

It takes a long time to learn a boat—the shroud, stay, sheet, and halyard tensions that make your boat go fast in various conditions. Maybe you're good enough to learn your boat's sweet spots every time you sail, but I'm not. A key to boat speed is repeating fast settings. Similarly, a key to safe sailing is knowing the limits of your rig and boat. For example, you don't want to overtension a backstay, because a fitting or even a mast can break. This speaks for coding or marking everything that can be tensioned or eased and then keeping a record of fast settings as well as those in the danger zone.

For example, mark your halyards so the sail and/or the Nicropress fitting on the shackle don't snag the masthead sheave (see FIGURE 5.9). Should the fitting foul the sheave, a sail can rip, the halyard can foul, and/or the sheave can be damaged. If it is a wire genoa halyard, tie a rope sheet or line to the genoa halyard and hoist it. When the Nicropress fitting is about 2 feet from the sheave, tie the sheet or line off. Then continue hoisting the halyard against the line with the winch. This causes the wire halyard to straighten. Then with someone at the masthead, properly secured in a

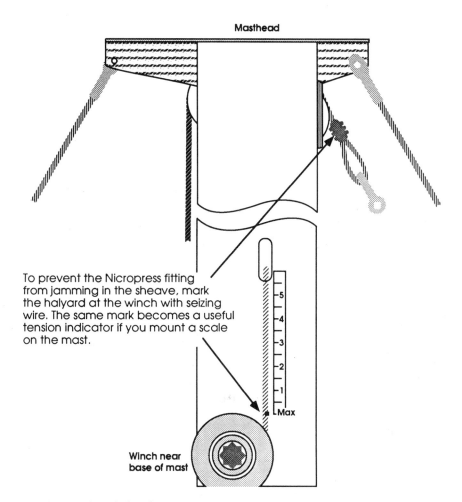

Masthead

To prevent the Nicropress fitting from jamming in the sheave, mark the halyard at the winch with seizing wire. The same mark becomes a useful tension indicator if you mount a scale on the mast.

5
4
3
2
1
Max

Winch near base of mast

FIGURE 5.9 *Marking halyards.*

bosun's chair, mark when the Nicropress is nearly touching the sheave. Make a temporary mark on the bottom of the halyard with tape, paint, or nail polish, etc.

A good way to mark a wire halyard like this permanently is with seizing wire (see FIGURE 5.10). Use two sets of vise grips above and below the temporary mark, and unwind the wire. Stick a marlin spike in the opening and then move it up and down to the proper mark. Then wind the seizing wire tightly several times through the halyard opening. Take out the spike and clean up the ends of the seizing wire, so it doesn't become a meat hook, rip-

Boat Speed

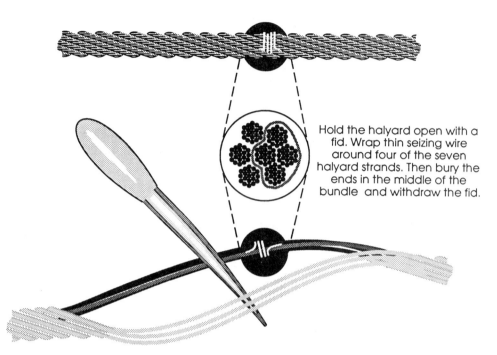

Hold the halyard open with a fid. Wrap thin seizing wire around four of the seven halyard strands. Then bury the ends in the middle of the bundle and withdraw the fid.

FIGURE 5.10 *How to mark wire halyards permanently.*

ping sails or hands. A corresponding coding on the mast is also important (see FIGURE 5.9). North Sails, for example, sells inexpensive and extremely handy marking strips that make such references clear and also look neat.

Mark the spinnaker and main halyard, too. It is helpful for identification if the halyards have different-colored rope tails; similarly, it helps if the genoa sheets are one color and the spinnaker sheets another. This also applies to the topping lift and the Cunningham.

If you sail a racing boat, remember there is typically a black band above which you can't hoist the main. In light winds, hoist a crew member to the top in a bosun's chair to mark precisely this position. Also mark reef positions for the main halyard. There are two halyard positions for every reef point. The first marks where the reef cringle can easily slip over the tack hook. The second marks the proper halyard tension for the reef point. Also mark the position of the reef lines, which tension the foot. When reefing, you want a flat sail to decrease heeling (see Chapter 6), so the marks should indicate when the foot of the sail is fully extended.

If you sail a boat with nonoverlapping headsails, or if you have a Number 3 genoa, which usually is nonoverlapping, mark the spreaders, at 2, 4, 6 inches, etc., from the spreader tip. This allows you to trim the headsail repeatedly to the optimum position. If you sail at night, use reflective tape for the marks, as the marks will then be more easily seen with a flashlight.

Mark the Cunningham, outhaul, and traveler with the previously described marking strips. This, again, will allow you to repeat fast settings. (The proper amount of tension for these items in different wind speeds and at different orientations must be determined by testing, which is discussed at the end of this chapter.) Speaking of the traveler, mark the traveler position when the boom is on the centerline, on both port and starboard tacks, as this is an important reference. Mark the appropriate genoa-lead positions by the lead itself. Also, mark them in waterproof ink on the clew of the particular sail. Mark maximum backstay tension, and the tensions for light winds and other points of sail. If you use a split backstay, put the marks on the rope tail; with a hydraulic backstay system, merely record the gauge

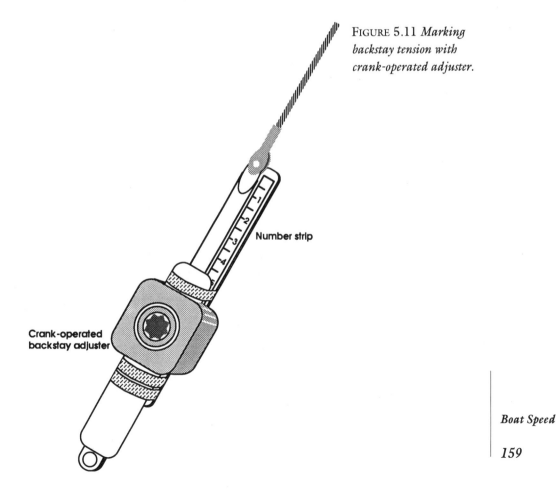

FIGURE 5.11 *Marking backstay tension with crank-operated adjuster.*

Number strip

Crank-operated backstay adjuster

numbers. If the backstay is operated by a crank, tape a batten to the back-stay and mark it with number strips (see FIGURE 5.11). Also mark the positions of the running backstays and babystay if you have them.

Then sail by the numbers: Have a 3-by-5 card entitled "7 Knots—Smooth Seas Upwind Trim." On it should be settings that have proven to be fast. For example: "Sail: Light Number 1 Genoa; Genoa halyard position: 7; Genoa Lead: 3; Traveler: 4 inches to windward; Backstay: 2,000 pounds." Sails and halyards stretch and Mylar and Kevlar sails wrinkle and shrink, for example, so be prepared to change these settings if you suddenly seem slow.

If you do a dip-pole jibe, mark the line on the pole-end fitting with nail polish or paint to show how high to raise the butt end of the pole so the front end clears the forestay. Also, note the proper topping-lift height so the

FIGURE 5.12 *How mast rake is determined.*

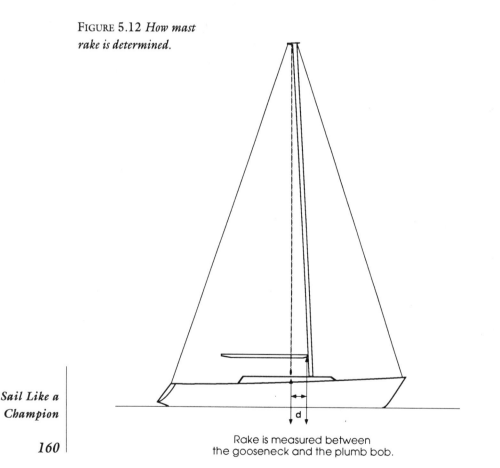

Rake is measured between
the gooseneck and the plumb bob.

outboard end of the pole just clears the forestay. Dropping the pole the same amount each time helps the bowman to grab cleanly the spinnaker pole as it swings toward his position at the bow and facilitates connecting the lazy guy to the pole. Knowing the proper topping-lift setting can speed your jibe; also, knowing what settings to return the spinnaker pole to after the jibe can make it easier to keep this big sail flying.

Write down or mark turnbuckle tensions, etc., to repeat fast rig settings. This is especially important if you trailer your boat, and the mast is often unstepped. Similarly, mark the fore-and-aft location of the mast.

To determine the degree of mast rake, use a fore-and-aft inclinometer to level the boat. Then tension the backstay as you normally would when sailing upwind (see FIGURE 4.16). Affix a heavy plumb bob on the main halyard (see FIGURE 5.12). Then measure the distance from the plumb bob to the gooseneck.

The amount of rake is a function of the length of the headstay, as described. Thus, it is helpful to know this distance, too. Hang a tape measure on your jib halyard. Hoist it to the top of the mast and measure to the lower pin in the forestay. When tuning the mast—whether once a season or once a week—reference points, like this, can come in handy to repeat fast setting.

WEIGHT-WATCHING

Excessive pitching of a hull in a seaway, described in Chapter 2, is slow. To reduce this, remove excess weight everywhere, but particularly at the top of the mast and the ends of the boat. Alternatively, concentrate weight, like sails, gear, food, etc., as low in the boat as possible and about in the center, provided, of course, that doesn't invalidate a rating.

Mast weight is important in terms of minimizing pitching but so, too, is where the weight is concentrated. Weight high—such as masthead fittings and antennae—has a greater impact on the pitching motion than weight low.

The debilitating effects of weight aloft are easy to see by focusing on heeling rather than pitching.[3] In FIGURE 2.5, we described how on a seesaw, a 60-pound child sitting 6 feet from a balance point can balance a 180-pound adult sitting 2 feet from the balance point. This is the concept of

---

[3]We shift from pitching to heeling, because heeling can be viewed in terms of pounds—a familiar measure—while pitching is measured in foot-pounds—a much less common measure. For those who are interested, the formula for pitching moment is: $PM = pounds \times ft^2$.

moments (weight times distance) and is demonstrated by the math: 60 x 6 = 360 and 180 x 2 = 360.

What happens to heeling if we replace a 20-pound radar antenna on the top of a mast that is 40 feet above the hull's fulcrum or center of gravity, as a yacht designer would describe it, with a 10-pound wind sensor? In this example, the masthead fitting is 40 feet from the center of gravity. The keel's weight is centered 5 feet below the center of gravity. If we reduce the weight of the radar antenna by half, it weighs 10 pounds. Therefore the weight of the keel could be reduced by 80 pounds (40 x 10 = 400 and 80 x 5 = 400). To say this another way, for every pound you save at the mast, you can save 8 pounds in the keel. Or since we aren't likely to reduce the weight of the keel, the yacht will be stiffer and can carry more sail area. When you reduce weight aloft, you similarly reduce pitching.[4]

Sails that hang near to or off the top of the mast contribute to pitching, too, and to heeling. Lightweight sails decrease pitching and heeling, and this is one reason for the popularity of Mylar, even lighter Kevlar sails, and perhaps carbon-fiber and liquid-crystal sails that debuted in the 1992 America's Cup. A Kevlar sail can weigh one-quarter as much as a Dacron (polyester) sail with the same low stretch. Also, sails stowed below deck in the ends can cause excessive pitching. Move them to the center of the boat unless your boat was measured with the sails in the ends.

Remove extraneous weight on the bow, provided it doesn't invalidate your measurement or isn't required by other rules or by safety considerations. That includes extra cleats, a fitting, or a towing ring. If the item is not essential to speed—if it does not help to get the boat around the race course, if it is not necessary for safety, or is not mandated by the rules—remove it. Cruisers, too, might consider removing at least one of the two anchors on the bow, the 200 pounds of extra chain in the forward locker, or, similarly, the barbecue on the stern.

Elsewhere, I commented that boats are like magnets for equipment. Don't allow excess gear to creep aboard your boat. If speed is your goal, remove what isn't absolutely necessary for safety or required by rules. Be a weight-watcher. Obviously, you can't remove something that affects your

[4]To put this into the context of foot-pounds, discussed in footnote 3: Imagine you have a 20-pound radar antenna at the masthead. And your mast is 40 feet from the hull's center of gravity, which is typically just below the waterline. According to the formula, PM = pounds x ft², that 20-pound fitting creates a pitching moment of 32,000 foot-pounds. If you could reduce the weight of that fitting by half, the pitching moment is half, or 16,000 foot-pounds. Thus, for every pound saved at the masthead, the saving is 1,600 foot-pounds.

rating without invalidating that rating. If you choose to, get your boat remeasured.

For the 1975 SORC, Carl Eichenlaub built a One Tonner for me, which became *Stinger*. The boat was built out of aluminum in just twenty-two working days. When it was time to add the interior, I got a frantic call from Eichenlaub, asking me what I wanted done to the interior. I told him to follow the designer's instructions. "There are no instructions," Eichenlaub said.

I went to Eichenlaub's yard in San Diego and roughed out an interior. I borrowed heavily from the Ranger 37, which had won the SORC in 1973. To reduce pitching, I asked for a minimum of accommodations forward of the mast. Eichenlaub only put a small enclosed head there. Also, to increase the righting moment, I wanted four bunks on either side. This way the sleeping off-watch of four men could increase the righting moment, which would decrease heeling. This was accomplished with a quarterberth and pipe berth above it and a settee with another pipe berth above it. *Stinger* won the SORC. I used the same interior on *High Roler*, which won Class A in the 1977 SORC. Dormitory-style interiors such as these became something of an IOR standard. Suffice it to say not everyone liked this kind of accommodation.

To reduce pitching, concentrate crew weight at the center of gyration, that is, the axis around which the boat pitches. The center of gyration isn't necessarily the center of the boat; rather, it is the balance point, which is influenced by weight in the ends, the placement of the engine, etc. In an offshore boat, I ask the designer for this location. In my 1992 America's Cup boat, for example, the center of pitching, or gyration, was aft of the winch pedestal. In most small boats, however, you have to sit near the sail controls, so knowing this point is less important but not unimportant.

Pitching, as indicated, isn't the sole motion that should concern sailors. Heeling is important, too. Indeed minimizing heel is more important than reducing pitching. This is why in my racing boats, the crews line weather rails. In light air, when there isn't much pressure on the sails, the crews are often positioned to leeward. This leeward heel allows the sails to sag into shape to catch the wind better; it also reduces wetted surface, that is, the area of the hull in contact with the water.

Fast Mast

A fast mast is light overall, with weight kept out of the tip, as mentioned. Also, it should be straight and aerodynamically clean. Addressing straight first, a straight mast is more the exception than the rule.

Aluminum masts are built through the process known as extrusion. Simply considered, a piece of aluminum is passed through a die. The die changes a little every time a piece of metal moves through it. Also, the die Alcoa uses may be slightly different from the die Reynolds uses. As noted in Chapter 3, if winning races is important to you, you should be meticulous about picking a boat—if you're buying a small boat, weigh it. You should be equally meticulous when selecting a mast. The best way to determine how straight a mast is, is to put it up in the boat. Then when all the rigging is connected and with equal tension on the shrouds, check the distance from side to side with a halyard or a tape measure. If the distances are the same, the mast is straight. Barring that, you can usually tell how straight a mast is by putting it on sawhorses with the sail-track side up. Make sure the mast is level, and the more sawhorses you support it with, the better. Then sight up the mast track.

To determine weight, obviously weigh a mast. It is also very helpful to determine the balance point or center of gravity—sometimes class rules define this point. You want a mast with the lowest possible balance point that is still within the rules. If the mast isn't too big or too heavy, put one sawhorse in the middle to support it. Two or more crew members can help to support it at either end. Then move the saw horse up and down the mast to determine its balance point. A lower balance point, or center of gravity, means a light tip, which reduces weight aloft and so diminishes pitching.

Alternatively, you can set the butt of the mast on a sawhorse and put a scale under the tip to weigh the top of the spar. (This is done in the Star Class to make sure the tip is not too light.) The mast with the lightest weight has the lightest tip. Be careful, however, that the balance point corresponds to class rules. A 12-Meter mast, for example, has a minimum weight and a minimum center of gravity specified in the rules.

As Lowell North taught us, the wind should smoothly flow past the mast. This is sometimes described as aerodynamically clean. This can speak for internal halyards, where the halyards run inside the mast until exiting through "exit boxes" near the winches and also at appropriate positions up the mast. With America's Cup masts, we try to make sure they are as smooth and as fair as possible, and we tape the halyard-exit boxes to lessen windage or turbulence. Also, we attempt to fair in the fittings—make them flush with the spar—so the wind can flow smoothly past.

SHAPING THE UNDERWATER FOILS

Now you've bought that J/24 or Etchells 22, and you've made sure it's perfect, from fit to finish. The ends are light and the mast straight. It is ready to win the Worlds, or isn't it? It probably isn't because the shapes of the underwater foils, the rudder and keel, which are critical to performance, have not yet been perfected.

As discussed in Chapter 4, sails are judged by depth, depth or draft position, shapes of the leading and trailing edges, etc. It may surprise you, but these factors are important for the underwater foils, as well.

The shapes are the responsibility of the designer and then the builder. However, what the designer wants and what the builder delivers can be two very different things. Also, since many boats aren't raced seriously if at all, many builders opt not to put in the hours that meticulous shaping of the underwater surfaces requires. Further, working with lead isn't fun. For safety, it requires special equipment and expertise, and should not be attempted unless you know what you're doing.

Shaping a keel properly is a lot like the old joke about Michelangelo. Asked his secret for carving marble sculptures, Michelangelo supposedly replied, "I just cut away everything that doesn't belong."

First, the shape of the underwater appendages has to fit class tolerances—many classes have templates (patterns) for the tolerances—and therefore keel, centerboard, or rudder shape needs to be measured accordingly. Other classes don't give you much room to maneuver. You can't, for example, do much with the shape of a Star-boat keel. It is essentially a flat plate. All you have to work with is the width, and with a 1/4-inch flat plate, there isn't much room for personal initiative.

Some other classes of boats are more liberal. If you sail an Etchells 22, Soling, J/24, or offshore boat, you shape these foils to some extent. Of course, consult class rules first. The first method described is the most difficult way to shape foils. I start with the hardest method—where you do all the work—because it describes the process well. Fortunately, there are easier ways to shape foils—the easiest of all is to pay someone else to do it! The other methods are also discussed.

First determine the optimum shape for the foils. To do this, measure your keel at 5 percent and 50 percent of its span (see FIGURE 5.13) to determine its depth at these two points. Then use parallel straight edges to measure its maximum thickness at these points. Divide the keel's maximum thickness by its chord length (the keel's horizontal or fore-aft dimension) to calculate its depth ratio. For example, a 4-inch thickness and a 40-inch

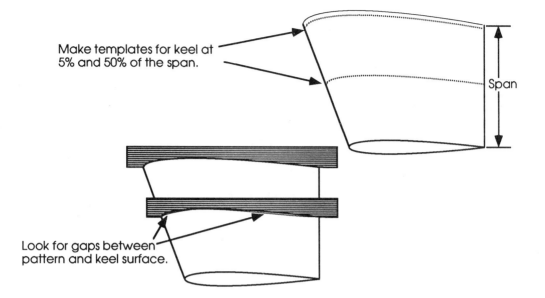

Make templates for keel at 5% and 50% of the span.

Span

Look for gaps between pattern and keel surface.

FIGURE 5.13 *Shaping a keel.*

chord (4/40), yields a depth or width ratio of .1. Expressed as a percentage, this is 10 percent.

To determine the optimum shapes for the foils (depth, draft location, and leading and trailing edge shapes), locate a copy of the book *Theory of Wing Sections*, by Abbott and Von Doenhoff (New York, 1949), available in most engineering libraries. Listed are NACA foil sections.[5] Find the numbers that correspond to the keel depth at 5 percent down from the top and at 50 percent from the top. From these numbers, it is possible to construct four templates, corresponding to the long chord at 5 percent, the shorter chord at 50 percent, and leading- and trailing-edge templates.

Then the fun begins: grind and sand the high spots, and fill the low ones accordingly. Your keel must be properly shaped but also symmetrical— the same shape side to side. When through, use epoxy to seal the keel. Be sure to protect your lungs while doing this work. In fact, since the materials and procedures used in such work may be hazardous, consult knowledge-able professionals in the marine field for information about safety before embarking on such a project.

[5]NACA was the acronym for the National Advisory Committee for Aeronautics. Shapes for lift-ing surfaces, as developed and/or tested by NACA, became a standard, first in aeronautics and then in sailing. NACA was eventually folded into NASA.

A better option might be Computer Keels Company, which sells ink-on-Mylar patterns for constructing the templates and will even construct the templates for you.[6] The company offers from eight to ten profiles, and provides a template for every 8 to 16 inches of keel height. Included are keel and some rudder templates for such popular boats as the J/24 and the rest of the popular J family, the Catalina 27, New York 36, etc.

Next, the grinding down and building up begin. Company principals say you should plan on six separate sessions of several hours. The good news is that once completed, the job is probably done forever.

SPEED DOCTORS

For sailors who lack the time, inclination, or skill to do such a job themselves, there are specialists, sometimes termed speed doctors, who will shape the foils, finish the bottom, set up the deck, even tune the mast. Some of the best-known people in the sport have provided this service from time to time. For example, Dave Curtis, loft manager of North Sails Marblehead, used to do this service on Etchells, through his company Curtis Boats.

As a world champion in the class and a two-time Yachtsman of the Year, Curtis had shapes for the underwater foils he felt were fastest. These came, he says, from trial and error. He then developed his own templates, which fit within the class tolerances. He describes the optimum Etchells keel as fine in the back, full forward, with maximum thickness in the middle. The boat that came from the factory had, he said, a thicker trailing edge and a fine leading edge, and the keel had its maximum thickness farther forward.

The service Curtis provided would add 10 to 15 percent to the cost of a boat. An Etchells with trailer and sails costs about $35,000 today. There is a rumor that one well-known Etchells sailor has a tricked-up Etchells, courtesy of a speed doctor, that cost $80,000. By way of comparison, I paid $12,000 for the Etchells that I sail in San Diego.

This tricked-up Etchells is used in San Diego, and the salient feature, at least according to the rumor mill, is that it has a minimum-weight keel. That's acceptable in San Diego, because there is little wind and, thus, the boat doesn't heel that much. In Perth and San Francisco Bay, however, where I recently sailed the 1990 and 1991 Worlds, respectively, it wouldn't

---

[6]Contact Computer Keels Company, P.O. Box 35757, Edina, MN 55435 (612) 829-5670.

be any good. This San Diego Etchells is the one-design equivalent of a "horse for the course" (see Chapter 2).

Curtis is no longer doing this work; who does it and more important, who does it well, vary over time. This speaks for going to regattas or chatting with the boatbuilder, manufacturer, or sailmaker to find out which speed doctor is hot in what class.

PRACTICE MAKES IMPROVEMENT

Pete Bennett was a journeyman sailmaker; he had been a sailmaker all his life. He started, I believe, at Murphy & Nye. When I met him, he was working for Lowell North, at his San Diego loft. Bennett was the best sailmaker I ever knew; he was even better than Lowell North, who didn't become a sailmaker until he was thirty.

Bennett was also a gifted sailboat racer; in the Star Class, he was almost on the same level as North and Malin Burnham. He won races in the Worlds. When I was coming up, Bennett, although several years my senior, was very important to me. He was, in some ways, my own private sailmaker. He and I used to test new ideas; we'd spend hours and hours testing sails on the water. Bennett tested sails because sailmaking was his livelihood. He did it with me because he liked me. Despite the difference in our ages, we were friends. I did it because I loved doing it. What I brought to the relationship was my attitude more than my ideas. I had the time, energy, and enthusiasm to help him develop better sails.

My pay back was considerable. I always had the best sails before anyone else did. As important, I knew how to use them. Some of the things we developed were extravagant. For example, rather than putting tape on the leech seam, Bennett would finish it off with a hot knife. This would melt and seal the polyester fabric, making for a smoother sail as the wind didn't have to jump over the little bump at the back of the sail. Without a tape, however, the sail's useful life was sorely limited. In time, the leech would get loose and start to flutter. Normally, sailmakers put a leech cord to quiet this motion, which wasn't possible without a fold in the cloth. A responsible sailmaker wouldn't do this with a customer's sail, but as a sailmaker, Bennett could afford to do it. I was often the beneficiary of such experiments. Also, I didn't have to pay as much for the sails, which was important because I had no money at the time.

Another thing he did was to put some extra reinforcing on the leech. In a Star, as in most classes, class rules limit the number of battens. Bennett put some extra material at the leech, to give the sail some added stability. It amounted to extra battens, but he made the case that the material kept the sail from tearing.

As our relationship progressed, sometimes I'd suggest things. He'd try some of them, and if one worked, he'd adopt it and sometimes he wouldn't, though it might have been a good idea. Bennett gave me the innovations, and let me have an edge. He didn't consider me a threat on the race course. He thought he could beat me. He could, too, particularly when I was young.

Better and cheaper sails weren't all I got out of the relationship, however. The sails were transitory, but the testing helped me to develop an eye for proper sail shape and gave me an opportunity to work on my boat speed.

Such practice made me a better sailor. Racing against Pete Bennett was like having a skilled sparring partner. Our time on the water and what I got out of it became the basis of my philosophy of "bludgeoning a problem to death."

To this day, I love to sail, and, thus, I love testing. To me, the two are the same. In a two-boat America's Cup program, Jack Sutphen, my long-time trial-horse skipper, and I will test one genoa for an hour straight to see if a particular sail design is faster than another. Or, when testing two identical sails, we want to know if one is faster when trimmed differently than the other. Not everyone shares our enthusiasm for testing, however. On starboard tack, the starboard-genoa tailer has nothing to do. On my boat, he'll be studying sail shape, or at least pretending to. On Jack's boat I've seen the starboard tailer dozing off. Jack pretends not to notice. He recognizes it's hard to keep everyone engaged all the time.

DETERMINING FAST SETTINGS

Earlier, I commented how you should code everything that moves. That includes backstay tension, halyards, sheet leads, traveler, etc. This coding allows you to develop and then to repeat fast settings. Then you should test these settings against another boat or boats, either in dedicated practice sessions or in a regatta. You probably don't want to do this in the season championship or when leading a race. But during less important races or when doing poorly, try easing the traveler a bit from the standard setting. If, as a result, you go faster in certain wind strengths, then maybe that should be the new standard setting. If, however, you're fast compared with the competition, don't change the standard—don't fiddle with boat speed for the sake of fiddling—but if you're slow, it's usually time to start changing things. Remember also that sails stretch and high-tech Mylar and Kevlar sails shrink, so standard settings will change, too. Try not to change more than one variable at a time, however; otherwise you can't be certain what caused the improvement.

If you sail an offshore boat and don't have a partner willing to test with you, you can test against target boat speeds for your design, provided by the yacht designer, private sources, or in this country by the United States Sailing Association (formerly United States Yacht Racing Union, or USYRU), which through its IMS VPP has target boat speeds, for eight hundred standard hulls (see Chapter 7). While not the best way to test settings, it can prove helpful.

RUNNING A PROPER TEST

1. Sail against an identical boat or one that is as similar as possible. It is probably a good idea that the crews be of similar abilities, too. A much better helmsman, for example, can easily invalidate a test.

2. Decide what you will be testing; the crews of both boats should be aware of it.

3. Line up properly: When sailing upwind, the two boats should be about two boat lengths apart and even, and with unobstructed air to windward. When sailing downwind, again line up two boat lengths apart. Make sure, however, that both boats have clear air behind them.

4. Before starting the test, sail together to see if one boat is faster than the other. Try to determine the difference. Say, for example, the white boat gains one boat length in 4 minutes. Use that number to factor in a correction.

5. Then one boat adjusts whatever is being tested. The other boat should not change anything.

6. Stop the test when one boat is clearly ahead. Remember, a wind shift of more than 10 degrees will likely invalidate the test, as will too much lateral separation between the boats.

7. Communicate with the other crew. If both boats agree a change was beneficial, it likely was.

6 | Crew and Crewing

For the 1980 America's Cup, I was named skipper of *Freedom*. I recognized that a crucial piece of the America's Cup puzzle would be the skipper of the trial horse—the sailing equivalent of a sparring partner in boxing or a batting-practice pitcher in baseball. As explained, the best way to improve, I believe, is to sail against another boat, a trial horse. Though the skipper of the trial horse is a very important position to me, it isn't the most glamorous job on the waterfront.

I had the names of about a half-dozen people who, I thought, might be good in the role. One was Tom Whidden, a young sailmaker from Connecticut. What impressed me about Whidden was that he had done a very good job with the boats he had, which were fairly ordinary. I also heard he was a good guy and a team player. I was interested because talent and loyalty are what I prize most in people.

I looked for Whidden during the 1979 Southern Ocean Racing Conference (SORC), which at this stage was in Miami. I introduced myself and told him I wanted to discuss my plans for the America's Cup. He was agreeable to such a conversation; however, he was on his way to the airport to fly home to Connecticut. I told him I'd come along for the ride to the airport if he didn't mind.

At the airport, I wanted to continue the conversation, so I asked if it would be all right if I flew with him to Connecticut. By now, Whidden was perplexed. He knew I had no other business or reason to go to Connecticut. He asked, "What will you do when you get there?" I told him, "I'll go home with you. . . . " On the flight north, I talked him into being skipper of my trial horse. With this most important position secured, I got off the airplane in Hartford and flew back to Florida.

Tom Whidden, now president of North Sails Group Inc., has been with me through every America's Cup, since 1980. True to his ability to make the most out of whatever he's given, Tom graduated from the trial horse, *Enterprise,* to sail on *Freedom,* the first-string yacht in 1980. In 1983, he sailed with me on *Liberty,* as tactician, when we lost the Cup. In 1986–87, he sailed in that slot on *Stars & Stripes '87,* in Western Australia, when we regained the Cup. In 1988, he sailed on the catamaran and sailed with me in the 1992 Cup. In all this time together—through the wins and the losses—he has become my best friend.

I tell this story for several reasons. One is because, intuitively, I figured out that it was important to follow Tom Whidden to Connecticut. I don't follow people to Connecticut very often, but I'd go almost anywhere to attract the right people to my program. Staffing has been one of my gifts. I wish I could tell you how it works other than to say that I trust my instincts about people.

Unless you sail a Laser or a Finn, yachting is a team sport. It is hard for a skipper to be much better than the people who surround him or her. There's a saying in the sport that skippers win races, crews lose them. I don't buy it. If you want to win on the race course or in the course of life, I think you should put considerable effort in recruiting the right people.

In an America's Cup campaign, we will sift through a couple hundred applications to fill about sixteen slots. With so many people willing to answer the call, it might be easy for us to get cynical or careless about the process. However, selecting crew is important. The other factors are keeping and properly using the people you've recruited. A large measure of my success can be traced to how I've handled these responsibilities. They are the focus of this chapter.

Having won the America's Cup three times, I can easily attract the right people to the program. Once upon a time, however, I hadn't skippered a winning America's Cup yacht. Nevertheless, I'd get on the telephone and ask Lowell North, Ben Mitchell, the noted navigator, or Ted Hood to sail with me. I figured, Why not start at the top? The worst thing they could say was no. I've never been one who believed a no could kill you.

Often, however, they said yes, and I trace much of my success to such yeses. Can you do what I've done? The answer is yes. I'm a salesman, and I use the so-called tools of this trade in recruiting crew. You must sell your program, be it a cruise to Bermuda, the Etchells 22 Worlds, or the America's Cup. At the risk of sounding trivial, a significant part of life is successful recruiting.

JOBS ON A SAILBOAT

The jobs on a sailboat can be loosely labeled skipper, steerer, tactician, navigator, mainsail trimmer, headsail trimmer(s), bowman, mastman/sewerman, pitman, and grinder(s).[1] This order of players also represents a common, if not universal, hierarchy on boats. Large boats may have a few of each, such as, grinders. Smaller crews on smaller boats obviously wear several hats. Labor-saving devices on cruising sailboats, such as roller-furling and roller-reefing devices, Stoway and Stoway-like masts, and self-tailing winches focus on reducing the number of jobs as well as the work load of the remaining ones.

Let's describe the roles separately and, in some cases, give some noteworthy examples. (The helmsperson is omitted in this discussion because this is the subject of Chapter 7.) Next, we'll describe how the jobs fit together when tacking, changing headsails, roller-reefing, mainsail jiffy-reefing, reefing with Stoway and similar masts, spinnaker sets (both cruising and racing), jibing, and dousing spinnakers.

Skipper

The skipper is the chief executive officer. Sometimes, he or she is the steerer; at other times, not. A major job, as described, is recruiting crew.

As I've said many times, when recruiting crew, my main concern is attitude. I don't look for the biggest, strongest, or most experienced person, but the one with the best attitude. Can this person take orders, not collapse under pressure, and make a complete and total commitment to the program? In an America's Cup program, I look for a person who's a team player: the captain of the football team, or a rower. Rowers are perfect. They go out at four in the morning, in the dark and cold and row until their hearts break. No one is cheering for them.

I demand a total "commitment to the commitment." I've used this line so much that it is parodied both within and outside the program. In truth, this commitment comes naturally to me. When I crewed for Gerry Bill on *Dolphin,* or Carl Eichenlaub or Alan Raffee in *Lightnings,* or Ash Bown on *Carousel,* I couldn't do enough. The more there was to do, the

---

[1]An attempt has been made throughout this book to avoid male-female stereotypes. In this chapter, however, we use pitman and sewerman, etc., since pitperson and sewerperson sound awkward.

happier I was. To me, this wasn't work; it was an ultimate pleasure.

The skipper is also responsible for working out crew schedules. Furthermore, it is the skipper's responsibility to go over, or see that someone goes over, the race instructions provided by the race committee before a race. Similarly, the skipper, or someone the skipper assigns, should check for sail limitations, if there are any. Also, this person should be sure that the boat is ready to race or to cruise.

Tactician

The tactician's primary job is strategy: where to go on the race course, in view of weather, competition, current, and course, etc. He or she should act as the steerer's eyes and ears. The tactician also has to motivate the crew and be a cheerleader for everyone. The tactician should be able to make quick decisions—think on his or her feet. The tactician must also be thick-skinned. This person should also be an extra set of hands, for example, operating the running backstays, if the boat has them.

In my first America's Cup in 1974, I was tactician as well as starting helmsman for Ted Hood, the famous sailmaker, on *Courageous*, following the demise of my ride, *Mariner*. On September 2, Labor Day, *Courageous* and *Intrepid* were deadlocked. In this, the last round of the defense trials, each boat had won four races in their matches against each other, although *Intrepid* led for the summer 11–8. It seemed certain that the New York Yacht Club's Selection Committee would name a defender at the end of this day. The day was made for drama. It was blowing 25 knots. Prior to Perth in 1986–87, America's Cup yachts never sailed in such winds unless caught out in them by accident.

Courageous started the summer with Hood sails, but by August changed over to mostly North sails. The new boat seemed faster with them. Before the start of this final race, Hood called for a Hood mainsail, rather than the North. Not only was the sail made by his company, but it was seven years old. It was also a light-air main—an unlikely choice since it was blowing 25 knots.

New York Yacht Club Vice-Commodore Robert McCullough ran the *Courageous* syndicate. He is an imposing man, to be sure. When McCullough saw the Hood mainsail, rather than the North, go up, he got on the radio. As tactician, I worked the radio. He said, "This is Commodore McCullough. Don't you think we ought to be getting the North sail on?" McCullough was trying to be polite and calm, despite the pressures of the moment. Ted said, "I need to look at this sail a little longer." McCullough called three times with the same request. The last call wasn't a request; it was a direct order to change to the North main. I relayed it to Ted. He said, "You tell Bob I'm skipper, and I'm going with what we've got up." Into the radio, I said, "This is *Courageous,* and Ted says we're going to use the sail we have up. *Courageous* out!"

Not only did Hood use his sail, but he started the boat. This was supposed to be my job, but I wasn't hurt and didn't withdraw. I felt Hood was the right man for the job in these particular circumstances. He was older and had far more experience sailing 12-Meters. As a sailmaker and sailor, Hood had been an integral part of the America's Cup since 1958. I'd never sailed on a 12-Meter when it was that rough before.

While not hurt, I wasn't decisive either in the subsequent call. I had the feeling we were late going for the starting line, but I wasn't going to tell that to Ted Hood. *Intrepid* was equally far away. If I was driving, I would have been going for it. In essence, saying to the other guy, You chase me up there. We were a minute late, as it turned out. Nevertheless, I didn't have enough confidence to speak up. I was the new kid on the block, in the boat, and in the America's Cup. Also, with Hood being so bold, this wasn't the moment to debate a point of order. In all ways, Hood took command on this fateful day.

This suggests that the tactician's skills and personality must complement the helmsman's. In our time together, Hood didn't do everything I suggested, but he did much of it. He gave me a large role to fill. Hood is such a quiet, introspective guy that it's hard to know what he's thinking. Therefore a tactician for Hood should be an active, up-front verbal person.

Being the tactician for me is different, however. When I have a plan, I tell the crew. When I don't, I tell them that, too. It is probably less interesting to be my tactician than Hood's, unless you know how to work with me, as Tom Whidden, my long-time tactician, does.

Tom's method of persuasion is interesting. When I don't agree with Tom, I pretend not to hear him. When he doesn't agree with me, he doesn't challenge me head-on. He's more obscure. He says, for example, "John Kolius is going over there, so is John Bertrand. I think we're kind of leaving the fleet here, getting over in a corner. Those guys up on our weather hip look like they're getting lifted, sailing in more wind. . . ."

Navigator

Navigation has come a long way since sextants, radio-direction finders, and the matching of sine curves on a primitive Loran-A screen while trying to figure out which are ground waves and which are sky waves. With space-age Loran and GPS, the answer to the question, Where are we? is straight-forward. Today, the navigator's role on a racing boat is more tactical. Indeed, often the tactician, mainsail trimmer, and navigator are one in the same.

We left that last *Courageous-Intrepid* race at the start. The most extra-ordinary and decisive tactical navigation I've ever seen was done by Halsey Herreshoff in that windswept Labor Day race. The wind, as described, was 25 knots with higher gusts. The seas were steep, making for ugly sailing conditions. The visibility was half a mile.

We went off the starting line to weather of *Intrepid*, but behind. Both boats continued on starboard tack. *Intrepid* was sailing faster. As tactician, I was responsible for calling aheads and behinds. I was sure that *Intrepid* would be ahead if she tacked to cross us. The only way we could beat this boat to the first mark was to make *Intrepid* overstand (this tactic is dis-cussed in Chapter 10). I kept asking Halsey how much farther to the lay-line. Using nothing but time and distance and a guess at leeway—a run-ning DR—he said, four minutes, three, and so on. Finally, he said emphati-cally, "We're there!" I was praying he was right, because *Intrepid* hadn't tacked yet. If Halsey was wrong—if we tacked short of the layline—our summer was likely over.

Halsey was, however, supremely confident. He instilled confidence in me, too. After sailing two minutes beyond the layline, I suggested to Hood that we tack. We did. Right away, *Intrepid* tacked, too. We sailed fifteen more minutes without seeing the mark and then, finally, were able to see it ahead and to leeward. We cracked sheets. *Intrepid* had to fall further off wind. We went around the mark with a forty-five-second lead, after being about fifteen seconds behind.

Mainsheet Trimmer

As mentioned in the previous chapter, the main affects both steering and speed. There are nine devices that shape the main and many of them over-lap. Also, mainsail and jib trim affect each other. Most notably, the mainsail causes the jib to sail in more wind and in a lift. The headsail causes the main to sail in less wind and a header.[2] Thus, this person must also take an overview of the sailplan by viewing the sailplan as one continuous wing, not two separate wings, or a biplane.

For the main trimmer, an artist's eye for shape is important. Not everyone can see three-dimensionally, and fewer still can remember three-dimensional shapes. (The difficulty in seeing things three-dimensionally accounted for the development of *New Zealand*'s computer, discussed in Chapter 4.) A mainsail trimmer also needs a critical sense—the ability to recall shapes that were fast in various conditions and duplicate them, using the tools of the trade (mast bend, sheet tension, Cunningham, etc.). It is clear from the above that this is one of the most important positions on a boat. On many boats, the mainsail trimmer is more important to success than the tactician and navigator. As I've said elsewhere, I'd rather be fast than smart.

Since mast bend is so essential to mainsail shape, as well as headsail shape, the mainsail trimmer's responsibilities typically extend to mast bend. As rigs have grown more complex, so, too, has the complexity of this job.

Sail Trimmer

This person trims the headsail and usually the spinnaker. Fine-tune the headsail before fine-tuning the mainsail (see Chapter 4). With a genoa, mast bend is the primary tool for controlling draft position and the amount of draft—particularly with low-stretch Mylar and Kevlar sails. On a main, in addition to mast bend, the outhaul, flattening reef, and Cunningham also control draft position and draft. Thus, the headsail trimmer should have the first word on mast bend as this control is of primary importance to this job. Mast bend is of secondary importance to the main trimmer, so this person shouldn't bend the mast to suit the main only. To put this another way, the sail trimmer is a specialist—interested primarily in the health of the headsail. The main trimmer is a generalist—interested in the health of both the headsail and the main. (Of course, on many boats this person is one and the same.)

Telltales are a primary system of checks and balances for a genoa trimmer. On larger boats, target boat speeds (discussed in the next chapter) are adjuncts or complements to telltales.

On big boats, where you have a selection of sails to choose from, a sail

---

[2]To see how the main and jib have an interactive relationship, start by trimming the two sails properly for upwind sailing. Then overtrim the jib (be careful, however, not to put the jib through the spreaders). If the jib can be trimmed enough, the main will luff.

trimmer should also know when the sail is getting out of its range. Then this crew member either reshapes it for the top end of its range (by easing the jib sheet and moving the lead outboard and aft), or suggests a sail change. Tacking is a major responsibility of the sail trimmer, and thus it helps if this person has good hand-eye coordination and quick reflexes.

Bowman

In a perfect world, the bowman would have the height of basketball-player Manute Bol, the strength of bodybuilder-actor Arnold Schwarzenegger, and the agility and light weight of gymnast Nadia Comaneci. The bowman also needs fabulous hand-eye coordination and must show an imperviousness to weather. This crew member should be able to hang on to a small triangle of real estate—the foredeck—in a confusion of seas and wind.

The bowman is the leader during sail changes and is the key person on spinnaker jibes. The bowman also checks the starting line to make sure you aren't over early. This can be critical, since in an International America's Cup Class yacht, the driver is about 65 feet away from the line.

If something breaks aloft, the bowman, by virtue of his or her light weight and physical prowess, is usually the first one up the mast. One of the most heroic aerial acts I've witnessed occurred shortly before the start of the fifth race of the 1983 America's Cup. On *Liberty*, we were ahead of *Australia II*, 3–1. The wind was about 18 knots, and the seas were lumpy, much bigger than the wind.

While testing sails before the start, John Marshall, our mainsheet trimmer, was pumping up the hydraulic ram, which controls mast bend at the top. He wanted the mast to be straighter there. Marshall was distracted and the wrong valve was opened, so rather than pumping the ram on the windward side at the top of the mast, he was pumping the one on the leeward side. Nothing was changing at the top of the mast, so he kept pumping. I tacked the boat. When the sail filled on the other side, the ram, now fully extended, broke.

We hoisted Scott Vogel, our foredeck man, and Tom Rich, to the top of the mast to make the repair. We didn't have a replacement part aboard *Liberty* or on the tender. Thus, our high-speed chase boat, *Rhonda*, had to go to shore to get it. Scott and Tom, nearly 100 feet off the deck, were taking a terrible beating. The only direction that was comparatively kind to them was downwind, but that was taking us away from the line at 9 knots and away from the start of the race.

To protect them, we ended up going downwind. To slow down, we trimmed the main to the centerline, stalling it, and put the trim tab (a second rudder on the keel) in one direction and the rudder in the other. This braking action made the best of a very bad situation. To complicate things further, the spare part that came out on *Rhonda* was 2 inches longer than the original. When ordering parts, we always specified spares. For some unknown reason, the spare part shipped with the original was not of the same size. Like a time bomb, it just sat in the container waiting to explode.

With the mast making awful circles in the sky, Vogel and Rich spent forty-five minutes almost 100 feet in the air replacing the fitting. They had enough to do just trying to hang on, but these two had to do that while making a fairly complex rigging repair with an America's Cup race looming. We got back to the starting line moments before the ten-minute gun. These two crew members had little left to give. When we came together with *Australia II,* we didn't even have a headsail up. John Bertrand, the Aussie skipper, engaged us immediately. I don't blame him; with a weakened opponent, I would have done the same thing. One more loss for *Australia II,* and their summer, which had been so glorious to this point, would have been over.

As we struggled to get the headsail up while heading downwind with *Australia II,* the luff tape on our sail ripped. The crew responded heroically to get a replacement sail up. I managed to drive Bertrand down to the leeward end of the line. He was over early by two seconds. By the time he sorted himself out, we had a commanding thirty-seven-second lead. However, four minutes into the race, the new ram, which was too long, broke. The mast sagged ominously. *Australia II* led at the first mark by twenty-three seconds and won the race by forty-seven.

That was likely the most frustrating moment of my sailing career, indeed my life. I still have "if only" dreams about that race. The broken ram was the first significant mechanical failure of the summer.

Mastman/Sewerman

This person—it is usually one person—is responsible for the halyards and bringing the proper sails up from below. The mastman's primary job is raising the halyards. Thus, height is important. If you're six feet, six inches tall and have an arm length of five feet, you can grab six or seven feet of halyard in a pull. That means it takes eight pulls to get a sail up a mast that it is 55 feet long. If, however, you're five feet, six inches, it is likely to take eleven pulls or more.

In addition to requiring height and wingspan, this crew member also needs the strength to raise the halyard without a winch. A good mastman can pull a jib halyard to the top of a 100-foot mast without benefit of a winch. That said, this is not the recommended procedure. A halyard not secured by a winch can be dangerous.

Height and strength are also important to the other half of this job. The so-called sewerman must drag the big and often heavy headsails, as well as spinnakers, and staysails up from below. A headsail on a Maxi can weigh 100 pounds or more when wet. The "sewer" designation has to do with the seawater that often slops through hatches into this crew member's working area below decks. This person also should have a strong stomach, as some cannot stand the typically stuffy below-decks working environment.

Part of the sewerman's job is to be familiar with every sail in the inventory and to select the correct one. Anticipation is extremely important, too. If the sail you want is under ten others, finding it and freeing it are going to add considerable time to a sail change. In fact, we discovered what took the longest time in a sail change was simply finding the correct sail and bringing it up on deck from below. If the sail had been on the top of the pile and close to the hatch, valuable seconds could be saved. The sewerman is also responsible for packing spinnakers and bagging headsails.

Pitman

On an America's Cup boat, the pitman is a separate position. On smaller boats, the mastman, sewerman, and pitman may be the same person. The latter designation has to do with this person's working area on a 12-Meter or an IACC boat, in a small cockpit behind the mast. There the pitman works the halyards from the perspective of sail trim. This person also works the topping lift of the spinnaker pole on jibes. On a dip-pole jibe, the pole should clear the forestay and come out on the other side in one continuous arc, stopping only for an instant as the bowman snaps in the lazy guy. From the position behind the mast, the pitman also monitors mast bend.

Grinders

The heavy work on a sailboat is done by the grinders. Here strength, size, endurance, and coordination are key. On an America's Cup boat, these people are the linemen: the offensive center and tackles.

BASIC MANEUVERS

Now that we have discussed the pieces, let's see how they fit together on a racing or cruising boat in the basic maneuvers: tacking, sail changes (both leeward and tack changes), roller-reefing, jiffy-reefing, reefing the Stoway and similar masts, reefing with the Stoboom and similar booms, packing the spinnaker, spinnaker sets, spinnaker jibes, and spinnaker douses.

Tacking

Though tacking is an essential part of sailing, most sailors don't give it much thought. However, there is a method to the maneuver that can spell the difference between a good tack and bad. If you can out-tack your competition, it can be an offensive weapon, like a better mainsail.

In the third race of the Challengers Finals in Perth, sailed on January 16, 1987, we had a lead at the first mark of twenty-one seconds over *Kiwi Magic*. Our mastman improperly attached the snap shackle of the spinnaker halyard to the sail. It fell into the water, and the Kiwis held the lead at the next mark. On the final 3.25-mile weather leg, we tacked fifty-five times—a record in the America's Cup trials—hoping for a mechanical or human error on the other boat. However, on this day, the Kiwis were as good at tacking as we were. They won the race.

I believe in the technique of visualization when tacking or doing other complex maneuvers. I try to get my crew to think about doing the perfect tack or jibe: think about their job, the jobs of the others, how all the pieces fit together, and how good they'll feel when they get it right.

Proper tacking works this way:

1. First, the helmsperson should get the boat up to speed. If you use target boat speeds (discussed in the next chapter), don't tack, if possible, until your boat is at the target speed.

2. The sail trimmer, or a grinder, flakes (clears), the loaded genoa sheet so it won't foul during the maneuver. On big boats, be certain that the primary winch is in its proper gear. Put the wraps on the winch—not too many that the sheet will foul or too few that it will not hold when under load. (If the sheet runs the wrong way, a finger can get trapped in a winch, which is extremely dangerous. So take more wraps in heavy air, fewer in light air.) Also, take out the slack in the windward sheet. If you use runners, take the slack out of the leeward runner.

3. Accelerate into the tack by having the mainsail trimmer pull up the traveler, which increases the mainsail's angle of attack (see FIGURE 4.12).

4. The sail trimmer or grinder should cast off the loaded sheet an instant before the luff of the headsail breaks. Precise timing of the release requires practice as well as a sense of the bow's angle to the wind and the speed of the turn.

5. Clear the genoa through the foretriangle. On boats over 45 feet or so, a tacking line can help to do this. A tacking line begins at a ring set into the middle of the foot of the headsail and then runs to the bow, and finally leads back along the deck to the mastman or pitman. (A foreguy can also serve as a tacking line.) The pitman or mastman trims the line as the sail begins to move through the foretriangle—in essence decreasing the size of the sail that must pass through the foretriangle—and eases the line once the sail is through. Note that improper timing can rip the sail.

6. With a small boat, the rate of turn is controlled by the helmsperson. The helmsperson should start the turn slowly and then speed it up when the boat reaches head to wind. With a large boat, however, you should be in slightly less of a hurry to get to the other side of the tack. Use the boat's inertia to take a little bite into the wind in the midst of a tack. As the boom starts to swing, grind the new windward runner, then ease the other.

7. The grinder(s) grind, the sail trimmer trims the sheet—and tells the grinders when to stop—and the foredeckman, or mastman, can take hold of the sheet and run aft with it if the boat is large enough to merit that kind of assistance. As loads build up on the sheet, the grinders shift winch gears—either by pressing a button or by changing the direction in which the winch is turned.

8. The bowman or mastman skirts the headsail's foot over the lifelines, if you have them.

9. The mainsail trimmer eases the traveler while the genoa is trimmed.

10. As speed builds, the sail trimmer trims the genoa the last few inches and checks for leech flutter, correcting it with the leech line. The helmsperson who has been footing off to aid acceleration comes up to the proper course.

11. The main trimmer raises the traveler to the proper spot.

12. The cockpit crew prepares the unloaded (windward) sheet for the next tack.

Roll Tacking

Roll tacking is used in smaller boats. Here the crew's body weight complements rudder action. Roll tacking isn't appropriate in larger boats as body weight has less of an impact on heel and thus turning speed than it does in smaller boats. Roll tacking works this way:

1. The boat is on port tack, for example, with the crew on the port, or weather rail. The boat is steered into the wind with the rudder, while the crew stays on the rail.

2. Once the boat reaches head to wind, the crew hikes hard (still on the port side), heeling the boat to port. The boat is, thus, "rolled" to port in this case—therefore the name.

3. Just before the backsides of the crew touch the water, they quickly move to the other side and flatten the boat through hiking. If the crew is too slow in moving to the other side, more than just their backsides may get wet.

Rule 54.3 of the International Yacht Racing Union (IYRU) Rules addresses limitations on kinetics, which includes roll-tacking. This rule describes what crews can do with their bodies to propel sailboats and what they cannot do. Roll-tacking is permitted if you don't come out of the tack faster than you went into it.

GENOA CHANGES

In small boats, it is common to have headsails that are hanked on the forestay. Larger cruising boats will often have a roller-furling and roller-reefing headsail. Big boats used for racing usually employ a double-grooved headstay to facilitate headsail changes. An advantage of a double-groove system is that the boat doesn't need to go "bare-headed" during sail changes, which a hanked system requires.

Racing boats typically change such headsails one of two ways: by a tack change or by a leeward set. A tack set is easier, as the "old" sail controls the "new" sail before the tack.[3] Then, the new sail controls the old after the tack. However, conditions, tactics, or which groove (port or starboard) the sail is in can make a tack change undesirable or impossible.

Before describing the two types of sail changes, a couple notes are appropriate: If close to the mark, you might want to forego the change, since the risks of a "fire drill" on the foredeck during a crucial moment in the race may be more costly than continuing to use the wrong sail. I've even resisted changing a partially ripped headsail when near to the mark. I bet that the sail change would be as costly to boat speed and our position in the race as a partially ripped sail. I also bet that the sail wouldn't totally self-destruct. It is a bet I've won on many occasions.

When trying to make a headsail work in winds below its range, you can ease the backstay, increasing the sag of the forestay, or move the jib lead forward, decreasing twist (see FIGURE 4.14). When trying to make a headsail work in winds above its range, ease the sheet and move the lead outboard and aft, increasing twist.

The tack change works this way:

1. The genoa trimmer, steerer, or a member of the afterguard decides to change the headsail and selects the proper size for the wind and wave conditions.

2. The sewerman brings the new sail on deck, typically in a zippered sausage-shaped bag.

3. The pitman flakes or clears the loaded jib halyard, so it will run smoothly when uncleated.

4. The bowman, and pitman if necessary, carry the replacement sail forward, and the bowman carefully secures the sail to the tack and feeds the top of the luff tape into the feeder and groove. It is helpful if the bowman has a knife to clean rough edges from the luff tape, if necessary, so it runs smoothly.

5. The bowman, mastman, or pitman removes the unloaded windward genoa sheet from the clew of the current headsail and ties it to the replacement sail. Alternatively, a third sheet can be used.

6. The sail trimmer adjusts the jib lead on the new side (currently the

---

[3]The "new" and "old" designations have to do with the order in which sails are hoisted, not their age.

boat's windward side) forward or back, and in or out, as is appropriate. (The proper lead position should be marked on the new sail's clew; see Chapter 5.)

7. The bowman checks aloft to make sure the halyard is clear of the old halyard, forestay, etc., and attaches the halyard to the sail. The new sail will be hoisted inside the old.

8. This is a "go, no-go" point, so the mastman or bowman should check with the afterguard before continuing.

9. On command, the mastman raises the halyard. Typically, the halyard is pulled hand over hand until friction builds up. Then the mastman pulls the halyard toward him, while another crew member, using a winch, takes in slack. This action is repeated until the sail is at or near the top. If the friction between sails becomes too great, the sail will have to be winched up the remaining distance.

10. Once the sail is up, the helmsperson initiates the tack.

11. The sail trimmer casts off the old sheet.

12. The sail trimmer trims the new genoa sheet.

13. The mastman uncleats and drops the old genoa halyard.

14. The bowman and pitman help pull the sail down and make sure the dropped sail doesn't fall overboard. It may have to be tied down with sail ties to keep it out of the water.

15. The helmsperson checks the speed after two minutes to determine if speed has improved and if the change was appropriate. If the boat doesn't have a speedometer, this must be done intuitively. Ask yourself, does the boat feel faster? Also look around at the competition and compare your speed to theirs.

16. The windward "lazy" sheet is tied to sail.

17. The cockpit adjusts the windward genoa lead in anticipation of the tack.

18. The bowman and pitman flake the old sail on deck—if possible—bag it, and stow it below. The halyard that is now free is checked to ensure that it isn't fouled aloft. It is cleared, if necessary, then coiled.

Crew and Crewing

185

The leeward change works this way:

1. The genoa trimmer, steerer, or a member of the afterguard decides to change the headsail, and the proper size sail is selected.

2. The sewerman brings the new sail on deck.

3. The pitman flakes (clears) the loaded halyard, so it will run smoothly when released.

4. The pitman brings the unused halyard *to leeward* of the old genoa and checks that it is clear.

5. The bowman, and pitman if necessary, carry the genoa forward. This person carefully secures the tack and feeds it into the feeder and the leeward groove of the head foil. It is helpful if the bowman has a knife to clean rough edges from the luff tape, if necessary, so it runs smoothly.

6. After double-checking that the halyard is clear, the bowman clips it onto the head of the new genoa. If the genoa has a Cunningham, use it to tension the bottom of the old sail. Then release the old sail's tack. This makes it easier to feed the new sail under the old.

7. The new genoa sheet is tied to the clew of the new sail, and the sheet leads are adjusted on both sides of the boat.

8. This is a "go, no-go" point, so the mastman or bowman should check before continuing.

9. Upon command, the mastman raises the halyard.

10. The new genoa sheet is trimmed.

11. The pitman eases the old halyard as the bowman pulls the old sail at the luff.

12. The helmsperson checks speed after two minutes to determine if speed has improved, and if the change was appropriate. Without instruments, this must be done intuitively.

13. A free crew member ties the windward sheet to the sail and adjusts other genoa lead, if it hasn't been done.

14. The bowman and pitman flake the old sail on deck, if possible, and stow it below. The unused halyard is cleared aloft and then its lazy end is coiled.

ROLLER-REEFING OF THE HEADSAIL

Roller-reefing offers many benefits, including increased space below decks (as one needs fewer headsails), reduced costs (again because of fewer sails), and easier sail handling. Also, reefing is typically done from the safety of the cockpit.

These tips can be helpful:

1. Before reefing, tighten the headstay by tightening the backstay adjuster—if your boat allows this—to flatten headsail. This is particularly important if your headsail does not have a foam luff or some other similar luff-shaping device to help flatten the reefed sail.

2. Reef the sail the appropriate amount. Too much sail exposed to the wind, and a boat heels excessively, is uncomfortable, and is difficult to steer, etc. Too little sail, and a boat can be sluggish at the helm and likewise uncomfortable. It is easy to overreef a sail with roller-reefing, as sail area is removed from the foot as well as the luff. To avoid this, have your sailmaker mark, for example, the Number 2 and Number 3 points on the foot of the sail and only reef to these marks. Better still, have your sailmaker add patches—a build up of material—at appropriate reef points on the foot and leech. Then stop when the patches are at the headstay. Sails are stressed when reefed, and such patches can help disperse the load. Some sailmakers will even sew in colored tape at appropriate reef points. Then you can match the genoa lead (see step 4) with identically colored tape.

3. With the sheet eased, but the sail not quite luffing, roll it to the desired size. Keep slight tension on the sheet, but ease it as the sail grows smaller. The sheet tension plus the wind pressure on the sail will help to reduce luff wrinkles. For an even smoother shape, try reefing the sail on a broad reach (rather than close-hauled or head-to-wind).

4. Adjust lead position: In general, move the genoa-lead block forward when the sail is made smaller, or reefed. Move it back when it is unreefed (see Chapter 4 for a complete description of the proper forward-and-aft lead position).

5. A boat shouldn't heel beyond 20 or 30 degrees. Beyond that, the keel is too horizontal to work efficiently, and the heel angle can be too uncomfortable. If reducing sail area in the genoa does not sufficiently depower the boat, reef the main (discussed next).

6. If still overpowered after reefing the headsail and main, hoist a storm jib or heavy-weather staysail on a detachable inner forestay. This is only appropriate if your boat allows this setup, and the mast and deck can handle the increased loads. Then roll up or drop the headsail—whichever is appropriate. Not only does this reduce sail area, but as the headsail moves back, so, too, does the sailplan's center of effort (see FIGURE 7.1). This counteracts lee helm, or the tendency of the bow to be blown away from the wind in storm conditions.

MAINSAIL JIFFY-REEFING

Beyond 20 or 30 degrees of heel, performance suffers. Speed isn't the only consideration, and for comfort or peace of mind, many cruisers prefer less heel. Before reefing the main, try adjusting sail trim as follows: The headsail and main should be flattened as much as possible, and the drafts moved forward. Also, the headsail's lead is moved to an outboard setting (see Chapter 4) to increase twist. Not only does proper sail trim reduce heeling, it improves speed and makes the boat's motion and handling much more pleasant.

Eventually, however, reducing sail area becomes necessary. The question is, Which sail to reef? Most often the correct answer is the headsail. A reef in the main not only reduces sail area, but causes more of the boat's sail area to be located forward. Moving the sail's center of effort forward in this way can upset the balance of the sailplan to the point where the wind can blow the bow to leeward (lee helm). It might even be impossible to sail to weather.

Also, with a 150 percent genoa on a masthead rig, the headsail represents 65 percent of the total area, with the main accounting for 35 percent. A change from a Number 1 (150 percent genoa) to a full-hoist Number 2 (130 percent genoa) accounts for a 9 percent reduction in total sail area. One reef—typically about 20 percent of mainsail area—accounts for only about a 7 percent reduction in total sail area.

Which sail to make smaller is also a function of rig type. Typically, a fractionally rigged boat might have its bigger main reefed earlier than later. A masthead boat might have its smaller main reefed somewhat later than earlier.

As reefing is done less often, many racing boats, particularly Maxis and 50-footers, now have an inshore main with no reef points and an offshore main with one or two. While reef points appear fairly harmless, the patching they require for strength and dispersing the load adds weight and stiffness.

This is particularly costly at the leech, or back, where the sail is the most highly loaded.

At some point, however, the mainsail has to be reefed. When that occurs varies from boat to boat, but these guidelines can be helpful. Reef if the headsail is down to a Number 3 or 4, and the heel angle is more than 20 or 30 degrees (whatever its maximum angle is from the perspective of speed or comfort). Also, reef if the crew has flattened the main and eased the traveler so the front half of the main is backwinding but not flogging. Or reef if the helm has become uncontrollable, or the boat tries to round up even when it is at an acceptable angle of heel.

Nevertheless, a larger headsail and reefed main combination can work when reaching, because with the apparent wind beyond 60 degrees, steering and balance are usually back under control.

Of course, you should reef when you've tried everything else, and the only way to control the boat is to flog the main regularly. Or you should reef for safety reasons.

Jiffy-Reefing

Jiffy-reefing is the method used on most racing boats and on many cruising boats, particularly those with full battens.

Before describing the process, first a caution: There is a man (or woman)-against-the-sea quality to reefing. Everyone likes to participate, feel useful, and get the blood circulating, but on a racing boat, in particular, reefing as a group activity should be avoided. Do it with the minimum number because keeping weight on the weather rail is also very important at such times.

Jiffy reefing goes like this:

1. Make sure all lines are free, and the crew understands their jobs and the sequence. Slow or improper reefing can cause reef lines to tangle, battens to break, or the sail to fatigue through flogging—the flagging back and forth that is the major cause of sail failure. An important note: If the boat doesn't have a vang that lifts or supports the boom when the crew eases the halyard, snug the topping lift, which supports the boom. Otherwise, the boom can fall on someone. If there is a leeward running backstay, ease it sufficiently so the sail doesn't beat against it when the sail is allowed to luff. If the vang doesn't support the boom, ease it as well.

2. Ease the mainsheet and lower the halyard to the correct height (see Chapter 5). Recall from Chapter 5 that there are two halyard positions

for every reef point: The first marks where the reef cringle can easily slip over the tack hook. (Proper height is one that permits the luff-reef ring to slip easily over the tack hook at the gooseneck, or positions the tack high enough for a block and tackle to provide further adjustment.) The second position marks the proper halyard tension for the reef point.

Follow the same procedure when reefing downwind. However, rather than easing the sail with the mainsheet, it may be necessary to *trim it* almost to the centerline. Then take a fair amount of tension on the clew-reef line before lowering the halyard.

3. When the new tack is fixed, the crew must strongly re-tension the halyard to the second position (see above). A polyester (Dacron) sail can usually withstand significant overtensioning—evidenced by a large overbend wrinkle. A laminated sail (Mylar, Kevlar, or Spectra) can withstand less, but the crew should stretch it more than might seem appropriate. If the halyard is not tensioned sufficiently, the crew must ease the sheet again and re-tension the halyard. Of course, if tensioned too much, the sail can stretch permanently, which is undesirable. Finding that "sweet spot" requires trial and error. Then mark it when correct.

4. While adjusting the luff, slowly tension the clew-reef line, which tensions the back of the sail. This reduces flogging and keeps the lines from tangling. Be careful, however, not to pull the reef tack away from whoever is trying to fasten it. (Note: Some yachts use a continuous reef line that shortens the luff and leech at the same time.)

Once finished with the tack, or luff of the sail, trim the clew-reef line. Pull it harder than normal to overstretch the foot of the sail. If it seems too difficult to tension the clew-reef line, make sure the line isn't sucking part of the sail into the block. Also check that the vang and sheet are well eased.

5. When finished with the clew, trim the mainsheet. Helm balance should be better, and the boat should be charging ahead rather than laboring. A crew member or two are usually sufficient to see to the remaining tasks.

6. Check sail depth. A reefed main should be very flat, no more than 8 percent deep at any draft stripe (see FIGURE 4.6). If the sail is too full, ease the sheet and increase luff or foot tensions.

7. After reefing, glance up the mast, and make sure the bend isn't extreme and the spar isn't flexing or pumping. In big seas, it is often a good idea to set up an intermediate headstay or ease backstay tension slightly

to reduce mast bend or compression. Also check mast bend from the perspective of sail shape. The amount of mast bend that was correct before reefing is often too much after reefing.

8. General housekeeping is done last. This means coiling loose lines and, if necessary, readjusting the topping lift or vang. Also, neatly tie the reefed part of the sail to the boom.

9. If the reef is going to be in for a long time and/or the conditions are rigorous, it is a good idea to tie a second line through the reef cringle and around the boom. This is a positive way to keep the clew close to the boom.

Reefing with the Stoway Mast

The popular Stoway mast—and masts of this type—are excellent laborsaving devices, particularly when reefing and stowing, or setting the main. Reefing with such a mast is very similar to the technique used with roller-reefing headsails. In fact, Ted Hood holds a patent covering both devices.

Compared with jiffy-reefing, the technique is straightforward:

1. Ease the mainsheet enough so the sail luffs but does not flog violently.

2. Roller-furling rod is then operated. This may work mechanically (with a winch), hydraulically, or electrically.

3. Keep slight tension on the outhaul so the sail furls under tension. It is also helpful if the wind keeps pressure on the luff of the sail. This means on starboard tack roll counterclockwise, and on port, clockwise. The electric Stoway mast has an alarm that sounds if it senses improper furling.

REEFING BOOMS

Reefing masts, discussed above, require compromises in terms of mainsail shape. For example, the sail must be loose-footed, that is, attached to the boom only at the clew. This contributes to induced drag since air will slip between the boom and the foot of the sail. Also, to facilitate reefing, such sails are typically built with concave roaches, which reduce sail area. (Roach is the extra sail area beyond a straight line drawn from head to clew.) Lastly, they don't allow effective battens, as the sail must furl in the mast or on a rod just behind it.[4] Because of this and the popularity of full battens, the Hood Stoboom and other reefing booms are becoming popular, particularly for boats with a P dimension (mainsail luff) of 50 feet or less.

In such systems, the sail winds around a rod within the boom. These systems have advantages. For example, full battens are possible, indeed necessary; the sail is not loose-footed and a fairly big roach is possible; there is no need for lazy jacks, reefing lines, and sail covers; the main stays relatively clean, since hands rarely touch it; and the sail doesn't direct rain water onto the crew in the cockpit, as the bunched sail by the boom in a jiffy-reefing system is wont to do. On the other hand, the mainsail must be cut precisely, or the system may fail to operate. Also, in my opinion, while these systems work well in the daytime, when it is easy to monitor the proper roll of the sail, they are trickier to reef or drop the sail at night, when visibility is limited. Of course, not everyone sails at night.

PACKING SPINNAKERS

This is typically the sewerman's responsibility. Before a race, it should be done ashore on a clean, grassy surface in calm winds. During the race and once a sail has been up, it is typically done aboard the boat. A larger spinnaker might require two crew members or even more to pack it. When packing a spinnaker, I try to imagine how the sail will come out of the bag, and that perspective helps me to pack the sail so it doesn't twist in the bag or upon exposure to the wind.

1. Gather the foot in accordion folds, starting at one clew and moving to the other.

2. Before stuffing the foot in the bag, give some thought to the bag's orientation. For example, is it clipped to the pulpit or life lines? Put the foot into its bag, turtle, bucket, or box, but leave the two clews outside.

3. Working up from one of the clews, gather one leech into accordion folds. Be sure the leech remains untwisted. Put this side in the bag. Keep the head, like the two clews, out of the bag.

4. Gather the other leech.

[4]Furling battens are now available from some manufacturers, but, at this time, must be considered experimental.

5. Once the three sides of the sail are in the bag and untwisted, pack the middle into the bag. You can be more casual about stuffing the belly of the sail into the bag as it is less likely to twist than are the sides. The two clews and head remain outside.

6. Finally, put the head and clews into the bag. Keep them together; even tie them with rotten twine.

Note: On a large boat, the top part of the spinnaker is sometimes girded in rotten twine or rubber bands. Occasionally, the two clews are also stopped with rotten twine or rubber bands. This partial stopping of the two clews of the spinnaker is known as frog-legging. It helps keep the sail from filling prematurely, while it's being hoisted.

Bear-Away Spinnaker Set

When racing, turning marks are most often left to port as they're passed. With marks to port—as will be discussed in Chapter 10—most often boats approach the weather mark on the starboard-tack layline. If the next leg is downwind and the wind hasn't gone right by more than 10 degrees, or if the next leg is a reach, you likely will set the spinnaker after bearing away at the mark; that is, you won't need to jibe before setting the spinnaker. Bearing away at the mark and setting the spinnaker without jibing is known as a bear-away set. (Jibing before setting the spinnaker is known as a jibe-set. The jibe-set will be discussed next.)

A bear-away spinnaker set works this way:

1. The bowman attaches the spinnaker bag to the lifelines, on the lee side or at the pulpit, whichever is appropriate. Small boats often launch the spinnaker from the cockpit.

2. The bowman attaches the sheet and guy to the two clews of the spinnaker. Make sure both are properly shackled and clear of lifelines, etc.

3. The bowman brings the pole forward and sets it on weather side of forestay. The guy is led through the jaws of the pole, and the pole's topping lift is attached.

4. The pitman trims topping lift, tensions the foreguy, and clears genoa halyard for the drop.

5. The cockpit crew gently trims the afterguy to get the clew closer to the end of the pole. So the sail doesn't blow out of the bag prematurely, it is helpful, particularly on larger boats, if the spinnaker's two clews are partially stopped with rotten twine or rubber bands.

6. The bowman, or mastman, attaches the halyard to spinnaker, making sure it is properly secured. Sometimes, the spinnaker halyard shackle is even taped shut. The mastman raises the halyard while the pitman tails it. A spinnaker can fill prematurely so a wrap or two on a halyard winch can prevent the sail from getting out of control.

7. The cockpit crew eases both the main and jib as the boat bears away after the mark.

8. The spinnaker guy is trimmed simultaneously by the cockpit crew.

9. When the halyard is fully hoisted, the spinnaker sheet is trimmed.

10. The mastman or pitman drops the genoa halyard.

11. The foredeckman and pitman help pull the genoa down quickly. A genoa blocking the foretriangle can prevent the spinnaker from filling or cause it to wrap.

12. Both the inboard and outboard end of pole are properly oriented (see Chapter 4).

13. Ease the backstay. Be certain the mainsheet is eased sufficiently and vang tension is correct.

14. Ease the Cunningham and outhaul on main to make the sail deeper and to move the draft aft. This is a more powerful setting.

15. The bowman ties the headsail to the lifelines if this particular sail is likely to be used again. If a change seems likely, bowman flakes and bags the genoa. Remember, however, that weight on the foredeck can hurt boat speed, so this maneuver might be delayed for a while.

JIBE-SET

1. The mastman attaches the spinnaker turtle to the lifelines on the (present) weather side.

2. The bowman and cockpit crew check that guy and sheet are on the

same weather side as spinnaker, and that the guy and sheet aren't fouling the lifeline, pulpit, etc. They should be outside of everything.

3. The bowman runs the guy through the jaws of pole. The pole is placed on the deck under genoa. The pole should be on the (present) leeward side of the forestay.

4. Mastman or pitman loads the halyard and topping lift on winches—if appropriate—and readies the jib halyard for the drop.

5. The bowman or mastman checks that halyards are clear.

6. The bowman attaches the guy and sheet to the proper sides of the spinnaker. Tension the topping lift, but don't hoist the pole. Be sure the weather jib sheet is forward and clear of the topping lift; otherwise you will be unable to jibe the headsail.

7. The helmsman jibes the boat.

8. The main is jibed.

9. The cockpit crew eases loaded genoa sheet and then releases it and trims the other sheet. The bowman helps the jib sheet clear the pole and pole lift.

10. Trim the guy to the end of the pole once the jib sheet has cleared pole. Don't, however, trim it so much that the spinnaker comes out of the bag prematurely.

11. Raise the topping lift.

12. At the same time, the mastman hoists the spinnaker halyard. Better crews will hoist the spinnaker earlier, in the midst of the downwind turn that initiates the jibe. The mastman working the halyard and the helmsman coordinate their respective actions to be sure the spinnaker doesn't blow the wrong way, perhaps causing a twist. If the halyard is ahead of the turn, the mastman slows or even stops the hoist; similarly, if the halyard is ahead of the turn, the helmsman turns the boat more quickly.

13. The guy, sheet, and pole height are adjusted.

14. The genoa is dropped.

15. Ease backstay. Be certain the mainsheet is eased sufficiently, and vang tension is correct.

16. Ease Cunningham and outhaul.

17. Bowman ties the headsail together and to the lifelines if this particular sail is likely to be used again. If a change seems likely, bowman flakes and bags genoa.

Setting the Cruising Spinnaker

Asymmetrical cruising spinnakers are usually hoisted from a sail-sock device. These devices vary, as do the sails, so the manufacturers' instructions for packing and flying should take precedent over the following suggestions, which are general in nature.

1. Secure the cruising spinnaker's tack fitting (on the bottom of the long luff) to the headstay. This is either a strap for a roller-furling headstay or a shackle for a wire headstay. This helps to keep the cruising spinnaker under control.

2. Secure the tack-pennant line to the bow cleat. It is useful to think of the tack-pennant line on an asymmetrical cruising spinnaker as the equivalent to the Cunningham in a mainsail. Pull on the Cunningham, and the draft goes forward and decreases somewhat, diminishing power. Ease the Cunningham and the draft goes aft and increases, increasing power (see step 8). This line can be run through a block at the bow and then aft, allowing easy adjustment from the safety of the cockpit.

3. Lead the cruising spinnaker sheet aft to a snatch block on the boat's stern quarter, passing outboard of all rigging and stanchions.

4. Hoist the cruising spinnaker and sock on the halyard. Be certain both the exit hole at the head of the spinnaker sock and the external control line, which is used to raise and lower the sock, face aft. The less sag there is in the sail and sock, the easier the sock will slide up and down. This can be overdone, however, as it is also important that sufficient space be allowed at the masthead for the hoops and the gathered sleeve.

5. Sail on a broad reach.

6. Pull the external control line to raise the sock. If the hoops that keep the sock open foul on the clew patch, carefully raise the hoops above the patch by hand before operating the control line.

7. When raising the sock, gently sheet in the cruising spinnaker. The sail, now exposed, will gradually fill and help push the hoop to the masthead. (The control line is continuous, and on boats bigger than 40 feet or on any boats in big winds, the bottom of the line should be run through a block and then to a winch. This is to control the sock's speed of ascent. When the sail fills in windy conditions, the spinnaker sock can possibly race upward. Should that happen, a crew member could suffer a rope burn. I've even heard of an example where this caused friction burns on the spinnaker.)

Continue pulling on the control line until the spinnaker sock is at the top. The mastman can walk aft while doing this and, when fully set, can secure the control line to the mast, like a halyard.

8. The height of the tack is determined by the apparent-wind angle (see Chapter 4). When close-reaching, the tack of the sail should be even with the bow pulpit. Ease the sheet until a slight curl develops. When beam-reaching, the tack of the spinnaker should be at the same height as the boom. When running, the tack should be between the boom and the first reef point on the mainsail.

SPINNAKER DIP-POLE JIBE

This is appropriate for large boats. A few years ago, boats bigger than about 25 feet or so would do a dip-pole jibe, and boats smaller than 25 feet would do an end-for-end jibe (discussed later). Now, however, this distinction isn't so clear. Today, even some 40-foot One Tonners are doing end-for-end jibes, as they are faster. Whether to do a dip-pole or end-for-end jibe on boat up to 40 feet now depends on the ability and strength of your crew and the wind speed.

The dip-pole jibe requires a guy and sheet on both sides. This allows the bowman to put an unloaded sheet into the pole. Thus, this person isn't fighting the spinnaker.

A dip-pole jibe works like this:

1. The bowman brings a loop of the (unloaded) lazy guy to the bow of the boat.

2. The pitman raises the inboard end of the pole to its mark (see Chapter 5 where coding is discussed). This allows the outboard end of the pole to clear the forestay.

3. The mainsail trimmer brings the main to the centerline.

4. The helmsman calls trip. The fact that this command comes from the helmsman is important because this person should control the rate of the turn and the maneuver.

5. Lower the topping lift to its mark (also see Chapter 5).

6. The bowman (in pulpit or in front of headstay) pulls the pole toward him or her. A short piece of line can be helpful in this regard. Don't allow the small piece of line, however, to foul in the jaws of the spinnaker pole.

7. Once the pole is on the other side of the forestay, the bowman snaps unloaded lazy guy into jaws at the outboard end of the pole being careful not to twist the line around the pole.

8. Helm steers into jibe. The steerer should try to keep pace with the crew. With a good crew, you can turn the boat relatively quickly; the crew can smartly move the sails from side to side. If the crew is fumbling, then slow the turn down. Note, however, if you jibe too slowly to keep pace with the crew, you go downwind too long. This can prevent the speed from building quickly on the new tack.

9. Jibe the main. Tension the new windward runner, ease the other one.

10. The sail trimmers keep the spinnaker square to the wind by trimming or easing the old guy and old sheet, as is appropriate. You want to keep the sail square to the wind.

11. The pitman raises the pole with the topping lift to its proper position for the wind direction and strength (see Chapter 4).

12. The pitman checks that the inboard end of pole is even with the outboard end—the standard position.

13. The pitman or someone in the cockpit tensions the foreguy.

14. The lazy guy is tensioned to take control of the sail. As the lazy guy is tensioned, the spinnaker sheet on the same side is eased.

15. At first, sail high of the intended course to build speed. Then ease off to optimum course.

JIBING THE CRUISING SPINNAKER

A cruising spinnaker is typically jibed by dousing it—particularly when you sail with a sail-sock device, and it is windy—and then it is raised on the new tack. It is possible, however, in lighter winds to walk the sheet around the forestay, as the boat slowly turns downwind. The sail billows out in front of the boat, but this usually isn't a problem in light winds.

An alternative method is to hoist the sail with an extra sheet on the clew, which is led around the forestay and then to the back of the boat on the weather side. Obviously, the sheets have to be more than double the length of the boat. On the jibe, the old sheet is eased, and the new one is trimmed as the boat slowly turns downwind.

It is helpful to mark both sheets, showing the places to both trim and ease to. Then the crew or even the helmsperson eases the leeward sheet to the predetermined mark. This allows the sail to clear the forestay easily without getting too far in front of the boat. Then this person trims the other sheet to the predetermined mark as the boat completes its turn.

END-FOR-END JIBE

A boat set up for an end-for-end jibe has only one line on each clew of the spinnaker. Also, when a boat is set up for an end-for-end jibe, the topping lift must attach to the center of the pole, and the fittings on the ends of the pole must be the same. For a dip-pole jibe, the topping lift runs to the end of the pole.

An advantage of the end-for-end jibe is that only two lines—rather than four in the dip-pole jibe—are attached to the sail. Two lines are less likely to weigh down a small spinnaker than are four. Also, as discussed, the end-for-end jibe can be faster.

An end-for-end jibe works this way:

1. A jibe on a small boat with a centerboard usually requires that the board be lowered in light and moderate air for stability. In heavy wind, however, it shouldn't go much beyond a third of the way down, as the boat can trip over the board. Different boats, however, behave differently, so if you are unsure, watch the competition.

2. The helmsman turns the boat downwind.

3. The bowman unhooks the inboard end of the pole from the mast. If it

Crew and Crewing

is windy, this can be an adventurous moment. When the spinnaker pole is released from the mast and the other end is still attached to the spinnaker, it can drive the pole back. It's a lot like holding onto a cocked arrow attached to a very long bow string.

4. The bowman affixes the sheet on the leeward side to the end of the pole without releasing the windward sheet. This can be difficult—particularly when it is windy—so ease the (windward) guy forward.

5. Jibe the boat after both lines are in the pole.

6. To jibe a small boat, the helmsman should steer into an S-turn. The timing works like this: the boat is turned off the wind, until the boom swings to the other side. As the boom starts its swing, the helm is turned slightly in the opposite direction. This correction, which should only be for a second or two, keeps the boat from heeling too much on the new board, possibly causing a capsize.

7. The foredeckman removes the old guy—now on the leeward side—from the pole and attaches the pole to the mast. Don't try to muscle the pole and spinnaker to weather (that is, perpendicular to the centerline of the boat), rather push the pole forward toward the headstay. This can give the bowman enough slack to get the pole onto the mast. Additionally or alternatively, the leeward sheet may have to be eased substantially—even to the point of collapsing the sail—to allow the pole to be attached to the mast.

   Note that some spinnaker poles are too short, in view of the length of the spinnaker foot, to keep the sail filled when end-for-ending the pole. Also, sometimes the wind is too strong to risk hooking the pole to both sides of the spinnaker at the same time, as the bowman can't control the sail. An alternative is to take the pole off the mast *and* the spinnaker before the jibe. The pole is removed first from the mast and then from the sail. With the spinnaker flying free, the boat is jibed. The cockpit crew keeps the spinnaker square to the wind with the sheets. The pole is hooked onto the sail's new weather sheet and then onto the mast. Again push the pole forward—of course, keep it on the weather side of the headstay—rather than in the athwartships direction. The sheet may have to be eased, too, to facilitate the hookup.

8. Trim the sheet and guy as appropriate. Tighten the foreguy or lead it under its hook to keep the pole from skying.

Dousing the Racing Spinnaker

1. The pitman makes certain the spinnaker halyard is clear for the drop.

2. The mastman hoists the genoa. It is better to do this early rather than late.

3. The sail trimmer trims the genoa.

4. When abeam of the mark, round up to a reach.

5. Trim main for a beat when boat is abeam of the mark. This helps to steer the bow closer to the wind. At the same time, ease the spinnaker halyard under control. Don't, however, ease the guy or sheet.

6. The cockpit crew gathers the spinnaker. After it is fully under control, ease the sheet first, then the guy.

7. Trim genoa for a beat.

8. Trim main for a beat. The traveler should be up.

9. Clean up so you are able to tack. Make sure the genoa sheets are clear of the spinnaker pole, lifelines, etc.

10. Remember to check mast bend, halyard, Cunningham, and outhaul tension, etc.

Jibe Takedown

An alternative to this is the jibe takedown, commonly done on small boats when moving from a run to a beat but also used on larger boats. The jibe takedown keeps speed up right to the mark. However, if there is a foul-up, it is usually very costly.

1. First, the genoa is raised.

2. The spinnaker pole is taken down, and the spinnaker is flown without a pole. (Err on the side of taking the pole down early rather than late.) Be certain that the spinnaker pole or its topping lift doesn't foul the genoa sheets, as the genoa must be jibed cleanly. (That is a particular trouble spot.)

3. Begin to take the spinnaker down on the leeward side, as is normal.

When the spinnaker is under control and the boat is at the mark, start the jibe. After jibing the mainsail and headsail, the spinnaker drop is completed with the spinnaker now on the weather side of the genoa. The genoa helps control the spinnaker. Then the main and headsail are trimmed for a beat.

DOUSING THE CRUISING SPINNAKER

1. Ease the sheet to collapse the spinnaker.

2. At the same time, pull the sail sock's control line down to snuff the cruising spinnaker. As in raising the sail, the less sag in the sail's luff, the easier this maneuver will be. Lower the spinnaker in the sock.

3. Raise or unfurl the headsail.

7 | Steering

S teering a sailboat upwind is not that difficult, at least in theory. With the sails properly trimmed, the windward telltales on the headsail should flick upward every second or every other second. If you can steer so the telltales do that in a variety of conditions, you'll be in the top one percent of boat drivers.

In smooth water and in enough wind so the sails are pressurized, practically anyone can get the windward telltales flicking every other second. That's one of the reasons why the difference between a good steerer and an ordinary one is least apparent in smooth water and a good breeze. The differences become more pronounced in rough water or when the waves are bigger than the wind—a typical San Diego condition.

Some boats are easier to steer than others. Today's boats, with their high-aspect-ratio foils (sailplans, keels, and rudders) are faster upwind but are more difficult to steer. Lift is quicker to develop around a high-aspect-ratio foil than a low-aspect-ratio one. Combine the accelerated lift of such boats with their deep keels, where ballast is concentrated low—providing a greater righting moment—and you get a boat with a jerky motion. As a result, it is more difficult to keep the boat in a groove, that is, steering relatively straight. This is why some cruising boats still show low-aspect-ratio foils, even a contiguous, or full, keel and rudder, as was popular in the pre-Cal 40 days (see FIGURE 2.3). While slower due to increased wetted surface and induced drag (see Chapter 2), boats with contiguous keels and rudders can be easier to steer. Also, their more robust keels help them resist underwater damage.

HOW SAILBOATS ARE STEERED

Three mechanisms steer: helm, sails, and degree of heel. How the rudder steers a boat is obvious to sailors. Sails and heel are less obvious, however. Sails work this way: To come up into the wind, trim the main and ease the headsail. To fall off, ease the main and trim the headsail. An exercise people sometimes do in small boats is to remove the rudder and steer with the sails alone.

Heel also turns a sailboat by changing the hull's underwater profile. Looking down from above, a boat without heel is symmetrical in the water. The hull generates the same amount of lift on both sides, and the boat steers straight. Then, imagine sailing on port tack in a breeze. The boat heels to starboard, making the starboard side of the hull longer, and the port side shorter. The result of this asymmetry—or unequal lift—is that the boat wants to turn into the wind. This is why the more a boat heels, the more weather helm it develops.

WEATHER HELM AND STEERING

To steer well, the three mechanisms—helm, sails, and heel—must complement, not fight, each other. The easiest way to get them to work together is through the proper amount of weather helm (discussed in Chapters 4 and 5). As you will recall, 3 to 5 degrees—maybe 6 degrees—of weather helm are optimum. (When reaching, more weather helm is acceptable; when running, a neutral helm is desirable.)

Recall from Chapter 2 that the sails, keel (or centerboard), and rudder are lifting surfaces, like an airplane wing. The total forces—the pushes and pulls—in any lifting surface can be reduced to one vector that emanates from one point.[1] In sails, the point the vector comes from is described as the center of effort (CE)—see primary drawing in FIGURE 7.1—in the hull, the vector comes from the center of lateral resistance (CLR).

How the sail and underbody forces line up fore and aft is also important to steering. If the center of effort in the sails and the center of lateral resistance in the keel line up—if CE is directly above CLR—the boat steers straight (see inset A in FIGURE 7.1). If, however, the sails' center of effort is aft of the keel's center of lateral resistance (as in the primary illustration and

---

[1]A vector is a line that shows both the speed by the arrow's length and the direction by its compass orientation.

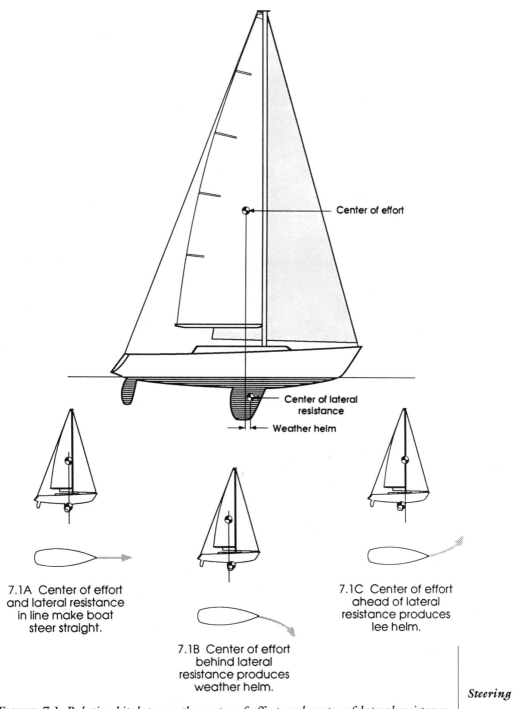

Center of effort

Center of lateral resistance

Weather helm

7.1A Center of effort and lateral resistance in line make boat steer straight.

7.1B Center of effort behind lateral resistance produces weather helm.

7.1C Center of effort ahead of lateral resistance produces lee helm.

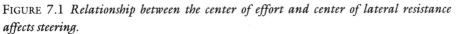

FIGURE 7.1 *Relationship between the center of effort and center of lateral resistance affects steering.*

inset B), the boat turns into the wind unless this action is corrected by the rudder. This is, of course, known as weather helm. If the center of effort of the sails is ahead of the center of lateral resistance of the keel (see inset C), the boat turns away from the wind, unless the action is corrected by the rudder. This is lee helm.

As indicated, this principle is clearly seen in a windsurfer—a rudderless sailboat. To turn into the wind, the rig on the windsurfer is tilted back. This moves the rig's center of effort behind the daggerboard's center of lateral resistance—as in inset B—and the board turns into the wind. To turn away from the wind, the rig is leaned forward, moving the rig's CE in front of the daggerboard's CLR (see inset C). To steer straight, the rig's CE is positioned over the daggerboard's CLR (inset A).

As noted in Chapter 2, a sail develops lift when it is trimmed at an angle to the wind, known as the angle of attack (shown in FIGURE 4.12). Also, a keel gets its angle of attack and, thus, lift from leeway, the difference between the course sailed and the course made good (see FIGURE 2.4).

What about lift from the rudder, however? In Chapter 6, it was mentioned that the headsail causes the main to sail in less wind and a header. The keel, likewise, causes the rudder to sail in slower flow and a very small angle of attack. A rudder on the centerline has little or no angle of attack so it provides only drag, not lift. With 3 to 5 degrees of weather helm—the optimum—the rudder must be turned to counteract this weather helm, that is, to turn the boat off the wind. This turning gives the rudder an angle of attack, too, like a sail or a keel. The angle of attack now provides the rudder with lift as opposed to just drag. The lift from the rudder is now added to the lift from the keel, and this moves the keel's center of lateral resistance aft (see FIGURE 7.1) until this point becomes lined up with the sail's center of effort. The forces are balanced, and as a result of this alignment, the boat steers straight.

With the proper amount of weather helm, you release pressure on the helm, and the boat turns into the wind. With a tug on the tiller or a turn of the wheel, the boat turns off the wind.

When the boat is trimmed so that there's an absence of both weather and lee helm—neutral helm—the boat must be steered up as well as down. This requires a push on the tiller to get the boat up and a pull to get it down, or two turns of a wheel. The result is that steering is much more difficult. At the other extreme, with too much weather helm, the helm must be fought too much. Not only is this exhausting, but turning a rudder too much is like overtrimming a sail. At some point, drag builds faster than lift, meaning the rudder will slow the boat. Also, the rudder can stall—that is, cease to generate lift. This, as we will see later in this chapter, can lead to a broach.

Three to five degrees of weather helm is so important to proper steering that a fundamental question when sailing is, How is the helm? Of course, as shown in FIGURE 5.8, it is important that you mark the wheel or tiller to know precisely how much helm you have.

If the correct amount of helm is the most important item for proper steering, there are other techniques and tricks that can improve your helmsmanship.

PRACTICE MAKES PERFECT

Becoming a good helmsperson is a lot like the old joke about the lost tourist in New York City who asks, "How do I get to Carnegie Hall?" The answer, of course, is "practice." If you have steered a sailboat for two hundred hours, you're going to be better than the person who has steered one for one hundred hours.

I have steered racing sailboats probably more than anyone alive. I'm not particularly proud of that admission, but when it comes to steering, there is no substitute for practice.

STEER FROM THE HIGH SIDE

Steering from the high side, that is, to weather, is better that steering from the low side. In this position, the skipper's weight helps to flatten the boat. Also, I find I can better observe the seas, the horizon, the heel angle, the telltales on the jib, the mainsail, and the other boats (at least those to weather), as well as feel the wind on my face. Steering on the low side is like steering in a cave. Indeed, the only world-class sailor I know who steers from the low side is Ted Hood, whom I sailed with on *Courageous* in 1974.

The one exception to this high-side-steering rule is very light air. Sometimes in drifting conditions, it is helpful to focus on the telltales while sitting on the low side. Such attention to the telltales can get the boat moving and allow the apparent wind to build. Also, in very light winds, low-side weight from the steerer as well as the crew can give the boat some heel, which reduces wetted surface. This leeward heel also increases weather helm—which translates to increased feel or feedback—something you almost can't get too much of in very light winds. Lastly, such leeward heel causes the sails to sag to leeward, giving them some shape. Sails with shape are easier to fill than sails that are flagging.

That exception aside, I think people who steer from the low side become too concerned with the telltales. They tend to sail too high and are at the mercy of waves that they can't see.

THE GROOVE

Earlier I talked about groove. The width of the groove is important to good steering. If there is a 1 or 2 degree difference between the windward tell-

FIGURE 7.2 *Draft location and leading-edge angle of the headsail influence steering.*

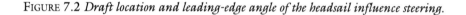

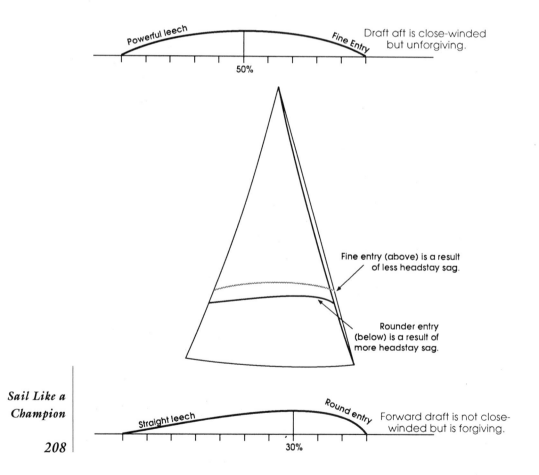

Powerful leech · Fine Entry · Draft aft is close-winded but unforgiving.

50%

Fine entry (above) is a result of less headstay sag.

Rounder entry (below) is a result of more headstay sag.

Straight leech · Round entry · Forward draft is not close-winded but is forgiving.

30%

tales fluttering and the leeward telltales fluttering, the groove is very narrow. On the other extreme, 10 degrees between windward and leeward telltales fluttering is a wide groove.

To compare the narrow groove and the wide groove, the boat with a narrow groove is—at least in skilled hands—closer winded and has a greater top-end speed, but demands precise steering. A small steering error causes the headsail to luff almost instantly, and the luffing extends deep into the belly of the sail. Even an immediate correction of steering and/or trim requires several seconds to get the sail filled again and the boat speed back up. A sail with a narrow groove is most appropriate in smooth water and sufficient wind.

A headsail with the draft aft (50 percent, for example), plus a fine entry or leading-edge angle, has a narrow groove (see FIGURE 7.2, top). To get this draft-aft shape, decrease luff tension with the jib halyard and/or move the genoa's sheet lead forward. To get a fine entry at the same time, straighten the headstay with the backstay or runner (see FIGURE 7.2, center).

A boat with a wide groove, on the other hand, is easier to steer and quicker to accelerate. Lost is 1 or 2 degrees of pointing and .1 or .2 knot of top-end speed. A headsail with the draft forward (30 percent, for example) and round entry will show a wide groove (see FIGURE 7.2, bottom). Such a sail will respond to a little wandering or lack of concentration with a gradual loss of power. Luffing is typically limited to the leading edge of the sail. The sail with the wide groove will also respond to sudden demands for power—as in falling off to accelerate after a tack or after big waves slow the boat—without needing major trim adjustments. This makes the draft-forward round-entry sail a better shape for sailing in waves or in wind chewed up by a competitor's sails. Since the draft-forward sail with a rounder leading edge makes fewer demands on the skill of the driver, this shape is also appropriate at night, when steering is less precise, or for use by cruising sailors who use self-steering devices and sail short-handed.

To get the draft forward in the headsail, increase halyard tension and/or move the genoa lead aft. To get the rounder leading edge at the same time, ease the backstay or runner, which causes the headstay to sag (see FIGURE 7.2, center).

At the top level of the sport, sea conditions and tactical considerations, rather than the skill of the driver, which is assumed to be excellent, dictate the size of the groove. In maximum pointing conditions—good winds and fairly flat seas—a narrow groove is selected with a draft-aft sail and fine entry. This shape is also appropriate in crossing situations—a boat on starboard tack trying to make the port-tacker tack away or duck, or a boat on port tack trying to cross a starboard-tacker. Not everyone can handle a narrow groove, however, so match the size of the groove to the skill of the steerer as well as to the conditions.

ELIMINATING PLAY FROM A STEERING SYSTEM

Imagine turning the wheel of your car and nothing happens for a second or two. In a car, this delayed reaction can be dangerous. In a sailboat, it can be slow. So remove all play from the steering system, be it a tiller or a wheel.

The link between the tiller and its extension can be a trouble spot. This attachment is often just a hole drilled through the tiller and secured with a bolt. Over the years, it loosens—the hole enlarges, and the nut securing the bolt is no longer tight. It rattles back and forth, and the steerer has grown used to it.

Everything in the steering system should be tight, from the extension to the tiller, to the way the tiller attaches to the tiller head. If this requires re-engineering of the extension or tiller, do it in the interest of proper feel.

It is easy to get used to a boat's flaws, like a loose tiller extension. Soon you don't even notice them. To guard against this, it is a good idea to let someone else steer your boat from time to time. This person may notice things you've grown accustomed to, perhaps flaws that are making you slower.

That's not to say you can't live with such imperfections. *Stinger* was a boat I had built for the Southern Ocean Racing Conference (SORC) in an extraordinarily short span of twenty-two days. The shaft, which connected the rudder to the tiller, was too small and rattled around. In this case, we made do. We won the 1975 SORC overall with this boat, but this was done in spite of the faulty steering system, certainly not because of it.

Similarly, with a wheel, you want to reduce the friction of the system and diminish play. If it's a chain-driven system, it's a matter of taking the slack out of the chain and all the attachment points. Don't, however, make the system so tight that the wheel doesn't turn easily. This is a balancing act. In an America's Cup program, we'll spend hours and hours working on the steering system in order to minimize friction and play and increase feel.

WIND INDICATORS

A small boat has maximum feel. On my Star, for example, I could feel a small increase in wind through increased pressure in the tiller, acceleration, and increased heel. Furthermore, I could see the wind pressure increase in the sails. I can probably sail a Star quite well with my eyes closed; just on the feel—the pressure on the helm and the heel of the boat. As long as your crew looks out for you to avoid danger, sailing with your eyes closed can be a useful exercise.

The clues in sailing are subtle, so it is important to heighten your sensory awareness. For example, before a big race or series, I get a short haircut. This allows me to feel the wind better on the back of my neck. Sometimes, I'll let my hairgrow long before a really big series, and then on race day, I'll have it cut short. This way I'm even more sensitive to the feel of the wind.

In drifting conditions, determining wind direction is very difficult and yet very important. Carl Eichenlaub, whom I crewed for in Lightnings as a youngster, claimed that he smoked awful-smelling cigars to find the wind. I think a large part of it was just an excuse to smoke those cigars, but they were helpful in finding the wind.

Speaking of smell, a sense of smell can come in handy, too, in finding wind and steering a sailboat. I've raced down Long Island Sound, for example, in a northerly, off the Connecticut shore. Often the breeze dies with the setting sun. You'll be drifting by Eaton's Neck on the shore of New York's Long Island in a dying or long-gone northerly and smell the power plant to the south of you on the New York shore. That means the wind has gone to the south. Often you'll smell the southerly long before it registers on the sails or on the wind indicator. As a result, you might steer the boat to the south to get the new breeze first. Races are won by such decisive actions.

A large boat, however, provides fewer clues, or feedback, than a small boat. This is why instruments, a speedometer and a wind-speed indicator, for example, are more important on a bigger boat. Those two instruments, which are certainly within the reach of most sailors, can provide a wealth of information. They will be discussed later in this chapter.

SAILING UPWIND IN A SMALL BOAT WITHOUT INSTRUMENTS

At the beginning of the chapter, I said that to sail fast, you should use the telltales. With the sails properly trimmed, the windward telltales on the headsail should flick every other second or every two seconds. Count 1,000, 2,000, flick. That, you may recall from Chapter 4, is the maximum point on the lift-drag curve. If, however, the windward telltales flip more often, you are probably sailing too high, which is known as pinching. Pinching takes you closer to a point upwind, meaning you sail less distance to get there. However, as you are sailing slower, you may take longer to get to the mark.

If the windward telltales never flick, you are probably sailing too low, which is called footing. While sailing faster through the water, you are sailing farther from the mark and, thus, must sail a longer distance. Again, you may take longer to get to the mark. Somewhere between pointing and footing is an optimum course and boat speed. It is important to note that this course or speed varies according to wind speed and boat design.

Also, the shape of a boat's sails can alter how high you sail. As mentioned, with a draft-aft sail, you can sail closer to the wind than you can with a draft-forward sail. Also, the shape of the keel can alter how high you can sail as well as how tight you trim the headsail. For example, some efficient but small keels work well, but only with a lot of flow over them. This means you are better off sailing low and fast to increase flow and, thus, lift. Moreover, on some boats you can't trim the headsail sufficiently (see FIGURE 4.15), because of the width of the spreaders or the deck layout. In such cases, you might as well sail low and fast.

If you sail a small boat or a boat without instruments, watch the competition to decide how high or low to sail in various wind speeds. If you're footing in about 10 knots of breeze and the competition is pointing and seems to be gaining, sail higher. Eventually you'll learn the optimum courses to sail your boat in various wind speeds. Then you'll be able to say, I want the windward telltale to flip every three seconds in 10 knots of wind and every other second in 17 knots. Better yet, practicing against a similar or an identical boat can also help to determine fast settings (this was discussed in Chapter 5).

Although it is impossible to be too specific about sailing a small boat upwind—as there are so many varieties of small boats and so many variables—these additional hints can prove helpful: In general, concentrate on building speed in light air. One of the mistakes to avoid while heading upwind in light air is oversteering—trying to follow the wind too much. Sometimes it is better not to get so greedy on every little puff. You might find yourself flopping onto the other tack or heading into the wind. After a traffic jam on the freeway, people tend to exceed the speed limit. That's why you often see speed traps just beyond traffic jams. Likewise, when you've been starved for wind, it is easy to want to speed—to chase the wind too much. I've been as guilty of such greed as anyone.

In medium air, watch the telltales and make sure the windward telltales are just flicking. This is the 1,000, 2,000, flip technique. The most skilled helmsmen I've seen can get the windward telltale lifting quite often without the boat slowing down.

In heavy winds, sailing fast isn't the problem. Rather, it's often too much wind that causes the boat to heel too much. So try to flatten the sails to minimize drag (see Chapter 4), or change or reef them to decrease weather helm. When it is windy, the windward telltale can be flipping up most of the time.

Also, when sailing upwind when the going is rough, focus on the seas. In rough water, lean toward footing; in smooth water, lean toward pointing.

I consider the action of the seas against my boat as a punch. I try to avoid the big punches—the big square seas. Try to pick the easiest path through the waves. Of course, you shouldn't be sailing all over the ocean or lake to avoid big seas. Also, I try to minimize the effects of the waves. If I were to turn the boat sideways to the wave, the punch could be felt along the entire boat. If I head the bow into the waves, however, the punch is limited to the bow, a much smaller target. To put this more formally: The proper technique for sailing in waves is to head up slightly into the wave (which usually means into the wind, as well) when approaching a wave and fall off the wind as the wave passes. Falling off the wind allows you to build speed for the next wave, which is important. The last thing you want to do is face a big sea without speed.

SAILING DOWNWIND IN A SMALL BOAT WITHOUT INSTRUMENTS

If the difference between high and slow and low and fast is 10 degrees when sailing upwind, the width of the proper steering groove will be 25 degrees when sailing down. (Of course, downwind sailing is the opposite of upwind sailing. When sailing downwind, you sail low but slow toward the mark, or high away from the mark but with good boat speed.) The 25-degree groove is why boats sail so many different jibe angles, or downwind courses, when heading downwind.

To complicate matters further, when running, one lacks consistent weather helm for feedback (the helm should be neutral when running). Also, there is no consistent heel angle. Even the telltales on the sails don't help, because when sailing downwind, the flow on the sails is stalled (telltales need attached flow to work). The pressure in a spinnaker can be a substitute for telltales, but not every one-design boat—a Star, for example—has a spinnaker.

To decide the optimum course—or jibe angle—in a small boat in various winds, again watch the competition. If you're sailing high but fast and the competition is sailing more toward the mark but slow, and appears to be gaining—getting closer to the mark than you are—sail lower. Eventually you'll be able to determine jibe angles in various wind speeds. Then you can use telltales mounted on shrouds (as opposed to sails) or a wind indicator at the top of the mast to repeat optimum jibe angles in various winds.

Most boats have a compass, and many small boats have a boat-speed indicator. With these two common instruments, selecting the proper jibe angle, or optimum downwind course, is fairly easy. To learn jibe angles, start by sailing the compass course to the downwind mark. Note boat speed. Let's say your speed is 5 knots. Then come up 20 degrees. According to the graph in FIGURE 7.3, the speed has to increase 5 percent to break even, or to justify the extra distance sailed. This means if you aren't going faster than 5.25 knots, your progress to the mark—also known as velocity made good

FIGURE 7.3 *How much faster you need to go to justify sailing a higher downwind course.*

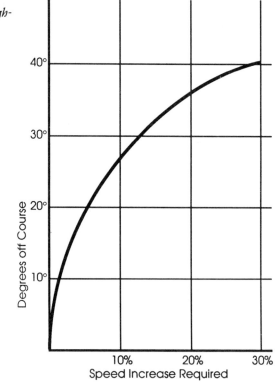

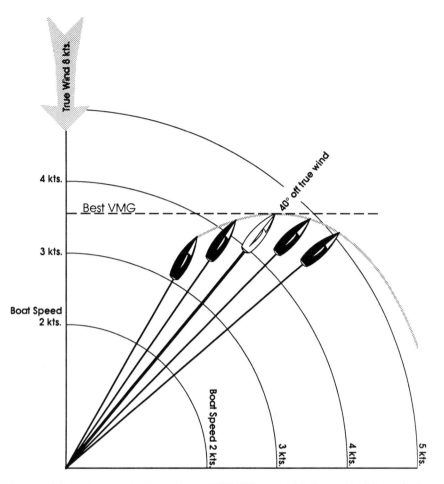

FIGURE 7.4 *Optimum velocity made good (VMG) upwind is determined from the formula boat speed x the cosine of the true-wind angle.*

(VMG)—is slow. To put this another way, you'd be better off sailing low and slow but more directly toward the mark. Similarly, one can purchase an inexpensive plastic course protractor that shows the same information. Like a slide rule, it does the math for you, and being plastic, it is waterproof.

TARGET BOAT SPEEDS UPWIND

A big-boat sailor has the same concerns as the small boat sailor. To mention one: Do I pinch or foot when sailing upwind? Since a big boat is less

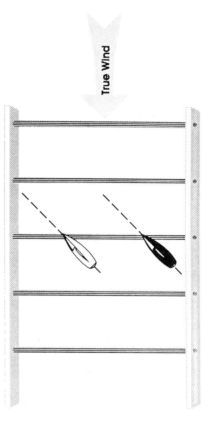

FIGURE 7.5 *Ladder rungs are helpful in visualizing VMG.*

responsive than a small one, big-boat sailors often rely on instruments. For those who sail boats with at least two instruments, with a boat-speed and a wind-speed indicator, the concept of target boat speeds provides a ready answer to the matter of upwind course as well as other similar questions.[2]

On a weather leg (where tacking is necessary to get to the weather mark), a boat can sail one of several courses, or angles to the wind. Again, the choices range from high and slow to low and fast (see FIGURE 7.4). Each of these courses can be evaluated to find the optimum course or speed using velocity made good (VMG) toward the wind. The formula for VMG when sailing upwind is boat speed x cosine of true-wind angle. The higher the

[2]The authors are indebted to Richard McCurdy, president of Ockam Instruments, for this discussion of target boat speeds. McCurdy has been part of our America's Cup team since 1983. Much of this work was developed during America's Cup campaigns during the 1980s.

VMG, the faster you get to a point upwind. Somewhere between low and fast and high and slow is a combination of course and speed that is best for a particular boat sailing in a particular wind strength. This course represents the highest, or optimum, VMG. In FIGURE 7.4, the white boat's course and speed are optimum. To put this another way, white will get to the weather mark first, provided all other factors are equal.

It is helpful to think of VMG in the context of ladder rungs (see FIGURE 7.5). The sides of the ladder are parallel to the wind and the rungs are perpendicular to it. The faster a boat climbs the ladder (when sailing upwind), the better the upwind VMG. Similarly, the faster it climbs down the ladder (when sailing downwind), the better its downwind VMG. (Ladders will be used in the next chapter, in the discussion of wind shifts.)

Upwind VMG can be computed by performing the above trigonometry (boat speed x cosine of true-wind angle).[3] Also, there are instruments that measure VMG, but neither formula nor instrumentation is particularly helpful in terms of figuring the optimum course. This is because VMG is a snapshot; it reflects an instant in time. For example, VMG can be maximized for a few seconds by turning a boat into the wind. The VMG will rise—and look beautiful when measured on an instrument or by performing the trigonometry—but can't be sustained. Soon the boat slows, and speed quickly drops.

TARGET BOAT SPEED

The principle behind target boat speed is that for each wind speed, there is a corresponding boat speed that is optimum. This is the target boat speed.[4] A target boat speed is used this way: If in 8 knots of wind the specified target

---

[3]For downwind VMG, the formula is VMG = Vs x Cosine θ. Vs is vessel speed and θ is the angle away from a dead run.

[4]Obviously, target boat speeds vary from hull to hull and in different wind speeds. The downwind target for a ULDB in 15 knots of wind is very different from that of a 12-Meter in the same wind. (Recall from Chapter 2 that a ULDB has a displacement-length ratio of 60–90, while a 12-Meter shows a ratio of 260.) Targets are developed after measuring a hull and then running it through a computer-driven velocity-prediction program (VPP), discussed in Chapter 2. US SAILING (P.O. Box 209, Newport, RI 02840) offers target boat speeds for more than eight hundred standard hulls. These were computed using the IMS VPP. Usable targets from IMS certificates can be purchased for fees that start at about $10. The organization also offers more sophisticated work-ups, which will be discussed later.

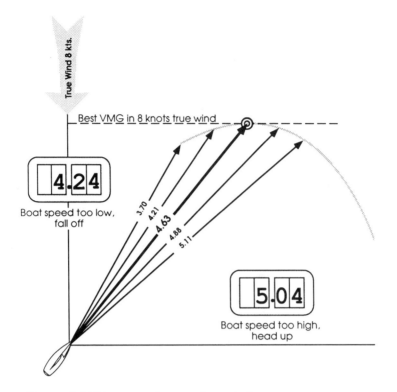

True Wind 8 kts.

Best VMG in 8 knots true wind

4.24

Boat speed too low, fall off

3.70
4.21
4.63
4.88
5.11

5.04

Boat speed too high, head up

FIGURE 7.6 *Using target boat speeds upwind.*

speed for the hull I sail is 4.63 knots (see the thick black line in FIGURE 7.6), and my knotmeter says the boat is going 5.04 knots, I'm going too fast for this wind speed. I'll reach my destination upwind more quickly if I sacrifice some speed for a heading that takes me more directly to windward. Thus, I would come up and point (trim sheets and maybe move the lead back at the same time), until the speed bleeds off to the target. Then I'd head off again before the boat gets too slow and would readjust sail trim.

If, on the other hand, my speed is 4.24 knots, I would fall off (ease sheets) and build speed until reaching my target speed and then would head up before the boat gets too fast. Thus, by focusing on boat speed, which because of momentum is slower to change than apparent-wind angle, we automatically make the proper response to apparent-wind angle. In practice when sailing upwind, I don't even need to know what the optimum sailing angle is; I just know that if I'm slow for this amount of wind, according to the speedometer and wind-speed indicator, I fall off and foot; if fast, I head up and point.

A rule, as noted, is that in rough water you foot and in smooth water, point. Target boat speeds reflect this. In smooth water in 16 knots of breeze, the target for our Puddlejumper 45 is 6.28 knots, for example. In these conditions, it is probably fairly easy to hit the target—even exceed it. Thus, the boat will likely be going too fast for this wind speed, and you'd turn up to bleed off speed until the boat approaches 6.28 knots. The result is that you're pointing in smooth water. In rough water in the same 16 knots of breeze, the target doesn't change; it is still 6.28. The boat would probably have trouble reaching that target in rough water, so you'd foot off to build speed to the 6.28 target. Thus, sail low, or foot, in rough water.

Target Boat Speed Work-up

As mentioned, target boat speeds are an outgrowth of velocity-prediction programs (VPP), discussed in Chapter 2. One of the first sailboat VPPs, you will recall, was done at MIT in 1973 and was used to write the International Measurement System (IMS) Rule.[5] A VPP uses such inputs as the lines of the boat, sail area, righting moment, displacement, and type of propeller to predict the best boat speeds in various winds and at various sailing angles.

This information is often plotted on a polar diagram, a circular graph, which looks like the North or South Pole on a globe—hence the name (see FIGURE 7.7). Wind angles, from beating to running (typically on one tack only), are plotted on the graph's perimeter. Plotted out from the graph's center in semicircles are boat speeds. Then the vectors showing the possible courses (beating, reaching, and running) and related speeds are plotted. Next a line is drawn connecting the tips of the vectors, and the vectors themselves are erased, so the graph is less cluttered.

Sometimes plots of several wind speeds are shown; sometimes only one wind speed is plotted to keep the graph uncluttered and easier to read. FIGURE 7.7 shows several wind speeds, and the bold face curves represent wind speeds of 3, 5, 7, 10, 14, and 20 knots, as read between 120 and 150 degrees. Target boat speeds—the optimum speeds when beating and running as determined by the aforementioned trigonometry—are denoted by the small concentric circles. So, for example, in 10 knots of breeze, the upwind target speed is 5.2 knots. In 20 knots of breeze, it is 6.2 knots. The downwind target in 10 knots of wind is 6 knots, and in 20 knots of wind, it is 8 knots.

As mentioned, US SAILING (formerly the United States Yacht Racing Union), offers target boat speeds in various forms for about 800 standard

---

[5]This was originally called Measurement Handicap System (MHS).

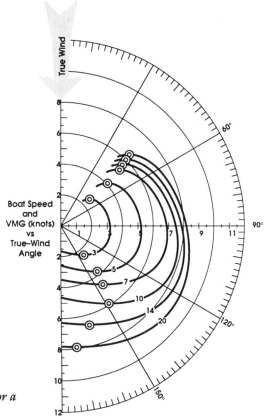

FIGURE 7.7 *Polar diagram for a typical 37-footer.*

hulls. If you have one of these standards hulls—and the likelihood is that you do—you can purchase an IMS certificate at a nominal charge. The certificate shows target speeds for six true-wind speeds and through the entire range of sailing angles. For the cruising sailor, this may be all the information you need.

For the racing sailor, IMS certificates are a good starting point. Much better still is the Performance Package, also from US SAILING. This shows such data as performance graphs for both true and apparent winds and tacking and jibing angles and considerable hydrostatic data about the boat, such as displacement, wetted surface, centers of gravity, pitching, and buoyancy. This hydrostatic data can help to optimize a design, that is, sail your boat better. For those with custom boats or those wishing for more complete hydrostatic information, a private source should be contacted, which will do a custom VPP run on your boat and provide target boat speeds and other useful information.[6]

Don't accept the numbers on faith, but confirm the theoretical targets with on-the-water testing. For example, if the target speeds are too easy to reach or too difficult, adjust them up or down, respectively. Or if you are really serious, try to find out why your boat doesn't measure up. You have to be something of a detective. If you could sail to the targets last year, but can't this year, maybe the rig is tuned differently. Alternatively, maybe your headsail has stretched out of shape. Or maybe your speedometer is off. You might want to adjust your speedometer, but don't get carried away with trying to make the instrument read perfectly.

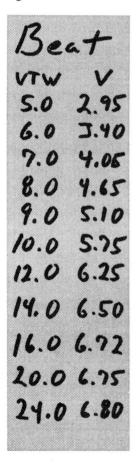

FIGURE 7.8 *Duct tape showing target boat speeds; VTW is true-wind speed, and V is boat speed.*

---

[6]In the United States, Design Systems and Services Inc. does such work for about $450. Contact them at 222 Severn Avenue, Annapolis, MD 21403 (301) 268-5551.

It is, of course, possible to develop your own targets. This requires meticulous record keeping of the three elements: wind angle, wind speed, and boat speed. In an America's Cup program, crews devote hours and hours of testing to develop targets. During the work-up for the 1986–87 Cup with *Stars & Stripes*, we carried along a computer to monitor boat speed, wind speed, and wind angle. Through this process we developed target boat speeds. They were refined and refined again. We did so much testing, that five years later, I can still recall the targets, for wind speeds ranging from 0 to 40 knots.

You can post target boat speeds on a piece of duct tape near the speedometer. (See FIGURE 7.8, where VTW is the velocity of the true wind, and V is boat speed.) Or Design Systems, mentioned in footnote 6, can "burn" the targets on a computer chip (EPROM), which presents targets automatically as an instrument reading for various wind speeds and apparent-wind angles. On *Stars & Stripes*, target boat speed instruments were available for sail trimmers as well as the driver. The instrument would say, for example, –.17, meaning we were .17 of a knot too slow of the target for this much wind. So if sailing upwind, I would fall off until the speed builds to the target, and then come up. The sail trimmers would know we were slow when I did, so they'd be easing and changing the lead as I was heading off to build speed.

UPWIND TARGETS AS A FUNCTION OF WIND SPEED

The graph in FIGURE 7.9 is a different representation of the information found in the polar diagram (see FIGURE 7.7). In FIGURE 7.9, target boat speed is plotted versus true-wind speed. Note that there are three areas: 0–10 knots of wind, 10–14 knots, and 14–24 knots. In the first zone, 0–10 knots, the curve is practically a straight line and very steep. A typical 37-footer will show a target boat speed increase of one-third knot for every knot of true-wind speed. That's a very significant increase, so it is important to pay attention to target boat speed in this area.

Above 14 knots, the curve is also almost a straight line, but it is just about parallel to the horizontal axis. Obviously, target boat speeds increase much less above 14 knots with an increase in wind speed. This is because the boat is at or near its hull speed (see Chapter 2). Near hull speed, the boat can't go much faster; all it can do is point higher. Target boat speeds are less useful in this area.

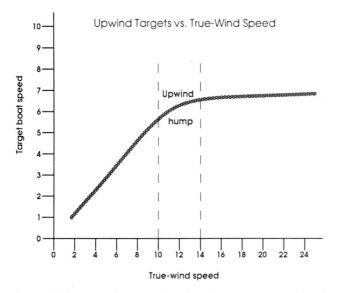

FIGURE 7.9 *Target boat speed is plotted versus true-wind speed.*

Ten to fourteen knots of wind represents a transition zone. This area features what is called an upwind hump. Here, a small difference in wind speed can mean significant variations in targets. Therefore, using target boat speeds in this area is particularly important. This is also the area, or wind-speed band, where most sailing is done.

There are tactical implications to upwind target boat speeds as well. When slow of the target, it isn't a good idea to come up to try to prevent a boat to windward and behind from passing you. It would be better to anticipate this passing attempt and fall off early to build speed, and then come up. Similarly, it often isn't a good idea to try to cross a starboard-tacker when your speed is below the target. If you anticipate a crossing, you might want to fall off and power up. Don't give away too much distance when powering up, however.

VELOCITY HEADER

One of the most difficult calls in sailing is determining the difference between a velocity header and an actual header and a velocity lift and an actual lift (the latter is discussed below). With target boat speeds, there is an improved likelihood of making the correct determination and the appropriate strategic response.

FIGURE 4.9 shows the familiar apparent-wind triangle. If you sail into a wind hole and the wind gets lighter, side TW (true wind) gets shorter. This changes the triangle. If we shorten line TW at the top, line AW (apparent wind) rotates clockwise. This clockwise shift on port tack is felt by the boat as a header. If the true wind hasn't actually shifted or changed direction but only the apparent wind speed has changed due to a drop in wind speed, this is a velocity header. In fact, once the boat loses inertia and slows—side VS gets shorter, too—the apparent-wind direction (AW) will show about the same angle as it did before the velocity change.

Imagine when sailing upwind, you sail into a hole where the wind speed suddenly drops from 9 to 5 knots. Again, a drop in wind speed moves the apparent wind forward. The windward telltales are fluttering and perhaps the jib is luffing—both of which are indicating that it's time to fall off. But should you?

If it's a velocity header, you shouldn't; you should come up. Putting this in the context of target boat speeds: With a velocity header, the likelihood is that you have too much boat speed for the new wind speed. Therefore rather than fall off, according to the telltales, head up. Use your boat's momentum to take a bite to windward—thereby increasing VMG for a time—until the boat slows to the target. Then fall off. If you had immediately fallen off—per the telltales or headsail luff—you would have lost several boat lengths of VMG.

The difficult part, however, is determining if you are in a velocity header or an actual header. To put this another way, has the wind decreased or actually shifted in direction?

To make this determination, there are several things to consider. First ask yourself, Is there less wind on the wind-speed indicator (assuming you have one)? Additionally or alternatively, ask yourself, Does the boat feel as if it has less power, or is it heeling less or are boats around you standing straighter? All of these conditions suggest diminished wind; that is, you're experiencing a velocity header. Also, are you observing what seems to be a small shift—less than 5 degrees—or one that is larger? A small shift can often mean a velocity header, not a real header. A larger shift is likely a real header.

If the shift is small and the wind light, the likelihood is that this is a velocity header. You can be bold and sail high until your boat speed bleeds off to the new target speed, or be conservative and sail straight. If you still don't know whether it is a velocity header or a real header, don't alter course immediately. Not altering course is better than falling off immediately according to the telltales. If it is a real header, however, without a change in wind speed, you should fall off with the telltales.

Note that this alteration of course due to a velocity header or lift (which will be discussed next) is a short-term response. Once your boat speed slows to a point where it is appropriate to the wind speed—side VS is the appropriate length—both the apparent-wind angle and the course steered are about the same as before the velocity header.

Note also that distinguishing between a velocity header and a real header and making the correct response are most important in light winds (0–10) knots. This is because in this region (see FIGURE 7.9), the curve representing the rate of change of boat speed is steepest, and target speeds change most dramatically when the wind speed varies. Above 8 or 10 knots, guessing wrong is less critical as boat speed won't alter that much.

VELOCITY LIFT

When you experience a puff of wind or when sailing into an area with more wind, you encounter what is known as a velocity lift. (This is again seen clearly in the apparent-wind triangle shown in FIGURE 4.9.) When side TW grows longer, side AW shifts counterclockwise. This counterclockwise shift is a lift to a boat on port tack. In a velocity lift, the leeward telltales on the sail will droop, signaling you to head up into the wind. Should you, however? If this is truly a velocity lift, you are—according to the concept of target boat speeds—likely sailing too slowly for the increased wind speed. So rather than come up, which is the sailor's normal instinct, head off and ease sheets to build speed. Then once you near the target speed for the new wind strength, head up again and trim sheets.

If you don't have a wind-speed indicator and a speedometer, a velocity lift, that is, a puff rather than a wind shift, is usually easier to see on the water or feel on the boat. With a puff, heel increases, the sails appear to have more pressure, the boat seems to accelerate, or the water grows darker with increased wind. Thus, it is often easier to distinguish between a velocity lift and a real lift than a velocity header and a real header. Again, if you don't know which it is, do nothing. Not altering course is better than coming up.

TARGET BOAT SPEEDS DOWNWIND

I find downwind sailing very difficult as there are very few clues to guide you. I haven't crewed for many people lately, but I do remember that Ted Turner, whom I crewed for in the 1974 America's Cup on *Mariner*, was very good at steering downwind. He had a natural ability to know when to go off and when to come up. I don't know how to describe it other than to say Turner had a great rhythm. He was, in my estimation, a much better driver downwind than upwind. I don't have a natural rhythm when sailing downwind, so for me target boat speeds have proved helpful.

When sailing downwind, there is an optimum boat speed for every wind speed. This optimum speed is the one that will cause you to arrive at a place as quickly as possible, be it a racing buoy or a cruising destination.

In FIGURE 7.10 note how the downwind target is 3.87 knots in a wind of 8 knots true. If I'm sailing 3.58 knots, I'm slow. So I would head up until I reach the target speed of 3.87. If, however, I am sailing 4.21 knots, I'm fast. Then I'd bear off and sail more toward the mark until the boat loses momentum, and its speed corresponds to the target speed. This downwind jog would give me the best VMG downwind, or the fastest run down the ladder.

Once the target speed is reached, begin sailing the proper sailing angle as delineated in the polar diagram. That would be the angle marked θ in this figure.

FIGURE 7.10
*Using target boat
speeds downwind.*

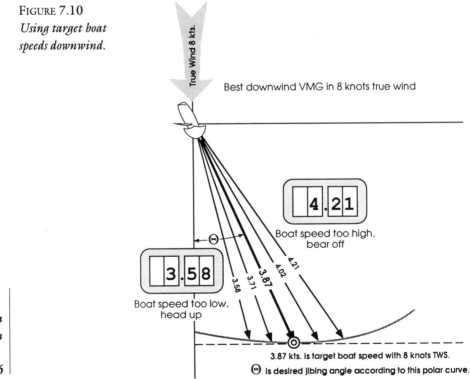

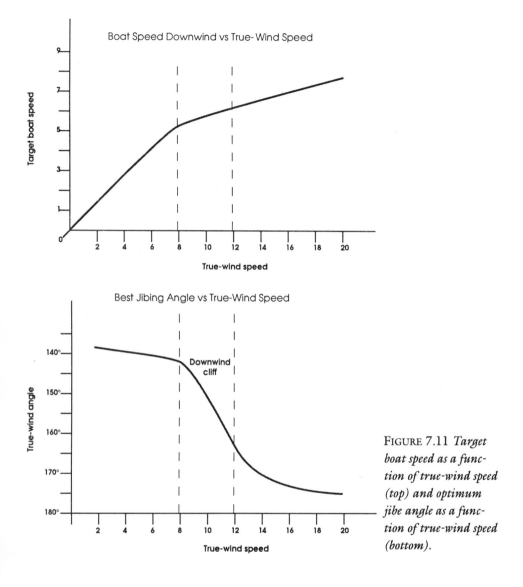

FIGURE 7.11 *Target boat speed as a function of true-wind speed (top) and optimum jibe angle as a function of true-wind speed (bottom).*

DOWNWIND TARGETS AND JIBING ANGLES AS A FUNCTION OF WIND SPEED

FIGURE 7.11 shows different representations of the information displayed in the polar diagram (see FIGURE 7.7). The top graph shows downwind target boat speed as a function of wind speed. The bottom graph shows optimum downwind sailing angle as a function of wind speed.

There are three zones in both graphs in FIGURE 7.11. In the top graph, where target boat speed versus true-wind speed is plotted, note that in the first zone, 0–8 knots, the curve is linear. Also, the curve is rather steep; in this zone, target boat speeds increase at a rate of about .5 knot per 1 knot of true-wind speed. That's a very significant increase. Thus, in the area between 0 and 8 knots, the emphasis is on maintaining the proper target boat speed. If you are slow or fast of your target boat speed when sailing downwind in 0–8 knots, you should steer up or down, respectively, and do it aggressively. Sails should likewise be trimmed aggressively in this area.

In the bottom graph, optimum sailing angle versus true-wind speed is plotted. Note in this graph that the optimum true-wind angles in the 0–8 knot zone do not change much. They are from 145 to 140 degrees. The import of this is that in light air, 0–8 knots, the emphasis is on target boat speeds, as mentioned above, not on sailing angle.

The middle zone in the bottom graph is interesting. While the top graph shows that target speeds do not change very dramatically in this wind range, the bottom curve shows that sailing angle does. This is called the downwind cliff. The graph shows that a 1-knot change in true-wind speed corresponds to a 5-degree difference in sailing angle for a typical 37-footer. That's a very significant increase. In this 8–12 knot area, concentrate on sailing angle. Above 12 knots, both curves are relatively straight and fairly level, which means there aren't big gains or losses to be had in this area. In summary, when sailing downwind in 0–8 knots, concentrate on target boat speeds. In 8–12 knots, concentrate on sailing angle. Above 12 knots, about the best you can do is to sail closer to the mark in the puffs to minimize distance to the mark, and higher in the lulls to increase speed. (This is discussed further in Chapter 8.)

VELOCITY HEADER DOWNWIND

As in upwind sailing, a drop in wind speed causes a velocity header. Since you are sailing from more wind to less, you are likely going too fast. Thus, use the excess speed to bear off—take a bite to leeward. By bearing off, you sail closer to the downwind mark, which maximizes VMG, or what has been referred to as the trip down the ladder. Don't be greedy, however. This is a short-term response. Come back up before your boat speed drops too much, because it is hard to build speed again when sailing downwind in light air.

As when sailing upwind, if you don't know if you're experiencing a velocity shift or an actual wind shift, the conservative approach is to maintain your current course.

VELOCITY LIFT DOWNWIND

With an increase in wind—a puff—the apparent wind goes aft, giving the impression of a lift. When you move from less wind to more, you are likely to find yourself slow of the target boat speed for the strength of the new wind. So head up to build speed. If you had borne off with the increase in wind, the apparent wind would move aft, making it much harder—and requiring more time—to accelerate to your new target.

Again, if you aren't certain if this is a wind shift or a velocity shift, don't alter your course.

REACHING

Steering is relatively straightforward in a light- and moderate-air reach. Just sail the compass course and try to dissuade boats from passing you on your windward side (discussed more fully in Chapter 10).

Weather helm is less of a problem when reaching than when beating, so power up the sails. Make them deep and draft aft. Sail trimmers should follow the lead of the helmsperson and trim the sails according to the telltales; both telltales should be flying aft most of the time.

Heavy-air reaching is somewhat more complicated. Sometimes it requires two people on the tiller to control all that power. And sometimes two aren't enough. The reason is that on a reach, increased sail area translates to increased speed. On the other hand, increased sail area translates to increased weather helm, which can make steering difficult or impossible. A broach, an uncontrolled turn into the wind, can result from too much sail area. (Usually the cause of a broach is a spinnaker, but even boats without spinnakers can broach.)

What happens is that the wind causes the boat to heel. This heeling, as discussed, creates weather helm, and the boat turns into the wind. Sometimes the steerer can do little to counteract it. You will recall from the Chapter 4 that on an overpowered reach, leave the outhaul on the main tight to minimize weather helm. It helps if someone plays the vang to keep the end of the boom out of the water.

HOW TO AVOID A BROACH

Avoiding a broach requires coordinated action between the steerer and the sail trimmers. Sometimes a broach comes with a warning—the boat rolls hard to weather or the helmsperson realizes he or she is on the edge of control. And sometimes a broach occurs quickly and unpredictably.

If there is sufficient warning, the key to avoiding a broach is to release the sails from the back of the boat to the front. Start with the mainsheet, then the boom vang. Next, ease the staysail sheet if flying this sail. Quickly ease the spinnaker sheet so the sail collapses, which can unload the rudder. Don't, however, release the spinnaker guy.

If none of this works and you can't avoid a broach, steer into the broach to collapse the chute. If you must broach, speed is an advantage. This is because the slower you go, the more the apparent wind moves aft, further heeling the boat. Rudder drag and heel are bad.

The following actions on the part of the steerer and sail trimmers can lessen the effects of a broach if it becomes unavoidable. If the rudder is stalled—that is, it is no longer steering the boat—straighten the rudder. Collapse the sails, as described above, from back to front. Once the boat straightens up, you should still have most of your speed. Then with the sails luffing, bear off sharply to a broad reach. This helps to avoid a second broach that often occurs once the spinnaker—assuming you are flying one—refills. Because of the lack of speed, the second broach can be a bigger problem. Once on a broad reach, trim the sails from front to back. Then build speed before trying to come closer to the wind again.

STEERING DURING A TACK

Steering a small boat through a tack, as described in the previous chapter, isn't that difficult. Start the turn slowly and then speed it up when the boat reaches head to wind. Tacking a big, heavy keelboat requires other techniques, however. Use the boat's inertia to increase velocity made good (VMG). As indicated, you can maximize VMG, at least for a time, by shooting the wind. (You also do this at the end of a race to shoot the finish line when it is an upwind finish, or to head dead downwind in a downwind finish, discussed in Chapter 10.) When tacking a keelboat in smooth water and in a good breeze—the optimum sailing conditions—you can take a little bite to windward, gaining distance toward the mark.

This is accomplished by tacking a little more slowly. To do this, use weather helm and less emphasis on the tiller or wheel to swing you into the wind. In light air, crew weight on the low side and sail trim (overtrim the main) can aid this process. After passing into the wind, accelerate the turning with the helm to fill the sails quickly on the new tack.

It is helpful for the steerer to stay on the old weather side, as when roll-tacking (see Chapter 6). From this vantage point, you can watch the headsail fill. Once you're on the new tack, if the wind is light, the sails should be eased slightly. Also, as discussed in Chapter 5, the leads can be positioned outboard on a tack and then, as speed increases, moved inboard while the sheet is trimmed. Furthermore, your initial heading can be briefly held below your intended course to build speed. In heavy air, you want to come out of the tack with flatter sails and an inboard lead, and point closer to the wind immediately after the tack. In choppy seas, you have to tack more quickly.

Tacking is often a tactical response. As such, it isn't something you want to advertise. Earlier in this book, I wrote about *Enterprise* in the America's Cup of 1977. Lowell North was skipper of that boat, and Malin Burnham steered it. In time, Burnham replaced North as skipper. Burnham, a Star sailor, wasn't comfortable with a wheel, so he steered *Enterprise* with a tiller affixed to a wheel. To tack the boat, Burnham would have to get off the weather rail. When he stood, the competition knew *Enterprise* was going to tack and could respond accordingly. It was like knowing when the other team in football is going to throw a pass.

PLANING AND SURFING

A light boat with a flat bottom can plane on the top of its bow wave when the boat is reaching or running (see Chapter 2). Planing is fast and therefore desirable. With enough wind, keep the boat flat through hiking and keep the crew weight aft. Also balance the helm with the sails, as using the rudder too much for steering causes the boat to slow, thereby inhibiting planing. Properly trimmed, the boat may now plane. If not, a pump on the mainsheet can facilitate planing. Be careful, however, as "repeated pumping" is forbidden in the International Yacht Racing Union (IYRU) racing rules. Ooching, the sudden movement fore and aft of the crew, can also cause a boat to plane. Ooching is, however, forbidden by the IYRU rules. When running and broad-reaching, waves, which provide a push from behind, can start your boat planing, too.

Larger keelboats will surf, that is, ride down and across the face of a wave like a surfboard, when broad-reaching or running. A surfer starts down a wave by paddling to build speed. Similarly, a sailboat is made to accelerate before a following sea reaches the stern. To do this, the steerer briefly heads up before an appropriate wave. To start surfing in light and moderate air, place crew weight slightly forward, which reduces the boat's wetted surface. In heavier air, the bow is often driven down by the spinnaker and the rest of the sailplan, so bring crew weight aft. Then when a wave is about to overtake the boat, head off. The bigger the wave is, the better. You can't ride all of them, so, like a surfer, be discriminating.

With the increase in speed, it is possible to run into the back of one wave after you've surfed down the one behind it. Before the bow digs in, bring the boat up and start the procedure again.

It is easier to surf with the seas running with the wind—the normal orientation. A quartering sea, however, can force the helmsperson to sail near to or by the lee (dead downwind), where the margin of error is very small. An accidental jibe can make a mess of things; indeed it can break equipment and threaten crew safety.

An accidental jibe is the flip side of broaching. Here, rather than the boat turning up as it does in a broach, it turns down. The sudden swinging of the boom across the boat can be deadly. A crew member, for example, was killed in such an accidental jibe in the 1979 SORC. Also, the running backstays, common on fractional rigs, can trap the boom after an accidental jibe, making it extremely difficult to clear the boom. If a boom is restrained with a preventer, which can protect the crew, this can cause the mainsail to back after an accidental jibe and pin the boat down. Then, an accidental jibe is often followed by a broach.

Unfortunately, there is no easy solution to these problems. A preventer should probably be used in light- and moderate-air sailing, when an accidental jibe is less likely. In heavier winds, however, whether or not to use a preventer is a more complicated choice. Without one, crews must protect their heads by ducking to avoid the boom during an accidental jibe. An alternative is to run the preventer line to a winch in the cockpit. Then, if the boat jibes accidentally, the boom can be released under control. If the running backstay(s) of a fractional rig traps your boom, the boom must be carefully walked through the backstay(s).

8 | Strategy: Wind, Weather, and Current

A large part of sailing and sailboat racing is mental—the on-the-water chess match that encompasses strategy and tactics. Strategy we will define as sailing in response to wind, weather, and current. Strategy involves decisions aimed at getting the boat around the race course or to your next landfall quickly *without* regard to other boats. Thus, it is an important topic for both cruising sailors and racers. Tactics, on the other hand, are defined more narrowly as the moves and countermoves you make to get ahead of other boats when you are racing.[1]

To put this another way: Strategy has to do primarily with the laws of nature; tactics primarily with the laws of humans, some might say the laws of the jungle.

While the focus of this chapter is racing strategy, the subjects covered—weather, current, and wind shifts—are appropriate for both racing and cruising sailors.

For those cruising sailors who doubt that, consider this: Imagine you're sailing west on Long Island Sound from Westport, Connecticut, to Greenwich. The wind is building from the southwest, and the tide is about to flood. According to the weather forecast, the passage of a cold front is imminent. Do you head on starboard tack and go for the Long Island shore where the seas might be smaller in the lee of the land or do you tack to port and favor the Connecticut shore? The correct answer: the port tack toward the

---

[1]The separation between strategy and tactics is somewhat artificial, done for clarity's sake. In practice, strategy and tactics overlap, as they will in Chapter 10. Also, the racing rules, discussed in Chapter 9, have a considerable influence on tactics.

Connecticut shore will get you to Greenwich sooner and probably in greater comfort than the tack to the Long Island shore.

Is that information valuable for racing or cruising? The answer: both. The tools to help make this and similar strategic decisions are presented in this chapter.

PLANNING

I can improvise in a sailboat when I have to—and that ends up being a fair amount of the time—but I prefer starting out with a fully realized plan. The result is a more even, more consistent performance.

My goal in sailing isn't to be brilliant or flashy in individual races, just to be consistent over the long run. For me, this philosophy has paid off.

To develop a plan for a race or a passage, some of the things I consider are possible courses, likely wind speed and direction, proper sails, current, tide, competition and sailing instructions—if racing—and ability of my crew. Long before a race or departure, I start to assemble the pieces into a logical plan.

I might use all the plan, some of it, or none of it. However, if you can't make sense of a race or passage slowly and thoughtfully on land, you'll never be able to do it well on the water, where there are so many distractions.

METEOROLOGY

An important part of prerace or precruise planning is figuring out the wind: its direction(s) and speed(s). In sailboat racing, knowing which way and how much the wind blows is like reading tomorrow's *Wall Street Journal* today. It's money in the bank.

We begin by showing how meteorologists forecast weather in an America's Cup campaign. Although the technology may be more ambitious than most sailors will ever use, the process is, or should be, much the same as that used by sailors, who have fewer resources.

Weather is the product of complex interactions among temperatures, clouds, oceans, landmasses, ice, dust, snow, volcanoes, water vapor, gases, etc. The challenge of predicting the weather keeps supercomputers humming and confounds them as well. Underlying the codes (programs) used in the supercomputers are "simplified assumptions." Meteorologists make simplified assumptions about the weather and see if they are valid. This methodology will be used in this chapter.

In an America's Cup campaign, for example, we might collect as much as twenty years of data, if it's available, from local weather sources to begin to assemble what the weather people term a regional-climatic analysis.[2] This information is analyzed by the computer to determine typical conditions at certain times of the year, and so forth. The value of the data varies. In some venues, for example, the readings are taken at quite some distance from the actual sailing sites. Sometimes you can easily extrapolate this information to the race course, and sometimes you cannot.

To determine its worth—to give the data some statistical weight—the sailing locale is monitored at the times of day the boats will be racing and at the appropriate times of the year. Thus, if the boats will race from 12:00 PM to 5:15 PM from January to May, as they did in the 1992 America's Cup in San Diego, that's when the data is collected. Monitored on a ten-minute or hourly basis are such things as wind speed, wind direction, and sea state, or waves.

For 1992, the work was done by Lee Davis and Chris Bedford, from Galson Technical Services, as it was in Western Australia.[3] In San Diego, Galson placed two sea buoys, one south of Point Loma and one west. Also in use was a 35-foot meteorological tower at the South Mission Beach Park and a monostatic Doppler acoustic sounder (SODAR) at the south side of San Diego Bay. (The use of Doppler as a tool in weather forecasting will be discussed later.)

This on-site monitoring typically begins two years before the start of the event. Collecting data for two years is important. Whereas one year could be an abnormal year, two years tends to smooth out statistical anomalies. Also, two years before an America's Cup, the yacht designers are starting their work. Meteorology influences many design decisions, such as sailing length, sail area, and ballast-displacement.

The weather information is summarized in several ways. One useful summary, for example, is a wind rose: a graphical device that shows wind speed and direction. (A wind rose for Newport, Rhode Island, is shown in

---

[2]The statistically minded sailor can obtain historical weather data from one hundred sites around the U.S.—many of them near popular sailing spots—from the National Climatic Data Center, Federal Building, Asheville, NC 28801. A computer spreadsheet program or something similar can be used to analyze the numbers, even graph them, which can be very helpful in determining patterns.

[3]The authors wish to acknowledge the kind help of Lee Davis and Chris Bedford in the writing of this chapter.

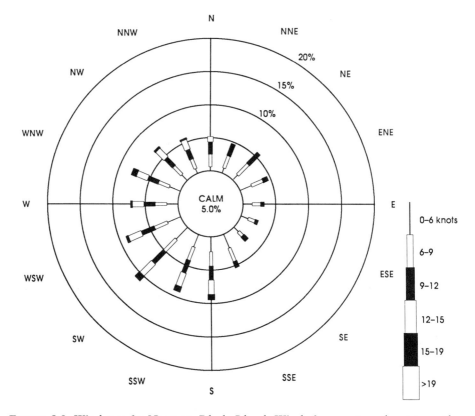

FIGURE 8.1 *Wind rose for Newport, Rhode Island. Winds from west-southwest to south-southwest are most common.*

FIGURE 8.1.) Then, using this and other models, a computer program tests yacht designs by "sailing" races based on gathered weather data. The computer might assume that at 12:20, when the race starts, the wind will be 10 knots from a bearing of 180 degrees. The seas will be choppy. At 12:50, the computer determines the wind will be at 13 knots from 225 degrees, and so on. From this weather modeling, the computer helps define critical yacht-design parameters.

After yacht design, the focus of the meteorological program moves on to weather forecasting. For the 1986–87 America's Cup in Western Australia, for example, we were able to model statistically thirty-two different weather events. Of these thirty-two events, eight occurred more than three-quarters of the time. We were then able to characterize the day in terms of one of the thirty-two models. This gave a very good indication of what to expect on the race course.

What we did in Perth and in San Diego is obviously ambitious—it cost several hundred thousand dollars. However, the process is not foreign to good sailors. A good sailor starts with a forecast and then tries to match the forecast to what was observed (clouds, temperature, wind shear, etc.), and then to what actually happened: Was the right side of the course favored, the left, or the middle?

Off Newport, for example, the forecast often calls for onshore winds—the southwest sea breeze. The southwest sea breeze usually starts in the south and shifts to the southwest. For indicators, you might watch for puffy cumulus clouds forming over land. If they are present, the land is usually heating up, and the breeze might come up and switch to the right. If, however, there's no buildup of clouds, the wind may stay in the south and show only small oscillations. Lastly, the good sailor must make the appropriate strategic response.

In Chapter 5, I commented how I don't care why something works, only that it works. There is enough to worry about in sailing without worrying about why. In this chapter, too, I have avoided some of the more complicated causes and effects of weather. If a sailor can match indicators, to winds, to strategy, everyone will think he or she is brilliant anyway.

WIND

Three types of wind have a direct bearing on sailing: gradient wind, thermal wind, and geographic wind.

Gradient Wind

Gradient winds are those caused by large weather systems, for example, the winds that blow from a high-pressure system to a low-pressure system (see FIGURE 8.2). They can be thought of as a big-picture factor, what a meteorologist describes as synoptic. Typically, a strong gradient wind works its way down to the surface and affects the winds in which we sail.

High-pressure air is colder, drier, and denser than low-pressure air. Colder, drier, and denser air is more stable, and, thus, high pressure is usually associated with fair weather. Low-pressure air is warmer, moister, and less dense. Warmer, moister, and less dense air is more unstable, and, thus, low pressure is usually associated with foul, even dramatic weather.

High-pressure centers are indicated on weather maps with an *H* and low pressure with an *L*. Typically, a high will have a central atmospheric pressure

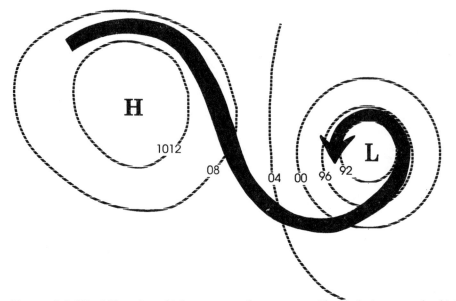

FIGURE 8.2 *Wind blows from high-pressure to low-pressure. Also clockwise around a high and counterclockwise around a low.*

of 1,016 millibars (mb) or more, whereas a low has a pressure of 1,010 mb or less.[4] With a little barometer watching, it becomes apparent that rapidly falling atmospheric pressure (1.7 millibars, or .05 inches, per hour) often foretells an approaching low-pressure system and a storm. A storm is also usually associated with the winds shifting counterclockwise from southeast to northeast. This is the infamous "nor'easter." Rising barometric readings signal fair weather, particularly when the wind goes to the west.

In the northern hemisphere, the winds move clockwise around a high and counterclockwise around a low (see FIGURE 8.2). Also, the wind moves from a (denser) high-pressure region to a (less dense) low-pressure region. Wind velocity is a function of the relative differences in pressure between the high and the low. It is like a rock tumbling down a hill: the steeper and higher the hill (high pressure) and the lower the valley (low pressure), the faster the rock falls—or the stronger the wind.

The direction of the wind depends on the positions of the pressure centers. If the center of a low-pressure system passes to your north when you're

[4]Air pressure expressed in millibars (a metric-system measure based on the dyne) is commonly used in meteorology. Another measure of atmospheric pressure is inches of mercury: 1 inch corresponds to 33.86 millibars, or 1 millibar corresponds to .03 inches of mercury.

in the northern hemisphere, the wind will likely shift clockwise—*veer* is the technical term for a clockwise shift. Alternatively, if the center passes south of you, the winds will shift counterclockwise—*back* is the formal term.

The passings of fronts are another synoptic weather phenomenon to which you should pay attention. On a weather map, the leading edge of a cold front is delineated by triangles. The passage of a cold front can mean dramatic weather: strong winds, lightning, thunder, and rain squalls. The approach of a cold front is swift and typically comes with little or no visual warning. Sometimes the approach of a cold front is heralded by the sudden appearance of towering cumulonimbus clouds—what sailors call thunderheads. Thunderstorms and squall lines often come next.

As the cold front approaches, the wind typically blows from the southwest and then shifts abruptly to the northwest. (Recall the Connecticut shore example at the start of this chapter.) After the cold front passes, the strong gradient winds tend to push down to the surface and control the local winds. Winds behind a cold front can be puffy and shifty.

If a dramatic weather event is brewing, such as the passage of a low-pressure system or a cold front, I save several weather maps from the newspapers. (Sources of weather information are discussed later.) I watch the system's movement relative to race day and my location. Isobars—lines on a weather map connecting points of equal pressure—give an indication of the wind direction. The wind blows basically parallel to the isobars. The spacing of the isobars is important, too. The closer they are, the more wind there will be.

Compared with the coming of a cold front, the arrival of a warm front is not, typically, a dramatic event. There is ample warning, usually anywhere from twelve to thirty-six hours. The clouds (see FIGURE 8.3), change (moving right to left) from cirrus to cirrostratus, to altostratus, to stratus (nimbostratus if it's raining), and then to cumulus. On a weather map, a warm front is designated by half circles. With the passage of a warm front, the winds are generally from the east and move to the south and then southwest.

An occluded front can best be described as a combination of a warm front and a cold front. The onset of an occluded front isn't a dramatic occurrence; as such it is similar to the arrival of a warm front. The passage of an occlusion, however, is often marked by a shift of winds to the west and northwest, as one would expect with a cold front. The symbol for an occluded front on a weather map is half circles and triangles on the same side of the frontal line. A stationary front, as the name indicates, moves slowly, if at all. It typically means light and variable winds. It is denoted by half circles and triangles on opposite sides of the front line.

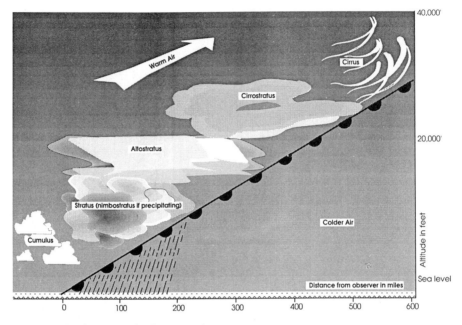

FIGURE 8.3 *The approach of a warm front.*

Thermal Winds

Land heats and cools more rapidly than water. This temperature differential causes what is called thermal winds. This is a more localized phenomenon, or, as meteorologists say, a mesoscale phenomenon, than the synoptic-scale gradient winds. On warm, sunny days, the land heats rapidly. This heating of the land causes the air above it to rise in thermals, under the same principles that cause a hot-air balloon to rise. As the warm air rises, it cools and can generate puffy cumulus clouds (see clouds in bottom left of FIGURE 8.3). Cumulus clouds are, in fact, an indicator that the thermal wind, known as a sea breeze, is forming. Cooler, denser air over the water moves in toward the land to replace the warm air that has risen, thus creating the onshore sea breeze. In turn, the rising, land-heated air moves aloft out over the water and cools and descends.

It is useful to think of this phenomenon as a wheel (see FIGURE 8.4). If the winds aloft—the gradient wind, discussed earlier—blow in the opposite direction to the winds on the surface, this helps turn the thermal-wind "wheel." Then as the warm air—driven by the gradient wind—moves over water, it cools and falls, or subsides.

Note, however, if the gradient wind is too strong, it will oppose the development of the thermal sea breeze, as it works its way to the surface. It affects the sea-breeze "wheel" like a brake. The trick in predicting the thermal sea breeze is understanding how the gradient winds interact with the development of the sea breeze.

The sea breeze usually starts offshore and then fills like a mini-front toward the shore. As there is typically more velocity in a sea breeze, this might call for a tack offshore to get into the stronger sea breeze first. Sometimes a sea breeze that starts offshore can be seen on the water as a wind line or even a wall of haze—both of which will move toward land.

The greater the difference in temperature between the air over the land and that over the water, the stronger the thermal winds. This is why the phenomenon occurs most often on warm spring or fall days when the water is significantly cooler than the land. Late in the summer, land and sea temperatures are closer. Other conditions important to the formation of thermal winds are little or no cloud cover and a gradient wind, as mentioned, that blows aloft in the opposite direction to the sea breeze.

This mechanism is what fueled the dramatic Fremantle Doctor—the strong, 18- to 26-knot or more southerly we enjoyed in Western Australia

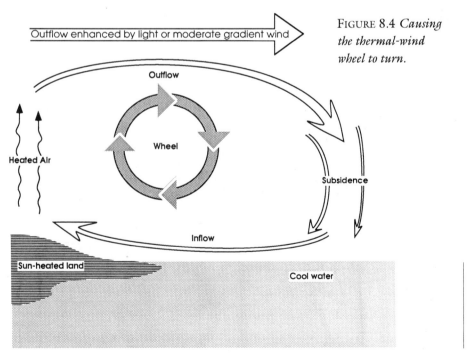

FIGURE 8.4 *Causing the thermal-wind wheel to turn.*

during the 1986–87 America's Cup. It supposedly derives its name from the relief it provides from the heat and flies. A lesser known version of the story is that the phenomenon was originally called the Fremantle Docker, because when the breeze came in from the southwest, the big sailing ships could dock in Fremantle.

If the name is obscure, the phenomenon is well documented. Off Perth, the cool Antarctic waters of the Indian Ocean meet the superheated air of the Western Australia desert. This hot land/cold water phenomenon also accounts for the onshore southwesterly, the typical breeze found in Newport and Buzzards Bay.

There is a tendency in the northern hemisphere for the thermals to veer (shift clockwise) when forming. In the southern hemisphere, the thermal wind backs (shifts counterclockwise). This is due to the Coriolis force, which affects all winds and currents. (According to the Coriolis Force, the rotation of the earth causes moving air to appear to be deflected to the right in the northern hemisphere and to the left in the southern.)

In the northern hemisphere, the sea breeze often veers (clocks) at 5 degrees an hour. This is why you typically favor the righthand side of the course during a sea, or onshore, breeze in the northern hemisphere (the lefthand in the southern). A shift in one direction is called a persistent shift, which characterizes a developing sea breeze. Once the sea breeze is fully formed, however, it often changes from a persistent shift to an oscillating shift—a shift that swings back and forth like a pendulum. The sea breeze starts to degrade in late afternoon as the sun sinks toward the horizon, and the breeze starts to veer, or back, again in a persistent shift. Cloud cover has the same effect as the setting sun; it can nullify the sea breeze.

At night, the land cools more rapidly than the water, and an offshore breeze—the opposite of a sea breeze—can develop. This wind, sometimes called a land breeze or a drainage wind, typically starts close to the shore. This is why after a hot, sunny day, it can sometimes pay to sail close to the shore, where the wind may be stronger. The land breeze is not as strong as the sea breeze, because the difference in temperature between the land and the water is not as great at night as it is during the day. This phenomenon, like the sea breeze, is less likely to occur when the day has been cloudy or cool.

Geographic Winds

Geographic winds—those breezes resulting from the steering effects of land—represent microscale meteorological effects. A useful rule is that wind, like any fluid, seeks the path of least resistance. It will flow down rivers, into bays, around buildings, and over islands. To the "tourist," or the visitor, the geography and its effects may be hard to discern. Thus, when it comes to geographic winds—as with thermal winds—there is probably no substitute for local knowledge, or experience.

Such natural and manmade features can affect both the velocity and the direction of the wind. For example, if the choice is between tacking toward shore or offshore, often the tack to shore will pay off with a lift (see the white boat in FIGURE 8.5). This is because the wind tends to run more perpendicular to the shore as a result of the greater friction encountered by air moving over land versus air moving over water. The danger, of course, is that you can get too close to the shore, where, in the lee of the land, the wind's

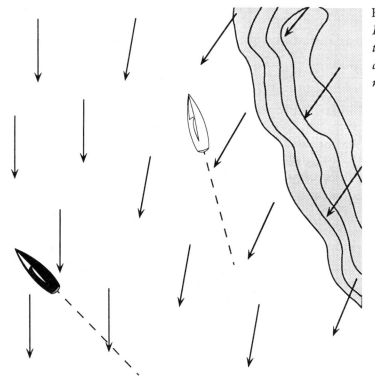

FIGURE 8.5
Land can bend the breeze, which can cause a lift near shore.

velocity is less. This assumes you're dealing with a gradient wind. If it's a thermal wind, for instance, a sea breeze, the wind can blow harder when you get closer to shore. Clearly, it's important to identify the type of wind you're sailing in before developing a strategy; thus, we will spend much of this chapter doing that.

In my three America's Cups in Newport, I've often sailed with Halsey Herreshoff, who has lived in Bristol, Rhode Island, all his life. Halsey is a descendant of the famous Bristol boat-building and yacht-design family. These days he is the town administrator of Bristol, in essence the mayor. Halsey is immensely knowledgeable about Newport weather, but put him in Perth or San Diego, and he may not have as much of an edge.

When I'm sailing in a new area, I seek the locals. In my experience, sailors are generally friendly. They're flattered that you care and usually are willing to talk. Fruitful topics of conversation include the thermal and geographic winds and currents (which will be discussed shortly).

FORMAL SOURCES OF WEATHER INFORMATION

Weather information comes from such mass media as the local TV or radio and even the maps in the newspapers. I pay some attention to these weather maps, although they often seem unspecific and irrelevant to sailboat racing. Also, the weather "news" in newspapers is fairly old by the time you see it. For sailing purposes, one of the best weather maps is found in the *Los Angeles Times*. Of late, isobars have been conspicuously absent from newspapers and most TV weather maps. Even wind direction is hard to discern. Still, these maps have some relevance to sailing. They show the average range of wind speeds, which can be helpful in planning whether to go, what to wear, and other general safety and comfort concerns.

Much better for sailors is the dedicated cable weather channel, which during the boating season gives coastal conditions, sea-breeze information, and isobars.

A good source for more tightly focused weather information is the continuous National Oceanic and Atmospheric Administration (NOAA) weather broadcasts available on a VHF radio (162.40, 162.475, and 162.55 MHz) or on an inexpensive dedicated weather radio. This information is updated every few hours. If you live in an area where buoy data is given, pay close attention to wind directions and speeds at various buoys. You may be able to discern patterns that are helpful in predicting the thermal winds, even geographic winds, in your area. Further, it is a good idea to compare

NOAA's predictions with what actually occurs. Remember, you are trying to develop your own data base—the key to local knowledge. (Be warned, however, that NOAA tends to overestimate wind speed, perhaps for safety or liability reasons.)

NOAA also provides weather information for pilots, and sailors can tap into this source. This is in the form of a conversation with a meteorologist, as opposed to listening to a tape.

There are, of course, different levels of weather forecasting. If your budget and boat will accommodate them, there are paper-recording weather-fax machines, which receive NOAA faxes by way of your vessel's single-sideband radio. An ocean-surface analysis is provided, as well as forecasts for twelve-, twenty-four-, thirty-six-, and forty-eight-hour periods.

As an alternative to the marine weather-fax, a relatively new service being offered by several private companies allows you to receive up-to-date NOAA charts on a normal fax machine for a modest fee.

More sophisticated, more advanced and—yes—more expensive is Automatic Picture Transmission (APT). Here infrared and visible images are received on a radio and displayed on a computer aboard a boat. The information comes from low-flying polar-orbiting satellites. They are real-time systems, meaning what you receive on your computer is what NOAA gets, and you get it when NOAA does. A weather fax, on the other hand, may be six to twenty-four hours old. Also, the stationary geopolar satellites, which feed the weather fax, are at 22,000 miles high, whereas the polar-orbiting satellites are at 500 miles. With lower satellites, the detail is much improved. You can see an area of 5 miles versus 100 miles.

Of course, you don't have NOAA as an interpreter, so skill is necessary to analyze it. However, the resolution is so much better with pictures from the low-flying polar-orbiting satellites that interpretation isn't that difficult.

The images can be stored and easily manipulated on a computer screen, through zooming, panning, and magnification. This allows you to get quite specific about where you sail. It is possible to see currents, Gulf Stream eddies, even differences in water temperature of 1°F. Also, with sophisticated VGA computer screens, the images are excellent, indeed visually arresting. They are the same as those that decorate TV news. A portable 286 computer with 640K of RAM and a 20-megabyte hard drive and at least an EGA screen are sufficient, although a 386 machine with more RAM and a VGA monitor are better. Pro-Tech Marine (297 Rhode Island Boulevard, Portsmouth, RI 02871) offers an on-board system, fed by single sideband radio.

Accu-Weather (60 Leveroni Court, Novato, CA 94949) offers a system based on the same satellite information, for at-home use. Information is fed through a modem, a device that allows a computer to receive and send data over telephone lines. It allows off-line analysis, graphing, and mapping. When your friendly TV weatherforecaster says, "Let's put the satellite into motion," the images are often provided by Accu-Weather. It is a great learning tool and good fun to use.

Some people have personal trainers. Others, like America's Cup sailors and BOC racers, have personal weather forecasters, sometimes called weather routers. In my America's Cup programs, I've used Lee Davis (Galson Technical Service, 6601 Kirkville Rd, East Syracuse, NY 13057) since 1983. Cruising sailors, for reasons of comfort and safety, are also beginning to take advantage of these and other private sources.

Living by your wits is important in sailing, and I've used informal sources for more localized weather forecasting. When racing from the Bahamas to Florida, in the Southern Ocean Racing Conference (SORC), for example, I've often monitored radio transmissions between pilots and airport control towers in Miami and Ft. Lauderdale. A VHF radio that can tune in 118–135.975 MHz can receive these transmissions. From them, you can learn whether the planes are taking off or landing using, for example, the east or west runways. Knowing that planes take off and land into the wind, you can tell the wind direction in Ft. Lauderdale or Miami, even when on the other side of the Gulf Stream in the Bahamas. That is as real-time a forecast as one can get.

The new weather forecasting technology may be impressive, but approach it skeptically. Although I'm certain it's better today than it once was, weather forecasts are far from perfect. Treat them as a guide, not the gospel.

CURRENT

If there is no current where you sail or if the current is the same everywhere you sail, strategy for coping with current isn't important. That said, current is more prevalent than you might think. It is not just an ocean phenomenon, for current occurs on rivers and lakes, too. That statement becomes clearer when we define some terms: *Current* is a horizontal flow of water. *Tide* is a vertical flow. You can't have tide without current, but you can have current without tide.

A strong wind blowing from the same direction for a day or two can pile huge amounts of water to one end of a lake or bay. The effect is analogous to lifting one end of a child's swimming pool. When the wind subsides—when the pool is level again—the water flows back to the other side. Both the buildup and subsiding can cause currents. Also, denser air in a high-pressure

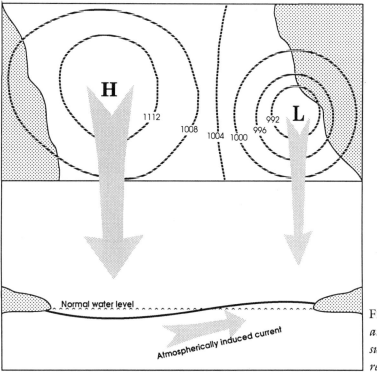

1112   1008   1004 1000   996 992

Normal water level

Atmospherically induced current

FIGURE 8.6 *How atmospheric pressure creates currents.*

system can push down on the water, causing it to bulge in areas of lower pressure (see FIGURE 8.6). This pressure causes current, as does its diminishing.

Another source of current is gravitational pull. This is, of course, common to rivers, which flow downhill. At the mouth of rivers, which empty into oceans, you can experience both tide and currents. This convergence zone can, at times, make for challenging sailing. The mouth of the Columbia River—America's second largest river—on the Pacific Ocean is a familiar example and can be a dramatic illustration of this phenomenon. In addition, there are ocean currents, such as the Gulf Stream and California Current, that can affect how we sail.

TIDE

The gravities of both the sun and the moon cause the water to bulge according to the moon's path around the earth (see FIGURE 8.7). The result is a high tide. There is a second bulge of water at the opposite side of the earth,

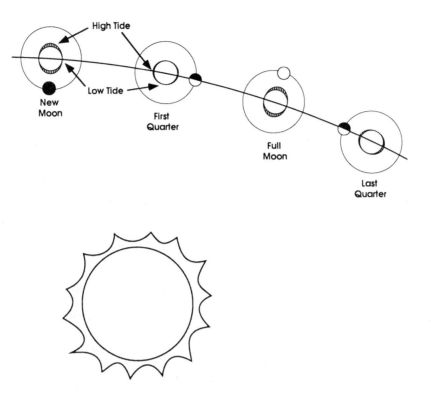

FIGURE 8.7 *How the sun, moon, and earth line up determines the heights of tides.*

with low tides between the two high tides. Sometimes all three bodies, the sun, moon, and earth, line up—during a new or full moon. At such times, tides may be much above normal. Smaller tides occur when the moon, sun, and earth form a right angle (see first quarter and last quarter in FIGURE 8.7).

There are times when tide, wind, and pressure exert their respective forces in the same direction. This can make for very high and very low tides and strong currents. It can be even more dramatic during the new or full moon.

The prerace tools you'll need to predict current deal primarily with tide. The equipment includes a chart of the area, a tide table, and, if available, a current chart. The navigational chart shows, of course, deep and shallow areas. Just as the land steers the wind, bottom contours guide the current. Usually, the current runs fast in deep water, slow in shallow water.

So, obviously, if the current is fair (heading in your direction of travel), sail for deep water: a shipping channel, for example. If it is foul (heading against you), head for shallow water: close to shore, for example. Also, current tends to change direction in shallow areas before it turns in deep areas.

(Recall the Connecticut shore example at the beginning of this chapter. If you had remained in the shallow water near the Connecticut shore, you would receive the favorable tide sooner than if you had tacked toward deep water.) So if you round the mark near when the tide is about to change from foul to fair (on your new course), it can pay to head to shallow water first. Current also flows more strongly around points of land or openings, such as rivers or harbor mouths. These can be places to avoid when the current is foul or to seek when the current is fair.

Waves can be a good indication of current and, thus, are important to strategy. When the current flows against the wind, the waves will be choppier than is normal. Since the current will help you when sailing upwind, look for choppier water (see the close-hauled boat in FIGURE 8.8). As an alternative, sail in smoother water when bucking a current (see the boat broad-reaching under spinnaker in the same figure). When the current flows with the wind, the water is smoother than normal. If you have a choice between smooth water and choppy water when sailing downwind, it can pay to head for the smoother water.

Tide tables show the period and degree of the tides. Current charts show the speed of the current and the direction at one hour after flood or

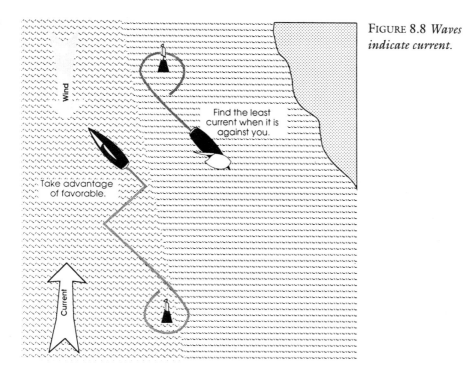

FIGURE 8.8 *Waves indicate current.*

Strategy: Wind, Weather, and Current

249

ebb, two hours, etc. (It should be noted that with current, we are concerned with the direction it is going; with wind, the direction it is coming from.) Such resource materials have their limits, however. They can't predict currents caused by other sources, that is, pressure or wind. Faced with these, one must again rely on local knowledge.

The National Ocean Service (NOS) is the best source for tide tables and current charts (available from NOS-authorized dealers or through the Distribution Branch [N/CG33], National Ocean Service, Riverdale, MD 20737, [301] 436-6990). Many of the popular current charts are based on NOS information.

For planning purposes, compare your expected starting time and expected times of mark roundings with the current charts. (A cruising sailor can factor in way points.) Then work out a plan for the legs of the race.

How important is current? In some venues, such as San Francisco Bay, where I have often raced Stars and more recently an Etchells 22, information about currents can be more important than wind information.

Currents can play a pivotal role in ocean racing and sailing as well. I often sailed with the noted navigator Ben Mitchell, now deceased. For the St. Petersburg–Ft. Lauderdale Race in the Southern Ocean Racing Conference (SORC), he would charter an airplane to fly around Key West to look for signs of the Gulf Stream. The Gulf Stream, charted by Ben Franklin in 1770, is a "river" of water that runs in the Atlantic from the Caribbean, along the East Coast of the United States, to Europe. It moves generally northeastward on a meandering and eddying course from 2 to 4 knots. It is a warm current, about 15°F warmer than the surrounding water, that is rich in fauna and flora, most notably the sargassum weed. This telltale weed, which floats on its surface, can signal the Gulf Stream's location. Ben Mitchell would look for the sargassum weed and then drop packets of dye from the airplane to determine precisely where the current was moving the fastest.

Much of the SORC strategy involves finding the Gulf Stream when a boat is heading north or avoiding it when going south. Similarly, in the biennial Newport-Bermuda Race, hitting the proper Gulf Stream eddy can profoundly determine your standing at the finish. This is because the stream breaks off into warm and cold eddies, which can go southeast, toward Bermuda.

Detailed charts of the Gulf Stream are available from NOAA and are issued about twice a week. Tune to NOAA VHF-FM weather radio at 162.55 MHz, broadcast from Wilmington, North Carolina. Being VHF, it is only a line-of-sight transmission, limited to about 30 miles. This is also tunable on single-sideband (SSB) frequencies ITU Channel 601 (USB 6501 KHz); ITU Channel 816 (USB 8764 KHz); and ITU Channel 1205 (USB 13089 KHz) at 1600 and 2200 GMT.

The previously discussed APT satellite system—with its infrared capability—is particularly adept at showing currents, such as the Gulf Stream.

THE PLAN

Wind and current information allows me to formulate a plan. It might go like this: The forecast calls for sunny and hot weather in the morning. This should cause a sea breeze to form. Look for it at 10:30—a half hour before the start. With the formation of the sea breeze, watch for a persistent shift to the right. If the forecast is accurate and the timing is correct, I'll start at the right side of the line on starboard—unless the port side is heavily favored with respect to the wind direction or mark placement—and immediately tack to port. Heading right on the course is also good because it gets me into shallower water, which should get me out of the adverse current on the leg. Remember, however, that a sea breeze starts offshore and fills in toward shore. So don't go too far in if the wind hasn't yet reached the shore. Factor the current into this decision of how far in to go.

Reality Check on Race Day

On race day, before the start, I test my prerace plan. Here, what I think is going to happen with the weather and current, for example, comes face-to-face with what is truly happening just before the race.

What happens if my plan is wrong? I'm looking for the southwesterly sea breeze, and it's blowing 15 to 20 knots from the northwest. If I'm out early enough, there is sufficient time to amend my plan. Most books and articles say to get out to the line an hour before the start. To me, that is insufficient. You almost can't get there too early. Just before a sailboat race, there's so much to do and so little time.

What Early Birds Do

I use the time before a race to work on my boat speed, sail the weather leg, and determine if my sail selection is correct. This is a good time to decide which end of the line is favored; which end I will go for (they aren't always the same); where on the course I will likely go; and whom I should watch for, that is, the competition. For example, if I'm racing an Etchells 22, and

Vince Brun, the great one-design sailor who runs North Sails One Design West in San Diego, is out there, I guarantee you I'll know what Etchells he's in. Or I might note boats with sailors who know more about an area than I do or are better than me. As the saying goes, imitation is the greatest form of flattery. Don't be afraid to "flatter" people outrageously when learning to race or looking to improve. I'd follow people to the ends of the course, if not the earth, who know more about an area or a boat than I do.

Before the race, I also check for current. Anchored buoys or boats are useful in this regard. For example, eddies around a buoy or lobster pot can be a sign of current. Be careful, however, because what looks like current around a buoy may, in fact, be caused by windblown waves. Also, if an anchored boat, like a committee boat or fishing boat, is not facing directly into the wind that can also signal current. It doesn't necessarily indicate the current's direction, however, as the wind may be exerting a force on the anchored boat at the same time.

The best way to determine current is with a current stick—a decidedly low-tech item that hasn't lost its usefulness. For a current stick, I prefer a broomstick with a weight bolted to one end to help keep it vertical. A hunk of Styrofoam, or similar material, affixed near the other end, provides some flotation. Then before the race, the stick is thrown overboard, and the drift is timed against a fixed (anchored) object. This provides the direction and speed of the current. For speed, use the formula .6 x amount of drift (measured in feet per seconds) = knots of current. Or to put this another way: an object that drifts 25 feet in 15 seconds is going about 1 knot.[5] I then compare the speed and direction of the current with the plan. If they differ significantly, I might have to amend my strategy. Don't forget to pick up the current stick when done.

Check the wind speed, too. Use this information to decide which headsail(s) and spinnaker(s), if appropriate, to use and, perhaps, whether to reef or not. Remember that the National Oceanic and Atmospheric Administration, the source of the official forecasts, tends to overestimate wind speed. That overestimation can be tricky if you're racing in a dinghy, as a small boat doesn't normally carry extra sails. With a dinghy, you normally have to decide on sail selection at the dock well before the start—often before the wind has begun to blow.

Getting out to the starting line early also allows me to see what headsails

[5]The current stick, for example, travels 25 feet in 15 seconds. To determine feet per second divide 25 by 15, which equals 1.66. Then 1.66 x .6 = 1 knot.

my competitors are using and, perhaps, to try these selections from my inventory. On the other hand, if you don't want the competition to see what sail you are using, don't tip your hand too early.

I also use the time before the race to sail up the first leg of the course, which is typically to weather. Often when you are out early enough, the course isn't determined and won't be for a while, but you can usually assume the race committee will set the first leg as squarely into the wind as possible. If the committee uses fixed marks, such as navigational buoys, imagine you are the committee, and sail to the mark that you would choose. (Obviously, these assumptions can be very wrong.)

One caution, however, about sailing a practice leg: in a dinghy or a boat without auxiliary power, when the wind is very light and/or the current is running strongly away from the starting line, or you are late getting out, don't wander too far from the line. You may not be able to get back in time.

While sailing a practice weather leg, I work on boat speed. To do this, it is extremely helpful if there is another boat to test against. Without a partner, sail against your target boat speeds, if available (see Chapter 7). Check your headsail leads, mast bend, battens, etc. While sailing upwind and back down to the line, it is a good idea to do some tacks, of course, but also perhaps a spinnaker set and a jibe or two. If your crew hasn't sailed together before, or several members aren't familiar with the boat, practice the common maneuvers. You can also practice on the way to the start. Don't, however, tire the crew before the race.

When sailing upwind before the start, try to determine if one side of the course has more wind or is favored. In a dinghy, it can be helpful to sail the practice weather leg while standing to see the wind better. Look for cat's-paws—the etching of the wind on the water—or dark spots, which can signal more wind. This is an acquired skill because cat's-paws and dark spots can also mean weeds, such as on the Pacific coast, or even schools of fish.

If you have a friendly competitor, you can head to the left while the other boat goes right to see which boat comes out ahead. This can indicate which side of the course is favored or has more wind. Remember, however, that the favored side can change during the race, due to wind shifts, puffs, or a change in current, etc.

As long as you're sailing with a friendly competitor, a good way to determine which side of the starting line is favored is to have one boat start at the starboard end on starboard tack and the other boat start at the port end on port tack. Whichever boat is ahead at the first crossing started at the favored end. If one boat would hit the other amidships, they are even—although I expect you'll want to call off the exercise before reaching that

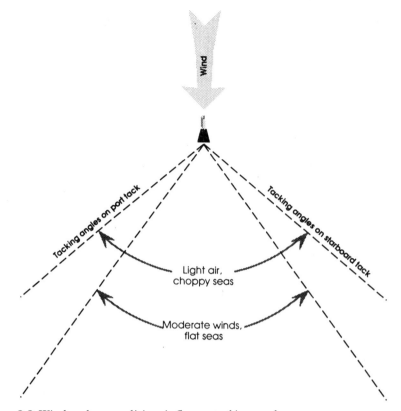

FIGURE 8.9 *Wind and sea conditions influence tacking angles.*

point. Beware of wind shifts, however, that can invalidate such testing. (Which end of a starting line is favored is discussed in more detail in Chapter 10.)

I also try to see if one side of the course has less current—if adverse—or more if favorable. Also, I try to determine whether one side of the course has smaller waves. When sailing upwind, waves, which can be considered a punch in the face (see Chapter 2), hurt boat speed. (Remember, however, that when the current opposes the wind, as shown in FIGURE 8.8, the water will be choppier. As this is a fair current for boats heading upwind, it can pay to sail in choppier waters.)

The angle between a boat's heading on either tack is called the tacking angle. Waves as well as light winds widen the tacking angle. FIGURE 8.9 shows this. Smooth seas and moderate winds narrow the tacking angle, getting you to a weather mark sooner. As waves vary on a body of water due to bottom contours, water depth, protection from the land, etc., consider sailing in smaller waves when heading upwind. Be warned, however, that smaller waves can also signal less wind or even an adverse current. In sailboat racing you have to prioritize, and usually more wind wins out.

Downwind, waves are a persistent push in the direction you want to go. So consider sailing in waves when sailing downwind. In heavy downwind sailing, however, waves can cause you to broach (see Chapter 7), so you might want to search for smoother water at such times.

Also while sailing on the practice first leg, make a mental note of any obstacles, such as buoys, lobster pots, or fishing boats, that can affect strategy or tactics.

CHARACTERIZING THE WIND

One of the most important things to do before the race is to check the wind direction by sailing close-hauled on port and starboard tacks. Every minute or two, write down your compass headings to assemble what is termed a two-number system. Eventually, you'll develop a table that looks like Table 8A.

Table 8A

	Port	Starboard
	355	265
	356	262
	358	270
	002	268
	355	260
	<u>346</u>	<u>252</u>
Average	355	263

Wind is almost never steady. It shifts in one of three ways. It *oscillates* like a pendulum. Or it shifts in one direction, called a *persistent* shift. Or it shifts primarily in one direction but also has oscillations back and forth, which is an *oscillating-persistent* shift. Each of these shifts requires a different strategic response, so it is critical to characterize the wind.

The two-number system allows you to do this. With an oscillating shift, the numbers swing between the lower and upper limits (see Table 8A). Average them, or more simply, find the median to determine the average or median wind on both tacks.[6] The average wind, as will be discussed shortly, helps to determine when to tack on a header.

Also, try to determine the time, or period, between shifts. The time can likewise help you to decide when to tack. The period can change the charac-

---

[6]Although there is a difference between average and median, it is not significant in terms of wind shifts. These terms will be used interchangeably.

terization of the wind and, obviously, your strategic response. Suppose before the start, you determine the period between oscillations is thirty minutes. The wind has reached or is nearing the end of its lefthand swing (perhaps you're sailing 346 degrees on port tack). The weather leg will take about fifteen minutes to sail. With thirty minutes between oscillations on a fifteen-minute leg, this is, as far as you are concerned, likely to be a persistent shift to the right.

If the wind has been oscillating for an hour before the start, you can conclude it will continue doing so, at least in the near future. Of course, that assumption can be dead wrong. All I can say is that's sailboat racing. Assume it is correct, however, until you have evidence to the contrary.

With a persistent shift, compass headings when close-hauled on both tacks will gradually get either larger or smaller. Table 8B shows a persistent shift, with the wind clocking, or moving right.

Table 8B

Port	Starboard
245	158
252	158
253	162
260	168
265	170
268	172

Likewise, if the wind shows a persistent shift for an hour, assume it will continue to happen. That assumption, too, can be very wrong.

With an oscillating-persistent shift, you get highs and lows on either tack, but the median wind changes gradually toward a higher or lower compass number (see Table 8C).

Table 8C

Port	Starboard
245	158
242	160
253	159
250	163
255	165
268	170

Adding to the Two-Number System

Some sailors prefer to "shoot the wind," go head to wind before the start, to determine headers and lifts and the wind direction.[7] However, after the start, this technique alone has less utility than the two-number system. With the two-number system, you can add to it when sailing, which keeps your information up-to-date. In fact, you absolutely should add to it, particularly when you have a new high or low. With a new high or low, you may also have to refigure the median wind.

Keep the numbers handy, indeed eminently visible. I write down the headings in grease pencil or nonpermanent marker near both the starboard and port compasses. Just after the start, I'm excited and operating on instinct. Having the numbers in view helps my concentration. Later, I can usually remember these headings.

One other point I'd like to make here: I find the excitement—the adrenaline rush before the start—a positive force in sailboat racing. I know what adrenaline level works best for me, and I monitor it carefully. If I'm overexcited before the start, I try to turn it down. If, however, I'm flat, I turn it up. To do this, I try to visualize how good I'm going to feel standing at the trophy presentation, or when hoisting the America's Cup in victory, or having a medal put around my neck at the Olympics.

CONDITIONS ASSOCIATED WITH AN OSCILLATING WIND

An oscillating shift, as described and as the name indicates, moves back and forth across an average direction (see Table 8A). An oscillating shift is the most common wind shift, so when you aren't sure what is happening to the wind, assume it's an oscillating breeze.

Oscillations are common to fully formed thermal winds, not to be confused with a developing thermal wind.[8] Oscillations are also a characteristic of

---

[7]A wind shift toward the bow is a header; away from the bow is a lift. Whether you experience a given shift as a header or lift depends on what tack you're on. A lift when you're on starboard tack is usually a header for a boat on port.

[8]As noted, land heats and cools more rapidly than the water. This temperature differential between land and water creates thermal winds. When the thermal wind starts to blow (developing), the wind shows a persistent shift. When it settles in (fully formed), it shows oscillations.

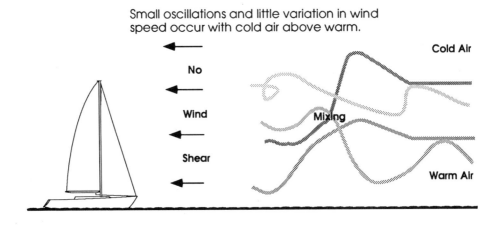

Small oscillations and little variation in wind speed occur with cold air above warm.

Cold Air

No

Wind

Mixing

Shear

Warm Air

FIGURE 8.10 *With cold air above warm, winds are fairly steady with but small oscillations.*

offshore breezes (winds that pass sun-heated land before moving over water).

Small oscillations are common when cold air is over warm. Normally, air cools with altitude. If you drive from "mile-high" Colorado Springs to the summit of Pikes Peak at over 14,000 feet in the summer, you should bring your down parka and mittens. With cold air above warm air, the hot air rises and cools, and the cool air, which is relatively denser, falls, and its temperature increases (see FIGURE 8.10). This causes considerable mixing from the top layer to the bottom. The mixing tends to equalize both wind direction and speed. The uniformity means that the air tends to move at the same speed and direction, no matter what the altitude. (Note how the arrows are the same length in FIGURE 8.10.) To be more specific: with cold air above warm—the typical condition—the wind shows but small oscillations and only the occasional small puff.

Strategy for an Oscillating Wind

In an oscillating shift, you tack when you detect a header in order to sail on the lifted tack as much as possible. In Table 8A, the average wind on port tack is about 355 degrees. If when close-hauled you are down to 358 or 002, you are being headed, and it is time to tack (see FIGURE 8.11). The faster a boat is able to tack, the smaller the header on which it will tack. A Star, for example, might tack when down to the median (355 degrees), while we wouldn't tack the catamaran we sailed in the 1988 America's Cup unless headed 10 degrees or more (005 degrees). This is because it is so difficult to

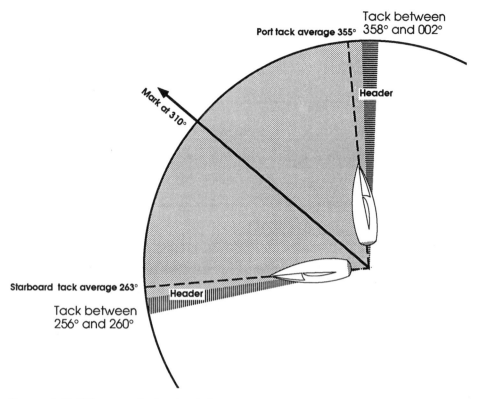

Port tack average 355°

Tack between 358° and 002°

Mark at 310°

Header

Starboard tack average 263°

Header

Tack between 256° and 260°

FIGURE 8.11 *When to tack when headed.*

tack a multihull. You're stopped in the water while the competition is going 15 knots. A boat going 15 knots is traveling 25.3 feet per second. Since you can easily lose 250 feet when tacking a catamaran, the wind shift must be sizeable enough for a tack to pay off.

To decide when to tack, focus on the median wind. If, for example, you're up 10 degrees on the median (345 degrees in Table 8A), and then you are headed by 5 degrees (350 degrees), you are still up 5 (the median is 355), so don't tack. Wait until your course drops at least to the median or below. Also, when headed, don't tack immediately. Wait until you're into it a bit before tacking. Otherwise, you'll likely sail out of the shift on the other side.

In an oscillating breeze, sail on the lifts—"stay in phase," as it is called. For example, if from your prerace testing and the two-number system you know that you are on a starboard-tack header when you start, you might want to tack to port immediately after the start to be lifted while on port tack (see white boat in FIGURE 8.12). In this instance, starting at the right side of the line is wise, as the white boat is. Here you can tack fairly easily without

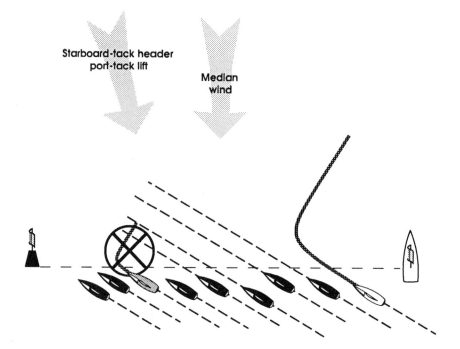

FIGURE 8.12 *In an oscillating wind try to get in phase immediately. Here white is positioned to tack to port to sail on the lifted port tack.*

having to worry so much about starboard-tackers who enjoy right-of-way. On the left side of the line, however, you might have dozens of starboard-tackers that can keep you from tacking. See the gray boat, with the "X" symbol, in the figure. (We will use this symbol to designate unwise, forbidden, or inappropriate actions.)

Also, while sailing in the optimum direction—on the lifted tack—you should probably take the sterns of boats, if need be, or put up with sailing in the disturbed air of a competitor heading in the same direction as you. This, of course, does not extend to match racing, where beating the other boat (tactics) takes priority over getting around the course the fastest. Also, it does not apply in fleet racing if there are one or more boats you have to beat for reasons related to scoring.

In an oscillating wind, stay in the middle and avoid the sides of the course. When you approach the layline take every opportunity to get back to the middle of the course. When sailing to one side in an oscillating shift, you might tack on smaller headers than you ordinarily would to get back into the middle. When sailing toward the middle, don't tack on small headers.

To say this another way, sail the long leg of the beat as early and for as

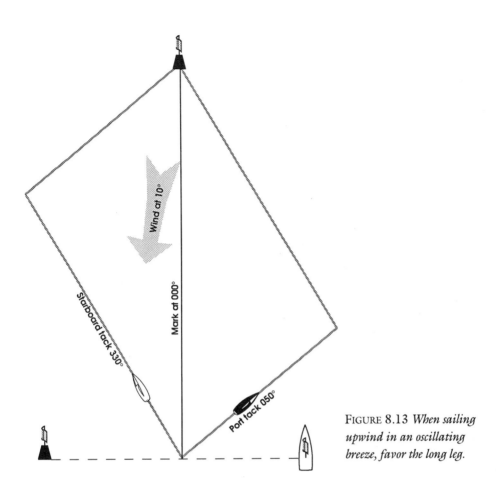

FIGURE 8.13 *When sailing upwind in an oscillating breeze, favor the long leg.*

much time as possible (see FIGURE 8.13). Usually, you will sail on one tack longer than the other. The long tack, or long leg of the beat, is the one on which your heading takes you closest to the mark. Say, for example, the mark bears 000 degrees, and the wind 10 degrees, as in the figure. On port tack you sail 50 degrees, on starboard, 330. Thus, starboard tack is the long tack because 330 degrees is closer to 0 than is 50. By emphasizing starboard tack (as the white boat does), you will be in the middle of the course and, thus, better able to take advantage of future wind shifts. The black boat gets off to a corner very quickly.

There are some exceptions to favoring the middle of the course in an oscillating breeze. In very light winds, the wind in the middle is often less than the wind on one or both sides. Also, the waves can be greater in the middle.

Eventually you'll have to sail on the layline to get to the mark, but do it later rather than earlier. Early laylines are poison—sailboat-racing death. They leave you no options. Thus, go to the point of no return late rather than early.

Strategy: Wind, Weather, and Current

CONDITIONS ASSOCIATED WITH A PERSISTENT SHIFT

A persistent shift continues moving in the same direction and does not return. Its causes are the passage of a front (gradient winds), a geographic shift, and the forming or decay of a sea breeze (thermal winds).

Strategy for a Persistent Shift

The strategy for sailing in a persistent shift is straightforward. With a persistent shift, sail toward the direction the new wind will come. If the wind is moving counterclockwise (to the left, as it is in FIGURE 8.14), you sail on starboard tack to the lefthand side of the course. With the counterclockwise wind shift, the white boat, on the left side of the course, is more upwind and, thus, ahead. Any boat on its right, no matter what the tack, is farther downwind and behind. Additionally, the boat farthest left in a lefthand shift comes out ahead.

Ladder rungs, such as in FIGURE 8.14, are helpful in visualizing this. Recall from Chapter 7 how the rails of the imaginary ladder are parallel to the wind, and the rungs are perpendicular to it. In FIGURE 8.14, the initial wind ladder is under the new ladder. With the initial wind, white and black boats are even. With the lefthand shift, white—the boat farthest left—is more upwind, on a higher ladder rung, and is ahead.

If, however, the wind is moving clockwise, sail on port tack to the right side of the course. To put this another way, with a persistent shift, you sail on the headed (or knocked) tack first, because that takes you to the correct side of the course. Also, in a righthand shift, the boat farthest to the right comes out ahead, as it ends up more upwind.

The danger of going to one side or another, however, must be made clear. If this isn't a persistent shift, but an oscillating shift, and the wind oscillates back, you're in big trouble.

Assuming this a persistent shift, however, the sooner you get to the new wind—to the appropriate left or right side of the course—the more boats you will be ahead of. Don't, however, go directly to the layline. At the layline, there is a good likelihood that you will overstand the mark if the wind continues shifting. Thus, as with an oscillating shift, it is best to tack well before the layline and make your final approach to the mark when much closer to it.

This is worthy of review. With an oscillating shift, you sail in the middle of the course and tack on the headers. With a persistent shift, you sail to one

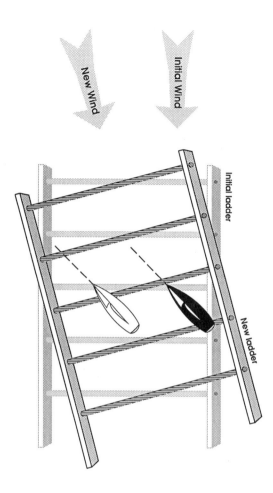

FIGURE 8.14 *Ladder rungs show the boat (white) closest to the new wind is ahead.*

side: the right (on the headed port tack) if the wind is going to the right or clockwise; the left (on headed starboard tack) if the wind is going left or counterclockwise. To put this another way: If you are lifted when sailing upwind in an *oscillating* wind, you should stay on this lifted tack until headed at least to the median before tacking. If, however, you are lifted when sailing upwind in a wind that is shifting *persistently*, you should tack. If you take nothing more from this book than this, you'll be a much better sailor.

Determining a Persistent Shift

If the strategy is uncomplicated, determining whether you're sailing in a persistent shift or another wind is the true challenge, however. For example, in the sixth race of the 1983 America's Cup, we were sailing with *Australia II* in a good northwesterly in Newport, a common gradient-wind (weather-system) condition after the passage of a cold front. It was blowing 15 knots. In Newport, the southwesterly thermal sea breeze often replaces the gradient northwest breeze on the second day, but the difficult call is when that will occur. A 15-knot wind is a good sign of stable gradient conditions. A southwest sea breeze would have trouble winning the battle of the breezes this day, or so I thought.

On *Liberty*, we were ahead in the series 3–2 at the time, needing but one more race to win. We won the start by seven seconds. *Australia II* tacked to starboard for the left side, and we followed to cover. *Australia* tacked, and we followed, putting ourselves directly in front of the Australian boat, as the book on match-racing tactics says. Both of us got a large port tack lift, and *Australia II* tacked (see screen in FIGURE 8.15).

FIGURE 8.15 Australia II*'s big lift.*

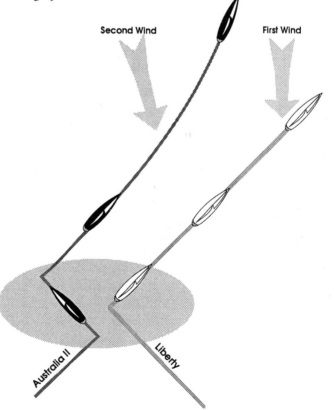

This was, presumably, to get clear air, as tacking on a lift is not the recommended strategy in what was, by all outward appearances, an oscillating wind.

The Australian boat just kept going and going, and finally tacked well to weather of us. Then *Australia II* got her own private sailing breeze. It was blowing several knots more in strength and at a better angle. *Australia II* was able to sail 15 to 18 degrees closer to the mark. This was the beginning of an extraordinary 100-degree persistent-wind shift. *Australia II* led at the mark by an insurmountable two minutes and twenty-nine seconds and at the finish by three minutes and twenty-five seconds.

I've often wondered how the Australians could have known that the shift was going to get there in time. We couldn't see it, nor had our prerace testing, including the Doppler system (discussed next), indicated anything of the sort. Also, the Australians weren't tentative or cautious about it. They just "headed for the hills" as if they knew what they were looking for. For me, it was the most singular occurrence in three America's Cup campaigns in Newport. Not even Halsey Herreshoff, as local as they come, had seen anything like it. That evened the series at three. At the end of the next completed race, the Australians owned the America's Cup.

As I've heard often enough, I should have covered the Australians. As so many have speculated, that's the reason I lost the America's Cup. In this series, I often broke the old America's Cup rule about covering the competition. I had a slow boat in *Liberty*. If I'd covered *Australia II*, which was faster, I'd have lost for sure. I can argue this the other way: rather than losing the America's Cup because I didn't cover *Australia II*, not covering made it a much closer series.

Wind Shear and a Persistent Shift

Over the years, particularly in the America's Cup, we've worked hard to improve our ability to forecast weather, in particular wind shifts. This was done with meteorologist Lee Davis and his Galson Technical Services. For us, the key to predicting wind shifts—the future, so to speak—was found by looking up. Winds aloft, especially wind shear, can be extremely helpful in this regard. The *Oxford American Dictionary*'s definition of shear is "successive layers being shifted laterally over each other." With wind shear, the wind direction changes rapidly with altitude. Incidentally, wind shear is very dangerous in aviation, as pilots think they are landing into the wind but suddenly they're not.

In sailboat racing, exaggerated wind shear can indicate a persistent shift.[9] Given certain conditions, the winds aloft tend to work their way down to the surface as the day progresses. Thus, it is important to know if there is abnormally large wind shear. In an America's Cup, this can be done by monitoring the wind direction, wind speed, and, as we will see, temperature at 100 feet, 500 feet, and 1,000 feet. (One need not have access to America's Cup technology; later we will see how monitoring wind shear can be done on any sailboat.)

As discussed, when on land, air usually cools with height; recall the Pikes Peak example. To put this another way, air is warmer on the ground, or surface, than above it. This cooling with height happens over water, too, particularly in the summer, when air and water temperatures are similar. With this temperature arrangement, the cold air falls and the hot air rises, and there is significant mixing (see FIGURE 8.10). This mixing tends to equalize both wind speed and direction top to bottom, making for consistent conditions: only small oscillations in direction and the occasional puff of wind.

However, when the water is much cooler than the air above it, the air near the water's surface can be colder than the air above. This is called a temperature inversion, and while it can happen anytime, it is most common over water in spring and fall. When this occurs, you tend to see a marked difference in wind direction (wind shear) and a difference in velocities with height (see FIGURE 8.16). This wind shear works its way down to the surface and can cause a persistent shift. In fact, exaggerated wind shear is an indication of a persistent shift. Velocities tend to work their way down to the surface as well.

Beginning in the 1983 America's Cup in Newport, we used a Doppler system to track wind speed and direction, that is, shear, aloft. It worked this way: An acoustical pulse was transmitted from a loud speaker–like device in a cone-shaped antenna. There were three of these antennae. One pointed vertically and the others pointed at small elevations and bearings off vertical. The sound pulses were reflected by turbulence and density changes in the air above the antennae in the atmosphere.

The same speaker became a microphone, listening for the backscatter echo. Then a computer analyzed the echo and determined frequency shifts. If the frequency of the initial pulse decreased, the air was moving (shearing) away from the speaker. If the frequency increased, the air was moving toward the

---

[9]As discussed in Chapter 4, there is a difference in wind speed, and, thus, direction, at the top of the mast when compared with the bottom, due to the friction between the wind and the water (see FIGURES 4.8 and 4.10). This difference accounts for a normal 3 to 5 degrees of twist, or shear, in the wind. What we are talking about here is a difference, top to bottom, of 10 or 20 degrees or even more.

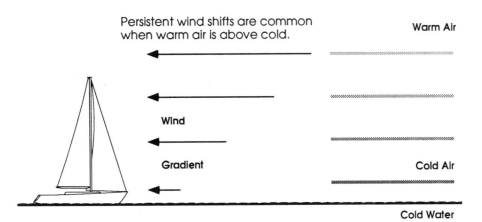

Persistent wind shifts are common
when warm air is above cold.

Warm Air

Wind

Gradient

Cold Air

Cold Water

FIGURE 8.16 *With warm air above cold, look for a persistent shift.*

speaker. Then, using trigonometry and physical laws governing the speed of sound in air, the horizontal and vertical wind aloft could be determined. Our Doppler system was used to measure winds aloft every fifteen minutes at 165-foot (50-meter) intervals up to .6 mile (1 kilometer) above the race course.

From the wind speed and direction measured aloft, we could determine how far left or right the oscillations would be as well as the timing. By using wind shear analysis, we were able to identify the formation of the sea breeze and the opposing return-flow aloft and figure when they would make their appearance. In 1983, this technology was only used in research or by NASA.

To see the future, looking up the course proved almost as good a crystal ball as looking up in the air. We'd send boats out to measure surface winds, halfway up the weather leg and at the weather mark. This information would come to us on *Liberty* by way of a coded radio report. (Up to the ten-minute gun, such outside contact is legal.) On a private radio channel, we received messages from the spotters that went like this, "We have a tuna on the hook at echo, bravo, whiskey, sierra, Nevada, tango." Messages like this would tell us the wind speed and direction on the surface of the water, as well as at various heights, and what we might expect over time. In addition to wind speed, wind direction, and sea state in thirty-minute intervals, we would also receive any other weather information that might prove helpful, such as when to expect the sea breeze, or cloud cover that might nullify a sea breeze, and the passage of frontal systems.

We would get a coded radio report at eleven minutes before the start—the "eleventh-hour" report. If we were too busy to decode it—which was often the case when we were about to lock horns with an opponent in a match race—it was decoded by those on our tender. Before the ten-minute gun, they delivered it to us on a small piece of paper inside a cut tennis ball, lobbed aboard *Liberty*.

Did I pay attention to the Doppler information and the weather information up the course? Yes. Were they accurate 100 percent of the time? No. However, the information was probably accurate 50 percent of the time. In the world of wind shifts, that's some crystal ball. We used a similar Doppler system in Perth in 1986–87. As indicated, we did something similar in San Diego for 1992 with the help of Galson Technical Services.

The winds-aloft theory has relevance to those without access to America's Cup technology. Sailors can compare the angular readings of the masthead fly with the sails or telltales down low, looking for abnormally large wind shear. Wind shear usually (90 percent of the time in the northern hemisphere) moves to the right (clockwise) at the masthead. With exaggerated wind shear, the top of the sail(s) is reaching (on starboard tack), and the bottom beating. (On port tack, the top is beating, and the bottom reaching.) Excessive wind shear is what makes the sails so difficult to trim, particularly on port tack. It also accounts for very different sail settings on opposite tacks. Also, one tack—typically the port tack—feels much more sluggish than the other. Exaggerated wind shear, difficulty in controlling twist (see Chapter 4), very different sail settings on one tack versus the other, sluggish feeling on one side versus the other, and odd instrument readings on one tack compared with the other are all indications of abnormally large wind shear and, likewise, a persistent shift.

Note that the degree of shear often corresponds to the amount of the shift. To put this another way: the greater the shear, the greater the shift. Also, the more the wind shears, the sooner one can expect the shift.

Obviously, wind shear is a good indication of a persistent shift. Its absence is a good indication of an oscillating shift.

With wind shear which, as indicated, is usually to the right in the northern hemisphere—the strategy is usually to sail toward the righthand side of the course (on the headed port tack). That said, with the typical righthand shift, as signaled by wind shear, the boat will feel awful on port tack. All you can do when on port with excessive wind shear is to move the headsail's lead forward and overtrim the mainsheet and/or raise the traveler to minimize twist at the top of both sails. And grin and bear it. If you identify a persistent shift properly and sail appropriately, you might well have more to grin about at the weather mark. If you don't, and the wind shifts back, there's always tomorrow.

Oscillating-Persistent Shift

The oscillating-persistent shift is the most challenging condition. Here, the wind oscillates in the midst of a persistent shift (see Table 8C). The proper technique when sailing upwind is a combination of the former two strategies. Work toward the direction of the new shift, while tacking on headers. Thus, if the wind is going left, lean toward the left side of the course (starboard tack), but also tack on the headers, as if it were an oscillating shift.

If difficult to respond to properly, the oscillating-persistent shift is the least common of the three wind patterns. Also, on a race course with short legs, which are now popular in sailboat racing, even when such a shift does occur, you tend to find yourself sailing an entire leg in what amounts to either an oscillating or a persistent shift. There often isn't time for both events to occur.

VELOCITY HEADERS AND LIFTS

In Chapter 7, we discussed velocity headers and lifts. To review that briefly: In a velocity shift, the true wind doesn't actually shift—it increases or decreases in strength—but on the boat, due to apparent wind and the boat's momentum, it appears to shift. A *drop* in wind moves the apparent wind *forward*. This is a velocity header. An *increase* in the wind moves the apparent wind *aft*. This is a velocity *lift*.

If you know you are in a velocity header—moving from more wind into less—the strategy is to head up rather than fall off, according to the telltales. If you know you are in a velocity lift—sailing into more wind from less—the strategy is to fall off rather than head up. Note that velocity headers and lifts are a short-term dynamic. Once the boat slows or speeds up, as is appropriate, both the apparent-wind angle and the course steered are about the same as before.

What follows are nine rules and postulates to help formulate an upwind strategy. (Be warned, however, they don't establish a priority; you must do that. For example, sometimes you should sail for more wind, or for less current, etc.)

1. Sail toward more wind, unless overpowered.

2. Sail toward more current (deep water) if it is fair, less current (shallow water) if it is foul. Of course, if the latter, don't run aground.

3. Sail for smaller waves when sailing upwind, larger waves when sailing

down, until steering becomes a problem. Note, however, that sometimes increased waves show current against the wind, which can be helpful when sailing upwind (see FIGURE 8.8).

4. If you are in an oscillating shift, stay on the lifted tack but tack on the headers.

a) Don't tack, however, until your course drops to at least the median or average wind (see FIGURE 8.11). The point at which you tack depends on how quickly your boat tacks.

b) Even then, don't tack immediately but sail into the header.

c) Because it is so important to sail on the lifted tack, take the sterns of boats, if need be, or sail in bad air.

d) Stay in the middle of the course; sail the long tack first (see FIGURE 8.13).

e) Avoid laylines until the very end.

5. If you are experiencing a persistent shift, sail on the headed or knocked tack first. The sooner you get to the new wind, right or left, the better. Also, the boat farthest left in a lefthand shift or farthest right in a right-hand shift comes out ahead.

a) Avoid the layline, however, or you'll likely overstand.

b) Make your final approach to the mark when closer to it.

c) Wind shear is a good sign of a persistent shift. The more shear there is, the more the shift will be and the sooner it will occur.

6. In an oscillating-persistent shift, go in the direction of the new wind, as if it is a persistent shift.

a) Tack on the headers, however.

7. If you know you are in a velocity header—moving from *more* wind into *less*—head up rather than fall off. This is a short-term response.

8. If you know you are in a velocity lift—moving from *less* wind into *more*—fall off rather than head up. This, again, is a short-term response.

9. If you don't know if it is a velocity shift or wind shift, don't alter course.

DOWNWIND SAILING

Downwind, a boat can sail straight to the mark; this isn't possible upwind. Nevertheless, sailing a dead-downwind rhumb-line course is usually slow. Thus, a boat almost always tacks downwind, that is, sails on a broad reach and jibes back and forth. Wind speed strongly affects this reaching angle, more properly called the jibe angle. In heavy winds, a boat can sail almost directly toward the mark. In medium and light winds, jibing angles should be progressively wider—that is, the boat sails higher. The jibe angle is very wide, too, with very fast boats, such as the catamaran that we sailed in the 1988 America's Cup described in Chapter 2. Even downwind in such boats, you typically sail at 30 degrees to the apparent wind because you're going so fast.

It is easy to approximate the proper angle when sailing upwind, as the width of the groove—between high and slow and low and fast—is so narrow, about 10 degrees. Downwind the width of the groove—between high and fast and low and slow—is closer to 25 degrees. This is why boats sail so many different angles when heading downwind.

As mentioned, upwind or down, there is an optimum combination of sailing angle and speed that is better than all the rest (see the white boat in FIGURE 8.17). This combination gives the maximum VMG (see the dotted line)—the

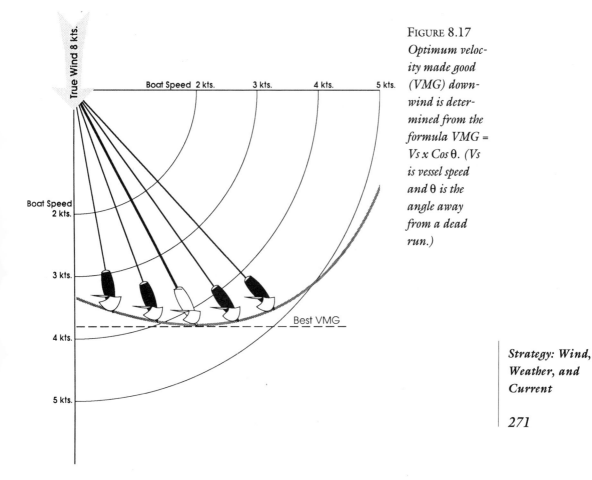

FIGURE 8.17
Optimum velocity made good (VMG) downwind is determined from the formula VMG = Vs x Cos θ. (Vs is vessel speed and θ is the angle away from a dead run.)

fastest course down (as in the figure) or up the ladder in a particular wind speed.

Big boats often have target boat speeds, discussed in Chapter 7, to determine jibe angles. In the heat of battle, however, the targets and/or angles might not be readily available. Small boats usually don't have targets; most of them don't even have boat-speed indicators. A useful rule after rounding the weather mark is to sail the reciprocal of the course sailed on the weather leg or parallel boats still on that leg. This will get you close to the optimum jibe angle. Then when things settle down, sail your targets if in a big boat, or if in a dinghy, sail at an angle where the boat feels and appears fast. In a small boat without instrumentation or a big boat without targets or some sort of course protractor that helps to figure jibe angles, the cardinal question is, Am I gaining on or losing to the competition?

Oscillating Shift: Downwind

As will be more apparent, upwind and downwind are opposites—mirror images—and much of what we've said earlier in this chapter is opposite to what is done when sailing downwind.

When sailing *upwind* in an oscillating shift, we tack on the headers. Then we sail on the lifted tack. When sailing *downwind* in an oscillating shift, jibe on the lifts to sail on the headed tack.

A lift can be determined by the compass, of course. An easier way to determine a lift is with spinnaker trim, if you sail with one. If the spinnaker trimmer is calling for the spinnaker pole to go back and/or is easing the sheet, you are being lifted. So jibe to sail on the headed tack (see FIGURE 8.18).

Also to get in phase with the oscillations, sail on the headed jibe first. As noted earlier, oscillating shifts are the most common wind shifts. Obviously this is true downwind as well. If there was an oscillating shift on the upwind leg, the likelihood is that there will be one on the downwind leg. Current or wind velocity (discussed later) and obviously a persistent shift can alter this strategy.

Sailing to the layline too early should be avoided when sailing downwind, too. To do this, sail the long jibe first. (Upwind, sail the long tack first.) Not only does sailing the long jibe keep you away from the layline, but it maximizes VMG—speed down the ladder to the mark.

An easy way to determine which is the longer jibe is to recall the weather leg. If you sailed longer on starboard tack on the beat (see FIGURE 8.13), start on the port tack on the run. Better yet, check the compass course on either jibe. The course closest to the mark heading is the longer jibe.

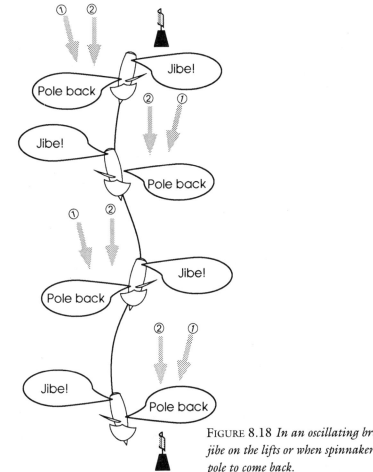

FIGURE 8.18 *In an oscillating breeze downwind, jibe on the lifts or when spinnaker trimmer calls for pole to come back.*

Persistent Shift: Downwind

When sailing downwind in a persistent shift, you should sail on the lifted tack first. (See the white boat in FIGURE 8.19.) If the spinnaker trimmer is asking for the pole to come back, you're going the correct way. Then jibe—before the layline—and sail the headed tack for the mark. Again, more wind on the "wrong" side of the course or more current if favorable, less if unfavorable, can alter this strategy.

Strategy: Wind, Weather, and Current

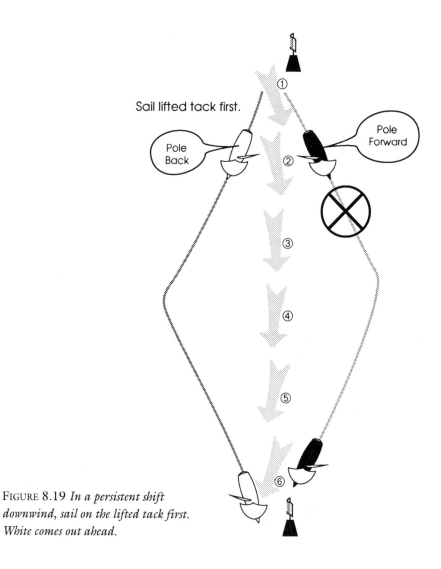

Sail lifted tack first.

Pole Back

Pole Forward

FIGURE 8.19 *In a persistent shift downwind, sail on the lifted tack first. White comes out ahead.*

Oscillating-Persistent Shift: Downwind

Downwind in an oscillating-persistent shift is a combination of the above two techniques. Sail on the lifted tack at first. However, jibe on the lifts. Again, current or more wind can alter this strategy.

Downwind Velocity Lifts and Headers

You will recall when sailing upwind, a lull moves the apparent wind forward, making it appear like a header. A puff brings it aft, making it appear like a lift. Velocity headers and lifts are factors downwind as well. As in upwind sailing, it isn't easy to tell the difference between velocity shifts and actual wind shifts. Nevertheless, misjudging them when sailing downwind isn't as costly. Suppose you jibe on a velocity lift—remember the rule of downwind sailing in an oscillating wind is jibe on the lifts. A jibe isn't nearly as costly in terms of speed as a tack. Also, you're jibing into more wind, and this is almost always the recommended technique.

Sail for Velocity: Downwind

Upwind, reacting properly to shifts is important—often *the* most important skill. However, when sailing downwind, looking for more wind and placing your own boat accordingly are often more important, at least until you are overpowered.

When running, your boat speed is *subtracted* from the wind speed to arrive at the apparent wind. This means that the apparent wind you sail in is considerably lighter than the true wind. Usually, you can handle an increase in wind speed. When beating, your boat speed is *added* to the wind speed. This means the wind you sail in is considerably higher than the true wind, and you get overpowered sooner.

In Chapter 7, I wrote about target boat speeds. When sailing downwind, if you are fast for the wind speed, you head off to bleed off speed. Similarly, with more wind, you have more speed, and you can head off and sail closer to the mark, that is, more downwind.

Watch for more wind on the water when sailing downwind. A good way to do this is to look behind you, and if you see it on the water, change course accordingly. Obviously, wind is harder to see when it is behind you than in front, as when beating. Hunting for wind when running is probably not a job for the steerer; if possible, have a crew member watch for it.

Once you find wind, do all you can to stay in it. To do this, you might sail a lower than optimum course. By paralleling the puff, you stay in it longer. If you see that you are heading out of the puff, jibe to stay in it. Jibing gives you more freedom to go wind hunting, particularly if your crew is up to the task of jibing.

CURRENT

When sailing downwind, as when sailing upwind, you want to sail in favorable current and avoid unfavorable current. When the current is favorable, consider heading for deep water, where it can be running faster. If the current is unfavorable, it can pay to head to shallow water. Remember that the current, resulting from a tide change, changes first in shallow water.

Waves or lack thereof can indicate where the current is foul or fair. When sailing downwind, you might look for a place that has smoother water (see FIGURE 8.8), as current running with the wind (your direction when running) makes for smoother water. (Of course, this can also mean less wind.)

The following are eight rules for downwind strategy.

1. Maximize VMG with the best combination of downwind angle and speed (see FIGURE 8.17).

2. In an oscillating shift, jibe on the lifts (see FIGURE 8.18).

3. In a persistent shift, sail on the lifted tack first (see FIGURE 8.19).

4. In an oscillating-persistent shift, sail on the lifted tack first. This is the strategy for a persistent shift; however, jibe on the lifts, as if you're sailing in an oscillating shift.

5. No matter what the wind pattern, avoid laylines until the end.

6. Misjudging a velocity lift or header is less costly when sailing downwind. This is because you are jibing into more wind.

7. More wind velocity and/or a favorable current can be reasons to violate rules 2, 3, and 4.

8. Sail for more wind and fall off or jibe to stay in it. Jibing doesn't have as significant an impact on speed as does tacking.

REACHING

Sailing has a special twist on geometry. Although the shortest distance between two points remains a straight line, rarely is it the fastest course. Sailing a straight line is impossible when beating and usually is not faster when running. On a reaching leg, however, the fastest course often is that straight line, so the basic strategy on a reach is to sail the rhumb line. That said, there are so many exceptions that the rule is nearly meaningless.

For example, a reach is the fastest point of sail, and so another principle on this leg is to sail for speed. This means sail the course that will get you planing or going fast, regardless of the rhumb line. If the rhumb line course is too close to the wind or it is too windy for a spinnaker, sail a lower course with the spinnaker. Allow yourself to sag down below the rhumb line until the course to mark is a tight reach. Then put up a reacher or a headsail, drop the spinnaker, and sail back up to the mark. Don't allow yourself to sag so low, however, that you must beat to the mark.

An alternative is not to set your spinnaker immediately at the mark. Stay high of the rhumb line and close-reach with your jib. Then, after working your way to weather, hoist the spinnaker and sail down to the mark with speed. Sailing high also puts you upwind of other boats, allowing you to pass them more easily.

Velocity Changes

Reaching is the same as running. You head up for speed. So in lulls, head up. Use puffs to head down to get back to the rhumb line. If the breeze has been increasing during the race, head high at the beginning of the leg when the wind is lighter, and head low later, when the wind should be heavier. When the wind is going light, sail low—when you have the most wind—and high later when there should be less wind (see FIGURE 8.20).

Perhaps, the most extreme example of this technique was done by accident in the awful Fastnet Race of 1979. Dennis Durgan, who would be my tactician on *Freedom* in 1980, was sailing an Admiral's Cupper for a European team. When the crew rounded Fastnet Rock and headed into the fury of the storm, they were too ill or frightened to come on deck to reef. Unable to reef, Durgan had to sail low—about 25 degrees low of course. His major concern was that he avoid running into England. After the storm passed, the wind lightened and went aft. I was on *Williwaw*, as a member of the U.S. Admiral's Cup team, and we were running in horrible seas in light winds. Meanwhile, Durgan just kept hardening up and was reaching along at 14 knots. He finished second or third in the race.

Wind Shifts When Reaching

The strategy for a persistent header when reaching is the same as sailing in a building breeze. Go high of the mark early when you can, and low later,

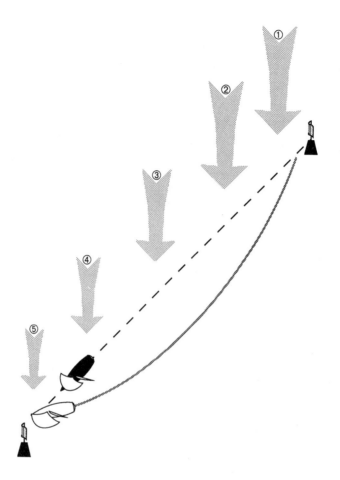

FIGURE 8.20 *Go low early, high later, when reaching in a dying breeze.*

when you have to, due to the wind shift. Do the opposite on a persistent lift: go low early, high later. Alternatively, treat a persistent lift as if you are sailing in a dying breeze (see FIGURE 8.20). In an oscillating wind, try to keep a constant apparent-wind angle. Go up in the lifts, off in the headers.

KEY TO LOCAL KNOWLEDGE

As should be clear, the strategies for oscillating, persistent, and oscillating-persistent shifts are different. Also, they are different when beating, running, or reaching. The difficulty is less in figuring out the strategy than in identifying the sailing wind, which is a combination of the gradient, thermal, and geographic wind.

The process starts with a weather forecast, and the better the forecast, the better off you are. Then work to match the prediction to what you saw and what truly happened. You aren't necessarily explaining it; you're just saying, I heard this forecast, saw that, this occurred, and I did this. The following chart can be helpful in this regard. The location where you sail may be a little different or a lot different, but try to match wind to causes, to indications, and to strategy. (Note that this chart is keyed to the northern hemisphere.)

Wind	Description	Causes	Indications	Strategy
Oscillating	Pendulum.	1. Cold air over warm.	Air aloft colder than air on surface. Absence of wind shear.	Upwind: Sail on lifts as much as possible. Tack on headers. Downwind: Sail on headed tack. Jibe on lifts. Reaching: Try to keep constant apparent-wind angle. Up in lifts, off in headers.
		2. Developed thermal conditions.	Sea breeze has had time to develop. Persistent shift changing to an oscillating shift.	
		3. Offshore breezes.	Buildings, trees, etc., that can cause wind to shift.	
Persistent shift	Swings in one direction.	1. Frontal passage.	Cold front is signaled by a shift of wind from southwest	Upwind: Sail to new wind or on headed tack first. Then sail lifted tack

Wind	Description	Causes	Indications	Strategy
			to northwest. Other signals include thunderheads and thunderstorms. Also associated with passage of warm front with wind shifting from east to southwest. Also clouds change from cirrus to cirrostratus, altostratus, nimbostratus (rain), and cumulus.	to mark. Running: Sail on lifted tack first. Sail headed tack to mark. Reaching: In a persistent header, go high early, low later. In a persistent lift, go low early, high later.
		2. Development of sea breeze.	Hot, sunny day. Heated land, cold water. Cumulus clouds.	
		3. Decay of sea breeze.	Air aloft is warmer than air on surface. Wind shear, sun setting, or clouds obscuring sun.	
		4. Geographic shift.	Shoreline can cause persistent shift.	
		5. Passage of a low-pressure system.	Rapidly falling barometer. If low passes to north, clockwise shift; to south, counterclockwise.	

Wind	Description	Causes	Indications	Strategy
Oscillating-persistent shifts	Persistent shifts with oscillations.	All the above		Upwind: sail toward new wind, as if a persistent shift, but tack on headers, as if an oscillating shift. Running: Sail on lifted tack first, but jibe on lifts.

9 | Rules

When I started sailing, I had an imperfect view of the racing rules. I knew that tacking too close wasn't allowed, but I didn't know exactly what "too close" meant. In truth, I didn't know what the rule meant by tacking. I thought tacking began when the skipper called "hard-a-lee," and the sails starting luffing.

Ignorance of the rules is no excuse. The United States Yacht Racing Union (US SAILING) Appeal 38 says exactly that. You want to be a law-abiding citizen, so you need to learn the laws of the land. You want to be a law-abiding racing sailor, so you need to learn the laws of the sea and, more specifically, the yacht-racing rules.

My learning of the racing rules has been ad hoc. I've grown comfortable with the rules through the huge number of races I've sailed. Moreover, I can remember clearly what happened last summer on the second beat on August 10—indeed, the second beat on August 10, 1974. For most people, however, experience isn't a very efficient way to learn the rules. Also, when educated in the school of hard knocks, the lessons can be costly.

The racing rules are about as complex as our legal system. They are the type of endeavor about which people can, and do, write books and make videos. Confining this discussion to one chapter, we will focus on the most important rules—those that are used the most often. An excellent way to understand the racing rules is through David Dellenbaugh's video, "Learn the Racing Rules," produced with *Sailing World* magazine. Dellenbaugh's video, as well as his writing on the rules, were helpful in the preparation of this chapter. Another good source is *Understanding the Yacht Racing Rules*, a book by Dave Perry, who was kind enough to review this chapter.

INTERNATIONAL YACHT RACING RULES

The International Yacht Racing Rules (IYRR), under which most of us race, are issued by the International Yacht Racing Union (IYRU) every four years, after the Olympic Games. Presently, we are racing under the 1989–92 rules. The following remarks confine themselves specifically to these rules. Nevertheless, the most important Right of Way Rules and those that apply to Rounding or Passing Marks and Obstructions don't typically change to any significant degree from one period to the next. Rule books can be purchased from national sailing authorities.[1]

There are seventy-eight rules, divided into six major parts. There are also sixteen appendices, as well as dozens of cases issued by the IYRU and appeals issued by national sailing authorities. Appeals, which are separate publications and not found in the rule book, are authoritative interpretations, not in themselves rules. Nevertheless, they are extremely helpful in penetrating the language, perhaps more important in penetrating the intent behind a rule. (Looseleaf binders of appeals can likewise be purchased from national sailing authorities.) The rules themselves span 134 pages. The most important ones fill eight pages. They are, however, a rigorous eight pages.

The rules aren't, for the most part, intuitive. If you want to learn them, you'll probably have to study them. Is it worth it? My guess is that many more people would race sailboats if they weren't frightened off by an imperfect or incomplete knowledge of the rules. When you're afraid to mix it up with another boat because you're unsure of the rules, you give away too much to an opponent who knows the rules and isn't afraid to use them.

Before delving into the rules, let's talk about attitude. You're going to make mistakes with the rules. Even the experts—the guys who write the books—make mistakes. I know I do on occasion. When too many boats are trying to occupy too little space, there are bound to be infractions of the rules. If you've made a mistake, take the penalty and get on with the game. Think of it as an object lesson. You're not a felon, after all; this is a sport, a game. Don't let a mistake with the rules ruin your entire day or let a fear of making a mistake keep you away. In the bygone days, one strike—one mistake with the rules—and you were out. As mentioned in Chapter 3, Alan Raffee and I needed to beat Lowell North in the last race of the 1968 Olympic trials in the Star class to make the Olympic team, but we hit a mark and were out of the race and the Olympics. More recently, alternative penalty rules for violators (such

---

[1] Contact US SAILING, P.O. Box 209, Newport, RI 02840 (401) 849-5200.

as a 720-degree turn or 20 percent penalty) have changed that. In fact, "keep[ing] yachts racing" is the expressed intent of alternative penalties.

UNDERLYING PRINCIPLES OF THE RULES

The modern yacht racing rules come to us from Harold "Mike" Vanderbilt, skipper of three America's Cup defenders when the J-Class boats raced for the America's Cup. Vanderbilt skippered *Enterprise* in 1930, *Rainbow* in 1934, and *Ranger* in 1937. He was a national champion in bridge and the inventor of contract bridge. Perhaps it was his love of complexity that accounts for the obvious complexity of the racing rules. One can say that the racing rules are contract bridge on the high seas. The rules are complex, but they work well in preventing collisions, even when racing in large fleets in tight quarters. Also, they promote fair sailing. Safety and fairness are the underlying principles of the rules.

The rules are designed to be a "shield," not a "sword." That very language appears in USYRU Appeal 233. In the real world, however, some use them as a sword—that is, to win races. In yacht racing, it's important to distinguish who uses the rules as a weapon and who uses them for protection. As the expression goes, Know thy enemy. That's a little strong for yacht racing. A better expression might be, Know thy competitor.

The late Tom Blackaller was one of my rivals whom I came to know well and admire in his fairness in applying the rules. If you crossed him on port (Rule 36), he wouldn't take a cheap shot. He wouldn't give you a thin inch either.

For example, in one America's Cup Trials race in Perth, his *USA*, on starboard tack, was ahead of *Stars & Stripes*. I had a chance to cross him on port at the finish and to pass him. I knew if I didn't take the shot, I wasn't going to win the race. I just seized the opportunity and crossed him. If I was wrong, I was going to lose the race and likely the rig. Or worse. With 65-foot boats, there' s a point—a very long point—of no return. It was so close as I crossed Blackaller that I had to close my eyes. We must have missed him by 6 inches. He didn't protest.

Suffice it to say that not everyone you or I race against is so scrupulous. In my experience, the younger, more aggressive competitors who are trying to make names for themselves are the ones who push the rules. There are some people I'd never try to cross on port tack, because I know they're going to take a cheap shot—by saying I forced them to alter course to avoid a collision. That's a place where umpiring, as used in the 1992 America's Cup, can make a difference.

FUNDAMENTAL RULES

Part I of the rules comprises the Fundamental Rules and Definitions. Their location—first in the rule book—and their weighty name—Fundamental Rules—are testimony to their importance. To reference them briefly:

Rendering Assistance: A yacht shall render all assistance to a person or other vessel in trouble when in a position to do so. If you do so, you can seek redress under Rule 69(b).

Responsibility of a Yacht: Whether to start or continue a race or not is the responsibility of the individual skipper, not the race committee. You know your boat and crew better than the race committee does.

Fair Sailing: This is a requirement to abide by the rules and to sail in recognition of the principles of fair play and good sportsmanship. A yacht is subject to penalty under this rule only when there is a "clear-cut violation" and no other rule applies.

Accepting Penalties: If you realize you have violated a rule, you must accept your penalty: either withdraw or accept an alternative penalty (for instance, the 720-degree turn), if prescribed in the sailing instructions. You can't just continue to sail as if nothing happened. If disqualified from a race under Fair Sailing or Accepting Penalties, you can't use this as your throw-out race, per Rule 74.5(c).

DEFINITIONS

The remainder of Part I consists of definitions of eighteen terms, such as starting, luffing, clear astern, clear ahead, and overlap. These might appear obvious, but the wording is very specific. Note that when applying or studying other rules, definitions—included in Part I—appear in italics. We will use that typographical convention here in the quoted material.

Take, for example, the definition of tacking. It reads, "A yacht is *tacking* from the moment she is beyond head to wind until she has *borne away* to a *close-hauled* course." So tacking doesn't start when the skipper calls "hard-a-lee," as noted at the beginning of this chapter. Rather, the rule book definition starts when the boat is just beyond head to wind and spans about 45 degrees, rather than 90 degrees. That distinction can be important, because when tacking you are, essentially, a man or woman "without a country." You have few rights. Also, note that completing the tack doesn't have anything to do with when the crew gets the headsail in. Rather, tacking ends when the boat is on a close-hauled course. That distinction, too, is important because it can sometimes take thirty seconds or more for a crew to trim a large over-lapping genoa.

RIGHT OF WAY RULES

Pages thirty-two to forty-six make up the Right of Way Rules. Nevertheless, they don't specifically address right of way; rather, they say which boat must keep clear. Before turning to which boat must keep clear, the right-of-way yacht is not completely devoid of responsibility. Rule 32.1 says that even when in the right, she must take evasive action, if possible, to avoid a major collision. The rules absolutely do not countenance collisions.

Note, also, that these are racing rules only. Sailboats that aren't racing or intending to race are subject to the International Regulations for Preventing Collisions at Sea or Government Right of Way Rules, which vary according to location. Appendix 9 of the book has excerpts from the International Regulations for Preventing Collisions at Sea.

The Right of Way Rules view all racing situations in one of three ways, and it is helpful to read and apply the rules accordingly: 1) boats are on opposite tacks; 2) boats are on the same tack, or 3) one or both boats are changing tacks.

Port-Starboard: Rule 36

Rule 36—the opposite-tack rule—is known to most racers. It says that a port-tacker (P) must keep clear of a starboard-tacker (S).[2] If P can't cross S, it has two options: duck or tack. Note that it is courteous for the starboard-tacker to hail "starboard," but such a hail isn't mandatory. All yachts are bound to keep a good lookout, according to IYRU Appeal Case 51. If the starboard-tacker has to alter course to avoid a collision, the port-tacker has infringed Rule 36. This was the essence of the Blackaller example, cited earlier.

Often, the starboard-tacker yells "starboard!" And the port-tacker yells "hold your course!" Neither of these hails is mandatory, and the latter is usu-ally inappropriate. As discussed above under Rule 32.1, the starboard-tacker doesn't have to hold its course if it thinks a collision will result. Rather, it

_____

[2]In this chapter, we will use the conventions P for the port-tack boat, S for starboard, W for windward, L for leeward, I for inside, O for outside, and M for middle.

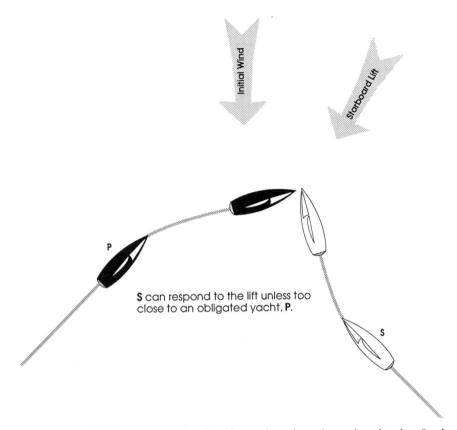

FIGURE 9.1 *Rule 36 says a port-tacker (black) must keep clear of a starboard-tacker. Starboard can also respond to a lift unless too close to port to allow the other boat from keeping clear.*

should alter course to avoid a collision and then protest the port-tack yacht.

A typical situation is when the boats are sailing in shifty winds. In FIG-URE 9.1, P (black) thinks she can cross S (white). Then S gets a lift, which is, usually, a header to P. The question is, Does S have to hold its course? According to IYRU Case 52, the starboard-tacker can respond to a wind shift at any time, "unless (starboard) is so close to an obligated yacht [port] in the act of keeping clear that her course change would prevent that yacht from keeping clear." So if on starboard tack and the lift occurs when close to P, you must, in effect, "hold your course." Other limitations on altering course are the subject of Rule 35, discussed later.

Opposite-tack Rule 36 is applicable downwind as well as upwind (see FIGURE 9.2, right). When the yacht clear astern is running or reaching on starboard tack, the port-tack yacht must keep clear. In Rule 37.2, however, the yacht clear astern must keep clear of a yacht clear ahead (see FIGURE 9.2,

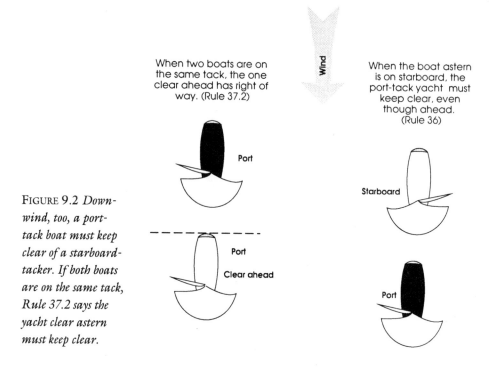

When two boats are on the same tack, the one clear ahead has right of way. (Rule 37.2)

Wind

When the boat astern is on starboard, the port-tack yacht must keep clear, even though ahead. (Rule 36)

Port

Starboard

Port
Clear ahead

Port

FIGURE 9.2 *Down-wind, too, a port-tack boat must keep clear of a starboard-tacker. If both boats are on the same tack, Rule 37.2 says the yacht clear astern must keep clear.*

left). While this may seem a contradiction, note that rule 37.2 only applies to yachts on the same tack.

There are some exceptions to the starboard-tack rule, for example, when the starboard-tack boat has started prematurely. Until the starboard-tack boat clears the line and starts properly, she must keep clear of all boats, including those on port-tack. Other exceptions include if the boat on starboard tack is in the midst of doing circles under the alternative penalty rule (discussed later), if the port-tacker is rescuing someone who fell overboard, and if port is capsized, anchored, or aground. Note that when anchored or aground, the port-tack boat must hail to that effect. Later, we will see that the port-tacker has rights over the starboard-tacker if the port-tacker is the inside boat at a leeward-mark rounding. This, however, is subject to some limitations.

Boats on the Same Tack: Rule 37

The second way the rule classifies racing situations is that boats are on the same tack. This is the focus of Rule 37—Same Tack, Basic Rule. The rule addresses two possible relationships: the boats are overlapped, or they aren't .

If they are not overlapped (see FIGURE 9.3, top left), one is "clear ahead," or the other is "clear astern." The definition of "Clear Astern and Clear Ahead; Overlap" reads: "A yacht is *clear astern* of another when her hull and equipment in normal position are abaft [behind] an imaginary line projected abeam from the aftermost point of the other's hull and equipment in normal position.... The yachts *overlap* [see FIGURE 9.3, top right] when neither is *clear astern*; or when, although one is *clear astern*, an intervening yacht *overlaps* both of them" (see FIGURE 9.3, bottom).

Note in the bottom of FIGURE 9.3 that A overlaps C because B overlaps both of them. You can't secure an overlap by letting off a spinnaker halyard or something similar. Further, the only time the overlap rule applies to boats on opposite tacks is at leeward mark roundings (that is, whenever Rule 42 applies).

According to Rule 37.1, when an overlap exists, the windward boat (W) must keep clear of the leeward boat (L). FIGURE 9.4 shows the possible overlap positions. In each case, black, as the windward boat, must keep clear. W must keep clear of hiking crew on the leeward boat as well as the boat itself.

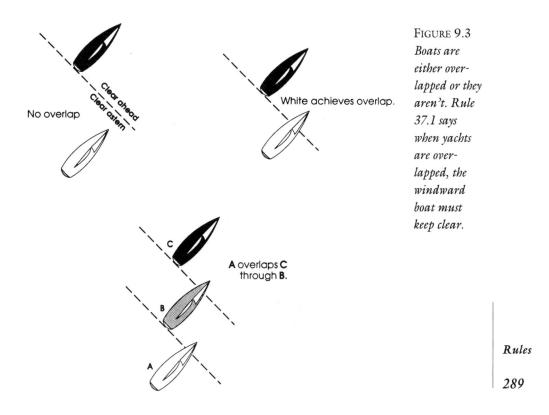

No overlap

Clear ahead
Clear astern

White achieves overlap.

A overlaps C
through B.

FIGURE 9.3
Boats are either over-lapped or they aren't. Rule 37.1 says when yachts are over-lapped, the windward boat must keep clear.

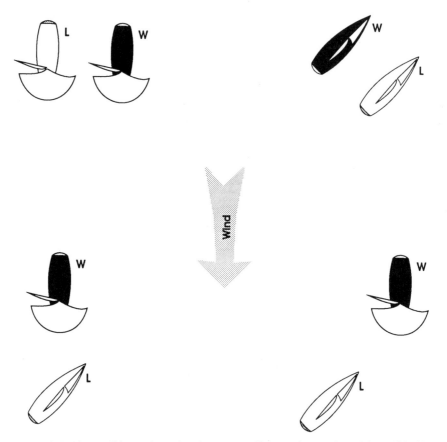

FIGURE 9.4 *The possible overlapped positions. In all cases, the windward boat (black) must keep clear.*

What happens when there isn't an overlap (see FIGURE 9.2, left)? According to Rule 37.2, when one yacht is clear astern, the yacht clear astern shall keep clear of a yacht clear ahead. Again, this presumes they are on the same tack. If on different tacks, the port-tack yacht must keep clear of the starboard-tacker (see FIGURE 9.2, right).

Before the start, there is a common transition, between Rule 37.2 and Rule 37.1 (see FIGURE 9.5). Black is luffing near the line, killing time, and white is overtaking to leeward. At first, there is no overlap. White, as the boat clear astern, must keep clear according to Rule 37.2. Often you hear this boat screaming for the windward boat to come up, before establishing an overlap. This is premature, because according to IYRU Case 115, a yacht clear ahead (black) need not anticipate that she may have to keep clear of a leeward boat (white). This means black doesn't have to take any action until the overlap exists.

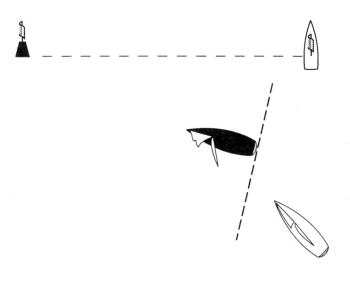

FIGURE 9.5 *A common transition before the start. The windward boat (black) need not anticipate the overlap. Once the overlap exists, the leeward yacht must allow "ample room and opportunity to keep clear."*

Once there is an overlap, black, as the windward yacht, must keep clear under Rule 37.1. This transition is the subject of Rule 37.3, which reads, "A yacht that establishes an *overlap* to *leeward* from *clear astern* shall initially allow the *windward yacht* ample room and opportunity to keep clear." Room means enough space; opportunity means enough time.

When One or More Boats Are Changing Tacks: Rule 41

The third way the rule categorizes racing situations is that one or both boats are changing tacks. This is the focus of Rule 41, which applies to tacking as well as jibing. Tacking has already been defined. The rule book definition of jibing says that it begins, "…the moment when, with the wind aft, the foot of her mainsail crosses her centerline, and completes the *jibe* when the mainsail has filled on the other *tack*."

Rule 41.1 deals with jibing or tacking too close: "A yacht that is either *tacking* or *jibing* shall keep clear of a yacht on a *tack*." This usually isn't a problem when jibing, as jibing is nearly instantaneous. Also, it usually isn't desirable to jibe directly in front of another boat.

Tacking too close is the subject of many protests, however. Note that timing is critical. If the tacking boat completes the tack—according to the

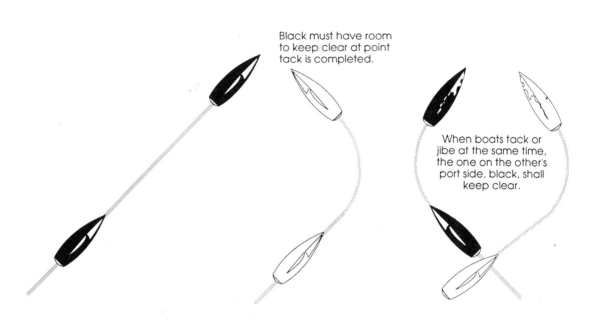

Black must have room to keep clear at point tack is completed.

When boats tack or jibe at the same time, the one on the other's port side, black, shall keep clear.

FIGURE 9.6 *(left) Rule 41.2 addresses tacking or jibing too close.*

FIGURE 9.7 *(right) When both boats are tacking or jibing at the same time, Rule 41.4 says the one on the other's port side (black) shall keep clear.*

definition, is on a close-hauled course—*before* the other boat turns to avoid her, then the boat that has tacked has fulfilled her obligations under Rule 41. If, however, a yacht on a tack has to alter course *before* the tacking boat completes her tack, then the tacking boat has tacked too close. While not mandatory, a hail by the tacking boat to the effect of "on course" or "close-hauled" can help to demonstrate that your tack was completed in sufficient time. It can also alert potential witnesses to this fact.

Rule 41.2 discusses another transition. Here, a yacht tacks (see the white boat in FIGURE 9.6) or jibes into a right-of-way position (that is, starboard) too close to a port-tack boat. The rule says, "A yacht shall neither *tack* nor *jibe* into a position that will give her right of way unless she does so far enough from a yacht *on a tack* to enable this yacht to keep clear without having to begin to alter her course until after the *tack* or *jibe* has been completed." Again, *when* the yacht completes the tack or jibe is critical. Similarly, hails such as "I'm tacking" or "close-hauled" can help establish the relationships.

There are two other parts to Rule 41. Rule 41.3 says that the "onus" of proof is on the yacht that tacks or jibes (the white boat in FIGURE 9.6). This boat has to prove to the protest committee that she didn't tack or jibe too close to the black, which is not easy to do without a witness.

Rule 41.4 deals with simultaneous tacking or jibing, that is, when two boats are tacking or jibing at the same time (see FIGURE 9.7). This can happen when the port-tack (white) boat ducks a starboard-tack (black) boat, and then both boats tack. (This often occurs when the starboard-tacker [black] tries to slam-dunk the port-tacker as in FIGURE 10.22.) When this occurs, the black boat, in this case, must keep clear, as according to Rule 41.4, "The one on the other's port side shall keep clear."

Limitations on Altering Course: Rule 35

As mentioned, the right-of-way yacht doesn't have free reign. We've already discussed that a boat on starboard is not permitted to follow a lift if too close to the obligated yacht (see FIGURE 9.1). Rule 35 is to protect the "burdened boat"—the boat that must keep clear—from sudden and unpredictable course changes. A typical example occurs before the start with two boats reaching at each other on port and starboard tack. The port-tacker falls off to pass to leeward of the starboard-tacker. Rule 35 says the starboard-tacker can't suddenly alter course, or, fall off, to hit the other boat. (Note: The Match Racing Rules—separate appendix in the IYRR book—have a more liberal interpretation of this rule.)

According to USYRU Appeal 167, this rule "doesn't shift the basic rights and obligations, it just puts certain limits on the right-of-way boat."

Exceptions to Rule 35: Rule 38.1

Most of the time the right-of-way yacht has to be well behaved—"reasonable" might be an appropriate description. There is an exception to this, however. For example, according to Rule 38.1, "After she has *started* and cleared the starting line, a yacht *clear ahead* or a *leeward yacht* may *luff* as she pleases...." The import of this is that once you are across the starting line, if another boat tries to pass you to windward, you can luff it sharply, even unpredictably. Note that the leeward boat can luff more than one boat, provided she has the rights to luff all of them. (See FIGURE 9.3, bottom. Here A can luff B and C, because B overlaps both of them.) Rule 38.2(e) goes on to say that all yachts must respond, "...even when an intervening yacht or yachts would not otherwise have the right to *luff*."

USYRU Appeal 42 approaches "luffing as she pleases" from the other perspective: "The windward yacht assumes an obligation to be prepared for the possibility that the leeward yacht will luff sharply, head to wind, as she

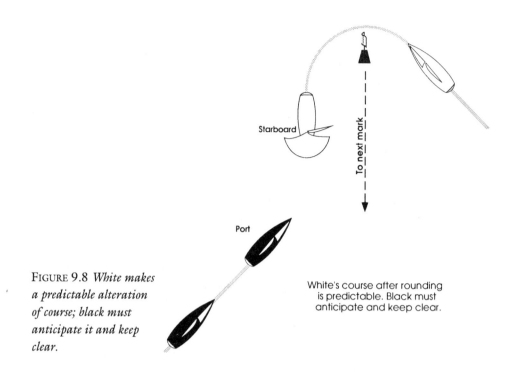

FIGURE 9.8 *White makes a predictable alteration of course; black must anticipate it and keep clear.*

Starboard

To next mark

Port

White's course after rounding is predictable. Black must anticipate and keep clear.

pleases. Therefore she should establish and maintain her overlap at a distance sufficient to be able to respond to a luff and keep clear."

Another common exception has to do with a "predictable alteration" of course by the right-of-way boat (see FIGURE 9.8). Rounding a mark to sail on a proper course to the next mark is a predictable alteration of course. As such, the black boat on port must anticipate white's alteration of course and keep clear.

Luffing After the Start: Rule 38.2

Rule 38.2 deals with proper-course limitations after clearing the starting line. This is the familiar "mast-abeam" relationship. In FIGURE 9.9, the leeward boat (L) can luff the windward boat (W) in position 1. Note that the rule book defines luffing as "altering course towards the wind." This luffing must stop, however, when "...the helmsman of the *windward yacht* (when sighting abeam from his normal station and *sailing* no higher than the *leeward yacht*) has been abreast or forward of the mainmast of the *leeward yacht*" (see FIGURE 9.9, position 2 and detail). (Note that the definition of mast abeam doesn't appear in Part I, but is found in Rule 38.2[a]. Also, IYRU Case 101 says, "The normal position of W's skipper may vary depending on wind conditions." Further, the windward boat cannot sail higher than the leeward boat to secure a mast-abeam position.)

When the windward boat calls "mast abeam" (position 2 in FIGURE 9.9), L must resume sailing her proper course. Once "mast abeam" has been called, W isn't completely without responsibility. Because according to IYRU Case 106, proper course for L doesn't necessarily mean a straight line to the next mark; it takes into account such variables as wind, current, and waves. Suppose the leeward boat decides her proper course is above the rhumb line to the mark because more wind or less current exists there. The leeward boat can sail high of the mark to sail for more wind, though "mast abeam" has

FIGURE 9.9 *The leeward boat can luff until the mast-abeam position is reached. Note the helmsman of the windward boat cannot sail a higher course than the leeward yacht—to secure an early mast-abeam call.*

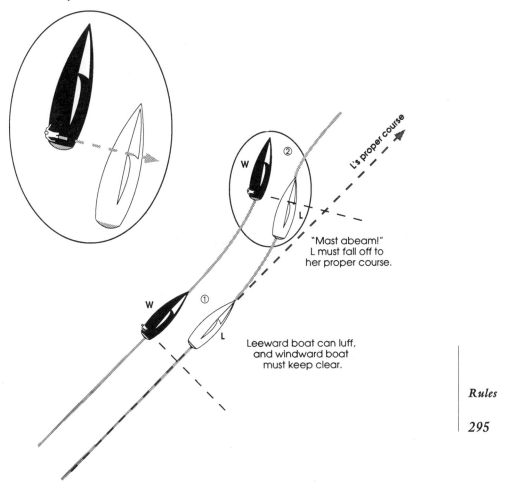

been called. The windward boat must keep clear under Rule 37.1. According to the definition of proper course, "The course sailed before *luffing* or *bearing away* is presumably, but not necessarily, that yacht's *proper course.*"

Obviously, securing mast abeam is crucial, and a hail to that effect is a good idea. The sole time such a hail is not mandatory is if there is no doubt that the windward boat has mast abeam. The skipper of the leeward boat may, in fact, assume he or she has luffing rights, unless hearing "mast abeam"—or words to that effect. If the skipper of the leeward boat doesn't agree with the hail, the only viable choice is to return to the proper course and then to protest.

The timing of the hail can be critical. If the windward boat hails "mast abeam" and contact occurs almost immediately after, the protest committee may decide that the windward boat didn't give the leeward boat enough time to respond to the hail.

Other limitations to luffing include an obstruction, such as an anchored boat or the shore, that prevents the windward yacht from responding to the luff. Another yacht in the race can be an obstruction, too.

The mast-abeam hail freezes the action. While the boats remain overlapped, nothing changes. Even if the leeward boat moves forward of the mast-abeam position, she doesn't regain luffing rights. To regain them, the leeward boat must pull clear ahead, breaking the overlap, or, according to Rule 38.2(b), by going more than two boat lengths to leeward. Also, luffing rights can be reestablished by jibing or tacking.

Often distance races will suspend luffing rights when offshore or at night. Mast abeam depends on being able to see precise relationships. Obviously, this is difficult at night. In one of my earliest SORCs (Southern Ocean Racing Conference), I sailed aboard Marty Gleich's Redline 41, *Hallelujah*. Aboard were all the San Diego "rock stars," such as Lowell North and Dick Deaver, but in those days, we didn't know much about ocean racing beyond the gentle confines of Southern California. Strangers in a strange land, some of us didn't even know enough to bring foul-weather gear while racing in Florida and the Bahamas. We weren't aware it was windy there, so we raced with a 190 percent genoa. The oversized sail sat in the bag for most of the series, taking up space and adding precious seconds, minutes, and hours to our corrected time as our rating was based on the 190 percent genoa.

I didn't know enough to read the race circular, specifically the "Race Continues After Sunset," addressed in Rule 3.2(b)(xxix), which, in this contest, suspended luffing at night. In the St. Petersburg–Ft. Lauderdale Race, we were being passed by *Alerion*, sailed by Halsey Herreshoff and Jack Sutphen. While both have come to sail with me in several America's Cups, I'd never heard of them then. So as they were trying to pass us to windward in the middle of the night, I was taking them up. Someone on their boat started swearing at me. Now that I've come to know Jack well, I am sure it was he. He gets fired up. He's a yeller—this was particularly true in those days.

SAILING BELOW A PROPER COURSE: RULE 39

While Rule 38.2 discusses sailing above a proper course, Rule 39 focuses on sailing below a proper course. The intent of this rule is to give a boat trying

FIGURE 9.10 *Rule 39 gives a boat trying to pass to leeward some chance of success. Since the white boat in examples 1, 2, and 3 is steering a course to pass to leeward, black can't sail below its proper course. Example 4 is the exception.*

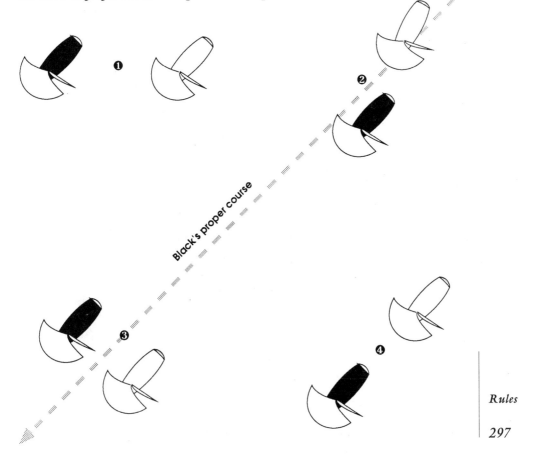

to pass to leeward some chance at success. The rule says, "A yacht that is on a free leg of the course shall not *sail* below her *proper course* when she is clearly within three of her overall lengths of a *leeward yacht* or of a yacht *clear astern* that is steering a course to *leeward* of her own."

The operative phrase is "steering a course to leeward." In FIGURE 9.10, the white boat is steering a course to pass to leeward in examples 1, 2, and 3. Thus, the black boat must not sail below her proper course. Only in example 4 can the black boat sail below her proper course, because white is not "steering a course to leeward."

If, however, the leeward boat is more than three boat lengths to leeward, then the rules allow the windward boat to sail below her proper course. (Here, too, the Match Racing Rules are more liberal.)

Rule 39 addresses a "free leg," one that doesn't require tacking to get to a mark. Upwind, however, the windward boat can sail below a proper course to impede another yacht with a tight cover. This tactic is discussed in the next chapter.

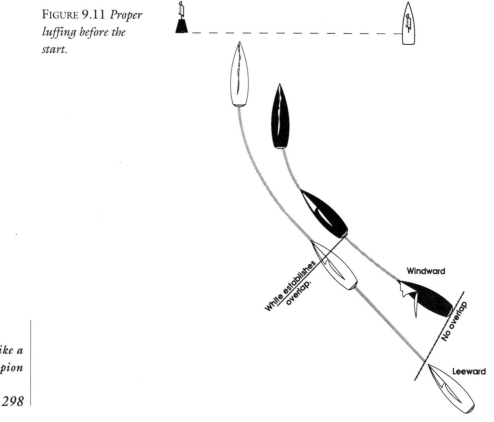

FIGURE 9.11 *Proper luffing before the start.*

LUFFING BEFORE THE START: RULE 40

Starting lines are crowded places, so to prevent collisions before the start, luffing, as described, must be done slowly, and initially in a way that gives the windward boat room (space) and opportunity (time) to keep clear. USYRU Appeal 233 puts this into perspective, however. It says the windward boat's right to room and opportunity is a "shield and not a sword." Thus, the windward boat should try to keep clear—not use the opportunity to get a better start.

FIGURE 9.11 shows the windward boat stalling before the start with the leeward boat approaching to leeward. As mentioned, windward doesn't have to anticipate the leeward boat's overlapping her. This is the aforementioned transition where the leeward, as the yacht clear astern and overtaking, must keep clear. When the leeward first achieves its overlap, she must allow windward ample room and opportunity to keep clear (Rule 37.3). Furthermore, leeward does not have luffing rights (the windward boat is in the mast-abeam position). Even without luffing right, leeward can, however, luff up to a close-hauled course but no higher. (If the mast-abeam position is broken—as it often is since the leeward boat has more speed than the recently luffing windward boat—L can then luff head to wind.) This applies until the yachts have started and cleared the starting line.

ROUNDING OR PASSING MARKS AND OBSTRUCTIONS: RULE 42

Rule 42 applies "when yachts are about to round or pass a *mark* on the same required side or an *obstruction* on the same side." The salient feature of Rule 42—familiar to most—is that "an outside yacht shall give each inside *overlapping* yacht room to round or pass the *mark* or *obstruction*." Note the word each. If more than one boat has an inside overlap, the outside boat or boats must give each inside boat or boats room to round the mark.

Rule 42 is the longest and most complex one in the book. It begins Section C. Section C Rules, "Rounding or Passing Marks and Obstructions," take precedence over rules in Section B, "Principal Right of Way Rules and their Limitations," as just discussed. The sole exception to a Section C rule not taking precedence over a Section B rule is Rule 35, "Limitations on Altering Course"—the rule that protects the burdened boat from unpredictable actions from the right-of-way yacht (see above).

Rule 42 does not apply before the start when one of the boats is "barg-

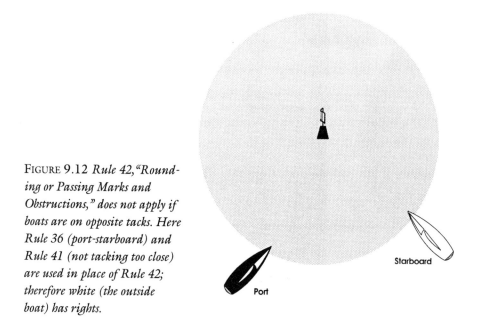

FIGURE 9.12 *Rule 42, "Rounding or Passing Marks and Obstructions," does not apply if boats are on opposite tacks. Here Rule 36 (port-starboard) and Rule 41 (not tacking too close) are used in place of Rule 42; therefore white (the outside boat) has rights.*

ing" (to be discussed) and when the "starting mark is surrounded by navigable water" (see Rule 42.4).

Rule 42 also does not apply if the mark the boats are rounding is a windward mark and both boats are on opposite tacks (see FIGURE 9.12). Notice that for Rule 42 not to apply, both of those conditions (windward mark and opposite tack) must be met. In the situation depicted in the figure, Rule 36 (port-starboard) and Rule 41 (not tacking too close) are used in lieu of Rule 42.

However, if two boats are on the *same* tack when approaching the windward mark, Rule 42 does apply. The outside boat must give the inside-overlapped boat room. If the leeward boat has to luff head to wind to round the windward mark, the windward boat must give her room do it, even when the windward boat has mast abeam.

WHEN OVERLAPPED: RULE 42.1

Rule 42.1, titled "When Overlapped," applies when two or more yachts are overlapped. First, it focuses on the responsibilities of the outside (O) yacht (see FIGURE 9.13) and then on the inside (I) yacht. Regarding the outside yacht, Rule 42.1(a) says when an overlap exists between two or more boats,

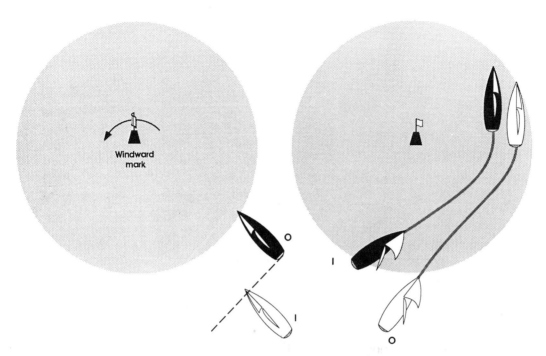

FIGURE 9.13 *(left) Rule 42.1(a) says that when an overlap exists between two or more boats on the same tack, the outside boat (O) must give each inside boat room to round a mark or obstruction. Thus I is entitled to room.*

FIGURE 9.14 *(right) Before reaching the two-boat-length circle, the windward boat (black) must keep clear. When about to round the mark, the outside boat (O) must keep clear. Here, however, black is making a wide "tactical" rounding—a violation of the rules.*

the outside boat (O) must give each inside boat (I) room to round or pass a mark or obstruction.

In FIGURE 9.14, two overlapped port-tack boats approach the mark. Before the two-boat-length circle, they are sailing under Section B rules. For example, the windward boat (black) must keep clear, per Rule 37.1. Rule 42 takes effect when the boats become "about to round the mark," which is generally about two boat lengths from the mark (see gray area) and continues until the boats round the mark.

Seamanlike Rounding: Rule 42.1(a)

When overlapped, the rule addresses how the inside boat can turn the mark. The second sentence of Rule 42.1(a) says that the inside boat is entitled only to a seamanlike rounding. It can't make a tactical rounding. Without other boats around, a yacht should take a mark wide on the near side and close on the far side. This is the optimum way to round a mark and, as such, is called a tactical rounding. When an overlap exists, the inside boat is not allowed to make a tactical rounding. In FIGURE 9.14, I is making a tactical rounding (going wide on the near side), a violation of the rules (USYRU Appeal 119).

Rule 42.1(a) also says that the outside boat must allow room for the inside boat to jibe or tack if it is integral to the rounding maneuver. In view of that, can the inside boat delay her jibe or tack? Rule 42.1(e) says if the inside boat does not have luffing rights, she "shall *jibe* at the first reasonable opportunity." In Figure 9.14, I obviously doesn't have luffing rights as it is the weather boat. Therefore, I must tack immediately. FIGURE 8.20, however, shows two boats at the mark on starboard tack. In this case, white, the inside-leeward boat with luffing rights can continue past the mark if she chooses, taking black, the weather and outside boat, with her. While not common, this sometimes happens in a match or team race.

Two-Boat-Length Circle: Rule 42.1(b)

Rule 42.1(b) addresses what happens if the outside boat breaks the overlap before going around the mark. The rule says that if overlapped when O comes within two of her overall lengths of a mark or obstruction, O must give I room.[3] Note in FIGURE 9.15 that I and O are overlapped in position 1, prior to reaching the two-boat-length circle. In position 2, O breaks the overlap, but it is too late as O, the lead boat, has already entered the two-boat-length circle. Therefore, even though the overlap was broken, O must give I room. If the outside yacht believes she broke the overlap just before reaching the two-boat-length circle, Rule 42.1(c) says that the onus is on her to prove it. Again, a hail, sounded four or five boat lengths from the mark, can help establish the relationships. It isn't mandatory, however.

Rule 42.1(d) addresses what happens if the inside boat thinks she establishes an overlap just before the outside boat reaches the two-boat-length circle. The onus is on the inside boat to prove it.

Hailing is the subject of the rest of Rule 42.1. It says that hailing, to signal an overlap or the breaking of an overlap, can help to support a claim in a

---

[3]Regarding the two-boat-length circle: if the boats are of different sizes, use the overall length of the boat outside.

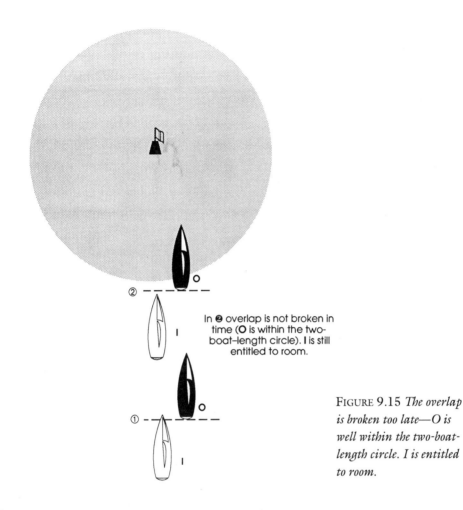

In ❷ overlap is not broken in time (O is within the two-boat-length circle). I is still entitled to room.

FIGURE 9.15 *The overlap is broken too late—O is well within the two-boat-length circle. I is entitled to room.*

protest hearing. Note, however, that the rule doesn't say hailing is mandatory. In fact, the rules keep hails to a minimum as they are hard to hear. Also, yachting is an international sport, and there can be misunderstandings due to language differences.

What happens if you're the inside boat, and you think you have an overlap, but the outside boat disagrees? Your only option is to slow down and let the outside boat round the mark ahead of you, and then protest. If you follow this procedure, you can't get tossed out of the race. You may lose the protest, but you can't get disqualified. If, however, you try to take what you believe is rightfully yours, there is a good chance of disqualification.

Obviously, securing or breaking an overlap is critical. If you end up in a protest hearing, the committee will often try to determine the relationship between the boats when they were farther away from the mark. If both com-

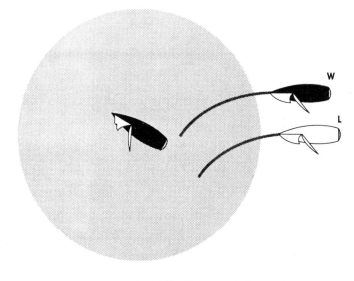

FIGURE 9.16 *If the inside boat (W) wants to pass an obstruction on the leeward side, the outside boat must give it room. This is an example of section C rules taking precedence over section B rules, i.e., windward-leeward.*

L and W wish to pass to leeward.
If W wants room, L must give way.

petitors—or witnesses—agree an overlap existed three to five boat lengths from the mark, for example, the committee may well decide an overlap existed at the critical two-boat-length circle. If both competitors—or witnesses—agree an overlap didn't exist three to five boat lengths from the mark, the committee may well decide an overlap didn't exist when the outside boat reached the two-boat-length circle.

This rule applies to passing obstructions, as well as rounding marks. A common obstruction is a right-of-way yacht. FIGURE 9.16 shows a starboard-tack yacht luffing near the line. Approaching it are two overlapped boats, both to windward of the luffing yacht and within two boat lengths of the obstruction. Both W and L want to pass the obstruction on the leeward side; therefore L, the outside boat, must allow W, the inside boat, room to do this.

Boats Not Overlapped: Rule 42.2

We've just discussed what happens when two overlapped boats approach a mark or obstruction. Rule 42.2 discusses what happens when two yachts that are not overlapped approach a mark or obstruction. Rule 42.2(a) says, "A yacht *clear astern* when the yacht *clear ahead* comes within two of her overall lengths of a *mark* or *obstruction* shall keep clear in anticipation of and during the rounding or passing maneuver, whether the yacht *clear ahead* remains on the same *tack* or *jibes*." (Note that this rule does not address tacking. This will be discussed shortly.)

What if the yacht clear ahead has a poor rounding, however, and goes wide of the mark? The yacht clear astern can try to sneak in, as long as she doesn't interfere with the boat ahead. According to USYRU Appeal 38, "It is an established principle of yacht racing that when a yacht voluntarily or unintentionally makes room available to another yacht that has no right to it, under the rules, the other yacht may take advantage at her own risk of the room so given."

If, however, the yacht clear ahead must tack to get around the mark, Rule 42.2(c) says she must be sure she doesn't tack too close to the boat clear astern (see Rule 41).

That addresses the yacht clear ahead. What about the yacht clear astern? There are limits to what the yacht clear astern can do to prevent the yacht clear ahead from tacking, however. According to Rule 42.2(b), the yacht clear astern cannot "*luff* above *close-hauled* so as to prevent a yacht *clear ahead* from *tacking* to round a *mark*." If when ahead you are worried about being able to tack, luff up to the mark. This is permissible because you are clear ahead and need not provide room to the trailing boat. Usually, the trailing boat will bear off, taking you stern. At that instant, you tack around the mark.

Limitations to Establishing an Overlap: Rule 42.3

There are limitations on establishing an overlap. Rule 42.3(a) says that when I secures an overlap from behind, two conditions must be met. O must be physically able to give room. Also, I's overlap must exist before the outside boat is within two of her overall lengths of the mark. Regarding "physically able": Imagine six boats approaching a mark. Just before the two-boat-length circle, a seventh boat gains an inside overlap. There probably isn't time for all six boats to respond, so in this case I can't claim room.

Limitation When an Obstruction is a Continuing One: Rule 42.3(b)

Rule 42.3(b) focuses on what happens when an obstruction is a continuing one, such as the shore, a shoal, or another yacht. As we learned in the last chapter, this can happen when boats are sailing in shallow water to avoid a foul current or to get in a fair current first. The rule says, "A yacht *clear astern* may establish an *overlap* between a yacht *clear ahead* and a continuing *obstruction*, such as a shoal or the shore or another vessel, only when, at that time, there is room for her to pass between them in safety."

FIGURE 9.17 *A right-of-way yacht can be a continuing obstruction.*

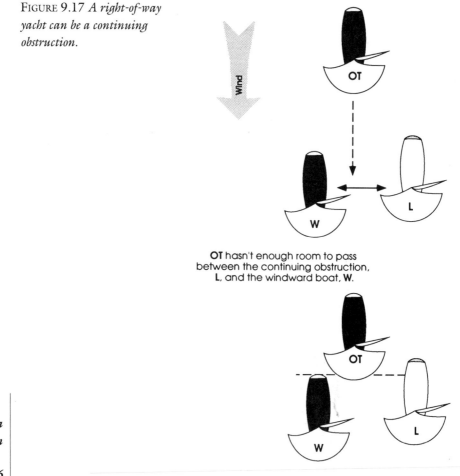

OT hasn't enough room to pass between the continuing obstruction, **L**, and the windward boat, **W**.

The rule focuses on the instant the boat clear astern gets an inside overlap. If the inside boat can, at that moment, pass between the outside boat and the obstruction without touching one or the other, she is entitled to sail between the boat and the shoal or shore. As the obstruction is a continuing one, so, too, is the right to room. If the shore or shoal comes out, the inside boat can get more room, as needed, under basic Rule 42.1(a).

A continuing obstruction can also be a right-of-way yacht. FIGURE 9.17, top, shows two overlapped boats on starboard tack (W and L). L is a continuing obstruction to W. As the yacht clear ahead, L is also a continuing obstruction to OT, the overtaking boat. Is OT allowed to pass between them, thereby establishing an overlap between W and L? IYRU Case 27 says this is not permitted. The reason is the same as discussed above. There isn't room for OT to pass between L and W (see FIGURE 9.17, bottom).

BARGING AT THE START: RULE 42.4

Barging is the focus of Rule 42.4. The rule reads, "When approaching the starting line to *start* until clearing the starting *marks* after *starting*, a *leeward yacht* shall be under no obligation to give any *windward yacht* room to pass

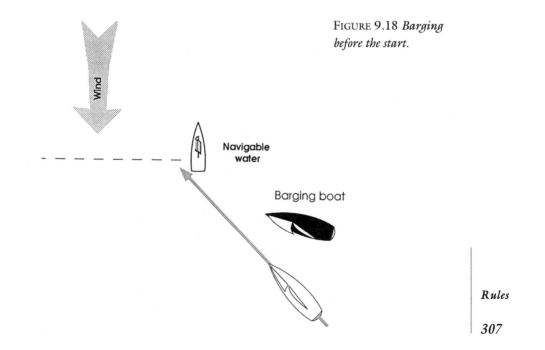

FIGURE 9.18 *Barging before the start.*

Wind

Navigable water

Barging boat

to leeward of a starting *mark* surrounded by navigable water…" (see FIG-URE 9.18). Note, first, that the boats must be starting. If four minutes before the gun, two overlapped boats are sailing by the committee boat (an obstruction), the outside (leeward) boat must give room to an inside (windward) boat. Also note that the starting line must be surrounded by navigable water. If the starting line is a pier, for example, Rule 42.4 doesn't apply.

As we learned earlier, the leeward boat can only luff the windward boat slowly, according to Rule 40. Also, if the windward boat secures mast abeam, the leeward boat cannot luff above a close-hauled course. The windward boat should remind the leeward boat of these limitations.

Rule 42.4 continues, "…but, after the starting signal, a *leeward yacht* shall not deprive a *windward yacht* of room at such a *mark* by sailing either: (a) to windward of the compass bearing of the course to the next *mark,* or (b) above *close-hauled.*" This means once the race committee hoists the starting signal, the leeward boat cannot sail higher than a close-hauled course if it is a beat to the first mark, or higher than the compass course to the first mark if it is a reach or run to the first mark. If this opens the door for the windward boat, so be it.

CLOSE-HAULED, HAILING FOR ROOM TO TACK AT OBSTRUCTIONS: RULE 43

Before asking for room to tack at obstructions, Rule 43 says three conditions must be met. 1) The boats must be on the same tack and sailing a close-hauled course. (FIGURE 9.19 shows two boats on opposite tacks, so white—the port-tacker—isn't entitled to room to tack.) 2) The boat that is to leeward or clear ahead must make a substantial alteration of course to avoid hitting the obstruction. If the yacht only has to alter her course slightly to miss the obstruction, she is not entitled to call for room to tack. 3) The boat that is to leeward or clear ahead cannot tack without a collision. (FIGURE 9.20 shows that the white boat can tack without causing a collision.)

If these three conditions are met, the rule outlines a specific sequence of hails and responses. 1) The hailing yacht asks for room to tack. This should be done early enough, so there is time for a second hail, if the first isn't heard. 2) The hailed yacht can either tack immediately or respond, "You tack." 3) If the hailed yacht tacks, then the hailing yacht must tack as soon as she can without hitting the hailed yacht. 4) If, however, the hailed yacht says, "You tack," then the hailing yacht must immediately tack, and the hailed yacht must stay clear.

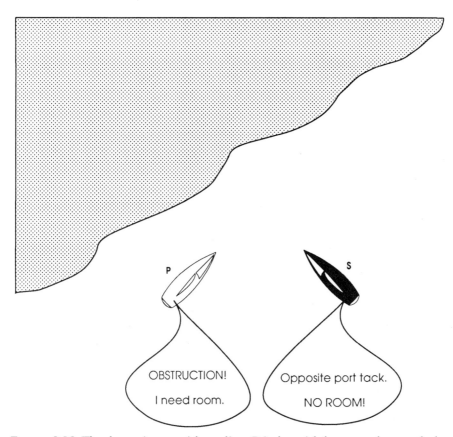

FIGURE 9.19 *The obstruction notwithstanding, P isn't entitled to room, because the boats are on opposite tacks.*

Don't deviate from this procedure. The hailing yacht can't ask for room to tack, receive a response, and then not tack (see FIGURE 9.21). Also notice in FIGURE 9.22 that according to USYRU Appeal 131, it is the leeward boat—not the windward boat—that decides whether to tack or to duck.

HITTING A MARK: RULE 52

In the old days, hitting a mark meant instant disqualification. More recently, you could exonerate yourself by rerounding the mark correctly. In the current rules, when you touch a mark, you must sail clear of other boats and do two 360-degree turns (that is, a 720-degree turn) in the same direction. This includes two tacks and two jibes. You lose most of your rights while doing

Rules

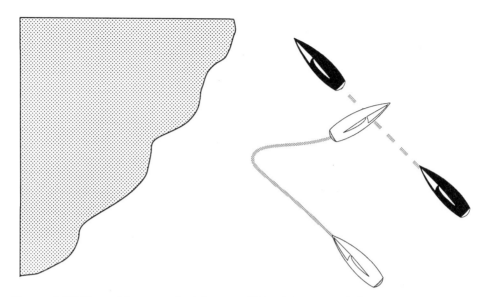

FIGURE 9.20 *Since white can tack without a collision, it is not entitled to room.*

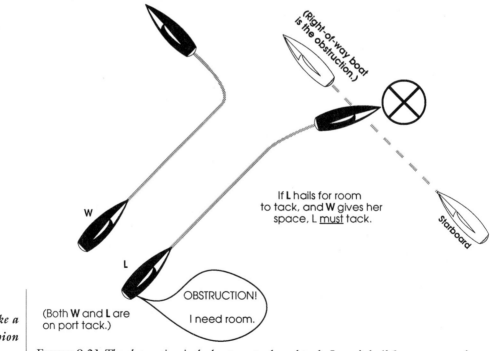

(Right-of-way boat is the obstruction.)

If **L** hails for room to tack, and **W** gives her space, L **must** tack.

Starboard

W

L

OBSTRUCTION!
I need room.

(Both **W** and **L** are on port tack.)

FIGURE 9.21 *The obstruction is the boat on starboard tack. L can't hail for room to tack, force W to tack, and then not tack.*

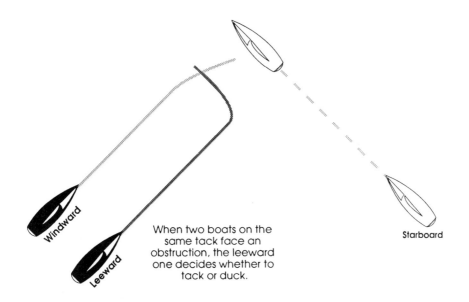

When two boats on the
same tack face an
obstruction, the leeward
one decides whether to
tack or duck.

Windward

Leeward

Starboard

FIGURE 9.22 *The leeward boat, not the windward, decides whether to tack or jibe at an obstruction.*

the turns. You regain all your rights when finished with the turns and sailing a proper course to the next mark.

Under the definition of a mark, ground tackle, such as the anchor line, is specifically excluded. Thus, hitting the anchor line with your centerboard, doesn't violate the rules. If, however, this action pulls you into the mark or the mark into you, then you must do your 720-degree turn or withdraw.

PROTESTS BY YACHTS: RULE 68

The rules of the game usually are enforced by competitors. Sailing aimed at a television audience or shoreside spectators often has umpires. The America's Cup is the obvious example.

If you think you've been fouled, you should protest. Make the decision to protest immediately. Rule 68.3(b) says the protest flag "shall be displayed at the first reasonable opportunity after the incident." In practice, this means almost immediately, so keep the flag handy. Note the all-red Code flag "B" is acceptable as a protest flag everywhere. Display the protest flag until you finish and until the race committee acknowledges the flag.

As long as we're discussing flags, Rule 4 of Part II, "Organization and

Management," outlines the visual signals. This includes postponement, change of course when racing, abandonment, replacement of a mark with a committee boat, shortening course, etc. The various international code flags are displayed in four colors on the inside front cover of the rule book. This is how the race committee communicates with the racers, so bring your rule book along when racing, if for no other reason than to have a flag reference.

Rule 68.2 says, "A protesting yacht shall try to inform the yacht she intends to protest that a *protest* will be lodged." If you can't contact the protested yacht on the water for some reason, you must inform the skipper before lodging the protest ashore. Rule 68.2 goes on to say, "When an alternative penalty is prescribed in the sailing instructions, [the protesting yacht] shall hail the other yacht immediately." Be sure your immediate hail clearly identifies which boat you are protesting. To be safe, you should always use the word "protest" in your hail.

Also, when the infringement occurs, look around immediately for possible witnesses. Ask crews in other boats if they saw it and will testify. It is also a good idea to comply with such requests. A cardinal expression in yacht racing is, What goes around comes around. You might need their help some time.

Lastly, fill out the protest form correctly and file it in time. Rule 68.5 outlines the particulars: 1) identity of the yacht(s) being protested; 2) date, time, and whereabouts of the incident; 3) particular rule or rules alleged to have been infringed; 4) description of the incident; 5) unless irrelevant, a diagram of the incident. If you fill out the wrong rules, you can amend your protest at the hearing. Lastly, under Rule 72, the boat you are protesting has the right to read your protest form before the hearing.

10 | Strategy, Tactics, and the Rules

In Chapter 8, we focused on strategy—the ways to get around a race course or to the next land fall as quickly as possible. It is the solution to the puzzle of wind, weather, and current. Strategy is as if one were sailing a time trial. Sailboat racing, however, is rarely a time trial. Strategy and tactics—the latter being the boat-on-boat moves and countermoves—interact constantly. Sometimes it is strategy; sometimes it is tactics; most of the time, it is both. In this chapter, we will unite strategy and tactics and add the third piece, the racing rules, discussed in Chapter 9. Obviously, the racing rules affect both strategy and tactics.

COUNTDOWN

The ten-minute countdown before the start is a busy time. First, you have to start your timer with the visual signal: typically, the raising of a white or yellow flag on the committee boat. Note that IYRU Rule 4.4 says there are two systems for starting races, unless otherwise prescribed. In the U.S., races are typically started according to System 2—the raising of a white or yellow shape or flag at ten minutes; the raising of a blue shape or flag at five minutes; and the raising of a red shape or flag at the starting signal.

Gun or cannon shots usually accompany the raising of flags, but the visual signals, the flags, are the governing factors. It is best to start your watch with the visual signals. If you are unable to see them, start your watch with the puff of smoke from the gun, rather than its report. You'll see the smoke before hearing the bang, and this delay can prove significant in a close start.

For timing the start, I prefer to use a prerecorded tape, rather than a stopwatch—although I make sure both are started. I use the stopwatch as a backup. Once started, a tape doesn't require monitoring. This frees up a crew member for more important tasks. This prerecorded voice calls the time every fifteen seconds until one minute to go where she calls the time every five seconds. Yes, the voice is of a woman. We've used a man's and woman's voice calling the time on the tape and find the latter calmer as well as higher pitched and, thus, better able to penetrate the din of wind, waves, conversation, and grinding machinery.

Be certain, however, that the timing of the tape is correct. Also, that the tape player is decent, without much "wow and flutter"—the irregular speeding up and slowing down of the tape mechanism and therefore the tape. Further, be certain that the batteries are up to the task. Tired batteries can cause you to be late at the start, and wow and flutter can cause you to be early or late.

Sometimes the race committee describes the marks and the order they must be rounded in the sailing instructions; more often the committee determines this at the last minute in view of the wind direction. In the latter case, note the marks, which with the ten-minute gun should be displayed on the committee boat. Compass courses can be displayed numerically or in code flags; if the latter, bring an IYRR book, for example, to interpret the code flags. Write down the course, preferably in grease pencil, in an obvious place on the boat. Also, if they are fixed marks have the navigator work out the compass courses—at least for the first and second legs. (Compute the courses for other legs at a less hectic time.)

Sail for a short time on the course to the first mark. Assuming this is a weather leg, check the upwind course against the two-number system (see Table 8A, 8B, or 8C in Chapter 8) and add to it or change it if necessary. Also, while near the starting line, sail the heading of the second leg to determine which tack you will likely sail on and what spinnaker is appropriate, if you carry more than one spinnaker. Be warned, however, the wind can be disturbed near the starting line; this can invalidate the test. Also, by the time you get to the weather mark, the conditions can be different, and your sail selection or tack can be wrong. Make sure the keel, centerboard, and rudder are clear of weeds, if weeds are a problem where you sail. If you sail a big boat, remember to feather the prop.

Make sure the tape or watch corresponds to the five-minute "preparatory" gun. If the watch or tape is slightly off, don't stop it; rather, factor in a correction in your head. At the five-minute signal, the racing rules are in effect, so the engine, if you have one, must be off. A bow lookout is critical during prestart maneuvering as the skipper is often distracted by other things and visibility forward is limited.

DETERMINING THE FAVORED END OF THE LINE

A race committee usually tries to set the starting line square to the median wind, and the first weather mark perpendicular to this line or directly into the wind. The starting line and the first mark are places where there are often too many boats trying to occupy too little space at the same time. A square line can help to minimize crowds at the starting line, and a good weather leg can spread the fleet out by the first mark.

Rarely, however, do starting lines end up being square to the wind. One reason, as noted in Chapter 8, is that the wind is constantly shifting. Also, racers should, and typically do, have a larger focus than just winning the start. Often they want to be in a position to tack right or left immediately, depending on their strategy.

Long Beach, California, is the familiar example. This was the sailing site for the 1984 Olympics. After the start, the wind typically shows a persistent shift to the right. As you will recall from Chapter 8, if there is a persistent shift to the right (clockwise), the recommended strategy is to sail on the headed port tack to the right side of the course. Thus, the racers would gather at the starboard end of the line to tack to port immediately and sail toward the new wind. The only way the race committee could get the fleet to spread out at the start was to make the port end of the line significantly favored, that is, closer to the windward mark. The lefthand end would be located as much as two boat lengths upwind to get boats to that side. Thus, boats starting at the pin end would be two boat lengths ahead at the start. To some, that head start was irresistible.

Obviously, it is important to determine the favored end of the line—farther upwind and thus closer to the windward mark when it is an upwind start; or farther downwind and thus closer to the leeward mark when it is a (less common) downwind start. Before doing this, however, if one end of the line is on a committee boat, you must determine the precise point on the boat to which the line is drawn.

For example, is the line drawn to a flagstaff in the middle of the boat or to the bow? That can make a difference when determining the favored end of the line or figuring out how to start. This is typically addressed in the sailing instructions.

There are many ways to determine the favored end of the line. One way is to shoot the wind and record its direction (see FIGURE 10.1). It is best to take a wind shot, as this is called, without a genoa. The flapping back and forth of this overlapping sail can confuse the reading. That said, a small (nonoverlapping) jib, such as that on an Etchells or Star, is usually less of a problem. The wind bears 340 degrees magnetic in the figure. Then go outside the line—for better visibility, it is better to go to pin end—and line up the pin and committee boat and record its direction. In the figure, the line bears 90 degrees. Then sketch it out. For the line to be square, the wind would have to be from the north, 0 degrees. At 340 degrees, the lefthand end is favored by 20 degrees.

Another way to determine the favored end of the line is to reach down the line from right to left, or from the committee boat to the pin. Let the jib luff to avoid affecting the trim of the mainsail, or better yet do this before raising the jib. Trim the mainsail perfectly; this sail should be just on the verge of luffing. Then tack or jibe and run the line again, this time from left to right or from the pin to the committee boat. Keep mainsheet tension the same. If the main is luffing on the second course, the favored

FIGURE 10.1 *Determining the favored end of a starting line.*

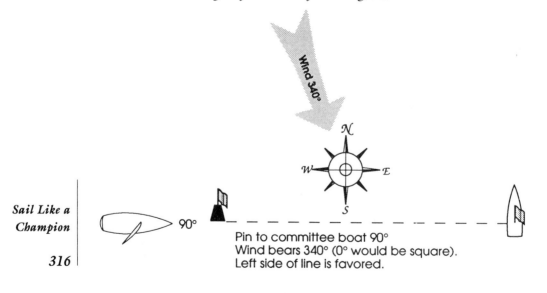

Pin to committee boat 90°
Wind bears 340° (0° would be square).
Left side of line is favored.

Sail Like a
Champion

316

end is the right—the committee-boat end—as it is more upwind. If, however, on the second run of the line, you can ease the main without it luffing, the favored end is the left (pin end), as it is more upwind. If the sail trim is correct on the second run, the line is square.

TWO MINUTES BEFORE THE START

With two minutes to go, be sure to check the favored end of the line one more time. This is also a good time to determine again where the wind is, according to your two-number system of testing. You will recall if it is an oscillating wind, you want to sail on the lifted tack immediately. If starboard tack is lifting, start on starboard tack and stay on starboard until headed at least to the median or average (see FIGURE 8.11). If, however, port tack is lifting, start on starboard near the righthand end. Then tack to port to sail on the lifted tack (see FIGURE 8.12). This gets you into phase with the shifts immediately. Alternatively, you could try a port-tack start, but this can be risky as the boats on starboard have right-of-way (Rule 36).

If, however, the wind is showing a persistent shift, start at the side closer to the new wind: right if the wind is going right, or clockwise (the Long Beach example, cited before), or left if the wind is going left, or counterclockwise.

Also determine who's who. You should have already memorized or written down the sail numbers of boats you want to beat or plan on following. It also helps to be familiar with what the boats look like. For example, is it a red boat when most of the others are white and blue? Or is their sail layout distinctive? On the other hand, if you're often followed because you have a talent for knowing where to go, don't advertise who you are. Blend into the crowd. Don't sail a boat with a distinctive paint job, a unique spinnaker, or an unusual team uniform, for example.

Determine where on the line the fast or important boats are planning to start. You can usually determine this with two minutes to go as it normally takes that much time to get from one end of the line to the other. If the good sailors are going where you are, your strategy is probably correct. If they aren't, you had better determine why and do so in a hurry. Maybe, it is a point in the regatta where they can afford to be conservative, while you must be aggressive, or maybe your strategy is wrong.

There is also a defensive reason for identifying fast boats. You absolutely don't want faster boats or bigger boat (if racing in a mixed fleet rather than one-design) on your lee side and ahead (see FIGURE 10.2). A

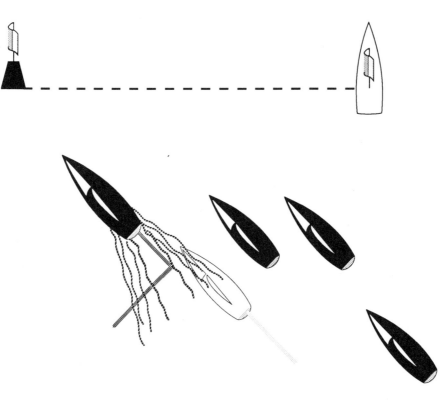

FIGURE 10.2 *When starting, a bigger or faster boat to leeward spells trouble.*

boat on your lee side and ahead is in what is known as the safe-leeward or lee-bow position. It changes the wind in which you sail: As the weather boat (white), you'll find yourself sailing in a header and in less wind. If you don't tack, the likelihood is the lee boat will foul you out of the race—recall that the windward boat must keep clear under Rule 37.1. The other alternative is to tack, which usually isn't easy to do because of the heavy starboard-tack traffic before and just after the start. Remember that under Rule 36, a port-tacker must keep clear of starboard-tackers. A faster boat to weather will roll over you too, but there is less likelihood of your fouling out of the race. Also you can minimize the damage of a boat passing you to windward by powering up in a hole left to leeward (discussed shortly).

STRATEGY VERSUS WINNING THE START

Winning the start isn't everything, however. Winning the first weather leg—even the first hundred yards of it—just might be. Thus, you have to decide where to start not just in view of the favored end of the line but according to what you think the wind will do on the first leg. This means that you shouldn't view the start as a win or loss but as the opening move, one that allows you to implement your strategy.

Experience, ability, and aggressiveness also count in the decision about where to start. The pin and committee boat ends are popular places to start. Ends are popular because, among other things, sailors can more easily tell if they're over the line early. Further, the committee boat end is popular because racers can often hear if they're over the line early, provided the committee is calling sail numbers of premature starters. To alert the fleet that there have been premature starters, the race committee must at least fly a Code-flag X, a blue cross on white background. This is accompanied by one sound signal. The flag remains flying until all improperly started yachts have restarted properly or for four minutes (see Rule 8.1 and 51.1[c]) With offshore boats, some race committees call sail numbers over the VHF radio. The procedure is described in the sailing instructions. Remember, however, that the onus is on the racer, not the committee, to start properly.

Suppose you're inexperienced and not yet ready to go for an aggressive start, but one end is so favored that it is irresistible? Don't start with the first group of boats but the second.

Alternately, you might consider starting in the middle of the line. This can be a good tactic in an oscillating wind or if you aren't sure which way the wind is going. A midline start will keep you in the middle of the course, allowing you to tack on the headers to sail on lifts—the recommended strategy in an oscillating wind. The middle of the line is, also, typically the least crowded place to start.

It is, however, very difficult to judge precisely where the line is from the middle. You turn your head in one direction to see one end of the line and in the other direction to see the other end. The result of this 180-degree turn is a significant misreading of the line, often reflected in a midline sag. Here boats in the middle think the line is closer than it actually is and are late.

That, of course, presumes you can even see both ends of the line from the middle—often other boats block your view of one or both ends. This misreading of the line and the difficulty in even seeing it, also result in a midline bulge, where boats are over the line early.

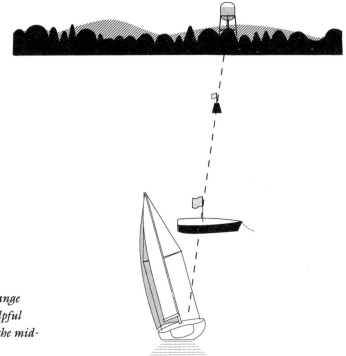

FIGURE 10.3 *A range on shore can be helpful when starting in the middle of the line.*

Thus when starting in the middle, it is helpful to use a range (see FIG-URE 10.3). For example, go outside the committee boat and line up the two flags, marking the line, with a discernible object on shore—assuming there is a visible shore with a discernible object with the proper orientation. You are safely behind the starting line, until the pin and the object ashore line up. Be warned, however, that other boats can obscure this range.

One-Minute or Black-Flag Rule

Being early when starting can be disastrous if there is a one-minute or black-flag rule in effect to control premature starters. (The use of either is typically noted in the sailing instructions.) When the one-minute rule is being used, if any part of the boat, crew, etc., is on the course side of the starting line with sixty seconds or less to go, the boat must return by going around either the pin or boat end. That penalty is particularly hard on boats that try to start in the middle of the line. From the middle, a premature starter must wait for the boats to weather or to leeward to clear the starting line, before being able to round either end of the line and start properly. If a boat is over early at the middle of the line with a one-minute rule in effect, a strong case can be made for just going home. The penalty is that severe.

The punishing "black-flag" rule says if any part of the boat is over the line with one minute or less to go, it is subject to disqualification, even if there is a general recall. This time you have no choice if you start prematurely; you can't sail this race.

Calling the Line from the Bow

A starting mark will appear close or far away, depending on the location of the viewer. When starting at the middle of the line—indeed, anywhere—it is very helpful to have a crew member at or near the bow calling the line. Even in small boats where a body on the bow can compromise the trim of a boat, this can be a good idea if you're close to the line or if the one-minute or black-flag rule is in effect. If you're going to be late at the start, however, get the crew member off the bow before the gun. Don't "plow" extra water when you're late.

All things being equal, I'd probably use the lightest crew member to call the line at the bow. Note, however, that not everyone has a good sense of time and distance. I think this talent should be prized in sailboat racing. In the 1986-87 America's Cup, for example, I changed my bowman, because I thought one was better than the other at judging the distance to the starting line.

Communications from the bow to the helm—stop, go, up, down, one-boat length—should be done with hand signals, rather than by voice. Shouted commands mean the information can be overheard by everyone. That, in effect, advertises what you intend to do.

Types of Starts

Now that you've planned where you want to start, how do you get there at the proper time? There are several commonly used starting techniques: Vanderbilt start, port-tack approach, luffing, dip start, port-tack start, and downwind start.

Vanderbilt Start

The Vanderbilt start is used most often by large cruising boats. If done correctly, you approach the line at the gun with a full head of steam. That makes it appropriate for large cruising boats that don't accelerate very quickly.

The start is named for Harold "Mike" Vanderbilt, also the author of the racing rules, discussed in the previous chapter. It works this way.

1. Begin the maneuver on the line at the place you want to start, while sailing on port tack (see FIGURE 10.4).

2. When you cross the line, note the time remaining until the start. Suppose it is 2 minutes and 10 seconds, which is 130 seconds.

3. Sail away from the line on a broad reach. (A sailboat travels about the same speed when broad-reaching and beating. This is the principle behind the Vanderbilt start.)

4. To determine when to tack or jibe, perform the following computation: Take the time remaining until the start (step 2) in seconds, i.e., 130 seconds. Add to it how much time it will take to tack or jibe, let's say 20 seconds. Then divide the total (150 seconds) by 2. The answer is 75 seconds, or 1 minute and 15 seconds. Thus when the *stopwatch says* there is 1 minute and 15 seconds *to go*, you start your turn back toward the line.[1]

5. Then tack or jibe and head on a close-hauled course to the line. Remember that in deciding whether to tack or jibe, tacking is slower. A jibe is faster, but riskier, particularly in heavier winds and heavier traffic. A jibe also takes you downwind—a little or a lot depending on the amount of wind.

   One important consideration in determining whether to tack or jibe is where you are in relation to the layline at the windward end of the starting line (see FIGURE 10.4). If you are on or above the layline, jibe. Otherwise you might find yourself barging, (see FIGURE 9.18). Below

---

[1]Many sailors have trouble with this math. The proof of the computation is that you sail 55 seconds on a broad reach, take 20 seconds to tack or jibe, and sail back 55 seconds upwind to the start. The total is 130 seconds, or 2:10 (see FIGURE 10.4). So if you start your turn for the line when the *stopwatch says* there is 1 minute and 15 seconds to go, in this example, you're right.

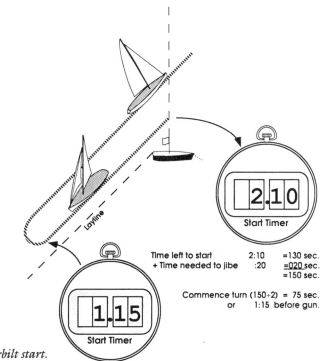

FIGURE 10.4 *A Vanderbilt start.*

the layline, tack or jibe, depending on where you want to be on the line. The boat in the illustration wishes to start about a third of the way down the line, so it jibes.

If, however, the boat in the figure were going for the perfect start at the committee boat, a tack would be in order. It is, however, usually foolhardy to try for the perfect start. Only one boat typically gets it. The risks of searching for perfection rarely balance the rewards. This speaks for starting somewhat to leeward of the mark, the windward third in this figure. The conservative approach is to think of the line in thirds: the windward third, the middle third, and the leeward third. If you're in the proper third when the gun goes off, consider the start a success. (That is, admittedly, one of those "do-as-I-say, not-as-I-do" lessons. The truth is that I enjoy mixing it up at the start. It gets my adrenaline flowing.)

The positions of other boats also determine whether you tack or jibe. When broad-reaching away from the line, avoid overlapping other yachts as they can restrict your ability to turn when, where, and how you want to.

6. The aim is to cross the line at the gun with full speed. If you are early, see luffing below; if you are late, you're late.

7. Choppy water, boats that blanket you or keep you from tacking or jibing, or disturbed winds can cause you to tack or jibe later or earlier, so adjust accordingly. Current, in particular, can alter the timing. Obviously, it is better to tack or jibe early rather than late as you can luff (described below) to kill time. You can't, however, speed up.

Ted Turner, sailing *Courageous,* used the Vanderbilt start with facility against me on *Freedom* in the 1980 America's Cup trials. Perhaps he wasn't comfortable challenging me before the start, but whatever the reason, after we entered the course from opposite ends, Turner would sail off on a broad reach away from the line. I'd try to chase him, but there isn't much you can do when the other boat is a football field away. He'd sail for four minutes or so and then jibe and head back to the line. I had a hard time attacking Turner. My only options were to jibe in front of him when he was coming back to try to slow him down, so he'd be late, or jibe behind him and try to push him over the line, so he'd be early. I can't say either tactic was particularly successful.

In Perth, we didn't have a very maneuverable 12-Meter in *Stars & Stripes '87.* The boat was comparatively long and heavy and, thus, not very maneuverable. Therefore, I used the Vanderbilt start, as Turner did, to avoid much of the prestart maneuvering. As mentioned, I enjoy the jostling at the start, and so I missed it, but obviously *Stars & Stripes '87* was the right horse for that windy course.

Port-Tack Approach

Differing from a Vanderbilt start, a port-tack approach is for those who are willing and able to think on their feet, that is, ad-lib. This start is very popular in dinghy racing, as these boats accelerate quickly, maneuver precisely, and don't require large quantities of space.

As the name indicates, you approach the starting line on port tack, looking for a place, or a hole, to tack onto starboard (see the black boat in Figure 10.5). When approaching on port tack, it is important to line up to keep your options open, that is, be able to tack when an opportunity arises. Boats overlapped to weather can prevent you from tacking. When and where you tack onto starboard has a direct bearing on when and where you

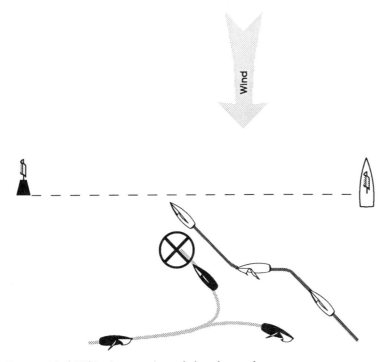

FIGURE 10.5 *White is protecting a hole to leeward.*

start on the line. Ideally, you want to tack close on the leeward side of starboard-tack boats. Also, you want to tack with enough speed so your bow sticks out enough to weather. This can prevent you from being blanketed, even give you the desirable safe-leeward position, discussed earlier. Further, you do not want any boat(s) close on your leeward side as you'll use this space to leeward to accelerate.

The problem is that when you open a hole to leeward, others try to fill it. Thus, don't make your hole too big or too obvious. Also, aggressively defend the hole against encroachers—those who have the "temerity" to do the same thing you did. If you see a boat on port tack about to tack onto starboard close and to leeward of you (as the black boat is doing near the "X" symbol), fall off (as is white), and aim at the black boat. Further, luff your sails, so you slow down and don't consume the precious space to leeward. This falling off might persuade the black boat to tack elsewhere, or tack to weather of you. From white's perspective, either of those options is perfectly acceptable.

A boat tacking from port to starboard isn't the only lurking danger for the starboard-tacker. A second danger is a starboard-tacker, sailing behind

Strategy, Tactics, and the Rules

you on a reach. This is, essentially, a sneak attack. So watch behind you for boats on the same tack who might try to fill your hole to leeward. No matter if attacking boats are tacking or heading up, the defensive maneuver is to fall off before the other boat gets an overlap to leeward (as in FIGURE 10.5). You might also luff your sails and let your boom out—like a blocker—to persuade further the attacking boat to take your weather side or someone else's lee side. If this boat takes the bait and tacks to weather, luff up to drive the other boat up. This opens more water for you to leeward, which is valuable real estate.

Luffing

Luffing can be a starting technique in itself or, more likely, a defensive maneuver when you are too early in attempting a Vanderbilt or a port-tack approach. As a starting technique, it is most appropriate to dinghies and small boats, which are quick to accelerate. No matter what type of boat you have, it is important to know how quickly your boat accelerates in various winds and, similarly, how long it takes to cover distances. This is the same mental exercise that you do when passing a car on a two-lane highway with another car coming from the opposite direction. You need to judge distances precisely.

I'm as good as anyone, I think, at estimating distances. I constantly practice judging time and distance, and not just in a sailboat. Wherever I go, such as in an airplane or in my car, I'm thinking about time and distance. In a boat, I'll ask people, How long it will take to get to that buoy? Or in a plane, How long it will take until the wheels touch the ground in San Diego? Or, How long it will take to drive or walk to the corner store? I like to carry dollar bills to place friendly wagers on the outcome, to give the contest some added significance.

Why bother? Because, as described, judging distance from the perspective of time is an important skill in sailboat racing, as well as sailing. It has relevance when docking a boat, when converging with another boat on a port-starboard situation, and, of course, at the starting line.

There are techniques for luffing at the start. Don't go head to wind. Rather, keep the boat at some angle to the wind and ease the sails. Then use the sails as your accelerator to get moving. For example, to accelerate, trim the jib first. This will drive the bow down in that hole you left open to leeward—you did leave a hole open, didn't you?—to a close-hauled course, at which point, trim the main. To force a boat to windward of you up and simultaneously to open a hole for you to leeward to accelerate into, trim only the main.

Dip Start

The dip start is appropriate when boats are likely to be late getting to the line, such as when the wind is light or the current foul. Here you wait on the upwind, or "course," side of the line. Then when there is a minute or less left, you reach below the line and come back up for the start. I saw Lowell North do this in the Star Worlds in Seattle in 1971, and he won the race. I remember this so well because I was down at the pin end fighting for room—slugging it out—and Lowell pulled this off. It was beautiful to see.

A dip start, however, can be disastrous if the fleet isn't late or, indeed, is early. It also obviously *isn't* appropriate if the one-minute or black-flag rule is in force.

Port-Tack Start

I've sailed in thousands of races, and if I've started on port tack in more than 1 percent of them, it would surprise me. A port-tack start can happen, however, when the lefthand end of the starting line is favored by a huge amount. A wind shift could cause that, although the committee would more likely postpone a start after a wind shift such as that. This is more

FIGURE 10.6 Liberty *port-tacking* Australia II.

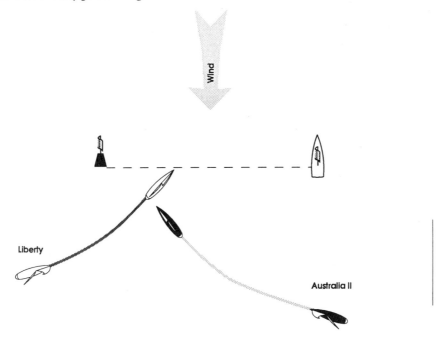

likely to happen in a distance race that has a predetermined start. Obviously, if it's a reaching start on port, you don't want to cross the line on starboard solely to have rights. You might not even be able to cross the line on starboard. With a good line, you have to be very brave to try this in the midst of starboard-tackers. This isn't usually something you plan; you just seize an opportunity. "Carpe diem," as Ted Turner might have put it.

In the fourth race of the 1983 America's Cup, I port-tacked *Australia II* at the start (see FIGURE 10.6). On *Liberty*, we were reaching on port tack at the port end of the line. *Australia II*, skippered by John Bertrand, was reaching on starboard tack from the starboard end. In my mind, I had to figure out what our course would be when we headed up, and what *Australia II*'s course would be when she headed up.

One other thing had to be considered. According to the Definitions in the IRYU rules, there is no proper course before the start. This meant *Australia II* could luff as high as she wished. Not only did I have to figure if we could cross ahead of *Australia II* on a close-hauled course, but I had to figure her course as she luffed up.

There was no time to ask anyone else whether they thought we could cross *Australia II*, nor was I interested in their opinions. As mentioned, I have great confidence in my ability to judge time and distance. I thought I could do it, so I tried it. Carpe diem.

Bertrand must have been amazed, because it took him a few seconds to respond. We passed ahead of him, winning the start by six seconds. That maneuver set the tone for the day. *Australia II* never got ahead of us, and we won the race by forty-three seconds to lead the series 3-1.

There's one other point I'd like to draw from this story. With a maneuver like this you can "own" someone for a day or even a lifetime. I don't presume to speak for Bertrand, but he sailed the rest of that afternoon as if he was embarrassed by what happened at the start. This was a short-lived victory, however. As history will recall, that was one of my best, as well as last, hurrahs in this series. The Australians won the next three races and the America's Cup.

Downwind Start

When starting downwind, first determine the favored end. (In a downwind start, the favored end is farthest downwind.) Then make the approach on starboard tack. Sail along the line on a beam reach. The closer you are to the line, the more the likelihood is you will be to leeward of the other boats and, thus, have right-of-way. Also, it is easy to judge time and distance when so close to the line. Finally, since you are beam-reaching—the fastest point of sail—you'll have good speed.

If you sail with a spinnaker, don't hoist it too early, particularly if there is a chance you will be early. With a spinnaker, it is very difficult to luff on the line, trying to kill time. If you're late, however, go for the spinnaker set before the gun. However, be very careful of leeward boats that don't have spinnakers up. They can take you up much higher than you can easily go, so give them plenty of room.

Table 10A   *Priority chart for tactical decision making*

Wind Type	Oscillating less than 10°			Oscillating more than 10°			Persistently shifting less than 10°			Persistently shifting more than 10°		
Wind speed (knots)	0-5	5-15	15-	0-5	5-15	15-	0-5	5-15	15-	0-5	5-15	15-
Clean Air	1	2	3	1	4	4	1	2	3	1	2	3
Correct tack	2	1	1	2	1	1	3	1	1	2	1	1
Ability to tack easily	5	5	5	4	3	3	5	5	5	5	5	5
Good Boat speed	4	3	2	5	5	5	2	3	2	3	3	2
Continue on correct tack	3	4	4	3	2	2	4	4	4	4	4	4

THE FIRST HUNDRED YARDS

When sailing upwind, the first hundred yards are probably the most important in sailboat racing. The rich get richer, and the poor, "asphyxiated." Thus, what you do in the first hundred yards can be telling. Sailboat racing is an ongoing process of choosing options: Do I want clear air? To be on the correct tack? The ability to tack easily? Good boat speed? The ability to continue on the correct tack? If you aren't in the lead, you usually can't have all of them, so hard choices are necessary. It is interesting that these choices differ in different types of winds and in different wind speeds.

Table 10A above, assembled by Ed Baird, a Laser and J/24 world champion, is helpful in determining a strategy for the first hundred yards. You can also use it on subsequent weather legs. First, characterize the wind. Are you sailing in an oscillating shift of more or less than 10 degrees or a persistent shift of more or less than 10 degrees?[2] Then, after characterizing the type of wind you're sailing in, select the proper wind speed along the top of the chart. The priorities go from 1, which is most important, to 5, which is least important.

UPWIND TACTICS

I commented that I like to be aggressive at the start. After the start, I am conservative, however. Risk and reward are the driving principles in sailboat racing. You want to lessen risks and maximize the rewards. In Chapter 8, we talked about a prerace strategy. Once it is determined, you have to decide how much you are willing to wager on it. An oscillating wind is a safer bet because this wind shift occurs most often. In fact, in Chapter 8 we commented that if you don't know what the wind is doing, assume it is an oscillating shift. A persistent wind is a tougher call—although abnormally large wind shear is helpful in predicting it. An oscillating-persistent breeze is a tougher call still. In sailboat racing, not only is the future hard to read, but, also, other boats very often won't let you go where you want to go. That is where strategy and tactics meet head-on.

Remember that you don't have to win the first weather leg to win a race; nor do you have to win this race or any races to win a series. After the start, I'd rather sail consistently—that is, conservatively—than chase long shots.

What this has to do with sailboat racing is this: Don't go toward corners or away from the competition. Stay in touch—sail conservatively. Corners are long shots—sucker bets.

For example, in the Star Worlds in 1976, I started on starboard in the middle of the line. You can't be more conservative than that. Then after crossing the starting line, I watched boats to windward and to leeward. If the boats to windward were sagging down toward me, and I was sagging down on the boats to leeward, I knew I was going in the correct direction, as the wind was persistently shifting in my direction or to the left. If, however, the boats to windward were beating me, and I was beating the boats

---

[2] The magnitude of the shift—less or more than 10 degrees—has to do with the time it takes to sail the windward leg. For example, if it is a persistent shift, do you expect it to shift more or less than 10 degrees by the time you finish the weather leg? This chart is published with the kind permission of Ed Baird.

to leeward, I knew I had to tack as the wind was persistently shifting toward the right.[3]

Nothing fancy or brilliant about it. I wasn't perfectly placed but I was well placed. Also, my boat speed was such that being well placed was all I needed. Using this strategy, I won all five races in the Star Worlds—my crowning achievement in the sport, in my estimation.

It was Carl Eichenlaub who taught me this tactical move, which I still use when racing in a large fleet in races characterized by persistent shifts. Eichenlaub was always very good at looking at other boats to determine which way to go. He used other boats to see the big picture. I have good tactical instincts from spending so many hours with Carl.

We did spend hours and hours together, too. I used much of our time together to become a much better sailboat racer. More of it, however, was just good fun. When I crewed for Carl in the Lightning class, we'd criss-cross the country with the boat on a trailer, just as people go camping today. Once Carl, Mike O'Brien, and I trailered a Lightning from San Diego to the Buffalo Canoe Club, in Canada, across the Peace Bridge from Buffalo, New York. While we came the farthest, I believe, we got there the earliest. We arrived at the Buffalo Canoe Club for this big Lightning regatta, and no one was there to greet us. There wasn't even a caretaker around.

We decided to launch our boat for some practice but couldn't locate the hoist to do it. Eventually, we noticed an old World War II Air Force flatbed truck, with huge tires. It had a crane on the back, which we figured was used to launch boats. We just appropriated it for our own use without permission—indeed there was no one around to ask for permission. Carl and Mike are both mechanically inclined, and somehow they got this old truck running without a key. We drove it into the water to launch our Lightning. It was very shallow so we must have driven out 100 yards. We didn't know the bottom and eventually drove the truck into a hole, where it got stuck.

Then we got concerned. Lightning sailors from around the country were coming to race in this regatta, and the only way to launch the boats was, as far as we knew, with this old truck that was now firmly planted in the water. Mike had an automobile club card, which he'd borrowed from his parents, so he called a tow truck. The driver took one look at the truck stuck 100 yards offshore, and said, "I'm out of here!" Eventually we persuaded him to wait while we scrounged up lines. Some were stronger than

---

[3]Obviously, that wouldn't work in an oscillating wind, but in the persistent shifts that characterized this series, it worked very well.

others and some were newer. Lines started breaking, and the little tow truck was hardly a match for this oversized Air Force truck stuck in the mud, but eventually the tow truck got the truck back ashore. The show went on. I'm not sure anyone even noticed.

AVOID LAYLINES

Obviously I believe in conservative sailing. To that end, the middle of the course is safe, the sides, and particularly the laylines, are too often sorry. Certainly, don't go to the layline early in a leg. Postpone it until you are five to ten boat lengths from the mark.

Suppose you think you're sailing in a persistent shift to the right. If you sail on port tack to the layline, the wind can continue shifting, and you will overstand (see FIGURE 10.7A). Or perhaps you've guessed wrong, and the wind oscillates back to the left (see FIGURE 10.7B). Now you are on the wrong side of the shift, and every boat to leeward or ahead will gain on

FIGURE 10.7 *When you're on an early layline, three things can happen, and all of them are bad.*

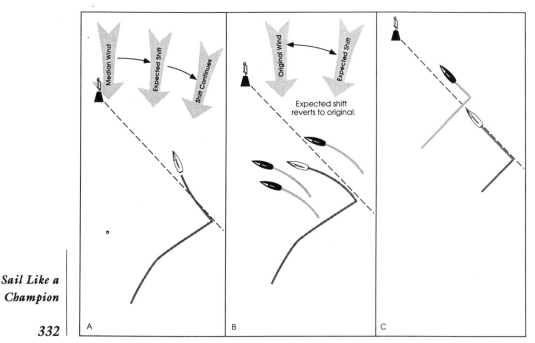

you. Also, if by some miracle you do pick the proper layline (see white boat in FIGURE 10.7C), every boat that crosses ahead of you will tack on your wind. In summary, when you're on an early layline, three things can happen to you, and all of them are bad.

The proper strategy with a persistent shift is to sail in the direction of the new wind, not, however, to the layline. To put this another way: lean toward the proper side, not, however, against the wall—the layline. If you're at the layline early in the leg or are the boat farthest to the right or left, you're chasing long shots. Sometimes long shots pay off handsomely, but to my mind not often enough.

GAINS AND LOSSES IN WIND SHIFTS

Gains and losses through wind shifts depend on three things: first, the direction of the shift, as discussed; also the degree, or amount, of the wind shift; and the degree of lateral separation between boats. The more the wind shifts to the left in FIGURE 10.8, the greater the gain for the boat(s) closest to it. If there is no shift (see "original wind" callout), the port- and starboard-tack boats are equal. With a 7-degree shift to the left, the lefthand boat gains approximately two and a half boat lengths. With a

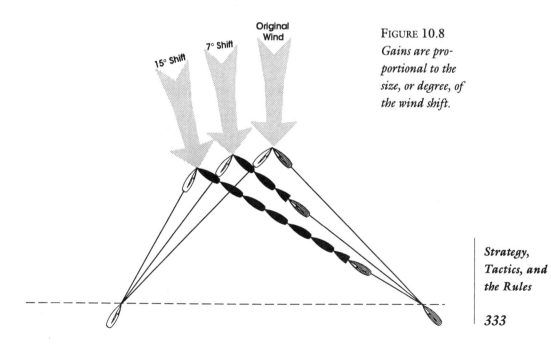

FIGURE 10.8
Gains are proportional to the size, or degree, of the wind shift.

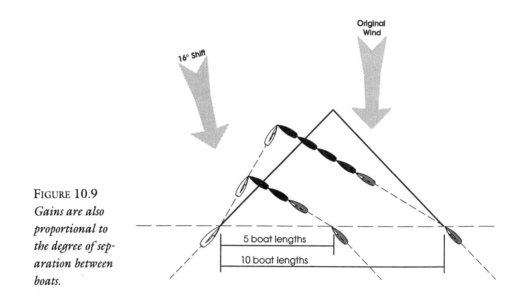

FIGURE 10.9
*Gains are also
proportional to
the degree of sep-
aration between
boats.*

15-degree shift, the lefthand boat gains six and a half lengths.

Similarly, the greater the lateral separation between the boats, the greater the gains and losses (see FIGURE 10.9). If five boat lengths separate the two boats in a lefthand shift of 16 degrees, the lefthand boat gains two boat lengths. If ten boat lengths separate them, the left boat gains four lengths.

Cross and Consolidate

Thus, if you realize a gain, that is, if you are on the correct side of a wind shift, tack and cross boats on the opposite tack to consolidate (see the white boat in FIGURE 10.10). If this were the stock market, you'd call it profit-taking. If you don't tack and the wind oscillates back, your gain is nullified—a profit on paper only, as they say on Wall Street if you don't cash out before a gain turns into a loss. The converse is true, too. If another boat tacks to consolidate a gain, don't let this boat cross you (see the gray boat in FIGURE 10.10). If you tack to leeward and ahead, you will be well placed to take advantage of the next oscillation.

Crossing and consolidating is particularly important in an oscillating shift; however, it ensures you some profit if you aren't sure if this is an

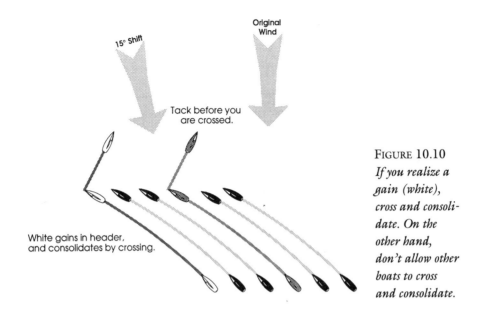

Original
Wind

15° Shift

Tack before you
are crossed.

White gains in header,
and consolidates by crossing.

FIGURE 10.10
*If you realize a
gain (white),
cross and consoli-
date. On the
other hand,
don't allow other
boats to cross
and consolidate.*

oscillating or persistent shift. As such, it is a good conservative bet. Of course, this may occur at a point in the regatta where it is time to chase longer shots. If late in a regatta and the boat(s) I have to beat are to the right of me, I'd tack for sure with a lefthand shift (see FIGURE 10.10). If, however, the boat(s) I have to beat are to the left of me, I'd delay tacking. If the wind continues left in a persistent shift, they win in the wind shift; if it oscillates back to the right, I win. No sense going farther right than I have to, however.

Foot to the Header; Pinch to the Lift

Similarly, if you can clearly see a header, foot to the header (see FIGURE 10.11). Footing to the header, that is, sailing fast rather than pinching, will increase your separation from a competitor who doesn't foot to the header and, as such, will increase your distance ahead with the shift. The tough part, of course, is "clearly seeing" that header. Boats to weather—the black boats in FIGURE 10.11—are a good indication of a header. On the other hand, if you can clearly see a lift, pinch to the lift. If you can't clearly see headers or lifts, the conservative approach is to do nothing.

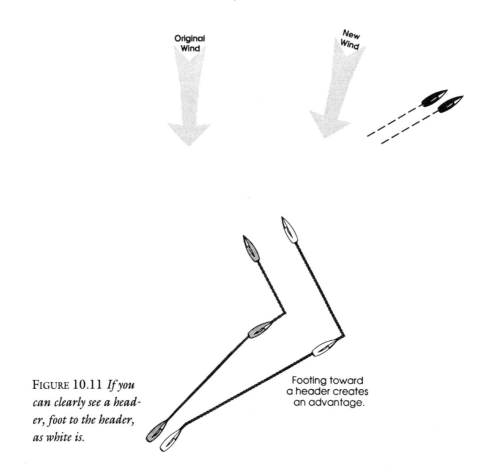

Original Wind

New Wind

FIGURE 10.11 *If you can clearly see a header, foot to the header, as white is.*

Footing toward a header creates an advantage.

"Take Your Medicine"

Suppose you bet on a persistent shift to the left, and it is a persistent shift to the right. Or you bet on an oscillating shift, and it is a persistent shift. If you've guessed wrong, you're likely behind, and it's time to go the right way.

The alternative to "taking your medicine," as that familiar expression goes, is hoping that the wind will shift back. Hoping is, in my estimation, an unproductive act in sailboat racing. If you've guessed wrong, go right. To use another common expression to characterize this situation, "Better late than never" is usually better in sailboat racing.

Cover When Ahead; Split When Behind

Depending on your perspective, lateral separation (how far to windward or leeward you are of other boats, discussed above), can be dangerous. On a

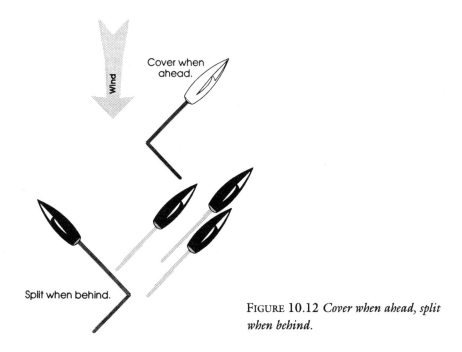

Cover when ahead.

Wind

Split when behind.

FIGURE 10.12 *Cover when ahead, split when behind.*

wind shift, you can win or lose "big." One way to reduce the risks of a shift when ahead is to stay close to the boat(s) behind you, thereby decreasing lateral separation. This speaks for covering when ahead (see white boat in FIGURE 10.12). This is very true in match racing and in one-design racing, where how much you win by isn't important. It has to be weighed in mixed-fleet racing, however, as you don't just race against other boats but against the clock.

If behind, however, do the opposite. Split—sail away from the leader (see FIGURE 10.12). That rule is more important toward the end of the race than the beginning, or toward the end of a series than the start. There is a time in sailboat racing to be a "contrarian"—rarely, however, is that on the first weather leg or in the first race(s).

LANES OF CLEAR AIR

According to Table 10A, being on the correct tack is most important, particularly when the wind is more than 5 knots. Next comes clear air. Thus, on the weather leg, you need to identify lanes of clear air and then sail in them. The apparent wind, not the true wind, determines where the area of disturbed air extends; this is true both upwind and down. Thus, if you are worried about "dirty air" from another boat, watch its masthead fly or, if close enough, its telltales to determine the envelope of disturbed wind. This is a danger zone: an area to avoid. Note that in light winds, the area of disturbed air is greater than in heavier winds.

On the weather leg, it is important that you look for lanes of clear air, and take them when and where you find them. He or she who hesitates may be lost. Of course, the lane you take should be on the favored tack. In very light winds, clear air is more important than being on the favored tack.

Tight Cover

If clear air is something you want to receive, dirty air is something you want to give. There are many ways a boat uses its wind shadow—or area of disturbed air—to slow the competition. Most obvious is the tight cover (see FIGURE 10.13). Here, the lead boat positions itself to weather and ahead of a leeward boat. (Remember that the area of disturbed wind

FIGURE 10.13 *Tight, light, and loose cover.*

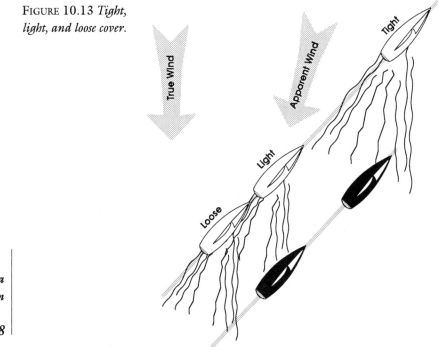

emanates from the apparent wind.) As the name indicates, a tight cover is an aggressive maneuver.

In FIGURE 10.13, the leeward boat (the first black boat) can tack away from white in the tight cover position. That's a good idea if the lefthand side of the course is favored because of more wind or a favorable shift. However, if the favored tack is to the righthand side of the course, a tack to starboard moves black away from the preferred side of the course. If the leeward boat wants to continue right, the tactic is to foot off. Of course, on a weather leg, the windward yacht can foot off, too, maintaining control. (To put this in the context of the previous chapter, Rule 39 does not apply on a windward leg.)

In match racing, the tight cover often precipitates a tacking duel, which is usually how a tight cover is broken. Tacking duels are less common in fleet racing as you usually have to worry about several boats. At the end of a series, when you have to beat one or a few boats—or they have to beat you—tacking duels are more common, however.

Use discretion when clamping on a tight cover, particularly in fleet racing. There are various familiar sayings that are appropriate for its measured use. For example, "What goes around comes around." A tight cover is about as friendly as a choke hold. If you are always clamping on tight covers, you aren't going to have many friends. There are, as we will see, other maneuvers that accomplish almost the same thing with greater subtlety.

Loose Cover

If a tight cover is corporal punishment, a loose cover is closer to friendly persuasion (see the back white boat in FIGURE 10.13). The idea is to stay between the boat(s) and the mark. White has a controlling position, but the control isn't hurting the other boat (black). One can put a loose cover on one boat or a group. Putting a loose cover on a group requires that the lead boat stay between the windward mark and the pack. This is another maneuver that lessens lateral separation.

Light Cover

A light cover is somewhere between the tight cover and the loose cover (see the middle white boat in FIGURE 10.13). The middle white boat tacks in a position where it isn't clear if its envelope of disturbed wind is affecting the second black boat. In essence, the lead boat tacks aft of the tight-cover position.

With the light cover, the leeward boat might fall off slightly to clear its air. This causes the weather boat to gain. A light cover allows the lead boat to herd the trailing boat in the direction it wants it to go. *Herding* is an accurate term for it. A tight cover would likely cause the leeward boat to tack away. That can be considered a stampede.

Covering When Match Racing

I've spent a large part of my life match racing, as practiced in the America's Cup. The truth is that it isn't my favorite form of racing. I find fleet racing more interesting. Match racing is like playing chess—sometimes with a grand master. Fleet racing is like playing chess against twenty competitors at the same time. Maybe not all of them are grand masters, but on any day any one of them can make it interesting. Too often very interesting.

Most people reading this book will never match-race. Nevertheless, we've given it some attention because it is easier to learn tactics through one-on-one situations. (However, the rules applied are fleet-racing rules.)

In a match race, you try to herd the other boat to the layline. When your opponent tacks away from the layline (toward the center of the course), you clamp on a tight cover. The typical response from your opponent is another tack. When, however, your opponent tacks toward the layline, you use a loose or light cover. Why herd the other boat to the layline? Laylines, as indicated earlier, are to be avoided. It is on the layline that the lead boat can inflict the most damage.

Earlier, I've written about the last race of the America's Cup trials between *Courageous* and *Intrepid* in 1974—my debut in the America's Cup. I sailed aboard *Courageous* as tactician, a role I assumed very late in the campaign. *Intrepid* caught us on the second beat. She was faster than *Courageous* when it was windy, as it was that day. Coming up on the layline, Intrepid was only two boat lengths behind. This race was so important—one final race would determine the success or failure of the entire summer—that my heart was beating furiously. There was a lot more current and sea running than I had realized. As a result, we had to pinch to get around the weather mark. A 12-Meter is a massive boat; as such, it has the momentum to pinch up to a mark quite effectively. *Intrepid* went from being two boat lengths behind to being four boat lengths, or thirty to forty seconds behind. All of this damage was inflicted on the layline. Further, at the mark, *Intrepid* had no speed, while we did a jibe set and were gone. That was the end of their summer. On *Courageous,* we advanced to the America's Cup.

LEE BOW

If on port tack and you can cross—or almost cross—a starboard-tacker, a lee-bow maneuver can be as aggressive and as devastating a maneuver as a tight cover. Rather than crossing ahead, the port-tacker tacks to leeward and ahead of the starboard-tacker (see white boat in FIGURE 10.14).

The principle behind the lee-bow maneuver was described in a different context earlier. In Chapter 5, we wrote how the main helps the jib by placing the jib in a lift and in more wind, and, also, how the headsail hurts the main by placing it in a header and in less wind. This is the principle of the lee-bow maneuver as well. The boat ahead and to leeward acts as the equivalent of a jib. It sails in more wind and at a more favorable angle, that is, in a lift. The boat behind is the equivalent of the main—it sails in less wind and in a header.

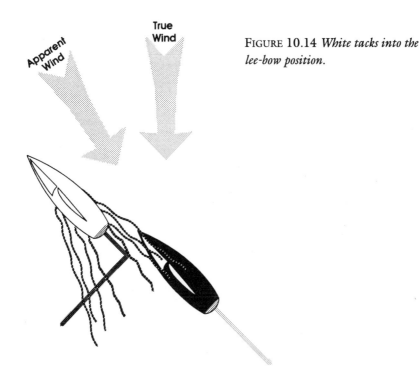

True Wind

Apparent Wind

FIGURE 10.14 *White tacks into the lee-bow position.*

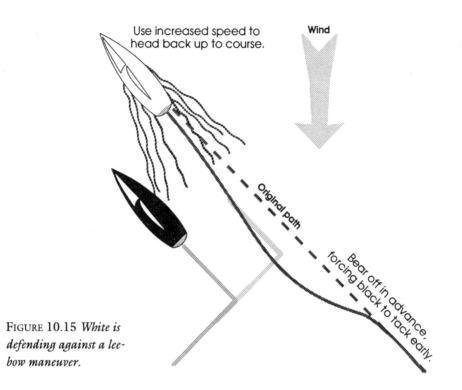

Use increased speed to head back up to course.

Wind

Original path

Bear off in advance, forcing black to tack early.

FIGURE 10.15 *White is defending against a lee-bow maneuver.*

In crossing situations, the lee-bow maneuver requires precise boat handling and timing. As such, it is best done in smooth water and moderate air. It can prevent a boat on the layline from making the mark. Like a tight cover, use it to force another boat away from the favored side of the course.

If you anticipate a lee-bow maneuver, you (the white starboard-tacker in FIGURE 10.15) can defend against it by bearing off before the crossing, which is legal on a weather leg. This causes the port-tack boat to tack prematurely. Then, as soon as the port-tacker tacks, the starboard-tacker uses the speed gained from bearing off to head up.

Crossing or Not?

The lee-bow maneuver depends on the port-tacker being able to cross or almost cross the starboard-tacker. Obviously, knowing whether you can cross another boat is important. Some sailors can just look at another boat on another tack and say with certainty whether they are ahead, behind, or even. Most of us aren't so gifted, however. In bigger boats, crossings are

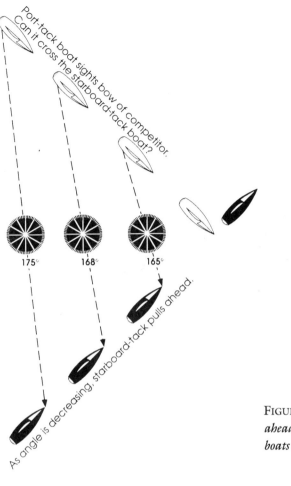

Port-tack boat sights bow of competitor.
Can it cross the starboard-tack boat?

175°   168°   165°

As angle is decreasing, starboard-tack pulls ahead.

FIGURE 10.16 *Determining aheads and behinds with boats on opposite tacks.*

often determined using a hand-bearing compass, those ever-useful "hockey pucks." Here, a sight is taken from the stern of the white port-tack boat to the bow of the black starboard-tacker (see FIGURE 10.16). Shortly after, two more sights are taken. If the bearings *decrease,* as they do in the illustration, the starboard-tacker is ahead. If the bearings *increase,* port is ahead. If the bearings stay the same, the boats will collide.

Don't, however, take your sights, draw your conclusions, and forget it. A wind shift, current, etc., can change the outcome dramatically. This technique doesn't obviate the need to keep a proper lookout.

You can also use this technique to determine whether you are pulling ahead or falling behind a boat on same tack (see FIGURE 10.17). When sighting a boat to your right (top left in figure), if the bearings are decreasing, as they are here, you (white boat) are falling behind. If they increase

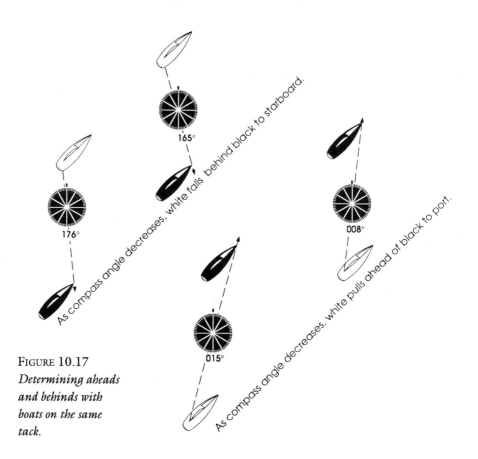

FIGURE 10.17
*Determining aheads
and behinds with
boats on the same
tack.*

you (white boat) are pulling ahead. When sighting a boat to your left (bottom right figure), if the bearings are decreasing, as they are here, you (white boat) are pulling ahead. If, however, the bearings are increasing, you (white boat) are falling behind.

TACKING LINES

Smaller boats don't normally have extra crew that can use a hand-bearing compass. If you race a dinghy, tacking lines, which are relevant angles scribed on the deck of a boat, are a useful graphic device to determine whether you can cross another boat on a different tack. Tacking lines can also tell you if you are ahead or behind a boat on the same tack and if you have reached a layline, that is, can tack for the windward mark. The use of tacking lines is not limited to small boats, however. Indeed, some larger

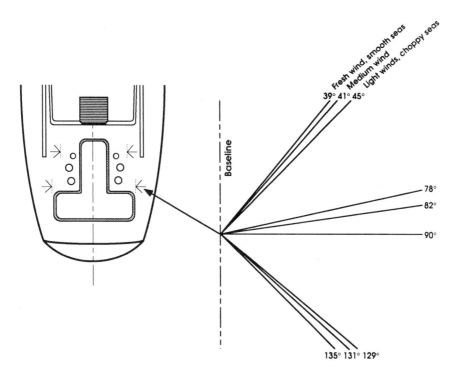

FIGURE 10.18 *Drawing tacking lines, laylines, and ladder rungs on a deck.*

boats use a hand-bearing compass and tacking lines to determine aheads and behinds.

To draw tacking lines, start by determining a line parallel to the center of the boat (see FIGURE 10.18). A string from the mast to the backstay can be helpful in determining this centerline. Mark the baseline(s) (parallel to the string) on either side (see the four dotted lines on the boat in the figure). Remember that the longer the lines, including the baselines, the easier they are to use.

Then determine your tacking angles in three conditions: light, moderate, and heavy winds. Note that the tacking angle will be wider in light winds and choppy seas and narrower in fresh winds and smooth seas (see FIGURE 8.9). Also, different boats have different tacking angles. (You might save or recopy the headings from the two-number system described in Chapter 8 to arrive at tacking angles. Average numbers from light-, medium-, and heavy-air days to determine your three tacking angles.)

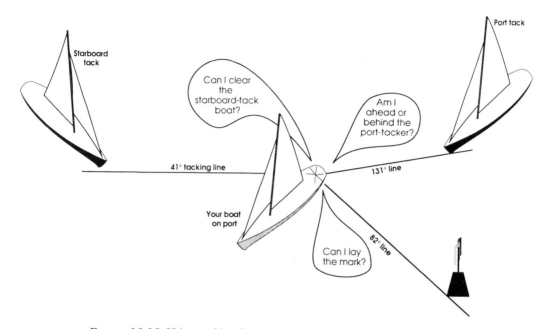

FIGURE 10.19 *Using tacking lines to determine aheads and behinds and whether you can lay the mark.*

Then take half of these angles and mark them on either side using a protractor (see the top three angles in the detail to the right in FIGURE 10.18). Perhaps they are 39 degrees in fresh winds and smooth seas, 41 degrees in moderate winds, and 45 degrees in light winds and choppy seas.

Next, take each of these three numbers and add them to 90. For example, add 45 to 90. That gives us 135 degrees. Draw this line and the other two (129 and 131 degrees). These bottom lines are ladder rungs, discussed in Chapter 7 and 8. Finally, double the tacking angles to determine the laylines (middle three angles).

Use the applicable forward angle to determine if you can cross a boat on the opposite tack (see FIGURE 10.19). If starboard (black boat at left) is behind this line, as it is in the illustration, the gray boat in the center will likely cross ahead. Gray might also be in a good position to clamp on a lee-bow maneuver (see FIGURE 10.14).

Use the applicable middle angle to see if you can lay the mark or are on the layline. If the mark is on or behind the layline, as it is in the illustration, you, the gray boat, can likely tack for the mark.

Use the appropriate aft angle to determine if you are ahead or behind a boat on the same tack, or, to use the terminology established in Chapter

7, on the same or different ladder rung. In medium winds, any boat aft of the 131-degree line is behind you, or on a lower ladder rung. Any boat ahead of this line is ahead, or on an higher ladder rung. Any boat on this line, as the black at right is, is on the same ladder rung or even with you on the gray boat.

This line also tells if there is room to tack and cross ahead of another boat. In the figure, if the gray boat tacked onto starboard, it would probably force the black boat at right to tack or duck—either way gray would be ahead. It might then be a good time for gray to tack to consolidate its lead over black.

Obviously, knowing whether you are ahead or behind is a powerful tool. In the 1986–87 America's Cup, for example, we used a handbearing-compass and tacking lines, as well as a stadimeter, hooked to an onboard computer, to determine aheads and behinds. The stadimeter—a new wrinkle in the America's Cup wars—worked this way: Our navigator in Perth, Peter Isler, would focus the stadimeter, a sighting device, on the draft stripes on an opponent's mainsail. The distance between draft stripes is a known dimension, thanks to the 12-Meter rule and the customary practice of sailmakers of putting draft stripes at the top, middle, and bottom quarter. From this known height, it was easy to compute range, or distance, to the opposing boat. Bearing came from an internal compass.

Stadimeters are commonly used in navigation. In fact, the stadimeter we used was a World War II surplus model, manufactured by Schick Razor Company in 1943. What was new about this application was that the computer would then compute the bearing and range into sailing distance, thereby describing whether we were ahead or behind and by how much. The readout could be in distance or in time.

This information helped to shape our tactics. I started conservatively in this series. I preferred to start to leeward of the competition but even, with both of us on starboard tack. On *Stars & Stripes,* we would sail our target boat speed for the wind speed (see Chapter 7) Then one of the first things we would do is determine if we were gaining or losing.

If we were gaining on the boat, per the stadimeter, we'd fall off a bit, increasing speed. This left the windward boat two tough options: foot with us or sail its own targets and separate from us. Footing with us wasn't easy, because *Stars & Stripes* was such a long boat with good stability. If an opponent chose this option, the boat would often sag into us, until the disturbed wind from our lee-bow position forced her to tack away. We'd be ahead.

Separating from us often ended up being an unpalatable choice, too. As described, separation is dangerous in a wind shift. As the leeward boat, we would be helped by a header. We would often take advantage of the header, the separation, and the knowledge we were ahead to tack to cross and consolidate (see FIGURE 10.10). Then, whether the wind continued to shift or oscillated back, we'd be ahead. A lift, of course, would help the other boat, provided it was a persistent shift. If, however, the wind oscillated back—which was very common in Perth—we'd make out in the next shift. (The weather boat can't very well cross and consolidate from an upwind position.)

Thus, if the boat wanted to match us in a drag race, we'd often win; if the wind shifted our way, we'd often win. But if the wind shifted the opponent's way, we might lose or we might not, depending on whether it was a persistent shift or an oscillating shift. Three out of four isn't bad odds.

Kiwi Magic misused this tactic against us in the fourth race of the challengers' finals. At this point, *Stars & Stripes* led the series, 2–1. The wind was blowing 26 knots and oscillating between 209 and 217 degrees. We started on starboard tack, near the pin (see FIGURE 10.20). We forced the New Zealand boat to tack, and they crossed the line on port near the committee boat. Eventually, we tacked to port and paralleled them. *Stars & Stripes* was to weather; *Kiwi Magic* to leeward. While the distance between us was 550 yards, according to our stadimeter, we were ahead by one and a half boat lengths. The wind, however, was on a righthand oscillating—a header for them—putting them ahead. The key to the leg, and likely the race, would be when they tacked. Ideally, they should tack when ahead and with the wind continuing its oscillating to the right. Then, when they converged with us after tacking to cross and consolidate, they'd be sailing on a lift, while we would be on a header.

Kiwi Magic didn't tack, however. Either they didn't know they were ahead, or they thought the wind would go farther to the right. We had an instrument (see the figure) that showed the history of wind direction on the computer screen as wiggly lines. Interestingly, *Kiwi Magic* had the same instrument. The wind was as far right as it would get at eight and ten minutes into the race. When the Kiwis tacked, at 14:30, the wind was oscillating back to the left to our side of the course. We were ahead.

From this point on, we tacked on the Kiwis when they tried to sail toward the center of the course on starboard tack, and gave them fresh air when they headed to the layline on port. We wanted to drive them to the layline, where, as mentioned, the lead boat can do the most damage. We rounded the mark with a thirty-two-second advantage.

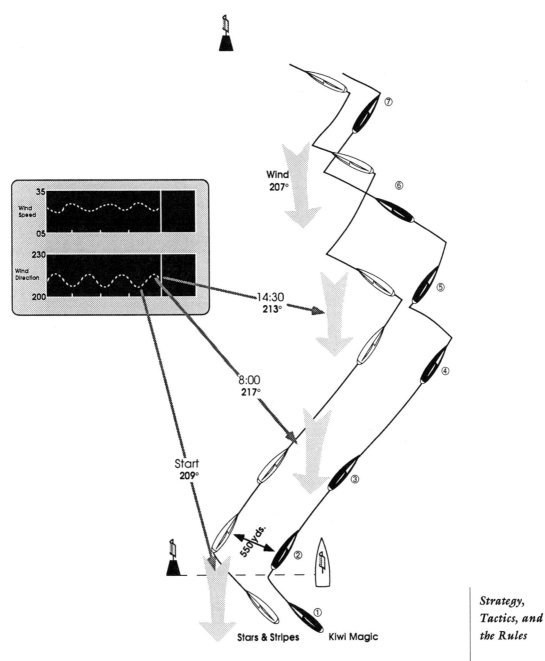

Wind
207°

35
Wind
Speed
05

230
Wind
Direction
200

14:30
213°

8:00
217°

Start
209°

550 yds.

② ⑦ ⑥ ⑤ ④ ③ ② ①

Stars & Stripes   Kiwi Magic

FIGURE 10.20 Kiwi Magic*'s tactical mistake in the challengers' final.*

DUCKING

If the port-tacker can't cross the starboard-tacker, ducking might be in order. You certainly would duck a starboard-tacker if on port-tack you are moving toward the favored right side of the course. There is a proper way to duck another boat. In fact, if ducking is done correctly, when the two boats meet again at the next crossing, the former port-tacker has a good chance of being ahead.

FIGURE 10.21 shows the proper and improper techniques for ducking another boat. The proper technique, used by the white boat, is to start the duck sufficiently early so this boat is close-reaching. Don't give away any more distance to leeward than you absolutely have to, however. If you ease the sails at the same time, speed increases. The burst of speed can cause the former port-tacker to be ahead when the two boats meet again. Also, there is a small lift off the sails of the starboard-tacker that can help you gain some distance to weather. If, however, the port-tacker ends up beam- or

FIGURE 10.21
*Proper and
improper
ducking.*

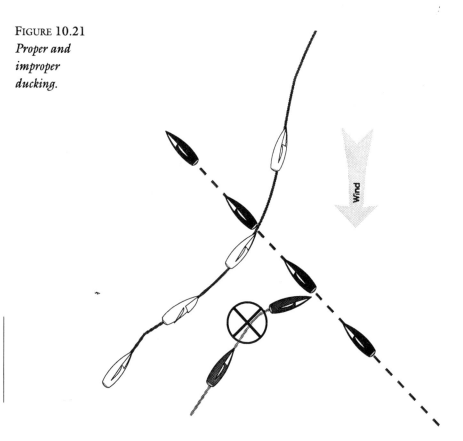

broad-reaching (see the gray boat), this port-tack boat will likely be behind on the next crossing.

CROSSINGS: NASTY AND NICE

The slam dunk is a crossing maneuver that the sailing press likes to write about, particularly in the context of the America's Cup. It has a wonderful name—borrowed from basketball—and, like its namesake, is unquestionably a dramatic maneuver. It is usually done when the boats are near the layline (see FIGURE 10.22). Here the port-tacker (black) ducks the starboard-tacker (white) at position 1. Immediately after the crossing, the starboard-tacker tacks on to port at position 2. If done properly, the white

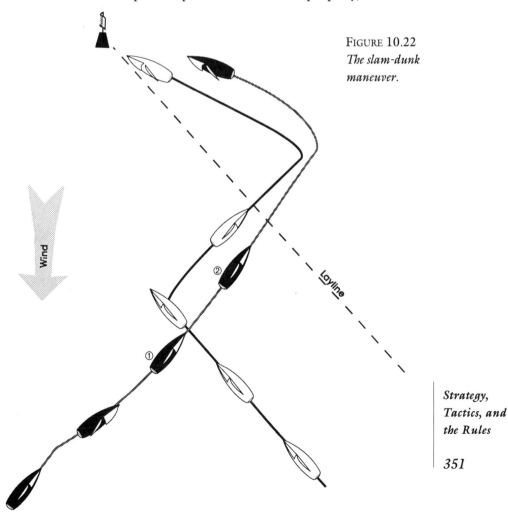

FIGURE 10.22
The slam-dunk maneuver.

Strategy, Tactics, and the Rules

351

boat in the diagram should be in a position to call "mast abeam," to prevent the leeward boat (black) from luffing (see FIGURE 9.9). Also black can't tack without violating Rule 41.2. Then in the controlling position, the white boat drives the black boat to or beyond the layline. The boats tack for the mark *when* the windward boat says so.

Lowell North was, I believe, the first to execute a slam dunk in the America's Cup. It happened in the 1977 America's Cup trials. When North's *Enterprise* threw a slam dunk on Ted Hood's *Independence,* Hood

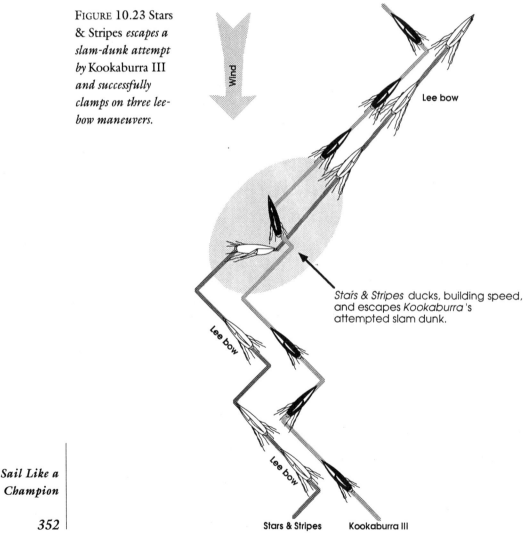

FIGURE 10.23 Stars & Stripes *escapes a slam-dunk attempt by* Kookaburra III *and successfully clamps on three lee-bow maneuvers.*

Wind

Lee bow

Stars & Stripes ducks, building speed, and escapes *Kookaburra*'s attempted slam dunk.

Lee bow

Lee bow

Stars & Stripes   Kookaburra III

was so surprised that he protested. The protest was disallowed. North used the slam-dunk maneuver to win two races in the trials, and this helped knock *Independence* and Hood out of the series. The slam dunk has since become a standard, particularly in match racing.

In the third race of the 1987 America's Cup, we escaped a slam-dunk attempt by *Kookaburra III* (see the gray oval in FIGURE 10.23). Notice how *Kookaburra III,* the black boat, couldn't quite get her nose in front of us after the slam dunk. Eventually we sailed into a lee-bow position (at the top of the figure), forcing her to tack away. Also note that before the slam-dunk attempt, we successfully clamped on two lee-bow maneuvers.

Remember, though, that might doesn't always make right. To put this another way, sometimes you can accomplish the same end, beating another boat, by using more diplomatic means. Imagine you are on starboard tack, heading to the favored lefthand side of the course. Using the tacking lines, hand-bearing compass, or good eyes, you know a port-tacker won't quite cross you. The port-tacker has two choices: tack or duck. You don't want your opponent to tack since, in your estimation, he or she is heading the wrong way. Go ahead, be a perfect gentleman or lady. Before the crossing situation, shout over to the starboard-tacker, "You're free to cross ahead." They'll think you're a wonderful person for doing it.

APPROACH TO THE WEATHER MARK

Particularly at the weather mark, you can make big gains or suffer big losses in the last 200 yards. People get lazy. They worry about the spinnaker set and whether they can lay the mark. This accounts for the popularity of the starboard-tack parade on the layline. A little aggressiveness at this juncture can pay off handsomely.

As noted, use the tacking lines to determine when to tack for the mark (see FIGURE 10.19). When the mark is on or behind the proper layline (one of the middle angles), you can probably tack for the mark. Remember, however, that current can change laylines. Bad air from other boats and wind shifts can also change the laylines. As such, laylines are movable targets.

The danger of laylines was obvious in a race we had with Tom Black-aller's *USA* in Round Robin III, in the 1986–87 America's Cup (see FIG-URE 10.24). Nearing the mark with both of us on port tack, we had a slight lead over *USA*. We were to weather. The wind shifted 20 degrees to the right, toward *USA*. Both boats tacked, and *USA* rounded the mark ahead.

As stated often, laylines are dangerous places. Avoid them until the

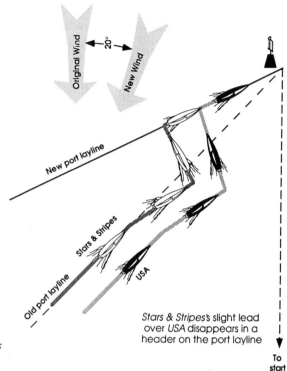

FIGURE 10.24 Stars & Stripes *shows why laylines are dangerous places as she loses in a wind shift to USA.*

Stars & Stripes's slight lead over *USA* disappears in a header on the port layline

very end (see FIGURE 10.25). When you're behind, don't go to the layline on starboard tack (see the gray boat with the "X" symbol). That is one of the most common errors inexperienced racers make. It is best to approach a weather mark to leeward of the starboard-tack layline (see white boat to leeward of the gray boat). White should tack, however, if it gets dirty air from gray or before a boat tacks on its weather quarter. The worst case is that white will have to tack twice; the best case is that it will be lifted to the mark if the wind goes right or will be on the proper side of the wind shift if it goes left.

The only time the starboard layline can pay is if boats there are getting big puffs of wind that the leeward boat isn't receiving. Also, if current is taking boats below the mark, the boats on the layline or above can be better positioned.

A boat approaching the mark on the port-tack layline can make up considerable distance by sailing in clear air all the way to the mark. One

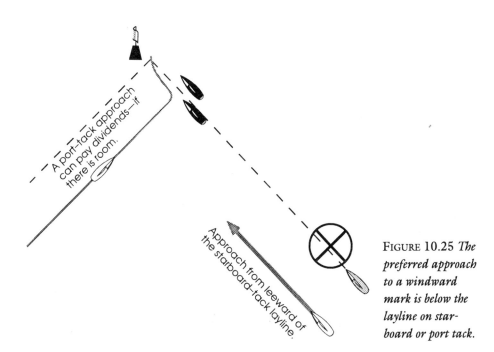

FIGURE 10.25 *The preferred approach to a windward mark is below the layline on starboard or port tack.*

problem, however, with this approach is finding a hole to tack into. In addition to the possibility of not finding a hole, a port-tack approach complicates the spinnaker set since you can't easily raise the spinnaker pole, etc., until rounding the mark. (Those doing a bear-away set on the starboard-tack parade can have the pole up, sheets connected, and spinnaker ready to go.)

Better than approaching the mark on the port-tack layline is to approach it one or two boat lengths below this layline (see FIGURE 10.25, left). From this angle, it is possible to sail to the mark in clear air and have a little more time for the spinnaker set.

Obviously, at some point, the port-tacker boat has to tack for the mark on the layline. One common maneuver is for this boat to tack ahead and to leeward of the weather boat(s) on starboard to establish the lee-bow position (see FIGURE 10.26A). The defense for this is for the starboard boat to reach down a bit. This can cause the port-tacker to tack early (see FIGURE 10.15), and starboard using its speed gained by close-reaching to break the lee-bow attempt.

More likely, port will duck rather than tack, if it can do so without interfering with other starboard-tackers (see FIGURE 10.26B). Assuming starboard is laying the mark, starboard is ahead with the duck. Further, if starboard has overstood the mark, reaching down a bit, this gambit—described as a head

Strategy, Tactics, and the Rules

355

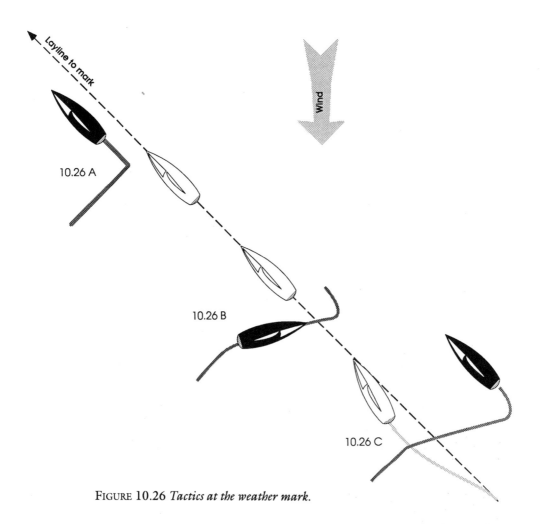

FIGURE 10.26 *Tactics at the weather mark.*

fake—can cause port to think starboard isn't laying the mark (see FIGURE 10.26C). This can cause port to overstand even more. Don't be obvious with this head fake, however. Also, don't fall off so much that you find you can't lay the mark.

Rounding the Weather Mark

Boats typically approach the weather mark on the starboard layline. (We are assuming the course is marks to port, which is most common.) This usually means that the leeward boat is entitled to buoy room, provided, among other things, that two or more boats are overlapped, and the overlap existed before reaching the two-boat-length circle from the mark. In FIGURE 10.27, the white boat will probably be entitled to room.

However, being entitled to something and being able to take it are two different things. The black boat can reach down to a tight-cover position and slow white so much that "room" becomes an academic issue. (The closer the two boats are to each other, the more devastating the wind shadow felt by white.)

Bear-Away or Jibe Set?

A bear-away or jibe set? is a familiar question at the windward mark. We will assume that the transition is windward-leeward. This is the transition after leg one and seven in the new America's Cup course and a common transition in round-the-buoys racing.

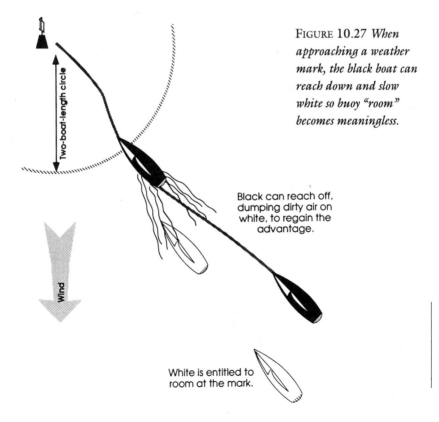

FIGURE 10.27 *When approaching a weather mark, the black boat can reach down and slow white so buoy "room" becomes meaningless.*

Black can reach off, dumping dirty air on white, to regain the advantage.

Two-boat-length circle

Wind

White is entitled to room at the mark.

If you are on a starboard-tack *lift* as you approach the mark, or the wind has gone right by 10 degrees or more from where it was at the start, a jibe set is likely. (Recall from Chapter 8 that the wind tends to go right in the northern hemisphere.) The weight of the boat (displacement) and amount of wind can change this dictum, however. With a heavy boat in light air, a jibe set can hurt boat speed too much. In those conditions, you might not jibe-set unless the wind has gone right 15 degrees or more. Also, don't jibe-set if it puts you on port tack while a wave of starboard-tackers is approaching the mark. Otherwise, you'll be sailing through the middle of these boats without much protection.

A jibe set can, however, give you the inside position at the next mark rounding. (This is discussed later.) A jibe set is usually faster in heavy air.

DOWNWIND TACTICS

In sailboat racing, it is, of course, better to be ahead than behind. Nevertheless, sailing downwind gives the trailing boat a reasonable opportunity to do something about it, provided this boat is close enough to the lead boat to affect its wind. Some advantages the trailing boat enjoys are that it receives puffs and wind shifts before the lead boat. Also, a boat's wind shadow extends downwind, often to the boat(s) ahead. (Upwind, the trailing boat's wind shadow has no effect on the leading boat.) For these reasons, there are those who believe that being slightly behind at the weather mark is an advantage. I don't subscribe to this—I think, more often than not, the boat ahead at the beginning of a run comes out ahead at the end. However, there are good opportunities to pass another boat when sailing downwind.

As mentioned, the trailing boat's apparent-wind indicator, or masthead fly, points to the center of disturbed air. Use this apparent-wind indicator (not a true-wind indicator) to blanket a boat that is ahead. The dirty wind usually affects the leading boat's mainsail first, but this is difficult to see. Most obvious is when the leading boat's spinnaker—assuming it has one—collapses or behaves strangely.

If a boat behind is affecting your wind, there are two tactical responses. Either head up to clear your air or jibe. Whether to jibe or to head up depends on strategy as well as tactics. If you are sailing on the favorable jibe in more wind, or out of a foul current, you might not want to jibe. So head up.

It is also possible to use a "fake jibe" to escape another boat's wind shadow. This is what we did against *Canada II* in the 1986–87 America's

Cup. *Canada II,* behind and to leeward, was biding her time, waiting for us to jibe. Such setting up in anticipation of a jibe is a common maneuver. Once we both jibed, her wind shadow would hurt us. I had the main brought amidships, squared the stern toward the wind, and loudly called for our bowman, Scott Vogel, to trip the spinnaker pole. *Canada II* immediately jibed to starboard, and *Stars & Stripes* fell back to course on port without jibing. We were off the hook.

Passing another boat is the obvious tactical use of a wind shadow. More subtle but often as effective, the trailing boat can also use its wind shadow to herd the lead boat to the wrong side of the course.

Protect the Inside

In the previous chapter, we learned that the inside boat has right-of-way at a mark rounding. Thus, a rule of downwind sailing is to protect the inside. To this end, you might jibe-set to port tack at the weather mark for the inside (lefthand side) of the course. Protecting the inside accomplishes other things, as well. It can put you on starboard tack at the next crossing, giving you right-of-way. It is hard—if often downright foolish—to take issue with a boat on starboard tack and on the inside near a mark as this boat is well armed by the rules.

If you are on the inside, try to stay there. When on starboard tack and approaching a port-tacker, don't cross the latter boat. The starboard-tacker can jibe early. As a defense against this, the boat on port tack can take the starboard-tacker's transom to get to the inside of the course.

Stay Between the Competition and the
Leeward Mark

Earlier in the chapter, we discussed a loose cover in the context of staying between the competition and the windward mark. The flip, or downwind, side of this is to stay between the competition and the leeward mark. Draw an imaginary line between the competition and the leeward mark. The farther you stray from this line when ahead, the more you risk in a wind shift.

The seventh race of the 1983 America's Cup Race has been called the "race of the century." Much of what we've just talked about occurred on the famous fifth leg, the run. At the end of leg four—a weather leg—*Liberty,* which I skippered, rounded the mark with a fifty-two-second lead over

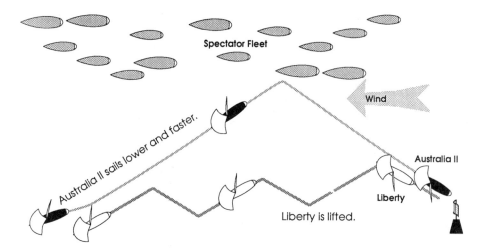

FIGURE 10.28 Liberty *losing to* Australia II *on the final run of the final race of the 1983 America's Cup.*

Australia II. The lead was less than it seemed since the Australian boat had gained on us an average of a minute on every spinnaker run.

Both boats did a bear-away set and sailed off to the right on starboard tack (see FIGURE 10.28). This put us between the competition and the mark, as the book says. The Australians started gaining. Also, the boat's wind shadow was starting to have an effect. Since *Australia II* had gained a minute on us on every run, if nothing changed, the boat would certainly be ahead at the leeward mark. We jibed away to port to escape her bad air. As described, jibing away from disturbed wind is recommended. This put us on the inside of the course, also recommended. Further, this got us away from the spectator fleet on this side that was churning up the water.

When we reached the inside, we received a small shift, a lift, and jibed on the lift—the recommended tactic in an oscillating wind—back to starboard and converged with *Australia II.* It was a grim sight to be sure. The Australian boat had enjoyed more wind on that side and had made up practically all the distance. It wasn't, as everyone thinks, a wind shift that made the difference; it was more wind on that side and a faster boat. Also, when we aimed at the spectator fleet while leading *Australia II* on starboard tack earlier in the leg, the spectator fleet was cleared out. It was as if we were a blocker for the Australian boat, driving the spectator fleet out of the way. Two quick jibes, and we paralleled *Australia II,* although we were still on the inside. This was, perhaps, our last hope. Then *Australia II* "shifted into overdrive" and started sailing lower and faster—a devastating combination (see FIGURE 8.17). In due time, this boat and the America's Cup were gone.

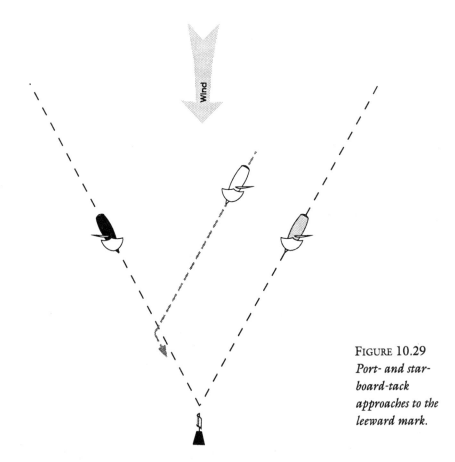

FIGURE 10.29
Port- and star-
board-tack
approaches to the
leeward mark.

Downwind Layline at the Mark

If you approach the downwind mark on the port-tack layline, a wind shift can cause you to lose to boats that aren't on the layline (see the black boat in FIGURE 10.29). For example, if the wind goes aft and you are lifted when on the port-tack layline, you'll have to fall off and sail a broader angle than boats inside you. As a result, you'll sail lower and slower. Also, there is a great likelihood that a boat on the port-tack layline will attract others—typically on your outside—that can give you bad air. Further, such boats will likely be entitled to buoy room. To be weighed, however, is the fact that a port-tack approach gives you ample time to get the jib up, spinnaker down, and things cleaned up. This accounts for its popularity.

A starboard-tack layline (see the gray boat in FIGURE 10.29) is also vulnerable to wind shifts and dirty air. It can, however, give you starboard-tack and inside rights at the mark. However, it requires a jibe takedown, a difficult maneuver (see Chapter 6), or an early spinnaker drop.

A compromise may be best. Here, you (the white boat) approach the

*Strategy,
Tactics, and
the Rules*

361

mark on starboard tack but sufficiently upwind to be able to jibe, raise a jib, and take down the spinnaker. This has the added advantage of keeping you off the layline until the very end.

ROUNDING THE LEEWARD MARK

Unless you are fighting to gain, maintain, or break an inside overlap, get your spinnaker down early rather than late. In fact, err on the side of early.

The optimum rounding is to take the mark wide—a boat length, for example—and then come onto the wind with maximum speed and no loss of distance to leeward (see FIGURE 9.14). Heading into the turn wide and coming out close to the mark is described as a tactical rounding, and, as discussed, has some limitations in the rule.

If another boat is close behind at the rounding, the lead boat should pinch a bit to close out the trailing boat. On the other hand, if you are the trailing boat and you don't want to tack to clear your air (discussed shortly), foot off through the disturbed air.

Heading more directly at the mark and coming out of the turn wide is described as a seamanlike rounding. It isn't as good as a tactical rounding because it can cause a wider turn and a corresponding loss of distance to windward. It can also open a hole for a trailing boat to stick its nose up into. If this happens, the lead boat may be unable to tack.

If you're on the outside and are going to have to give room to the inside boat, it can pay sometimes to slow down (see white in FIGURE 10.30). Take the spinnaker down early to slow down, even alter course. The inside boat makes a seamanlike rounding, and you make a tactical rounding and come up hard at the mark. If your timing is right, the boat ahead (black) will be—it is hoped—to leeward and perhaps unable to tack due to your presence to windward. This technique is known, somewhat optimistically, as slow down and win.

Upwind Strategy and the Leeward Mark

When rounding the leeward mark, upwind strategy counts, too. Before approaching the mark, you should determine how you want to sail the beat. The priority chart (Table 10A) is helpful on subsequent beats, too. Decide what you want to do, in view of the wind speed and direction, as well as your place in the race or the regatta. If you're up there or ahead and

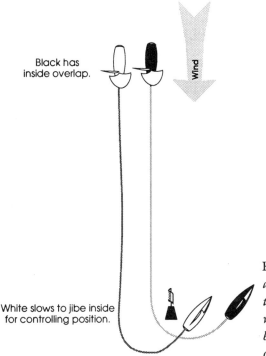

Black has
inside overlap.

Wind

White slows to jibe inside
for controlling position.

FIGURE 10.30 *The tactic "slow down and win," as used by white, can sometimes allow this boat to stick its nose to weather. White takes control because black can't tack too close, a violation of Rule 41.2.*

protecting your position, going the right way is probably less important than covering the competition behind. If the boat you have to beat tacks on a lift, you might want to tack, too, even if in an oscillating shift where tacking on the lifts isn't the recommended strategy. If behind, however, this might be a good point to tack on lifts and break the rules. This may be the time to be a "contrarian" or may not be.

If you chose to go left on starboard tack after rounding the leeward mark, there is always the danger of bad air from boats still on the run, so pick your spot carefully. Also, remember to go left requires a tack. Make sure the spinnaker gear, if you use a spinnaker, is properly put away. Sometimes when you are in a hurry to tack, the genoa sheet finds its way under the spinnaker pole or is otherwise fouled. This can ruin the maneuver as well as the pole.

REACHING TACTICS

Without other boats, the shortest distance on a reach is a straight line, the rhumb line (see Chapter 8). Other boats complicate matters mightily. I believe the goal of a reaching leg is to open distance on the boats behind and to close distance with the boats ahead. I don't see it as a place for big gains or losses. Not everyone, however, agrees with me.

By going up, you go faster and get the puffs first. Also, by taking other boats up, the leeward boat protects itself from being rolled over. However, it's where you are at the end of the leg that counts. Know, first, that what goes up must come down. That's fine if you can work your way down to course in more wind. It can be awful, however, if you have to work your way down in a dying breeze.

Also, the inside boat (typically the boat below the rhumb line) has the inside position at mark roundings and thus buoy room (see the white boat in the top grouping in FIGURE 10.31). Therefore, on the first reach, sail low for the inside position at the mark. If the triangle is beat, reach, reach, that applies to the first reach only. At the end of the second reach, the windward boat—the boat that sails higher (see the white boat in bottom grouping)—will be inside.

Whether you go high or low on a reach also depends on the boats immediately ahead and behind. Take the "high road" as white is doing in FIGURE 10.32 if the boats behind you are close. If you sail merrily down the rhumb line, the first boat may roll over the top. Once that boat rolls you, you lose speed. Then comes the "lynch mob."

Take the "low road," as gray is doing in FIGURE 10.32, if you have a large pack of boats ahead of you and no boats immediately behind you. The leading pack will likely fight its way high, and you may be able to sneak through by sailing low. Make the high-road low-road decision early and act on it in a timely fashion to maximize separation from the fleet.

If you choose to pass someone on a reach, the passing lane is to windward, but not so close that you will be vulnerable to a luff, however. On the other hand, if someone is passing you to weather, luff them immediately and aggressively, too. If the luff is too late, the weather boat may gain the mast-abeam position, which curtails the luff (see FIGURE 9.9). The danger of a luff is that you can easily lose to the boats behind you.

I don't like people sailing over the top of me. I try to communicate my displeasure to them. If they wish to take themselves out of the race by going high, they're talking to the right guy. "See you in China," I'll say. I try to explain the facts of life while they're trying to pass me to weather. It

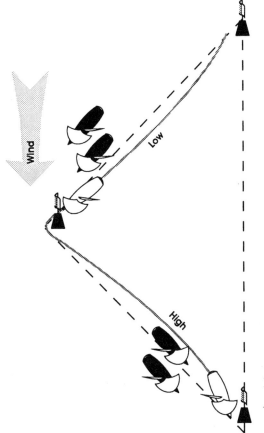

FIGURE 10.31 *Securing the inside position and, thus, rights at the mark on reaching legs.*

often works because going high on a reach is a great way to take yourself out of a race. There's a saying, "When all else fails, the truth can prevail."

DRAFTING IN A MIXED FLEET

I don't like being passed. Indeed, I've made a career out of that theme. I particularly don't like bigger boats passing me to weather. Use a word or a luff, or both, to get the big boat to pass you to leeward. If you are successful, it is possible to draft off a bigger boat, as automobile or bicycle racers do off another vehicle. As the big boat passes you to leeward, fall in right

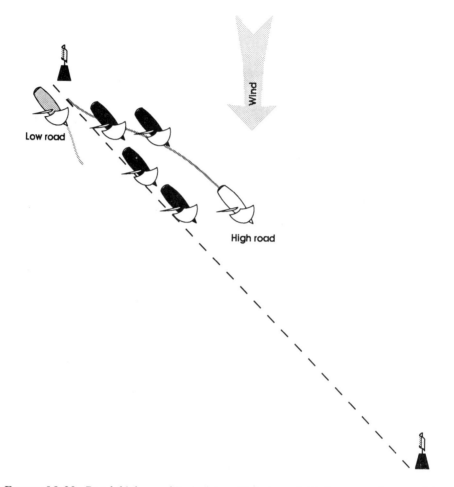

FIGURE 10.32 *Reach high, as white is doing, if the boats behind you are close; reach low, as gray is doing, if no boats are close behind you.*

behind it. Ideally you want to stay behind the big boat, riding on its stern wave, like a surfer.

If you are in a big boat, this speaks for allowing little boats some extra room, particularly if you are racing them. If passing too close to leeward, you may find yourself dragging the small boat along. (Also, passing to leeward isn't easy, even for a big boat, and a big boat might be unable to break through.) If passing too close to windward, the big boat is vulnerable to a luff.

ROUNDING THE REACH MARK

As indicated, it is preferable to be inside (leeward) at the first reach mark (see FIGURE 10.31). It is better to be inside (weather) at the second reach mark. These positions allow right-of-way at the respective marks.

Obviously there is much to recommend securing an overlap before the mark, and, from the other perspective, much to recommend breaking it. The weather boat, on the first reach, for example, should work hard to break the overlap before both boats reach the two-boat-length circle (see FIGURE 9.15). This can mean heading up just before the circle for speed, as well as for a more favorable angle, to break the overlap. Remember, however, that the outside boat has to prove the overlap was broken in time, which is hard to do without a witness. This is a situation where a hail can be important. As you approach the two-boat-length circle, tell the leeward boat in no uncertain terms, "No overlap!" This is no time to be shy.

The inside boat, on the other hand, should work hard to maintain the overlap. In a big boat, send a crew member to the bow, where the overlap begins, and be equally forceful in announcing, "We have an overlap!" Again, don't be shy, speak up.

FINISH

Finding the finish line is the first challenge. You can usually see the committee boat but are unable to see the buoy at the other end. You will recall that most races are marks to port. This means that when you started the race, the starting marker was on your port side, the committee boat on your starboard. You usually finish a race with the same orientation, that is, marks to port. Look for the pin to the left of the committee boat unless an instruction is to the contrary.

Once you've located the line, then you must figure out which end is favored. As a starting line is rarely square to the wind, so, too, the finish line is rarely square. Therefore, the favored end of the finish line must be determined. When finishing upwind, the favored end is farthest downwind. If one end is obviously favored, flags on the committee boat make this easy to determine. If the flags are pointed to the pin end in an upwind finish, that side is favored. The problem with this method is that this is very hard to read if the line is nearly square; also, you can't determine it until nearly at the finish, which can be too late.

Alternatively, sometimes the finish line will be set well before you have

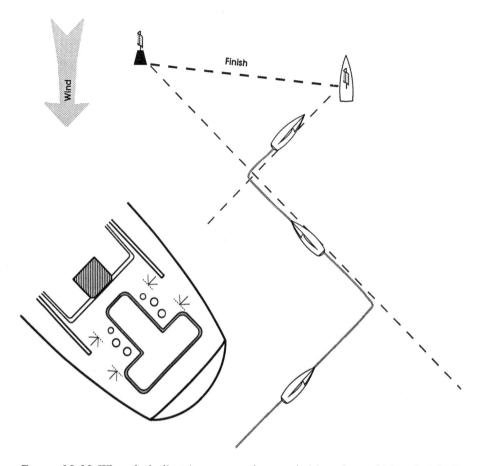

FIGURE 10.33 *When the laylines intersect, make your decision about which end of the line you are closest to. This is the favored end.*

to cross it. If possible during passings, shoot the line with a hand-bearing compass. You can draw this finish-line orientation (similar to FIGURE 10.1). Then as you near the line for the actual finish, draw in your starboard and port headings, to the pin and committee boat. Finish on the tack that is closest to being perpendicular to the line.

Another way is to watch the boats ahead of you finish—particularly if two or more are close. The likelihood is that they will finish at the favored end on the favored tack.

The longer you can delay making the decision about which end to finish on, the better. Thus, don't commit yourself until the very end. As you keep to the middle of a beat when you aren't sure what is happening, keep to the middle of the finish line until you make a decision. At some point, you'll be on a layline to one end (see FIGURE 10.33). When you continue on that layline and cross the layline to the other end, you have to make your decision. Otherwise, you may overstand. At the intersection of lay-lines, simply choose the end that appears closer to you.

Once you've made the decision, treat the favored end as a weather mark, not a line. Try to pass it close aboard. Remember, however, that in traffic there are times when crossing the line on starboard tack can be advantageous.

Once nearly at the line, you can increase VMG by "shooting it." When finishing upwind, shoot the wind—head directly into it—from one or two boat lengths to leeward of the line. The idea is to use the boat's momentum to cross the line most directly. In rough seas, you carry, or drift, less; in smooth seas, more. A massive boat carries more than a lighter boat, as indicated. Some sailors will even drop the jib when shooting the line. With the jib down—rather than flagging back and forth and causing windage—the boat will carry farther. Make sure, however, you are able to clear the finish line after finishing, according to the rules.

When finishing downwind, shoot the line by turning directly downwind to optimize VMG. Do this when one or two boat lengths from the mark.

That brings us to the finish of the race and the finish of this book. If you've gone the distance, I'm sure you'll be a better sailor. Writing this book has made me a better sailor. After sailing so long and so much, a great deal of the information has become instinctive—second nature. It is instructive to think about why I do something, not just what I do.

Glossary

Abaft: Behind.

Abeam: Perpendicular to the boat's center line.

Aft: Toward the stern or rear of the boat.

Aloft: Overhead in the rigging or on the mast.

Amidships: The middle of the boat.

Angle of attack: The angle of attack of a keel or centerboard stems from leeway, the difference between the boat's center line and the course made good. The angle of attack of a sail is the angle between the apparent-wind direction and the sail's chord line. The angle of attack increases as the sail is trimmed or its lead brought inboard.

Apparent wind: The apparent direction and strength of the wind as perceived from a moving boat. Movement alone creates the impression of wind coming from straight ahead, even if there is no wind. That plus the actual direction and velocity of the true wind combine to make what is called the apparent wind. See also *true wind.*

Aspect ratio: The height of a sail or underwater foil (keel or rudder) divided by its width.

Astern: Behind the boat.

Back: A counterclockwise wind shift. When the wind fills the sail from what ought to be its leeward side (given the way the sheet is trimmed), the sail is said to be *backed.*

Backstay: A stay running from the upper part of the mast to the stern. Keeps the mast from moving forward. Two types: permanent and running. The latter can be adjusted during a race to alter the shape of the mast, and therefore the shape or trim of the sails.

Ballast: Weight put in the bottom of the boat or keel for stability.

Barging: Attempting to squeeze between a starting mark and a close-hauled boat. Can be a violation of IYRU Rule 42.4.

Batten: A strip of plastic, wood, or carbon fiber used to stiffen the rear edge of the mainsail.

Beam: The width of the boat at its widest point. See also ***abeam.***

Bear away: To alter course away from the wind.

Bear-away set: Hoisting the spinnaker at a mark without jibing first.

Bearing: The angle between the center line of the boat or a point on the compass and another object, such as a mark or an opponent. To *gain bearing* is to point closer and closer to an object. For example, in a race a wind shift might allow you to sail more directly toward (gain bearing on) a mark.

Beat: To sail to windward close-hauled, that is, pointing as close to the wind as is efficiently possible. To reach an upwind mark in a race one *beats to windward* by tacking back and forth.

Before the wind: Sailing in the same direction that the wind blows.

Beneath: To sail beneath is to sail to leeward of another boat.

Bilge: The lowest, rounded part of a boat's hull.

Black flag rule: If a boat is over the starting line with a minute or less to go, it's out of the race, even if there is a general recall.

Block: Nautical word for pulley.

Boat speed: A boat's speed through the water. Compare with ***VMG, velocity made good.***

Boom: The horizontal spar that holds the foot or bottom of the mainsail.

Boom vang: A system using tackle or hydraulics to keep the boom from rising up, which would cause the mainsail to luff, and slow the boat.

Bosun's chair: The wooden or canvas seat used to hoist a crew member aloft.

Alternately, a crew member can wear a web harness throughout a race that can easily be clipped to the line that will haul him or her aloft when the need arises.

Bowman: The crew member who works on the foredeck. Duties include attaching the jib to the forestay, bringing the jib onto the foredeck when it is lowered, managing the spinnaker pole, and calling distances to a mark or an opponent.

Broach: An uncontrolled turn into the wind; it usually occurs when flying a spinnaker in heavy winds.

Broad reach: Sailing with the wind coming from astern over one quarter or the other.

Center of effort: The total forces in any lifting surface can be reduced to one vector that originates from one point. In sails, the point the vector comes from is described as the center of effort (CE).

Center of lateral resistance: The total forces in any lifting surface can be reduced to one vector that originates from one point. In the hull, the vector comes from the center of lateral resistance (CLR).

Center line: An imaginary line from the tip of the bow to the middle of the stern.

Chord: The measurement of a foil, like a keel or a sail, front to back or horizontally.

Chop: Seas with short, angular waves.

Chute: Another term for spinnaker.

Clew: The aft corner of a sail and the lowest corners of a spinnaker.

Close-hauled: Sailing as close to the wind as one can.

Cockpit: The recessed area aft in which the helmsman, tactician, and navigator work during a race.

Come about: To change directions from one tack (direction) to another while sailing to windward. To *tack* is to come about. Compare with *jibe.* See also *port* (tack) and *starboard* (tack).

Cover: To maintain one's lead in a race by staying between one's opponent and the next mark, even if one must sail a longer or slower course to do so.

Depth: The deepest point of a keel or sail.

Displacement: The weight of the water that a floating boat displaces; also weight.

Downwind: To leeward, the direction in which the wind is going.

Draft: In a sail, draft is described as depth divided by chord length and expressed as a percentage. If, for example, the draft of a sail is 1 foot and the sail's chord is 10 feet, draft is 10 percent. Keels can also be viewed this way. Also, the vertical distance between the waterline and the lowest part of the keel.

Draft position: Draft position is the location of maximum draft divided by chord, expressed as a percentage. If, for example, the draft is 4-1/2 feet back and the chord is 10 feet, draft is 45 percent.

Drag: Resistance. There are several types of drag: induced, form, and wetted surface.

Drag resistance: There are several types of drag resistance: frictional, form, and induced drag. Frictional drag is a function of wetted surface, i.e., how much boat touches the water. Form drag—or streamlining—is associated with the bluntness of the shape. Induced drag is the leakage from the high-pressure side to the low-pressure side.

Duck: To pass behind the stern of a boat.

Flattening reef: A control line that flattens the mainsail at the bottom.

Foot: A sail's lower edge. To foot is to steer slightly off of a close-hauled course, which, since a reach is the fastest point of sail, allows you to increase boat speed.

Foredeck: The part of the deck between bow and mast.

Foreguy: A line attached to the outer end of the spinnaker pole. It keeps the force of the wind on the spinnaker from raising the pole.

Forestay: The stay running from bow to mast on which the jib is set.

Forward: Toward the bow.

Fremantle Doctor: See *sea breeze.*

Freeboard: The distance from the water to the deck.

Genoa: A large jib whose clew (aft corner) extends aft of the mast. Larger genoas are designated by lower numbers.

Geographic winds: Those winds resulting from the steering effects of land.

Gradient winds: Those winds caused by large weather systems, for example, the winds that blow from a high-pressure system to a low-pressure system.

Grinder: Crew member who operates the winches used to trim the sails. A grinder must have great strength and endurance.

Halyard: A line used to hoist a sail.

Header: A wind shift whose direction moves farther forward relative to the center line of the boat. The usual response to a header is to tack or to bear off to leeward. The opposite of a lift.

Headsail: A jib or genoa, which are sails set forward of the mast.

Headstay: See *forestay.*

Head to wind: To point directly into the wind.

Heel: A boat heels or tilts over on one side due to the force of the wind on the sails.

Helm: The boat's steering wheel.

IMS: International Measurement System. A handicap system used to rate racer/cruisers, based on a computer-driven velocity-prediction program (VPP).

IOR: International Offshore Rule. A series of specifications that govern the design of a certain class of racing yachts.

IYRU: International Yacht Racing Union.

Jib: Alternate term for headsail or genoa.

Jibe: To jibe is to change course while sailing downwind. Requires that one move the mainsail and spinnaker from one side of the boat to the other. When, for example, the sails are trimmed on the port side of the boat with the wind coming over the starboard side, the boat is said to be *on starboard jibe.*

Jibe angle: The optimum downwind sailing angle as a function of wind speed.

Jibe set: Hoisting the spinnaker at a mark after jibing.

Jumper: A forward stay in the upper part of the mast.

Keel: A protruding section under the boat that provides stability and prevents sideways drift.

Kevlar: A material that ounce for ounce is stronger than steel. The gold-colored synthetic fiber is used in sailcloth, particularly in high-stress areas, and in ropes.

Lateral resistance: Resistance to sideways drift. It is provided by the keel.

Layline: An imaginary straight line tracing the course along which a boat can fetch a mark while sailing close-hauled. When racing to windward, competitors tack back and forth until they come to either the starboard or the port laylines and then, unless the actions of the opponent dictate otherwise, each boat heads directly for the mark along the layline. If a boat sails upwind beyond the layline, it will have gone farther than necessary (overstood) and, presumably, lost time. *Starboard layline:* layline to the mark that is sailed on starboard tack. *Port layline:* layline to the mark along which one sails on port tack. The position of these imaginary lines is determined by wind direction.

Leeward: Downwind.

Leeward mark: The downwind mark. Approached on a *run*.

Leg: The passage sailed between two buoys on a race course is known as a leg.

Lee bow: To maneuver in order to direct the disturbed, weakened air spilling aft and to windward of one's sails toward the sails of one's opponent, thereby slowing the opponent down. The correct position for using this tactic is just ahead and to leeward of one's rival.

Lee helm: When a boat tends to head downwind unless steered up, it is said to have a lee helm.

Lift: When a wind shift moves aft or away from the bow, it is called a lift. Sailing to windward allows one to steer more directly toward the mark. The opposite of a header.

Light cover: A windward boat tacks into a position where it is not clear whether its envelope of disturbed wind is affecting the leeward boat. Between a tight and loose cover.

Loose cover: Controlling a leeward boat from an upwind position; however, the wind shadow of the windward boat doesn't hurt the leeward boat.

Luff: A sail's leading edge. To luff is to point up into the wind so that the boat slows—sometimes a useful maneuver before the start of a race or when being passed to windward.

Mainsail: The sail hoisted *aft* of the *mast.* Its *foot* is attached to the *boom.*

Mainsheet: The line used to *trim* the *mainsail.*

Mark: A buoy that one must sail around in a race.

Mast: The vertical spar that holds up the sails and that is itself held up by stays.

Masthead: The top of the mast.

Mastman: Crew member situated near the base of the mast whose responsibilities include control of halyards.

Mast abeam: If the helmsman of the windward boat is sitting in his or her normal position abreast of, or ahead of, the mast of the leeward boat, luffing by leeward boat must be curtailed under IYRU Rule 32.8 (a). Usually a hail is sounded to that effect.

Match racing: Races involving two boats only as opposed to a fleet.

MORC: Midget Ocean Racing Club. A handicap system for boats that are 30 feet or less.

Mylar: A light, translucent material used in some sails and spinnakers.

Navigator: The navigator assesses the boat's position, speed, and bearing with respect to the opponent and to the marks that must be rounded to complete the course.

Off-the-wind: On a reach or a run you are sailing off-the-wind.

On-the-wind: Sailing as close to the direction the wind is coming from as you can. Close-hauled.

One-minute rule: If over the starting line with a minute or less to go, you must sail around either end of the line according to IYRU Rule 51.1(c).

Oscillating wind shift: A wind shift that oscillates back and forth, like a pendulum. The most common type of shift. See ***persistent shift.***

Oscillating-persistent shift: A wind shift that is persistent in one direction; however, it shows oscillations as well. Occurs least often.

Outhaul: A line or tackle that pulls outward, for example, the mainsail outhaul pulls the mainsail toward the aft end of the boom.

Overstand: To overstand a mark is to sail past the mark's port or starboard laylines, that is, to sail farther than necessary to round the mark. When the wind shifts, the laylines leading to the mark change too, and so a skipper may find that he or she unintentionally overstands the mark.

Persistent shift: A wind shift that continues shifting in one direction.

Pin: A buoy.

Pinch: To sail too close to the wind.

Pitch: Alternate rising and falling of bow and stern.

Point: To sail close to the wind. The points of sail are the terms assigned to the directions you can sail with respect to the wind.

Polar diagram: A graph of a hull's performance as a function of wind speed and wind angle.

Port: The lefthand side of the boat as you look forward.

Port tack: Sailing with the wind coming over the starboard side of the boat.

Preventer: A line running from the foredeck to the end of the boom that keeps the boom from jibing accidentally as the boat sails downwind.

Proper course: The course a boat would sail in the absence of other boats to finish a course as quickly as possible.

Rail: The deck's outer edge.

Rake: To bend the mast forward or aft by adjusting the rigging.

Reach: To sail with the wind *abeam*. On a *close reach*, the wind is somewhat forward of *abeam*. On a *beam reach*, the wind is directly abeam. On a *broad reach*, the wind is somewhat aft of abeam.

Rhumb line: A direct line between one mark and the next.

Rivlets: Microscopic grooves on plastic sheets applied to the boat. The grooves run iengthwise along the hull and are meant to increase boat speed by reducing friction between the water and the moving boat.

Rig: The way the spars, standing and running rigging, and sails are arranged. Spars and stays constitute *standing rigging*. Sheets and halyards are part of the boat's *running rigging*.

Rudder: An underwater flap operated by the wheels in the cockpit or the tiller that changes the boat's course.

Run: To sail directly downwind, which occurs on the leeward leg.

Runner: Running backstay.

Sailplan: A boat's inventory of sails.

Sea breeze: Breeze blowing toward the shore as heated air over the sun-baked land rises and draws the cooler offshore air inland.

Set: To hoist and then trim a sail.

Sewer: The area under the foredeck where sails are stored. The sewerman organizes the sails down below and helps the bowman hoist and take them down.

Shackle: A fixture that fastens a line to a fitting, or one line to another.

Sheet: The line used for trimming sails.

Shift: See *header* and *lift*.

Shoot the mark: If you are sailing toward the windward mark on a course just below the layline, you may avoid an extra tack by luffing up. This is *shooting the mark*. Ideally, you will be able to round the mark before the boat loses way.

Shrouds: Supporting wires on both sides of the mast. They give the mast lateral stability.

Slam dunk: Maneuver used to deny a trailing opponent wind when maneuvering in close. After port-tacker ducks starboard-tacker, starboard tacks into controlling position.

Spinnaker: A light sail with three corners used when sailing to leeward. When set it has a balloon shape. It is flown with the aid of a spinnaker pole.

Spreaders: Struts on both sides of mast that spread the *shrouds* out from the mast as they travel down to where they're fastened to the edge of the deck amidships. Spreaders enhance the stabilizing effect of the shrouds.

Starboard: The right side of the boat as you face forward.

Starboard tack: Sailing with the wind coming over the port side of the boat.

Starting line: An imaginary line between the mast of the boat of the committee that supervises the race, and a buoy. The ideal starting line is set at a right angle to the wind direction and is directly downwind of the first *windward mark*. This is meant to ensure that boats have an equal distance to sail to the first mark regardless of where they cross the line. But, for example, if the wind shifts to the right after the line has been established, a boat starting on the right will have a shorter distance to sail on the *beat* to the first *windward* mark. In such a case, the right side of the line is said to be favored.

Stay: A wire that provides fore and aft support for the mast; part of the standing rigging.

Staysail: Most often used during a run or a reach; it is a small jib flown between the spinnaker and the mainsail.

Stern: The part of the boat farthest aft.

Tack: To tack is to change directions while sailing to windward by steering the bow of the boat through the wind from port tack (wind coming over the boat's port side) to starboard tack (wind coming over the starboard side) or vice versa. Tack also denotes the foremost corner of the foot or bottom of a sail.

Tacking angle: The angle between a boat's heading on either tack is called the tacking angle. Good wind and smooth seas narrow the tacking angle; light wind and lumpy seas widen it.

Tacking duel: In a close race, a tacking duel occurs when the boat that is ahead tries to maintain its lead by tacking whenever its opponent does in order to stay between the trailing boat and the next mark that they both must round.

Tackle: An arrangement of ropes and blocks (pulleys) that yields a mechanical advantage and so makes it easier to pull or hoist.

Tactician: The crew member who assesses the actions of the opponent and the wind and offers tactical advice to the skipper, who concentrates on steering the boat.

Tailer: The crew member who trims the headsails.

Target boat speed: For each wind speed, there is a corresponding boat speed that is optimum.

Tender: A motorboat that holds spare equipment and sails for a yacht.

Thermal winds: Winds caused by the fact that land heats and cools more rapidly than water. This temperature differential causes thermal winds. A sea breeze is a familiar example.

Tight cover: The lead boat positions itself to weather and ahead of a leeward boat. Considered an aggressive maneuver as the wind shadow of the lead boat has a profound effect on the leeward boat. Often used to dissuade a boat from going to the favored side of a course.

Time on distance: The act of precisely controlling one's boat speed, course, the distance to the mark, and the time remaining before the starting gun in order to cross the line with the greatest speed exactly when the gun sounds. When maneuvering against another boat, the fight for the controlling position tends to prevent one from attempting a perfect time-on-distance start.

Transom: The back or the stern.

Traveler: A track perpendicular to the center line along which the travel car can slide. Used to adjust the angle of attack of the mainsail.

Trim: One trims a sail by pulling in on a sheet.

True wind: The actual velocity and direction of the wind. True wind combined with the wind one senses solely due to a boat's forward movement yields *apparent wind.*

Tuning: The act of adjusting a boat's sails, the shape of the hull and or keel, and the rigging to optimize performance.

Turtle: A bag that holds a folded spinnaker before that sail is set.

12-Meter: A 12-Meter yacht is not 12 meters long; rather, the term applies to a complex series of measurements and ratios having to do with various dimensions of the hull and mast, which, when fed into a certain equation, must yield a sum of 12 meters.

Two-boat-length circle: The imaginary two-boat-length circle that surrounds racing marks. Used to determine which boat is entitled to room at the mark.

Upwind: Toward the direction from which the wind is blowing, to windward or to weather.

US SAILING: The national authority, formerly United States Yacht Racing Union.

Vang: See *boom vang.*

Veer: A clockwise windshift.

Velocity header: If the true wind hasn't actually shifted or changed direction, but the apparent-wind speed alone has changed due to a drop in wind speed, this is a velocity header. Wind seems to have shifted forward, that is, a header. A short-term dynamic.

Velocity lift: When you experience a puff of wind, you encounter what is known as a velocity lift. Wind seems to have shifted aft, that is, a lift. A short-term dynamic.

VPP: Velocity prediction program. A computer program used to equate the physical characteristics of a yacht—sailing length, beam, displacement, etc.—to its speed.

VMG: Velocity made good. The actual speed one is making toward a mark as one tacks or jibes back and forth. VMG is affected by such factors as ocean current, leeway (side slippage), boat speed, and course sailed.

Wake: The turbulent waves a boat creates as it passes through the water.

Weather: In addition to the word's normal meaning, there is a nautical usage: to weather means to windward (upwind). The weather mark, therefore, is the windward mark.

Weather helm: When a boat tends to head upwind unless steered away, it is said to have a weather helm.

Winch: A drum around which one passes sheets or halyards; it enables one to trim or ease these lines even when they're under great strain from the pressure of the wind in the sails.

Wind shadow: The area of weakened, turbulent wind to leeward of a sail.

Windward: Upwind, to weather, the direction from which the wind is blowing.

Winglets: Roughly horizontal wings at the bottom of a keel that, when used on *Australia II* in the 1983 America's Cup, gave the boat increased speed and maneuverability. Winglets appeared on the keels of all 12-Meters in the 1987 America's Cup except the yacht *USA*. They were also on several yachts in the 1992 America's Cup.

Wing mark: The mark one must round between the two reaches.

Bibliography

Conner, Dennis, and Claflin, Edward. *The Art of Winning.* New York: St. Martin's Press, 1988.

Conner, Dennis, and Rousmaniere, John. *No Excuse to Lose.* New York: W. W. Norton, 1978.

Conner, Dennis, and Stannard, Bruce. *Comeback.* New York: St. Martin's Press, 1987.

Gentry, Arvel. "The Application of Computational Fluid Dynamics to Sails." Paper presented at the Symposium on Hydrodynamic Performance, at Newport, Rhode Island, 1988.

Hubbard, David W., and MacLane, Duncan T. "The Engineering of the Wingsail for *Stars & Stripes*, 1988 America's Cup Defender." Paper presented at the New England Sailing Yacht Symposium, New London, Connecticut, 1990.

Jobson, Gary; Whidden, Tom; and Loory, Adam. *Championship Tactics.* New York: St. Martin's Press, 1990.

Knapp, Arthur, Jr. *Race Your Boat Right.* 3d ed. New York: Grosset & Dunlap, 1973.

Levitt, Michael, and Lloyd, Barbara. *Upset: Australia Wins the America's Cup.* New York: Workman Publishing, 1983.

Marchaj, C. A. *Aero-hydrodynamics of Sailing.* New York: Dodd, Mead, 1980.

Marchaj, C. A. *Sailing Theory and Practice.* New York: Dodd, Mead, 1982.

North Sails Group Inc. *Fast Course, Smart Course,* and *Cruising Course* books. Milford, Connecticut.

Ockam U. Seminar Manual. Milford, Connecticut, 1990.

Rousmaniere, John. *The Annapolis Book of Seamanship.* New York: Simon and Schuster, 1989.

Sleight, Steven. *Modern Boatbuilding Materials and Methods.* Camden, Maine: International Marine Publishing, 1985.

Vaughan, Roger. *America's Cup XXVII, The Official Record 1988.* San Diego: Dennis Conner Sports, 1988.

Whidden, Tom, and Levitt, Michael. *The Art and Science of Sails.* New York: St. Martin's Press, 1989.

Willis, Melvin D.C. *Boatbuilding and Repairing with Fiberglass.* Camden, Maine: International Marine Publishing Company, 1972.

Videos

Dellenbaugh, David. "Learn The Racing Rules." New Haven, Sea TV/*Sailing World* magazine.

North Sails Group Inc. "Trim for Speed." Milford, Connecticut, Sea TV.

Sail magazine. "Spinnaker Sailing."

Magazine Articles

Baird, Ed. "Finishing Techniques." *Sailing World* (February 1985), p. 79.

——. "The First 100 Yards." *Yacht Racing/Cruising* (now *Sailing World*) (February 1981), p. 47.

Deaver, Dick. "Downwind Control—Not Disaster!" *Yachting* (January and February 1977), p. 83.

Dellenbaugh, David. "13 Minutes to Go." *Sailing World* (July 1989), p. 18.

Hopkins, Robert, Jr. "Tracking Every Move." *Sail* (May 1987), p. 80.

Isler, Peter. "Strategy on the Run." *Sailing World* (May 1988), p. 26.

Marshall, Jim. "Wind Shear and Wind Gradient." *Sailing World* (May 1988), p. 26.

Olson, Walter. "Ounce of Prevention." *Sail* (June 1990), p. 67.

Pittman, Freeman. "A New Look at Blister Repair." *Sail* (April 1989), p. 94.

Spranger, Jeff. "The Healthy Hull." *Sail* (April 1990), p. 80.

Index

waves:
  added resistance in, 25
  current and, 249
  sailing downwind and,
    255, 276
  steering into, 213
  stern, 20–21
  surfing and, 232
  tacking angle and, 254
  yacht design and, 25
weather, 250
  monitoring of, 234–237
  sources of information on,
    244–246
weather helm, 115, 139, 145
  boat speed and, 153,
    155–156
  degree of, 153
  heel and, 229
  mast tune and, 153,
    155–156
  running and, 213
  steering and, 204–207,
    229
  tacking and, 230–231
weather mark, 314, 353–357
weight:
  of boat, 71–72
  boat speed and, 161–163
  of crew, 145–146, 163,
    183, 232
  displacement and, 17–18,
    20
  of mast, 164
  of sails, 84

weight: *(cont.)*
  spinnaker and, 125
Whidden, Tom, 1, 9,
  171–172, 175
Whitbread Round the World
  Race, 117
White Crusader, 146
Williams, Ted, 2, 3, 5
Williwaw, 12, 61–63, 277
wind:
  apparent, 97, 207, 338
  downwind targets and,
    227–228
  geographic, 243–244
  gradient, 237–239, 241,
    244
  indicators of, 210–211
  jibe angle and, 227–228
  light, 207–208, 212
  tactics and, 333–337
  thermal, 239–242, 244
  upwind targets and,
    222–223
  see also downwind sailing;
    oscillating-persistent
    wind; oscillating wind;
    persistent wind; upwind
    sailing
wind rose, 235–236
winds-aloft theory, 268
wind shadow, 359
wind shear, 265–268, 330
  persistent winds and,
    265–268
  reaching and, 277–278

wind shear *(cont.)*
  separation and, 347
  strategy and, 265–268
wind speed, 222–223,
  227–228
  indicator for, 216, 225
wing sail, 48–49
wood, 74–75
World Ocean Racing Cham-
  pionship, 10

yacht design, 15–50
  America's Cup of 1988
    and, 43–50
  aspect ratio and, 27–28
  of *Australia II,* 33–37
  axes of motion and, 32–33
  computers and, 36–37
  displacement and, 17–18,
    20
  drag and, 22–27
  IMS Rule and, 40–43
  lift from keel and, 28–29
  rating rules and, 38–40
  right moment from keel
    and, 30–31, 33
  sailing angles and, 27–28
  wave-making resistance
    and, 18–22
  waves and, 25
  weather monitoring and,
    235–236
  winged keel and, 36–37
Yachting, 11, 55
yaw, 33